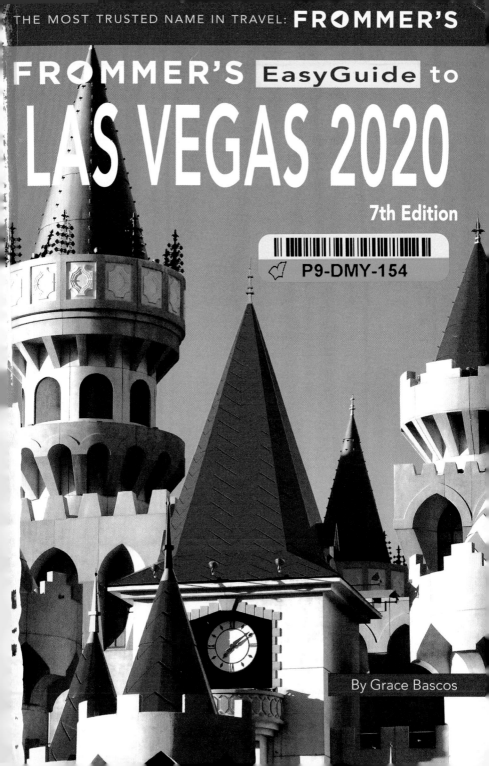

THE MOST TRUSTED NAME IN TRAVEL: **FROMMER'S**

FROMMER'S EasyGuide to
LAS VEGAS 2020

7th Edition

P9-DMY-154

By Grace Bascos

FROMMER'S STAR RATINGS SYSTEM

Every hotel, restaurant, and attraction listed in this guide has been ranked for quality and value. Here's what the stars mean:

★   Recommended
★★   Highly Recommended
★★★   A must! Don't miss!

AN IMPORTANT NOTE

The world is a dynamic place. Hotels change ownership, restaurants hike their prices, museums alter their opening hours, and busses and trains change their routings. And all of this can occur in the several months after our authors have visited, inspected, and written about, these hotels, restaurants, museums, and transportation services. Though we have made valiant efforts to keep all our information fresh and up-to-date, some few changes can inevitably occur in the periods before a revised edition of this guidebook is published. So please bear with us if a tiny number of the details in this book have changed. Please also note that we have no responsibility or liability for any inaccuracy or errors or omissions, or for inconvenience, loss, damage, or expenses suffered by anyone as a result of assertions in this guide.

Previous page: Excalibur hotel casino on the Strip. Above: Artist Dale Chihuly covered the ceiling of the Bellagio (p. 56) with a garden's worth of exquisite, hand-blown glass flowers.

CONTENTS

1 THE BEST OF LAS VEGAS 1

2 SUGGESTED LAS VEGAS ITINERARIES 10
Iconic Las Vegas 10
Over-the-Top Las Vegas 14
Guys' Getaway 17
Girls' Getaway 19
Unlikely Las Vegas 20
Eating Las Vegas 22
City Layout 24
Neighborhoods in Brief 25

3 LAS VEGAS IN CONTEXT 27
Las Vegas Today 27
Looking Back: Las Vegas History 29
When to Go 36
Las Vegas Calendar of Events 38

4 WHERE TO STAY 41
Practical Information 41
South Strip 45
Mid-Strip 56
North Strip 68
Downtown 73
Just Off the Strip 80
South & East of the Strip 88
North & West of the Strip 91

5 WHERE TO EAT 94
Restaurants by Cuisine 94
South Strip 96
Mid-Strip 108
North Strip 125
Downtown 128
Just Off the Strip 135
North & West of the Strip 142
Buffets 144

6 EXPLORING LAS VEGAS 152
Seeing Las Vegas 152
South Strip 153
Mid-Strip 156
North Strip 159
Downtown 162
Just Off the Strip 166
South & East of the Strip 169
North & West of the Strip 171
Casino Gambling 174
Outdoor Activities 184
Fore! Great Desert Golf 186
Spas 188
Getting Married 190

7 SHOPPING 195
South Strip 195
Mid-Strip 198
North Strip 200
Downtown 201
Just Off the Strip 202
South & East of the Strip 204

8 ENTERTAINMENT & NIGHTLIFE 205
The Performing Arts 205
The Bar Scene 219
The Club & Music Scene 229
The Gay & Lesbian Scene 238
Strip Clubs 239

9 DAY TRIPS FROM LAS VEGAS 242
Hoover Dam & Lake Mead 242
Valley of Fire State Park 247
Red Rock Canyon 249
Mount Charleston 253

10 PLANNING YOUR TRIP TO LAS VEGAS 258
Getting There 258
Getting Around 260
Fast Facts: Las Vegas 267

INDEX 275

MAP LIST 282

ABOUT THE AUTHOR 287

Bellagio's fountains, spectacular at night.

A LOOK AT LAS VEGAS

Glitzy, gritty, gaudy, glamorous, and sometimes goofy, Las Vegas may well be the most colorful city in America. That goes for the people who call it their home (or make it their home for the weekend), the lights and playful structures, the multi-hued desert and mountain scenery that surrounds it, and the ever-changing cityscape. Las Vegas is constantly in flux: new attractions and restaurants constantly appearing, new efforts to challenge the normal standards of morality that some cities cherish. That's why we revise this guidebook yearly. Our author, Grace Bascos, has captured the very latest and most outrageous Las Vegas efforts to shock, amuse and intrigue you. What follows now are some of the sights you'll see, the adventures you'll have, and everything else that "Vegas" provides in such awesome amounts.

Arthur Frommer

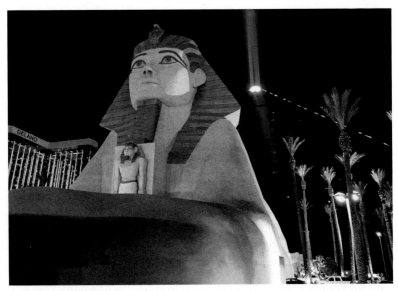

The myth about the pyramid-shaped Luxor (p. 52), with its sphinx out front, is that the beam of light shooting from its peak can be seen from outer space. That isn't true, but it makes quite an impact on the Las Vegas Strip.

THE LAS VEGAS STRIP

Hand-painted frescoes, 25-foot-high Bottocino marble columns, and a floor that's an exact replica of the one in Venice's Santa Maria Rosario greet guests checking into the Venetian (p. 61).

Singing gondoliers serenade visitors inside and outside the Venetian.

Glam chandeliers are draped throughout the lobby of the Cosmopolitan (p. 58).

The façade of New York–New York (p. 53) features a 150-foot replica of the Statue of Liberty, a 300-foot long "Brooklyn Bridge," and a taxi-themed rollercoaster—just for fun.

At Best Friend (p. 98) in Park MGM, celebrity chef Roy Choi delivers his Korean-Mexican mashup with Vegas style, including this flavorful tamarind black cod stew—or try tostadas topped with caviar.

Elvis and the "Welcome to Fabulous Las Vegas" sign (p. 161), two icons in Sin City. You'll be expected to tip if you pose with the King.

Sting is one of the many megastars who brighten the city's stages during Vegas residencies.

Cirque du Soleil's eye-popping spectacle *O* (p. 211) uses a vast pool for its acrobats, swimmers, and dancers.

Although *Absinthe* (p. 206) is not a Cirque du Soleil show, it features the same jaw-dropping acrobatics.

America's Got Talent winner Terry Fator (p. 218) performs his singing, joking ventriloquism act four times a week.

The music and dancing are always high-energy at Drai's Nightclub (p. 232) at the Cromwell. The highest rollers can get their bottles presented with Vegas flair, complete with sparklers and pictures on the LED screens.

ABOVE: At the Cosmopolitan's Marquee Dayclub (p. 233), DJs, food, and fun keep the poolside beach party lively. BELOW: For free entertainment, the colorful Eiffel Tower Light Show (p. 160) at Paris Las Vegas can't be beat.

The casino floor at Caesars Palace (p. 57). Vast, labyrinthine, and impressive hotel casinos are designed to captivate guests—and their wallets.

Gamblers play craps, one of the fastest-moving and most exciting games on the casino floor, at the Strat Hotel and Casino (p. 72).

Getting hitched can be a thrill ride: a bride and groom on the Stratosphere's Big Shot (p. 160).

The High Roller (p. 157) is the world's tallest observation wheel.

Luxury brands are the focus of the Shops at Crystals (p. 196) in City Center. Nearby are stunning works of contemporary public art.

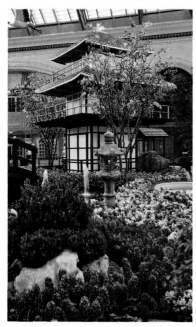

The Conservatory Gardens at the Bellagio (p. 160).

Elegant and extravagant: the Forum Shops (p. 198) at Caesars Palace.

DOWNTOWN LAS VEGAS & OFF THE STRIP

Outdoor bars, with photogenic bartenders, are part of the scene at the Fremont Street Experience (p. 163) in the heart of Downtown.

The LED above the Fremont Street Experience plays high-tech sound and image shows.

Guests "swim with the sharks" at the Golden Nugget pool (p. 74).

La Comida (p. 131), serving up worthy Mexican fare and fruity margaritas, is one of the cool restaurants spicing up Downtown's culinary scene.

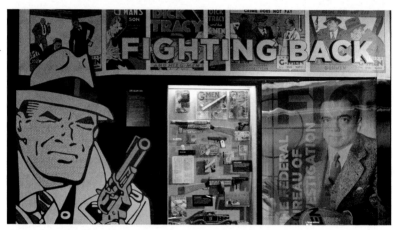

The thought-provoking Mob Museum (p. 163) explores the role of organized crime in history and popular culture.

The 20,000-seat T-Mobile Arena (p. 215) is Vegas's newest venue for big-name concerts and is the home of the city's Golden Knights hockey team.

At the new, adults-only Cannabition Cannabis Museum (p. 162), colorful murals, art installations, and exhibits turn you on (not literally) to the nuances of pot culture.

Visitors can play out NASCAR fantasies at SpeedVegas (p. 168). Anyone with a license—and the cash—can take an exotic muscle car or supercar out for a zoom around the 1.5-mile Formula One–inspired track.

A set of dazzling, historic stained-glass ceilings cap the casino at Main Street Station (p. 78), Downtown's hub for fans of Victorian architecture and design.

More than just a driving range, Topgolf (p. 168) features an entertainment stage, plus multiple kitchens and bars.

At the Neon Museum (p. 165), you see many of the spectacular vintage signs that once adorned Las Vegas.

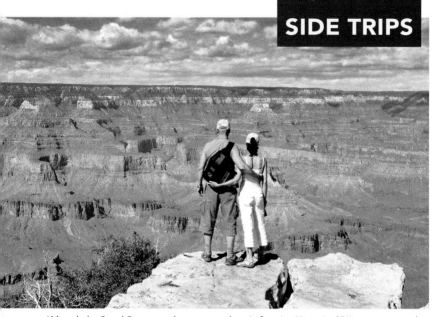

Although the Grand Canyon can be seen on a day trip from Las Vegas (p. 254), we recommend a several-day stay, allowing you to climb below the rim to see its turrets, buttes, and striations in different lights throughout the day.

Hoover Dam (p. 243), an engineering marvel completed in 1936, transformed the landscape and the lives of people in the West. It's beautiful anytime, including at dusk.

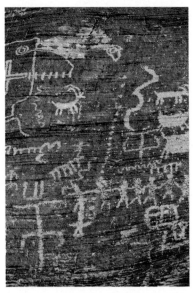

Handsome Red Rock Canyon (p. 249) is only a 25-mInute drive from the Strip.

Ancient petroglyphs dot the striated rocks of the Valley of Fire (p. 247).

A Vegas ski vacation?! It's doable if you add a visit to nearby Mount Charleston (p. 253).

THE BEST OF LAS VEGAS

The flamboyant showman Liberace once said, "Too much of a good thing is wonderful!" He may very well have been talking about Las Vegas, a city in which he was a frequent headliner and one that has built its reputation on the concept of excess.

There's too much to look at, too much to do, too much to eat, too much to drink, and certainly too many ways to lose your money. Indulgence is the level at which most people start their visit, and why not? You can run out of room on your memory card trying to snap pictures of all the postcard-worthy sights, from dancing fountains to blasting volcanoes; the hotels are so big that getting from your room to the front door requires rest periods; the dining scene has turned this town into a culinary destination; and the nightclubs have elevated Sin City to the biggest, most successful party spot in the world. And all of that is before you get to the shows, the shopping, and the sheer madness of glittering casinos. Look at the faces of those waiting for their flights out of town: tired, maybe a little hung over still, but then there's that little smile when they think about one of those "what happens in Vegas . . ." moments they had. When it comes to Las Vegas, Liberace may have had a point.

THE best AUTHENTIC LAS VEGAS EXPERIENCES

o **Strolling on the Strip After Dark:** You haven't really seen Las Vegas until you've seen it at night. This neon wonderland is the world's greatest sound-and-light show. Begin at **Luxor** and work your way past the incredible hotels and their attractions. You'll probably be exhausted both physically and mentally by the time you get to the halfway mark around **Caesars Palace,** but forge ahead and you could go all the way to the **Stratosphere Tower** for a bird's-eye view of the city from more than 1,000 feet up. Make plenty of stops en route to see the **Mirage Volcano** erupt, take a photo of the full moon over the **Eiffel Tower,** and marvel at the choreographed water-fountain ballet at **Bellagio.**

o **Casino-Hopping on the Strip:** The interior of each lavish hotel-casino is more outrageous and giggle-inducing than the last. Just when you think they can't possibly top themselves, they do. From Venice to Paris, from New York City to the Manhattan-style chic of the Aria mega-resort complex, it is all, completely and uniquely, Las Vegas. See "The Best Las Vegas Casinos," later in this chapter.

o **Sleeping In:** Come on! You're on vacation! Yes, there are lots of things to see and do in Las Vegas, but with tens of thousands of the most luxurious hotel rooms in the world, don't you just want to stay in one of those big fluffy beds and maybe order room service? We know we do. See "The Best Las Vegas Hotels," below.

o **Visiting an Only-in-Vegas Museum:** Take a breather from the casino floor and learn something new about Sin City: Go nuclear at the **National Atomic Testing Museum** (p. 167), get "made" at the **Mob Museum** (p. 163), or get lit up at the **Neon Museum** (p. 165). And even though the pastime is not a purely Vegas-only thing, there is only one interactive cannabis museum, the new **Cannabition** (p. 162), and it's in Downtown Las Vegas.

o **Spending a Day (& Night) in Downtown:** Glitter Gulch is undergoing a renaissance with fun, modern hotels and casinos like the **Downtown Grand** (p. 74); terrific and affordable dining options such as **Eat** (p. 133) and **La Comida** (p. 131); fun and funky bars like the **Commonwealth** (p. 226) and **Atomic Liquors** (p. 225); and must-see attractions like the **Fremont Street Experience** (p. 163). Oh, and there's a giant, fire-breathing praying mantis at the **Downtown Container Park** (p. 201), a shopping and entertainment center. If that doesn't make you want to go, nothing will!

o **Shopping Until You're Dropping:** Take what Napoleon called "the greatest drawing room in Europe," replicate it, add shops, and you've got the **Grand Canal Shoppes** at the Venetian (p. 199)—it's St. Mark's Square, complete with canals and working gondolas. See chapter 7 for the low-down on the shopping scene.

o **Dressing Up for a Show:** Even though you'll see plenty of cats in Bermuda shorts, hoodies, and Hawaiian shirts, there's something about putting on your best suit or fanciest dress for an evening at the "thea-tuh" that can't be beat. See chapter 8 for reviews of the major shows and check out "The Best Las Vegas Shows," later in this chapter.

o **Breaking Some Records:** You can find thrills in many parts of the United States, but a few of the adrenaline-pumping attractions here are worthy of spots in *Guinness World Records*. **High Roller** (p. 157) is the world's tallest observation wheel; the **Stratosphere Tower & Thrill Rides** (p. 160) are the highest in the United States; and **SlotZilla** (p. 166), the world's tallest "slot machine," is the launching platform for zip lines down Fremont Street.

o **Getting Away from It All:** Las Vegas can be overwhelming, so be sure to create some time in your itinerary to find your Zen at such scenic spots as the **Valley of Fire State Park** or **Red Rock Canyon**. See chapter 9 for more ideas for day trips from Vegas.

THE best LAS VEGAS RESTAURANTS

o **Best Strip Restaurants: Restaurant Guy Savoy** (p. 113) is a legend in Paris, and this offshoot is just as stellar. A second choice? **Estiatorio Milos** (p. 110), which serves impossibly fresh Mediterranean seafood.

o **Best Downtown Restaurants:** The gourmet-yet-cool specialties at the **Kitchen at Atomic** (p. 130) and the funky, homemade-style Mexican dishes at **La Comida** (p. 131) prove that the dining scene in Downtown has arrived.

o **Best Off-Strip Restaurant: Sparrow + Wolf** (p. 143) is a 10- to 20-minute drive from the Strip, but the exciting American- and Asian-influenced fare here make it totally worth the trip.

o **Best Comfort Food:** The heaping portions of classic American comfort food at **Hash House a Go Go** (in the LINQ; p. 120) will satisfy even the most ravenous of eaters, while the eclectic mix of Korean, Mexican, and American down-home fare at **Best Friend** (p. 98) will charm the most jaded.

o **Best Theme Restaurant:** Generally speaking, we think theme restaurants are overpriced tourist traps, but **Hell's Kitchen** (p. 111) lets you feel (and eat!) like you're on the set of Gordon Ramsay's TV cooking competition of the same name.

o **Best Steakhouse:** The Vegas staple restaurant is alive and well in the hands of modern chefs like José Andrés, whose **Bazaar Meat** (p. 125) celebrates the one thing that matters in a steakhouse: the meat. One of the stars of the show is the open kitchen with its wood-fired grill in the center of the dining room, surrounded by a butcher counter showcasing huge cuts of meat. The only better look you'd get of that beef is if you were face to face with the cow itself.

o **Best Cheap Meal: Flock & Fowl** (p. 134) serves one of the quintessential Asian comfort foods—Hainanese chicken rice—in the cool backdrop of Downtown Las Vegas.

o **Best Splurge:** Food should not cost as much as it does at **Joël Robuchon** (p. 100) and its slightly less expensive sibling **L'Atelier de Joël Robuchon** (p. 101), but a few bites of the exquisite cuisine will make you understand why it does.

o **Best Buffets:** It's expensive, but the **Bacchanal Buffet** (p. 147) at Caesars Palace serves high-quality food worthy of tablecloths and candlelight. Bargain hunters, however, won't need to sacrifice quality at the **Garden Court Buffet** (p. 150) in Main Street Station.

o **Best Hamburgers: bBd's Burgers, Beers, Desserts** (p. 138) grinds it out at Palace Station, putting out their take on your favorite burgers from around the country, cooked by different methods, from the steakhouse burger over the wood-charcoal grill to a griddled burger. Throw in an amazing craft beer selection, and it's just about the perfect burger joint.

- **Best Desserts:** An offshoot of the NYC original restaurant, **Black Tap** (p. 116) is known for its Instagrammable and enormous milkshakes. We think the Brooklyn Blackout shake is not just wacky looking but also the best treat in town on a hot Vegas day.
- **Best Views:** You can see the entire city and big chunks of southern Nevada from the revolving **Top of the World** (p. 128), situated more than 800 feet up the Stratosphere Tower, while at **Rivea,** at the top of the Mandalay Bay, you get a virtually unobstructed view of the Strip and delightfully crafted Mediterranean-inspired cuisine that may make you forget the vista entirely.
- **Best Breakfasts:** Don't let the long lines at the cheekily named **Egg Slut** (in the Cosmopolitan; p. 123) deter you. We didn't think egg sandwiches were worth the wait until we came across these bad boys.

THE best LAS VEGAS HOTELS

- **Best Classic Vegas Hotel:** Most of historic Las Vegas has been imploded (often spectacularly), but at **Caesars Palace** (p. 57) you can still get a taste of it as themed Roman decadence meets classic Sin City opulence.
- **Best Modern Vegas Hotel:** The **Cosmopolitan of Las Vegas** (p. 58) offers a blueprint for what the next generation of Las Vegas hotels will be like: as over-the-top visually as any theme hotel, but with a sexy, contemporary edge.
- **Best for a Romantic Getaway:** It may not be in the Mediterranean, but the gorgeous ceiling frescoes, faux canals and stellar shopping at the **Venetian** (p. 61) will transport you straight to Italy. Massive, luxurious suites provide a romantic retreat that really puts you in the mood for *amore.*
- **Best for Families:** Las Vegas is not a family destination, but if you can't leave the little ones with Grandma, your choice for a major Vegas hotel is **Circus Circus** (p. 71), where there are almost as many things for the wee ones to do as there are for adults.
- **Best for Business Travelers: Westgate Las Vegas**'s (p. 83) location next to the Convention Center makes this a no-brainer from a geographical perspective, but the large rooms, classic casino, and raft of restaurants give it a decidedly Vegas spin.
- **Best Rooms on the Strip:** There are fewer than 200 rooms at the **Cromwell** (p. 60), and compared to more modern hotels, they can run on the smaller side. But cool design touches (art! real books!) and a prime location center Strip make up for what you lack in space.
- **Best Rooms Downtown:** The **Golden Gate** (p. 77) is the oldest hotel in Las Vegas, but renovation of its old bones has transformed it into a modern yet comfortable resort that is keeping up with the rapid changes of this neighborhood.
- **Best Rooms Off the Strip: Red Rock Resort** (p. 92) lives up to the resort part of its name as a true desert retreat, complete with gorgeous, modern rooms that you'll never want to leave.

o **Best Bathrooms:** This one is a toss-up for us, with the bigger-than-many-apartments-size retreats at the **Venetian** (p. 61) and the sumptuous luxury fixtures at **Aria Las Vegas** (p. 45) both winning our, er, hearts.

o **Best Bang for Your Buck:** Almost everything you can find at a Strip hotel (nice rooms, full casino, multiple restaurants, former Las Vegas mayor/martini aficionado Oscar Goodman!) can be gotten at the **Plaza** (p. 79) in Downtown Las Vegas for a fraction of the cost.

o **Best Non-Casino Hotel:** They can't get your money gambling, so they get it through high room rates, but to stay at the **Four Seasons** (p. 46) is to immerse yourself in luxury.

o **Best Splurge:** Rooms at **Wynn/Encore Las Vegas** (p. 69) will almost always be among the most expensive in town, but you'll totally feel like you are getting your money's worth, especially with the gorgeous spas, pools, casinos, and other amenities at your disposal.

o **Best Hotels for Spas:** The **Spa at Encore** (p. 189) is a 70,000-square-foot oasis for the mind, body, and spirit, with gorgeous Moroccan-infused design and a full menu of pampering delights. Meanwhile, we only wish our own gym were as handsomely equipped as the one at the **Canyon Ranch SpaClub** (p. 188) in the Venetian, which also has several other high-priced treatments on which you can blow your blackjack winnings. For more great spa options, see p. 188.

THE best FREE THINGS TO DO IN LAS VEGAS

o **Watching the Waters Dance:** The intricately choreographed water ballet that is the **Bellagio Fountains** (p. 160) would be worth repeated viewings even if they charged to see it. The fact that they don't makes it an almost perfect Vegas experience.

o **Enjoying the Changing of the Seasons:** There are five seasons in the elaborately designed botanical gardens of the **Bellagio Conservatory** (p. 160): Winter (holiday), Chinese New Year, Spring, Summer, and Fall. No matter which is on display during your visit, make sure your digital camera has a full battery charge. You'll want lots of pictures.

o **Seeing a Volcano Erupt:** When the free **Mirage Volcano** (p. 160) first "erupted" in 1989, shooting flames and faux lava into the sky, it literally stopped traffic on the Strip. That it doesn't today only means that it has more competition for your attention, not that it is any less fun.

o **Watching the Sky Light Up:** Many people considered it almost sacrilegious to convert the famed Glitter Gulch in Downtown Vegas into a pedestrian mall with a free light-and-sound show broadcast on a massive LED canopy overhead. Now the **Fremont Street Experience** (p. 163) is considered a must-visit.

- **Playing a Penny Slot:** Yes, in order to win the big bucks—sometimes millions of them—on a modern penny slot, you must bet much more than just one penny. But if you're okay with smaller rewards and losses, you could stretch a dollar into 100 spins.

- **Beating the High Score:** It's free to just look at the restored classic machines at the **Pinball Hall of Fame** (p. 170), and if you want to do more than just look, it'll only cost you a couple of quarters. What other museum lets you play with its works of art?

- **Making Your Own Postcard:** Nearly every hotel now has some sort of clever wall or giant piece of art that's meant to help you populate your social media feed. But just down the road from the southernmost edge of the Strip is the original Insta-worthy installation, and one of the most photographed and imitated signs in the world. Get a picture of yourself at the **Welcome to Fabulous Las Vegas Sign** (p. 161), and you'll have a postcard-worthy souvenir—even if you've never sent a postcard in your life.

THE best WAYS TO SEE LAS VEGAS LIKE A LOCAL

- **Gambling on a Budget:** Finding a local at a Strip casino is rare. Why? Because Vegas residents know the limits are lower and the payback is often higher at neighborhood casinos like **Red Rock Resort** (p. 92) and **Green Valley Ranch Resort** (p. 88).

- **Eating off the Strip:** Those same locals who don't gamble on the Strip usually don't eat on the Strip either, unless they are trying to impress visitors. Instead, they dine at the less expensive but still fantastic local eateries such as **EDO Gastro Tapas & Wine** (p. 138).

- **Becoming an Arts Lover:** Leave the tacky Las Vegas snow globes for the souvenir-hunting tourists and get yourself some unique Vegas keepsakes at one of the arts collectives instead. The **Arts Factory** (p. 162) is leading the charge for the burgeoning arts scene in the city.

- **Hunting for Treasure:** It may be surprising to find out that in a city like Las Vegas, where history is often disposed of with carefully timed implosions, antiques shopping is a favored pastime of locals and visitors alike. Check out the fun finds at **Retro Vegas** (p. 202).

- **Catching a Broadway Show:** The stunning (visually and aurally) **Smith Center for the Performing Arts** (p. 218) is a boon to the cultural life of Las Vegas, giving a proper home to everything from the philharmonic and dance troupes to the popular Broadway Series featuring shows like *Book of Mormon* and *Hamilton*.

- **Walking the Streets:** No, not that way. Instead, check out the fun **First Friday Las Vegas** street fair (p. 165), which brings the local (and tourist) community together with live entertainment, art vendors, and lots of state fair–type food. Did we mention deep-fried cookie dough? We thought that would get your attention.

THE best LAS VEGAS CASINOS

○ **Best Classic Casinos:** On the Strip there is no place that honors its history quite like **Caesars Palace** (p. 57), where you can still enjoy the classic Roman splendor that has been wowing gamblers since 1966. Serious players still head directly to **Golden Nugget** (p. 74) for its 1990s *Swingers* vibe and lively table game action.

○ **Best Modern Casinos:** When we first saw the contemporary, cutting-edge decor at **Aria Las Vegas** (p. 45), we thought that nothing could top it in terms of modern casino luxury. But then along came the bold, artistic statement of the **Cosmopolitan of Las Vegas** (p. 58), and we realized we just might have a competition on our hands.

○ **Best Glitter Gulch Casinos:** Downtown Las Vegas casinos often have lower limits and friendlier dealers, two things that can make losing money less painful. The best of the breed in the area are the **Golden Nugget** (p. 74), all warm hues and laid-back fun, and **Downtown Grand** (p. 74), which manages to be both modern and charmingly retro at the same time.

○ **Best Local Casinos:** Most neighborhood casinos are low-limit, no-frills joints, but the casinos at **Red Rock Resort** (p. 92), **Green Valley Ranch** (p. 88), and **Palace Station** (p. 85) are as stylish as many on the Strip. That they can be that visually appealing, and still maintain most of the thrifty attitude that the locals' casinos are known for, is almost a miracle.

○ **Best Budget Casinos:** You won't find any ostentatious opulence at the **Orleans** (p. 85), but you will find thousands of low-limit slot and video poker machines and dozens of gaming tables that won't cost you an arm and a leg to join. Meanwhile the **Four Queens** (p. 76) in Downtown Las Vegas offers similarly low-priced gambling options in comfortable and friendly surroundings.

○ **Best Splurge Casino:** Yes, you can find high-limit slots and table games pretty much anywhere, but why not surround yourself with the opulent decor and high-class furnishings of **Wynn/Encore** (p. 69)?

○ **Best Blast from the Past Casinos:** Both the **D Las Vegas** (p. 73) and the **Eastside Cannery** (p. 86) have a selection of "classic" machines that still take and dispense actual coins!

THE best LAS VEGAS SHOWS

○ **Best Overall Show:** A perfect intersection of music and artistry can be found at *Michael Jackson ONE* (p. 209), featuring the music and choreography of the King of Pop and the stunning visual theater of Cirque du Soleil.

○ **Best Big Shows:** The wow-factor winner is a toss-up between **Cirque du Soleil's** *KÀ* (p. 208) and *Mystère* (p. 210). The latter is more traditional—if you can call a human circus that mixes dazzling acrobatics with dramatic visuals "traditional"—in that it has only a loose semblance of narrative, whereas *KÀ* actually has a plot. Both are dazzling and, given the extremely high production values, seem worth the extremely high-ticket prices.

o **Best Small Show:** Only the space in which *Absinthe* (p. 206) is performed can be called small; the over-the-top acrobatics, stunts, dance, comedy, and mind-blowing originality of each certainly can't be beat.

o **Best Classic Show:** Fare thee well, huge stage sets; pointless production numbers; showgirls; nipples on parade; and Bob Mackie headdresses. If you want more than just a musty blast from the past, check out *Vegas! The Show* (p. 219), which celebrates multiple eras of classic Sin City entertainment in one spectacular package.

o **Best Magic Shows:** This town isn't good enough for **Penn & Teller** (p. 216) and their master class in the art and artifice of illusion taught by guys who will both amuse and amaze.

o **Best Music Show: Human Nature's** *Jukebox* (p. 212) will shock you with how well four white Australian dudes can sing classic Motown songs, boy-band hits, and pop classics.

o **Best Daytime Shows:** It's almost as much of a comedy show as it is a magic show, but the set done by **Mac King** (p. 216) will leave you astounded while watching some great close-up tricks and laughing your head off at the same time. A similar mix of laughs and gasps can be found at the comedy juggling show done by **Jeff Civillico.**

THE best OUTDOOR EXPERIENCES IN LAS VEGAS

o **Best Pools:** There are acres of water park fun at **Mandalay Bay** (p. 48), including a wave pool, lazy river, beach, regular swimming pools, and even its own open-air casino. Meanwhile, the lush landscaping, fountains, and water slides at the **Mirage** (p. 64) will make you feel like you're in a tropical paradise. For more picks for our favorite pools, see p. 66.

o **Best Golf:** "Real" golfers head to **TPC Las Vegas** (p. 188) for its challenging holes, eye-candy scenery, and occasional Justin Timberlake sightings. If you're more into hitting a few golf balls as a social exercise, **Topgolf** (p. 168) is a driving range, bar, dining destination all in one.

o **Best Drives:** The 13-mile **Red Rock Scenic Drive** (p. 249) provides a way to enjoy the colorful rocks and canyons without leaving the air-conditioned comfort of your car. On the other hand, you could get a good breeze going at about 140 mph in one of the race or exotic cars you can drive yourself at the **Las Vegas Motor Speedway** (p. 172).

o **Best Retreat:** If you need a respite from the hustle and bustle of Las Vegas, head north to **Mount Charleston** (p. 253) for a relaxed mountain retreat, or to work up a sweat while hiking or snowboarding.

o **Best Man-Made Wonder:** One of the greatest engineering feats in history is the 726-foot-tall **Hoover Dam** (p. 243). You can take tours of the mighty facility and learn how it made Las Vegas (and much of the American Southwest) possible.

SUGGESTED LAS VEGAS ITINERARIES

The Strip alone has hundreds of restaurants, dozens of shows, and more attractions, sights, and sounds than can easily be catalogued, much less visited. So yes, when you come to Las Vegas, you certainly won't be lacking in things to do. But the sheer enormity of the city and its laundry list of items for your daily to-do list could leave even the most intrepid traveler feeling a little overwhelmed.

The itineraries in this chapter are designed to help narrow down the big list a little while maximizing your time. This way you can spend less energy planning and more having fun. Each itinerary has a theme, but you can always mix and match to create your perfect Las Vegas getaway.

Instead of a step-by-step tour, the itineraries are broken down by morning, afternoon, and nighttime activities with multiple suggestions for each, again allowing you to customize your vacation in a way that makes sense for you.

ICONIC LAS VEGAS

There are many things with which Las Vegas has become synonymous: Gambling and all things indulgent and excessive are probably at the top of the list, but there are also the dancing waters, the dolphins, the buffets, the Cirque du Soleil shows, the steakhouses, the offbeat museums, the wild nightlife, and much more. This itinerary will guide you to the must-see and must-do, all of which are fun for first-timers or repeat offenders. Have your cameras ready!

Mornings

Start your day with a photo opportunity at the **Welcome to Fabulous Las Vegas Sign** (p. 161), perhaps the city's most iconic symbol. Then keep your "say cheese" smile in place as you take a driving tour past the only-in-Vegas, social media post–worthy exteriors of hotels (see chapter 4) like the pyramid-shaped **Luxor,** the castle-themed **Excalibur,** the Gotham recreation of **New York–New York,** the modern wonder of **Aria,** the Italian villa charm of

Bellagio, the Gallic splendor of **Paris Las Vegas,** and the Roman decadence of **Caesars Palace.**

If you started early enough and still have time before lunch, check out one (or preferably both) of the city's more colorful attractions with the glorious botanical gardens at the **Bellagio Conservatory** (p. 160) or the majestic animals at **Siegfried & Roy's Secret Garden & Dolphin Habitat** (p. 158) at the Mirage. Both are fun to look at, but more importantly, offer a bit of a peaceful respite from the madness that is Las Vegas. Trust us, you'll need a break every now and then!

Afternoons

You can go one of two ways for lunch, either with a classic Vegas buffet or a view of the throngs of humanity that crowd the Strip. For the former, check out the **Spice Market Buffet** (p. 149) at Planet Hollywood or the **Buffet at Bellagio** (p. 147). Both offer a seemingly endless array of well-prepared food; while they may not be the cheapest buffets in town, neither are they the most expensive, so you can have your proverbial—or literal—cake and eat it, too.

The other way to go would be to have a nosh at a Strip-side cafe so you can do some people-watching. The best of the bunch are **Mon Ami Gabi** (p. 122) for Americanized twists on classic French bistro cuisine at Paris Las Vegas, and **Eataly** (p. 104) at Park MGM, with Italian favorites such as Roman-style pizza or even a quick cannoli and espresso.

After you have refueled, head to one of the city's offbeat, unique museums. Tops on our list are the **National Museum of Organized Crime and Law Enforcement,** aka the **Mob Museum** (p. 163), which takes a look at the Mafia and its influence on the country and Vegas in particular; or the **National Atomic Testing Museum** (p. 167), which explores the history of the nuclear age with a special focus on the nearby Nevada Testing Site.

Close out your afternoon with some shopping, window or otherwise. Even if you can't afford to buy, a stroll through the highly themed malls like the **Forum Shops** (p. 198, ancient Rome) or **Grand Canal Shoppes** (p. 199, Venice canals complete with gondoliers) is a hoot.

Nights

If you didn't eat the buffet at lunch you may want to consider one for dinner, but our preference would be to send you to a steakhouse. The best of the bunch are **StripSteak** at Mandalay Bay, Michael Mina's version of a modern steakhouse, which not only serves some of the best Japanese beef on the Strip but also has a really exciting non-steak menu; don't confuse this with **Strip House** (p. 115) at Planet Hollywood, which has fantastically flavorful cuts of meat and a peek-a-boo bordello theme; and the simply named the **Steakhouse** (p. 127) at Circus Circus, which has an old-school charm, terrific food, and affordable prices.

We hope you didn't eat too much, because your night is just getting started. Next, it's on to one of the shows by Cirque du Soleil, the French-Canadian

Suggested Las Vegas Itineraries

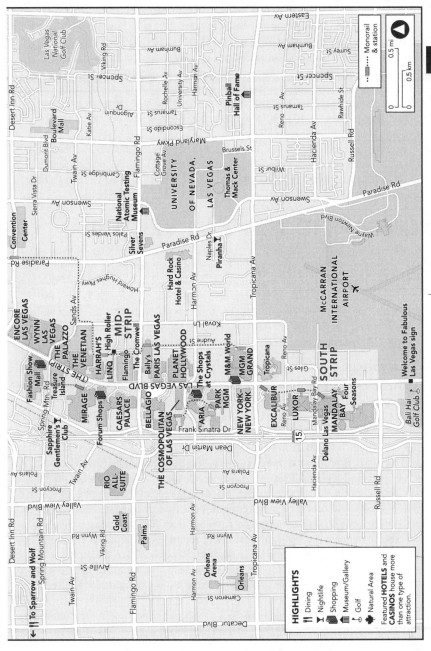

Monorail & station

0.5 mi

0.5 km

HIGHLIGHTS

🍴 Dining

🍸 Nightlife

🛍️ Shopping

🏛️ Museum/Gallery

⛳ Golf

🌲 Natural Area

Featured **HOTELS** and **CASINOS** house more than one type of attraction.

circus troupe that reinvented and now rules the Las Vegas entertainment scene. There are many to choose from, but our favorites include the dreamy wonder of *Mystère* (p. 210) at Treasure Island, the martial arts spectacle of *KÀ* (p. 208) at MGM Grand, the water ballet of *O* (p. 211) at Bellagio, or the King of Pop spectacle that is *Michael Jackson ONE* (p. 209) at Mandalay Bay.

From there it's on to the truly iconic Las Vegas experiences, which are all best viewed at night. The dancing waters of the **Fountains of Bellagio** (p. 160) are worth visiting no matter how many times you have seen them; the **Mirage Volcano** (p. 160) is still a lava-spewing delight; and the **Fremont Street Experience** (p. 163) in Downtown Las Vegas will immerse you in the neon-lit glory that is Glitter Gulch.

End your day dancing the night away at one of the city's hot nightclubs like the technologically innovative, LED-laden **Light** (p. 233) at Mandalay Bay or the enormous nightclub **Hakkasan** (p. 232) at MGM Grand. Or put some money down in the casino: It doesn't get more iconic Vegas than that.

OVER-THE-TOP LAS VEGAS

Las Vegas was built on the idea that "average" and "normal" were adjectives that should never be used to describe the city. They don't just build hotels here; they build some of the biggest hotels in the world. And then they throw a roller coaster, a volcano, a $500-per-person golf course, or a $400-per-meal restaurant into the mix. Vegas is all about extravagance, so this itinerary will help you find the biggest of the big, the wildest of the wild, and the most outrageous, over-the-top experiences the city has to offer.

Mornings

You're going to have a busy day of excess, so it's important to start out with an ample breakfast to keep your energy level high. Room service is always an option—there's nothing quite as extravagant as having servers bring you food without ever getting out of bed—but if you feel like getting out and about, try the sumptuous **brunch buffets at Wynn Las Vegas** (p. 150) or **Caesars Palace** (p. 147). Both offer a mind-boggling number of food choices (Caesars' Bacchanal Buffet claims over 500 individual dishes at any time), all of which are a cut above your standard buffet. Handmade omelets and crepes, freshly baked breads, and heaping mounds of bacon, sausage, and even steak will go well with your unlimited mimosas. At more than $60 per person (for the weekend champagne brunch), the price will remind you that this is no pedestrian all-you-can-eat experience. The **Sterling Brunch at BLT at Bally's** will set you back nearly $100 for the weekend meal, but with all-you-can-eat caviar, lobster tails, and free-flowing Perrier-Jouet champagne, it's worth every penny.

The morning hours are the best time to schedule your outdoor activities. Not only are crowds often lighter, as a lot of people sleep in (it is a vacation, after all), but temperatures are also more moderate. This is especially true in

VEGAS BY air

Most people are satisfied with the views of Las Vegas from terra firma. Walking or driving up the Strip, especially at night, is a requirement for the first-time Vegas visitor. But, for some, there is no better way to see Sin City in all its neon glamour than from the air. If you are one of these intrepid souls, then look for a helicopter tour of Las Vegas.

More than a dozen competing companies offer tours of the city and surrounding areas, and most offer the same type of services at very similar prices. We're including a few of the more well-known companies below, but comparison shopping is highly encouraged. **Maverick Helicopters** (www.maverick helicopter.com; ✆ **888/261-4414**) is one of the most well-known tour operators in Las Vegas. Its large fleet of ECO-Star

helicopters has one of the best safety records in the business, and various packages are available, including twilight and night flights over the Strip. If you want to venture farther, Hoover Dam and Grand Canyon packages are available. Rates start at around $119 per person and go up from there, depending on the length and distance of the tour. Most include transportation to and from your hotel.

VegasTours.com (www.vegastours. com; ✆ **866/218-6877**) features a similar list of air adventures, including a nighttime flight over Vegas and several to the Grand Canyon, while **Papillon Tours** (www.papillon.com; ✆ **888/635-7272**) not only offers helicopter tours, but airplane and ground excursions as well.

the summer, when an afternoon stroll down the Strip can emulate a trek across the desert. So use this time to catch some rays poolside or, if you are recreationally minded, work up a moderate sweat with a round of golf. If you are a guest of **Caesars Palace,** you can play the tony links at **Cascata** for a princely sum of $295 per person (or more).

End your morning with a visit to a spa for some pampering and luxuriating. The **Spa at Encore** (p. 189) offers virtually every massage, aromatherapy, skin-care treatment, and relaxation technique known—some of which will cost you more per 30-minute session than your hotel room. Soak in the Jacuzzi or dip in and out of the hot and cold pools before heading out again.

Afternoons

Then it's off to the shopping malls, where the true excess can really begin (see chapter 7). The **Forum Shops at Caesars Palace,** the **Grand Canal Shoppes at the Venetian,** the **LINQ Promenade, Grand Bazaar Shops,** the **Shops at Crystals, Fashion Show,** and the **Miracle Mile Shops** at Planet Hollywood are all filled with high-end retailers designed to drain your checking account and max out your credit cards. If those are a little out of your price range, consider going the opposite direction at the **Bonanza Gift and Souvenir Shop** (p. 200). Billed as the largest souvenir shop in the world, this is the place where you can find pretty much anything—from tacky to, well, *more* tacky—emblazoned with the words "Las Vegas" on it. The kitsch factor here is off the charts.

Finally, experience some of the quintessential, only-in-Vegas attractions, such as riding a gondola through a shopping mall at the **Venetian** (p. 61) or watching the water ballet at the **Fountains of Bellagio** (p. 160).

Nights

Start your evening with a meal at **Joël Robuchon** (p. 100), an outpost of the late, multi-Michelin-star-winning chef, who deserved his constellation of awards. The degustation menu will only cost you a mere $445 a person (and that's before wine). Or if your extravagance knows no bounds, try the Fleur-Burger at **Fleur by Hubert Keller** (p. 99). Made from Wagyu beef, topped with foie gras truffle, and accompanied by a bottle of 1995 Chateau Petrus, it costs a measly $5,000.

Next, you'll want to see a show, and you should focus on those that can only be seen here. If **Lady Gaga** or **Gwen Stefani** is in town, you should seize the opportunity to catch one of their performances at Park MGM and Zappos Theater at Planet Hollywood, respectively, because these shows are exclusive to Vegas. Or check out any of Cirque du Soleil's Vegas-only productions, the best of which are *O* at Bellagio and *KÀ* at MGM Grand. Each is set in its own multimillion-dollar theater, with stage sets—a giant pool and an enormous revolving platform, respectively—unlike anything you've seen before.

Nighttime is the best time for getting the true Strip experience, so how about renting a limousine (maybe one of those superstretch Hummers, if you are feeling really crazy) and instructing the driver to just cruise Las Vegas Boulevard? Hanging out of the sunroof with a cocktail in your hand is discouraged, but people do it anyway.

An after-dark stop at the **High Roller** (p. 157) is in order to give you a bird's-eye view of Las Vegas from the top of the world's tallest observation wheel, and then it's off to the party spots.

Most of the Vegas club scene starts late (11pm or midnight), so have your driver take you to one of the hip hot spots, such as **XS** at Encore, **Light** at Mandalay Bay, or **Marquee** at the Cosmopolitan of Las Vegas (all in chapter 8). These are see-and-be-seen places, so dress to impress and be on the lookout for a celebrity or three hanging out in the VIP areas. You can easily drop a grand if you want to sit at a table with bottle service.

Help for Troubled Travelers

The **Travelers Aid Society** is a social-service organization geared to helping travelers in difficult situations. Its services include reuniting families separated while traveling, feeding people stranded without cash, and even providing emotional counseling. If you're in trouble, seek them out. In Las Vegas, services are provided by **Help of Southern Nevada**, 1640 E. Flamingo Rd., Ste. 100, near Maryland Parkway (www.helpsonv.org; ☎ **702/369-4357**). Hours are Monday through Thursday 7am to 5pm.

If it's more of the classic Las Vegas vibe you're looking for, try **Peppermill Fireside Lounge** (p. 225), with its retro-'70s/'80s interior. So cheesy—it's hip again.

Your final destination should be in the spot that makes Vegas tick, the casino. Yes, there are casinos all over the country now, but there's nothing quite like tossing the dice at a craps table at **Caesars Palace** (p. 57) or spinning the reels in the high-limit lounge at **Wynn Las Vegas** (p. 69).

GUYS' GETAWAY

Not every trip to Vegas with the guys needs to get as crazy as the movie *The Hangover*, but if you're looking for a real man's–man experience, no other city does it quite like this one. Whether it's a bachelor blowout weekend or just an excuse to blow off steam without your significant other's disapproving glances, this itinerary is designed to explain why they call this place "Sin City."

Mornings

You were probably out late the night before and there may have been alcohol involved, so start your morning with a hearty guy's breakfast at **Hash House a Go Go** (p. 120). Its huge portions of reimagined farm food are chest-poundingly substantial, and there is even a specialty called O'Hare of the Dog—a Budweiser served in a paper bag with a side of bacon.

To get your body in shape for the day ahead, spend the morning taking advantage of the various sports and recreation options available around town. Nearly every hotel has a fitness center, and some, such as Bally's, offer full tennis courts. If you're a fan of the fairway, head over to **Bali Hai golf course** (p. 187), located conveniently on the Strip, for 18 holes and some wheeling around in their GPS-enabled golf carts. Or, if you need something more extreme, a visit to **Red Rock Adventures** at Red Rock Resort, where you can arrange everything from rock climbing to horseback riding to river rafting. Need something even *more* extreme? Take a few laps around the track with the **Richard Petty Driving Experience** at the **Las Vegas Motor Speedway** (p. 172), an interactive attraction that puts you behind the wheel of a 600-horsepower NASCAR car at speeds of 155 mph.

Afternoons

Continue your guys-gone-wild day with a stop at **Gilley's** (p. 119) for some great down-home grub and even a ride on the mechanical bull if you feel like proving your machismo.

Daytime is playtime in Las Vegas, where the big trend is to have nightclub-worthy experiences during the afternoon at some of the hotel pools. **Daylight Beach Club** (p. 234) at Mandalay Bay, **Wet Republic** (p. 235) at MGM Grand, and **Encore Beach Club** (p. 235) at Encore Las Vegas are all open to the general public (for a cover charge) and include everything from live DJs to fully stocked bars, and certainly a bevy of bikini-wearing partiers. If that's not enough to appeal to the guy in you, **Sapphire Gentleman's Club** (p. 240) now has its own daytime pool party complete with strippers. Next, head back to the casino for a little sports-book action. You can place a wager on just about any type of sporting event in existence (cricket, anyone?), and depending on the season and the day of the week, you might be able to catch a game in action. The **sports books** at the Mirage and Caesars Palace are always good options for their huge screens and high energy, but you may want to consider the M Resort, the Venetian, or the Palazzo, which offer in-running betting. Popular in the U.K., this means that you can not only wager on the outcome of the game, but place bets during the action as well.

If that isn't enough to get your adrenaline flowing, consider one of the serious thrill rides in town, such as the extreme adventures atop the 1,000-foot **Stratosphere Tower** (p. 160) at the Strat. You can play a little game and make whichever friend screams the loudest while on **Insanity** or **SkyJump** buy the first round of drinks later that night. Or take a run at **SlotZilla** (p. 166) a zipline attraction in Downtown Las Vegas that features both seated and superhero flying position rides.

Nights

We know. We already sent you to some sports books, but you should go back to the only one that is a real restaurant. The 45,000-square-foot **Lagasse's Stadium** (p. 121) at the Venetian is a sports bar on steroids, with 100 flatscreen TVs and a menu crammed with highlights from Emeril's American and Creole cuisine.

Is it hockey season? You'll definitely want to catch the Vegas Golden Knights play at **T-Mobile Arena** (p. 215). After a stellar first year in 2017–2018, the team has proved that a) this town can carry a professional sports team and b) Las Vegans care about hockey.

Now for some nighttime entertainment. Topless revues are becoming an endangered species around Vegas—which you can probably blame on the Internet—but there are still a couple left that will allow you to get your (not-so-cheap) thrills. Sadly, you won't catch too many of the traditional showgirl headdresses anymore, save for street buskers and the occasional appearances with former Mayor Goodman, but their modern, equally topless counterparts are still shimmying away at **Fantasy** at Luxor or **X Burlesque** at Flamingo.

The party gets started late in Vegas, and you might want to start at a bar or two, such as the **Commonwealth** (p. 226) on Fremont Street or **Gold Spike** (p. 78), both in Downtown Las Vegas. Then it's time to hit the dance floor. **Marquee** (p. 233) at the Cosmopolitan is an obvious place to start, but give **Jewel** at Aria or **Intrigue** (p. 232) at Wynn a shot.

What's that? You haven't had enough gambling? Well, head over to Planet Hollywood's **Passion Pit,** complete with lingerie-clad dealers at the blackjack tables and go-go girls.

And if you want more girly action, Vegas has **strip clubs** aplenty. The best of the best is detailed in chapter 8.

GIRLS' GETAWAY

With the plethora of strip clubs and showgirls in this town, you'd think that Vegas is a man's world. Not so! There are plenty of activities and attractions for the ladies—from wild, bachelorette-style craziness to relaxing, leave-your-cares-at-home-style getaways. Here are just a few suggestions.

Mornings

If you dream of a leisurely breakfast, skip your hotel buffet and head to the Cromwell and **Giada** on weekends. You know chef Giada di Laurentiis from her Food Network shows where she made home entertaining and cooking look light and breezy. The food is not cheap, but it is high quality, generously portioned, and just plain delightful.

Vegas is retail heaven, and you could spend your whole day going to branches of pretty much every designer name you can think of in the major hotel malls (the **Shops at Crystals,** the **Forum Shops** at Caesars Palace, the **Grand Canal Shoppes** at Venetian/Palazzo, **Miracle Mile** at Planet Holly-wood, and shops at Bellagio and Wynn Las Vegas). Bargain shoppers will want to check out the **Las Vegas Premium Outlets North** near Downtown. Truth be told, there are not a lot of bargains there; but it's an outlet, so something will turn up. See chapter 7.

Afternoons

You can have a fabulous girly lunch at the elegant **Bouchon** (p. 110) at the Venetian. Thomas Keller's brasserie is tucked away into a private tower so you don't have to be inundated with the dinging of the casino floor as you tuck into your eggs Benedict and mimosas.

Okay, it's time for some serious pampering. You could just stretch out by the pool (didn't you just buy a new bikini this morning?), but it's hot outside. So make your way to the spas at **Caesars Palace, Bellagio,** or the **Venetian** (which has a branch of Canyon Ranch) for a full menu of massages, facials, weird treatments imported from countries you've never heard of, and lots more—all designed to make you feel as relaxed and limp as an al dente noodle.

Nights

If your girls' getaway weekend is of the rowdy bachelorette variety, have din-ner at **STK** at Cosmopolitan. It's kind of like eating a steak in a loud night-club, surrounded by really beautiful people. If it's a sultrier, femme fatale atmosphere you're after, get a big table at **Red Square** (p. 102) at Mandalay Bay and drink cold vodka while noshing on upscale Russian fare.

Hey, speaking of getting rowdy, if you're tired of all those signs with scant-ily clad women all over Vegas, equal time can be attained at such shows as the male-stripper review *Thunder From Down Under* (p. 223) at Excalibur or the tried-and-true **Chippendales** (p. 223) at Rio. Or, if that's not risqué enough, try the delightfully profane circus of *Absinthe* at Caesars Palace. Just don't allow the host to pull you up on stage for audience participation. You'll thank us later.

Rosina (p. 224) at Palazzo is a calm, sophisticated spot to have a tipple to gear up for the rest of your evening. Peruse one of three secret cocktail menus to expand on your Manhattan, old-fashioned, and mojito vocabularies. And do feel free to press the Champagne Call Button at will so that you glass never runs empty.

Finally, strap on that pair of Christian Louboutins you bought earlier today (lucky you), because it's time to go dancing. If you're single and looking to mingle (or whatever, we don't judge), the scenes at **Light** at Mandalay Bay, **XS** at Encore Las Vegas, and **Omnia** at Caesars Palace are such that people will stand in line for hours (and pay outrageous cover charges) just to get inside. We have to admit they are awfully fun.

Wanna just go dance and not be bothered by the meat-market scene? Consider going to gay clubs, such as **Piranha** (p. 238), just off the Strip. They welcome women, but remember that you aren't going to be the priority.

UNLIKELY LAS VEGAS

It's really hard to overlook the Strip—after all, a number of people have spent billions and billions of dollars to ensure that you don't—but there are still some surprisingly unusual and captivating sights to see in and around Las Vegas. This itinerary is designed to help you discover them. You will need a car to do this tour.

Mornings

Those pricey buffets at the casinos may offer you truckloads of food, but even the ones at the out-of-the-way hotels are the very definition of "discovered." Instead, go down-home for the delightful Southern cooking at **M&M Soul Food Café** (p. 142). Chicken and waffles, biscuits and gravy, or anything with grits is a great way to start the day as far as we're concerned.

Walk off that breakfast by exploring the nearby **18b Arts District** (p. 165), home to several art galleries and studios, bravely taking a stance against pre-fab, soulless Vegas. You might take special note of **Retro Vegas** (p. 202), a fun and funky store celebrating Sin City and midcentury modern furnishings (they work remarkably well together). If it's the first Friday of the month, you could come back and stroll here in the evening, as that's when the galleries come into the streets for a food, art, and entertainment festival.

Springs Preserve (p. 173) is a remarkable destination, focused on nature and ecological concerns. The interpretive center examines the history of the region as related to water consumption, which sounds "dry" but isn't. Need proof? Try the so-real-you-are-there flash flood exhibit or the 3-D movie theater that puts you atop the Hoover Dam being built. Outside are animal habitats and trails through the wetlands, as well as other exhibition halls dealing with the environment and recycling. The place is informative, entertaining, and absolutely vital in this day and age, and you can't believe that something of this quality and social significance is anywhere near Vegas.

Afternoons

Although Las Vegas is obviously our favorite city, New York comes in a close second, and a lot of that has to do with the food. Downtown is becoming Brooklyn-esque, with great independent restaurants such as the **Kitchen at Atomic** (p. 130) and **Flock & Fowl** (p. 134) becoming neighborhood hangouts. Great for the residents of Downtown, even better for you since you get a taste of what you'd be eating if this were your town.

From there, we recommend a trio of only-in-Las Vegas museums. Begin with the **National Atomic Testing Museum** (p. 167). It's about more than just the 5 minutes when the bomb was awesome (apparently people really thought that—they have photos that you won't believe, like the one of Miss Atomic Bomb). The museum traces the history of the atomic age, focusing specifically on the aboveground nuclear testing that occurred just outside of Las Vegas. It's a fascinating and sobering experience.

Head Downtown for a fun yet educational hour or so at the **Cannabition Cannabis Museum** (p. 162) near Fremont Street Experience. Wander around immersive art installations dedicated to Nevada's newest favorite weed.

Then you're off to the **Pinball Hall of Fame & Museum** (p. 170), where you can not only appreciate but actually play, classic machines and arcade games from the 1960s to the present day.

If you want to skip the latter, consider taking in the afternoon show by **Mac King** (p. 216) or Wednesday shows by **Jeff Civillico** at Harrah's Las Vegas and Paris Las Vegas, respectively. Both are considered among the best shows in Vegas and are good values for the money. King is an illusionist and comedian of great personal charm who still practices magic that doesn't require computer technology, while Civillico is a comic-juggler with a family-friendly and very funny patter. You can often get discounted (or even two-for-one) tickets for both shows in local magazines or online.

Nights

Now we'll send you far west to a place only foodies tend to know: **Sparrow + Wolf** (p. 143), a favorite hangout in Chinatown for many of the chefs in town when they're off the clock. And surprise: It isn't Asian food. Alternately, if you do have a taste for Asian, head even farther down Spring Mountain to **Other Mama** (p. 142), a local favorite that features modern cocktails and Japanese fare.

After dinner, why not do something completely "unlikely," like perform on the Las Vegas Strip? There are several hotel lounges that offer karaoke, but the sing-along fun at the stand-alone casino **Ellis Island** is probably the best. Or, instead of a show in one of the casinos, see what's playing at the **Smith**

Center for the Performing Arts (p. 218) in Downtown Las Vegas. You might be able to catch a Broadway touring show, a big-name concert, or a jazz set in one of the many theaters at the complex.

End your night exploring the booming bar scene of Downtown's **Fremont East Entertainment District** or the **Main Street Arts District** with funky taverns like **Downtown Cocktail Room,** the **Commonwealth, Vanguard Lounge, Velveteen Rabbit,** and more, all within steps of each other (see chapter 8). Each has its own vibe and is mostly populated by locals, so try each on for style and see what fits.

EATING LAS VEGAS

Las Vegas is a mecca for food lovers, offering endless opportunities to gorge on virtually every type of cuisine, from cheap eats to gourmet meals. This itinerary presumes you are very hungry and want to at least sample as much of it as you can, throwing waistlines, cholesterol counts, and common sense to the wind. You'll need a car to do this tour, although you may want to consider walking as much of it as you can . . . to give the illusion that you're getting a little exercise in between binges.

Mornings

There are plenty of ways to overdo it from a food perspective first thing in the morning. You could go big with the super decadent and deliriously over-the-top selections at the **Pantry** (p. 65) at Mirage, or get an entire day's worth of calories at an inexpensive buffet like the **Garden Court Buffet** (p. 150) at Main Street Station in Downtown Las Vegas—but let's be reasonable, shall we? After all, you don't want to get too full before the day has really even started.

If you don't mind standing in line, go for something a little lighter but still packed with flavors, like the sumptuous soft scrambled egg sandwich or the namesake dish at **Egg Slut** (p. 123). Both come in very satisfying portions, yet they'll keep you from getting too loaded down.

If you decided to sleep in a bit (and really, who could blame you?), then you could go for brunch at **Sadelle's** (p. 122) at Bellagio, which offers the best of the New York favorite's menu (including a tower of smoked fish and bagels made in-house) in a luxe, spacious setting.

Otherwise the rest of your morning could be spent exploring various sweet shops so you can stock up on quick hits of sugar to get you through the rest of the day. **M&M's World** (p. 196) allows you to mix and match your own selection of candy, while local favorite **Ethel M Chocolates** (p. 169) serves a finer brand of confections. Or you could visit **Carlo's Bakery,** which, in addition to being across from its full-service restaurant **Buddy V's** (p. 117) in the Grand Canal Shoppes at Palazzo, has a window where you can watch the bakers in action as they create cookies, cannoli, and other pastries.

Afternoons

For lunch, we're going to suggest something a little more substantial. **Yardbird** (p. 123) offers a Southern-inspired menu, featuring some of the best fried chicken on the Strip, as well as down-home fried green tomato sandwiches.

Speaking of sandwiches, we'd be totally remiss if we didn't mention **Capriotti's** (p. 140) as a perfect place to have lunch. Their divine submarine sandwiches (we're partial to the Bobbie, which is like Thanksgiving on a bun) will make you consider getting the epic 20-inch size and calling it a day.

Burgers are another way to go, and there are lots of options in Vegas including the fantastic offerings at **bBD's Burgers, Beers, Desserts** (p. 138), **Gordon Ramsay Burger** (p. 124), **Black Tap** (p. 116), and the nationally beloved **Shake Shack** (p. 108).

As you are digesting, take a stroll over to Bellagio to visit its **Patisserie** (p. 144) and sample the finest chocolate available in Las Vegas, or get a quick fix from **Sprinkles** (p. 200) and its cupcake ATM at the LINQ Promenade!

If you're lucky enough to be visiting on the first Friday of the month, be sure to go to the **First Friday Las Vegas** (p. 165) street festival in the Arts District, where you'll find a parking lot's worth of food trucks and vendors serving everything from pizza to sushi to barbecue and more. Don't miss the state fair–style selections, including the genius deep-fried chocolate chip cookie dough. Missing this will haunt you—trust us.

Nights

Finally, it's time to go whole hog, or cow as the case may be, so head to dinner at one of the city's steakhouses. The **Steakhouse** (p. 127) at Circus Circus is a local favorite, offering full meals at the same prices that others charge for an a la carte selection. **Strip House** (p. 115) at Planet Hollywood puts a modern spin on things with a charming peek-a-boo bordello theme and fantastic cuts of meat. But for our money you can't beat **Old Homestead Steakhouse** (p. 112) at Caesars Palace, a sister of the legendary New York City restaurant. The portions here are huge, which is appropriate since this is the restaurant that claims to have invented the doggie bag.

If a steak seems like too much of a commitment to you, you could try one of the restaurants that serve small bites instead of full meals. Chief among them would be **L'Atelier** (p. 101) at MGM Grand, created by the late master chef Joël Robuchon, where you can get various-size tasting menus or order small plates, each of which will be better than the last. Also at MGM, **Crush** (p. 99) has fantastic gourmet small plates and a fun environment in which to eat them. Another great choice in this category would be **EDO Gastro Tapas & Wine** (p. 138), featuring the best bites of Spanish fare along with killer gin and tonics. Just be warned that even though the portions are small, you'll wind up ordering a lot of them, and it could end up costing you more than just a standard meal.

But wait, we're not done. This is a 24-hour town, and lots of restaurants are open all night to satisfy those 2am cravings. **Peppermill Fireside Lounge** (p. 225) is an institution for late-night/early-morning bites, with a massive menu and fun takes on classic diner food; or you could head back to the **Pantry** (p. 65) for the 24-hour restaurant's night shift of food.

CITY LAYOUT

Located in the southernmost precincts of a wide, pancake-flat valley, Las Vegas is the biggest city in the state of Nevada. Treeless mountains form a scenic backdrop to hotels awash in neon glitter. Although bursting with residents and visitors, the city is quite compact, geographically speaking.

There are two main areas of Las Vegas: the **Strip** and **Downtown.** The former is probably the most famous 4-mile stretch of road in the nation. Officially called Las Vegas Boulevard South, it contains most of the top hotels in town and offers almost all the major showroom entertainment. First-time visitors will, and probably should, spend the bulk of their time on the Strip.

Downtown, meanwhile, is where Vegas started its Glitter Gulch fame, complete with neon ambassadors Vegas Vic and Sassy Sally watching over the action.

For many people, that's all there is to Las Vegas. But there is actually more to the town than that: Paradise Road, just east of the Strip, and Boulder Highway on the far-east side of town, are home to quite a bit of casino action; Maryland Parkway boasts mainstream shopping; and there are different restaurant options all over the city. Many of the "locals' hotels," most of which are off the regular tourist track, offer cheaper gambling limits plus budget food and entertainment options. Confining yourself to the Strip and Downtown is fine for the first-time visitor, but repeat customers (and you will be) should get out there and explore. Las Vegas Boulevard South (the Strip) is the starting point for addresses; any street that crosses it starts with 1 East and 1 West at its intersection with the Strip (and goes up from there).

All major Las Vegas hotels provide comprehensive tourist information at their reception and/or sightseeing and show desks.

Other good information sources are the **Las Vegas Convention and Visitors Authority,** 3150 Paradise Rd. (www.visitlasvegas.com; ✆ **877/847-4858** or 702/892-7575), open Monday through Friday 8am to 5:30pm; the **Las Vegas Metro Chamber of Commerce,** 6671 Las Vegas Blvd. S., Ste. 300 (www.lvchamber.com; ✆ **702/735-1616**), open Monday through Friday 8am to 5pm; and, for information on all of Nevada, including Las Vegas, the **Nevada Commission on Tourism** (www.travelnevada.com; ✆ **800/638-2328**), open 24 hours.

NEIGHBORHOODS IN BRIEF

South Strip

For the purposes of organizing this book, we've divided the Strip into three sections. The **South Strip** can be roughly defined as the portion of the Strip south of Harmon Avenue, including the MGM Grand, Mandalay Bay, Park MGM, New York–New York, Luxor, Aria, and many more hotels and casinos. First-timers should consider staying here or in the Mid-Strip area simply because this is where the bulk of the things you're going to want to see, do, and eat are located.

Mid-Strip

The **Mid-Strip** is a long stretch of the Las Vegas Boulevard South between Harmon Avenue and Spring Mountain Road, which includes such big-name casinos as Planet Hollywood, the Cosmopolitan of Las Vegas, Bellagio, Caesars Palace, the Mirage, Treasure Island, Bally's, Paris Las Vegas, Flamingo Las Vegas, Harrah's, and more. As mentioned above, this is a great area for newbies, and it's also the preferred location for people with mobility issues since fewer steps will get you to more places.

North Strip

The **North Strip** stretches north from Spring Mountain Road all the way to the Strat and includes the Sahara, Wynn/Encore, the Strat, and Circus Circus, to name a few. Although there are certainly things to see along this chunk of the Strip, development has mostly stalled, so you'll see more things closed or partially constructed in this area than you will see open and completed. Except for Wynn/Encore and the Sahara, it is the lower-rent part of the Strip, with all the good and bad that comes along with it.

Downtown

Also known as **"Glitter Gulch"** (narrower streets make the neon seem brighter), Downtown Las Vegas, centered on Fremont Street between Main and 9th streets, was the first section of the city to develop hotels and casinos. Except for the Golden Nugget, which looks like it belongs in Monte Carlo, this area has traditionally been more casual than the Strip. But between the **Fremont Street Experience** (p. 163), the **Fremont East Entertainment District** (p. 165), and a general resurgence, Downtown offers a more affordable yet still entertaining alternative to the Strip.

The area between the Strip and Downtown is a seedy stretch dotted with tacky wedding chapels, bail-bond operations, pawnshops, and cheap motels. However, the area known as the **18b Arts District** (roughly north and south of Charleston Blvd. to the west of Las Vegas Blvd. S.) is making a name for itself as an artists' colony. Studios, galleries, antiques stores, bars, small cafes, and the fun **First Friday Las Vegas** festival (p. 165) can be found in the vicinity. Eventually the area may warrant its own neighborhood designation, but for now we include it in the Downtown category.

Just Off the Strip

With land directly on the Strip at a premium, it isn't surprising that veritable cottage industries of casinos, hotels, restaurants, nightclubs, attractions, and services have taken up residence in the areas immediately surrounding the megaresorts. Within a mile in any given direction, you'll find major hotels such as the Orleans, Rio, Palms, Westgate, and Hard Rock, to name a few, as well as important visitor destinations such as the Las Vegas Convention Center. You'll also find many smaller chain/name-brand hotels and motels offering reliable service at rates that are usually cheaper than you'll pay in a big casino-hotel on the Strip.

South & East of the Strip

Once you get a little bit of distance between you and the Strip, you'll start getting into the types of neighborhoods that will look much more familiar to you—except, perhaps, with a lot more desert landscaping. Shopping centers and housing tracts dominate the landscape of the bedroom community of Henderson, while lower-priced motels and chain restaurants take up a lot of space along the Boulder Highway corridor on the far-east side of town. In addition to the luxurious Green Valley Ranch Resort, sprinkled throughout are fun, low-cost casino-hotels, and some out-of-the-way attractions worth knowing about.

North & West of the Strip

The communities of Summerlin and North Las Vegas are where many of the people who work on the Strip live, shop, eat, and play. Yes, there are some major casino-hotels in the area, including the stunning Red Rock Resort, and a few notable restaurants, but for the most part what you'll find here are dependable chain stores and eateries that offer shopping and comfort food at better-than-Strip prices.

LAS VEGAS IN CONTEXT

N o major city in America has reinvented itself as many times, especially in such a short period, as Las Vegas. Just look at the recent decades. In the '80s, it was a discount afterthought. In the '90s, it was family and theme heaven. The new millennium brought in ultra-luxury and sky-high prices on everything from rooms to shampoo in the sundry stores. Visitors and even residents of the city always have the same question on their minds: What's next?

LAS VEGAS TODAY

At the beginning of the new millennium, the watchword was "expensive." The average room rate soared to over $200 a night, significantly higher than what visitors, once lulled by lower double-digit bargains, were used to paying. It was not unusual for the high-end hotels to charge $400 or even $500 for a standard room.

And why not? The crowds kept coming. Occupancy rates in Vegas were well over 90%, nearly 30% higher than the national average. Flush with big returns on their stock investments, equity in their home, or simply easy-flowing credit, those who could afford it flocked to the city in record numbers, generating record profit for the casinos. Vegas became hip, drawing a younger, more affluent demographic that lined up to pay for the fancy hotel rooms, the exclusive nightclubs, the celebrity-chef restaurants, and the high-limit gaming tables.

The Average Joe, on the other hand, got priced right out of town. For a lot of people—the people whose money helped build those massive hotels and casinos—the idea of a Vegas vacation became cost-prohibitive.

But then came the global economic meltdown in 2008, and Vegas was hit hard. The number of visitors coming to the city dropped dramatically, and those who came spent a lot less money in the casinos. By 2010, the average room rate plunged to the lowest level in nearly a decade and more rooms were going empty, with occupancy rates in the low 80% range—still good when compared to the national average, but scary for a city that depends on filling those rooms to keep its economy going.

Many gaming companies fell into bankruptcy, and while their casinos have remained open, their bank accounts have slammed shut. Just like many Americans who ran up too much credit-card debt, the gaming companies are operating under obligations that run into the billions, and they were having a hard time paying the bills.

Once the economy improved, resorts began to focus on padding their bottom line even more. Along came the resort fee. Now a standard attached to all hotel room bills, the resort fee was once scoffed at by most of the major hotel groups in town, one of which notoriously announced, "No resort fees ever!" That didn't last long. Before we knew it, almost all the hotels tacked and additional $10 to $15 per night to the daily room rate, intended to cover amenities such as usage of fitness and business centers, phone calls and Wi-Fi. Yet these fees quietly rise about $5 every year, and as far as we can tell, the amenities have stayed the same. It's not unheard-of to find nightly room rates less than $100 at some of the nice hotels, but that can be misleading. Add to it the average resort fee of about $35, and suddenly the room rate doesn't seem like such a bargain.

An even bigger heartbreak was when casinos started charging for parking (which is not even included in the aforementioned resort fees!). It started with MGM Resorts in 2016, and many of the hotel groups fell in line. The rationale was that other major cities charged for parking, so tourists would accept it. And they have, but not without a lot of grumbling. What used to be the most expensive real estate in the world where you could park for free is often a mighty pricey place to park.

As Las Vegas was shifting its focus, so were its visitors. Gambling took quite a dive after the economy tanked, as people obviously wanted to be more careful with their money. They still wanted to spend their money on a good time, just something more tangible. Conversely, the dining scene exploded, and entertainment headliners became bigger and bigger. Las Vegas transformed into a major nightlife destination in a matter of years, and at its height, had 7 of the 10 top-grossing nightclubs in the United States, thanks to the introduction of electronic dance music (EDM) to the city. Suddenly anybody with a few stacks in their pocket could be a high roller for the night and party with some of the most famous DJs in the world.

Adapting to Las Vegas

Las Vegas is, for the most part, a very casual city. Although there are a few restaurants that have a restrictive dress code, most of them—and all the showrooms, casinos, and attractions—are pretty much come as you are. Some people still choose to dress up for their night on the town, resulting in a strange dichotomy where you might see a couple in a suit and evening gown sitting next to a couple in shorts and sandals at a show or in a nice restaurant.

Generally speaking, spiffy-casual (slacks or nice jeans, button-up shirts or blouses, or a simple skirt or dress) is the best way to go in terms of what to wear, allowing you to be comfortable in just about any situation. Go too far to one extreme or the other and you're bound to feel out of place somewhere.

The only exception to this rule is the nightclubs, which often have very strict policies on what you can and cannot wear. They vary from club to club, but, as a general rule, sandals or flip-flops, shorts, and baseball caps are frowned upon. Think "business casual," but your business is getting into the club: That nice pair of jeans or slacks, a collared, pressed shirt, and leather dress shoes will get you in the door; fancier clothes (jackets, cocktail dresses) may get you past the velvet rope a little faster.

Yes, it does get hot in Las Vegas, so you really should factor that in when you're planning your wardrobe for your trip. It's important to note that every enclosed space (casino, showroom, restaurant, nightclub, and so on) is heavily air-conditioned, so it can actually be chilly once you get inside. Think light layers and you should be okay.

Las Vegas is a 24-hour town, so you can find something to eat or drink all the time; but many of the nicer restaurants open only for dinner, with 5 or 6pm to 10 or 11pm the standard operating hours. Nightclubs usually open around 10pm and go until dawn, with the bulk of the crowds not showing up until midnight at the earliest. There are a few afternoon shows, but most are in the evenings and often run two performances a night with start times that range from 7 until 10:30pm. Casinos and most regular bars are open 24 hours a day.

LOOKING BACK: LAS VEGAS HISTORY

The Early 1900s: Las Vegas Takes Shape

For many years after its creation via a land auction in 1905, Las Vegas was a mere whistle-stop town. That all changed in 1928 when Congress authorized the building of nearby Boulder Dam (later renamed Hoover Dam), bringing thousands of workers to the area. Although gambling still happened in the back rooms of saloons after it became illegal in 1909, the lifting of those prohibitions in 1931 is what set the stage for the first of the city's many booms. Fremont Street's gaming emporiums and speakeasies attracted dam workers. Upon the dam's completion, they were replaced by hordes of tourists who came to see the engineering marvel called "the Eighth Wonder of the World." But it wasn't until the early years of World War II that visionary entrepreneurs began to plan for the city's glittering future.

The 1940s: The Strip Is Born

Contrary to popular lore, developer Bugsy Siegel didn't actually stake a claim in the middle of nowhere—his Flamingo opened in 1946 just a few blocks south of already-existing properties.

The true beginnings of what would eventually become the Las Vegas Strip started years earlier. According to lore, Thomas Hull was driving toward

Downtown's already-booming Fremont Street area when his car broke down just outside of the city limits. As he stood there sweating in the desert heat, he envisioned, or perhaps just wished for, a cool swimming pool in the scrub brush next to the highway. Luckily, Hull was a hotel magnate, and he put his money where his mirage was. El Rancho Vegas, ultraluxurious for its time and complete with a sparkling pool facing the highway, opened in 1941 across the street from where the Sahara now stands. Scores of Hollywood stars were invited to the grand opening, and El Rancho Vegas soon became the hotel of choice for visiting film stars.

Beginning a trend that continues today, each new property tried to outdo existing hotels in luxurious amenities and thematic splendor. Las Vegas was on its way to becoming America's playground.

Las Vegas promoted itself in the 1940s as a town that combined Wild West frontier friendliness with glamour and excitement. Throughout the decade, the city was Hollywood's celebrity retreat. The Hollywood connection gave the town glamour in the public's mind—as did the mob connection, which became clear when notorious underworld gangster Bugsy Siegel built the fabulous Flamingo, a tropical paradise and "a real class joint."

While the Strip was expanding with major resorts like the Frontier, Bugsy's Flamingo, and the Thunderbird, Downtown kept pace with new hotels such as the El Cortez and casinos like the Golden Nugget. By the end of the decade, Fremont Street was known as "Glitter Gulch," its profusion of neon signs proclaiming round-the-clock gaming and entertainment.

The 1950s: Building Booms & A-Bombs

Las Vegas entered the new decade as a city (no longer a frontier town), with a population of about 50,000. Hotel growth was phenomenal, with legendary names like the Sahara, the Dunes, the Sands, and the Tropicana all gaining neon-lit fame.

The Desert Inn, which opened in 1950 with headliners Edgar Bergen and his dummy Charlie McCarthy, brought country-club elegance (including an 18-hole golf course and tennis courts) to the Strip.

In 1951, the Eldorado Club Downtown became Benny Binion's Horseshoe Club, which would gain fame as the home of the annual World Series of Poker.

In 1955, the Côte d'Azur–themed Riviera became the ninth big hotel to open on the Strip. Breaking the ranch-style mode, it was, at nine stories, the Strip's first high-rise. Liberace, one of the hottest names in show business, was paid the unprecedented sum of $50,000 a week to dazzle audiences in the Riviera's posh Clover Room.

Elvis appeared at the New Frontier in 1956 but wasn't a huge success; his fans were too young to fit the Las Vegas tourist mold.

In 1958, the $10-million, 1,065-room Stardust upped the stakes by importing the famed *Lido de Paris* spectacle from the French capital. It became one of the longest-running shows ever to play Las Vegas. Two performers whose names have been linked to Las Vegas ever since—Frank Sinatra and Wayne Newton—made their debuts there.

Mae West not only performed in Las Vegas but also cleverly bought up a half-mile of desolate Strip frontage between the Dunes and the Tropicana.

In the 1950s, the wedding industry helped make Las Vegas one of the nation's most popular venues for "goin' to the chapel." Celebrity weddings of the 1950s that sparked the trend included singer Dick Haymes and Rita Hayworth, Joan Crawford and Pepsi chairman Alfred Steele, Carol Channing and TV exec Charles Lowe, and Paul Newman and Joanne Woodward.

On a grimmer note, the '50s also heralded the atomic age in Nevada, with nuclear testing taking place just 65 miles northwest of Las Vegas. A chilling 1951 photograph shows a mushroom-shaped cloud from an atomic bomb test visible over the Fremont Street horizon. Throughout the decade, about one bomb a month was detonated in the nearby desert (an event, interestingly enough, that often attracted loads of tourists).

The 1960s: The Rat Pack & the King

The very first month of the new decade made entertainment history when the Sands hosted a 3-week "Summit Meeting" in the Copa Room that was presided over by "Chairman of the Board" Frank Sinatra, with Rat Pack cronies Dean Martin, Sammy Davis, Jr., Peter Lawford, and Joey Bishop (all of whom happened to be in town filming *Ocean's Eleven*). The series of shows helped form the Rat Pack legend in Vegas and, in many ways, helped make the town hip and cool—the ultimate '60s swinging retreat.

It needed the help. After nearly a decade of almost constant building and expansion (no fewer than 10 major resorts opened in the 1950s), a crackdown on the Mafia and its money, which had fueled the city's development, brought construction to a halt. Only two major properties opened during the decade— the Road to Morocco–themed Aladdin in 1963 and the Roman Empire bacchanalia that was Caesars Palace in 1966. Perhaps trying to prove that the mob was gone for good, Las Vegas became a family destination in 1968, when Circus Circus burst onto the scene with the world's largest permanent circus and a "junior casino" featuring dozens of carnival midway games on its mezzanine level.

Elvis officially became part of the Vegas legend with the release of the film *Viva Las Vegas* in 1964. This not only furthered the city's "cool" quotient but also gave it an enduring theme song that remains a part of the city's identity more than 50 years later. But it was not until 1969 that the King's place in Sin City history would be cemented with his triumphant return to Las Vegas at the International's showroom with a series of concerts that made him one of the city's all-time legendary performers. His fans had come of age.

The 1970s: The Glamour Fades

The image of Las Vegas that emerged in the 1970s was one that would take decades to shed: a tacky tourist trap with aging casinos, cheap restaurants, and

THE mob IN LAS VEGAS

The role of the Mafia in the creation of Las Vegas is little more than a footnote these days, but it isn't too bold of a statement to suggest that without organized crime, the city would not have developed in the ways that it did. Its past would have certainly been less colorful.

Meyer Lansky was a big name in the New York crime syndicate in the 1930s, and it was largely his decision to send Benjamin "Bugsy" Siegel west to expand their empire. Although the Strip had already begun to form with the opening of El Rancho in 1941 and the Frontier in 1942, it was Bugsy's sparkling Flamingo of 1946 that began a Mafia-influenced building boom and era of control that would last for decades. Famous marquees, such as the Desert Inn, the Riviera, and the Stardust, were all built, either in part or in whole, from funding sources that were less than reputable.

During the '60s, negative attention focused on mob influence in Las Vegas. Of the 11 major casino hotels that had opened in the previous decade, 10 were believed to have been financed with mob money. Then, like a knight in shining armor, Howard Hughes rode into town and embarked on a $300-million hotel- and property-buying spree that included the Desert Inn itself (in 1967). Hughes was as "Bugsy" as Benjamin Siegel any day, but his pristine reputation helped bring respectability to the desert city and lessen its gangland stigma.

During the 1970s and 1980s, the government got involved, embarking on a series of criminal prosecutions across the country to try to break the back of the Mafia. Although not completely successful, it did manage to wrest major control of Las Vegas away from organized crime, aided by new legislation that allowed corporations to own casinos. By the time Steve Wynn built the Mirage in 1989, the Mafia's role was reduced to the point where the most it could control were the city's innumerable strip clubs.

These days, strict regulation and billions of dollars of corporate money keep things on the up and up, but the mob's influence can still be felt even at the highest levels of Las Vegas government. Former Mayor Oscar B. Goodman, first elected in 1999, was a lawyer for the Mafia in the 1960s and 1970s, defending such famed gangsters as Meyer Lansky and Anthony "Tony the Ant" Spilotro. The popular and colorful Goodman cheerfully refers to his Mafia-related past often, joking about his desire to settle conflicts in the desert at night with a baseball bat like "in the good old days."

As if to bring things full circle, Goodman championed the **Mob Museum** (p. 163), a stunning facility that examines the history and influence of the Mafia in America and Las Vegas in particular. It is located in a former courthouse that was the site of the Mafia-related Kefauver hearings of the 1950s.

---

showrooms filled with performers whose careers were on their last legs. With a few exceptions, investment had slowed to a crawl and Vegas didn't seem as exciting anymore, especially when it was forced to compete with the sparkling newness of Atlantic City, where gambling was legalized in 1976.

There were some bright spots. In 1971, the 500-room Union Plaza opened at the head of Fremont Street on the site of the old Union Pacific Station. It had what was, at the time, the world's largest casino, and its showroom specialized in Broadway productions.

The year 1973 was eventful: Over at the Tropicana, illusionists extraordinaire Siegfried & Roy began turning women into tigers and themselves into legends in the *Folies Bergere*. Meanwhile, just up the street, the original MGM Grand (now Bally's) trumped the Plaza as the largest hotel and casino in the world, with Dean Martin as the opening evening's host.

Las Vegas made its way into America's living rooms with two very different television programs. Merv Griffin began taping his daytime talkfest in 1971 at Caesars Palace, taking advantage of a ready supply of local headliner guests. Then, in 1978, *Vega$* debuted, instantly emblazoning the image of star Robert Urich cruising down the Strip in his red Thunderbird convertible on the minds of TV viewers everywhere.

As the decade drew to a close, an international arrivals building opened and turned McCarran Field into McCarran International Airport, and dollar slot machines caused a sensation in the casinos.

The 1980s: The City Erupts

As the '80s began, Las Vegas was suffering an identity crisis. The departure of the mob and its money, combined with a struggling economy and Reagan-era conservatism, put a damper on the shining star of the desert. There was little new development, and a lot of the "classic" hotels became run-down shadows of their former selves.

A devastating fire in 1980 at the original MGM Grand killed more than 80 people, and just a few months later a fire at the Las Vegas Hilton killed eight more. In some ways these tragedies helped further the transformation of the public's view of the entire city. Las Vegas became tacky, desperate, and possibly unsafe.

Even the showrooms, once the magnificent Elvis/Sinatra klieg light that lured people from around the world, had become something of a joke. For entertainers, Vegas was where you played when your career was over, not when you were on top.

What Las Vegas really needed was a white knight, and they got one in the form of Golden Nugget owner Steve Wynn and his $630-million gamble on the Mirage. Financed mostly through the sale of junk bonds, the hotel's construction would eventually change the course of Las Vegas history.

The hotel opened in 1989, fronted by five-story waterfalls, lagoons, and lush tropical foliage—not to mention a 50-foot volcano that dramatically erupted regularly! Wynn gave world-renowned illusionists Siegfried & Roy carte blanche (and more than $30 million) to create the most spellbinding show Las Vegas had ever seen, and he brought in world-class chefs to banish the idea that all you could eat in the town were all-you-can-eat spreads and $4.99 prime rib.

It was an immediate success; financially, of course, but more importantly as a matter of perception. Almost overnight, Las Vegas became cool again and everyone wanted to go there.

The 1990s: King Arthur Meets King Tut

The 1990s began with a blare of trumpets heralding the rise of a turreted medieval castle, fronted by a moated drawbridge and staffed by jousting knights and fair damsels. Excalibur reflected the '90s marketing trend to promote Las Vegas as a family-vacation destination.

Was that trend successful? Well, Chevy Chase did take his family on a *Vegas Vacation* in 1997, but the city kept the Sin part of its name alive, at least in popular culture, with Robert Redford making an *Indecent Proposal* (1993); Nicholas Cage hitting rock bottom in *Leaving Las Vegas* (1995); and Elizabeth Berkley strutting her stuff in the widely derided but now cult-classic *Showgirls* (1995).

Canadian circus/theater group Cirque du Soleil transformed the entertainment scene in Las Vegas with the 1993 debut of *Mystére* at the newly opened Treasure Island. It would be the first of no fewer than eight Cirque shows that would launch over the next 2 decades.

The era of megahotels continued on the Strip, including the *new* MGM Grand hotel, backed by a full theme park (it ended Excalibur's brief reign as the world's largest resort), Luxor Las Vegas, and Steve Wynn's Treasure Island.

In 1993, a unique pink-domed 5-acre indoor amusement park, Grand Slam Canyon (later known as Adventuredome), became part of the Circus Circus hotel. In 1995, the Fremont Street Experience was completed, revitalizing Downtown Las Vegas. Closer to the Strip, rock restaurant magnate Peter Morton opened the Hard Rock Hotel, billed as "the world's first rock-'n'-roll hotel and casino." The year 1996 saw the advent of the French Riviera–themed Monte Carlo and the Strat, the latter with a 1,149-foot tower that makes it the highest building west of the Mississippi. The unbelievable New York–New York arrived in 1997.

But it all paled compared with 1998 to 1999. As Vegas hastily repositioned itself from "family destination" to "luxury resort," several new hotels opened, once again eclipsing anything that had come before. Bellagio was the latest from Vegas visionary Steve Wynn, an attempt to bring grand European style to the desert, while at the far southern end of the Strip, Mandalay Bay charmed. As if this weren't enough, the Venetian's ambitiously detailed re-creation of everyone's favorite Italian city came along in May 1999 and was followed in short order by the opening of Paris Las Vegas in the fall of 1999.

The 2000s: The Lap of Luxury

The 21st century opened with a bang as the Aladdin blew itself up and gave itself a from-the-ground-up makeover, which in turn only lasted for a handful of years before Planet Hollywood took it over and changed it entirely. Steve Wynn blew up the Desert Inn and built a new showstopper named for himself. Along the way, everyone expanded, and then expanded some more, ultimately adding thousands of new rooms. The goal became "luxury," with a secondary emphasis on "adult." Little by little, wacky, eye-catching themes were phased out (as much as one can when one's hotel looks like a castle), and generic sophistication took its place. Gaming was still number one, but the newer hotels were trying to top each other in terms of other recreations—decadent nightclubs, celebrity chef–backed restaurants, fancy spas, and superstar shows.

"More is more" seemed to be the motto, and its embodiment was the massive CityCenter, now generally referred to as the Aria resort, perhaps the most ambitious project in Las Vegas yet. Composed of a 4,000-room megaresort, two 400-room boutique hotels, condos, shopping, dining, clubs, and more, it covers more than 60 acres and, as such, is a city-within-the-city. Gone are the outrageous themes, replaced by cutting-edge modernism—all sleek lines of glass and metal designed with the future in mind, not only from an architectural standpoint but from an ecological one as well. Sure, building the massive CityCenter probably made the earth shudder a bit, but its advanced green building and sustainable operating systems helped ensure that the planet didn't just collapse in on itself from the weight of it all.

The excess of Vegas was spotlighted in popular culture as well. *Ocean's Eleven* got a new millennium makeover in 2001 with a cast of superstars like George Clooney, Brad Pitt, and Julia Roberts. Then in 2009, *The Hangover* took it all to a new level with a raunchy morality tale of a Vegas bachelor party gone horribly awry. The 2013 *Hangover 3* brought the action back to Vegas to close out the trilogy.

Even Las Vegas's motto, which became a popular part of the American lexicon, was a winking nod to the town's seemingly endless ways to satisfy the id: "What happens here, stays here."

Once known solely as an outpost of all-you-can-eat buffets and $4.99 prime rib specials, Las Vegas became one of the top dining destinations in the world. Every celebrity chef worth his or her sea salt had a restaurant here, and the level of culinary quality rose almost as fast as the prices. Take a look at some of the famous names attached to Vegas restaurants: Emeril Lagasse, Wolfgang Puck, Gordon Ramsay, Bobby Flay, Hubert Keller, the late Joël Robuchon, Thomas Keller, David Chang, and Roy Choi. It's a veritable who's who of the culinary world. Dining in Las Vegas has become one of the top reasons people want to visit the city.

And proving that Las Vegas really is a 24-hour town, the nightlife scene exploded in Vegas. Megaclubs such as **Intrigue** (p. 232) at Encore Las Vegas, **Marquee** (p. 233) at the Cosmopolitan, and **Hakkasan** (p. 232) at MGM Grand (billed as the largest nightclub in the world) pull in droves of the young and beautiful (or people who think they are, or who just want to be around them), who do not seem to be deterred by the eye-popping high prices ($20–$50 cover, $10–$15 drinks), long lines (expect to wait at least an hour), and lack of personal space. It's a see-and-be-seen scene, where you better dress to impress or expect to be relegated to the darker corners.

Céline Dion made it safe to be a Vegas headliner again as she kicked off a 5-year residency at Caesars Palace in 2003 (and came back in 2011). She would be followed by big-ticket names like Mariah Carey, Lady Gaga, and Bruno Mars, all of whom have made Vegas their performing home for a while.

Clearly, no one can rest on their laurels in Vegas, for this is not only a town that never sleeps but also one in which progress never stops moving, even for a heartbeat.

WHEN TO GO

Most of a Las Vegas vacation is usually spent indoors, so you can have a good time here year-round. The most pleasant seasons are spring and fall, especially if you want to experience the great outdoors.

Weekdays are slightly less crowded than weekends. Holidays are always a mob scene and come accompanied by high hotel prices. Hotel prices also skyrocket when big conventions and special events are taking place. The slowest times of year are parts of January and February; late June through August; the week before Christmas; and the week after New Year's.

If a major convention is to be held during your trip, you might want to change your date. Check the box on p. 38 for convention dates.

Climate & Current Weather Conditions

First of all, Vegas isn't always hot, but when it is, it's *really* hot. One thing you'll hear again and again is that even though Las Vegas gets very hot, the dry desert heat is not unbearable. We know this is true because we spent a couple of days there in 104°F (40°C) weather and lived to say, "It wasn't all that bad, not really." The humidity averages a low 22%, and even on very hot days, there's apt to be a breeze. Having said that, once the temperature gets into triple digits, it is wise to limit the amount of time you spend outdoors, and to make sure you are drinking plenty of water even while you are inside enjoying the blessed and omnipresent air-conditioning. Dehydration and heatstroke are two of the most common ailments that affect tourists—don't be a victim of one of them. Also, except on the hottest summer days, there's relief at night, when temperatures often drop by as much as 20 degrees.

But this is the desert, and it's not hot year-round. It can get quite cold, especially in the winter, when at night temperatures can drop to 30°F (–1°C) and lower. Although rare, it does snow occasionally in Las Vegas. The winter of 2008 to 2009 dropped nearly 3 inches of snow on the Strip. There's nothing quite like the sight of Luxor's Sphinx covered in snow. The breeze can also become a cold,

Las Vegas Average Temperatures (°F & °C) & Rainfall

	JAN	FEB	MAR	APR	MAY	JUNE	JULY	AUG	SEPT	OCT	NOV	DEC
Average (°F)	49	54	60	67	78	87	93	91	83	70	57	48
(°C)	9	12	16	19	26	31	34	33	28	21	14	9
High Temp. (°F)	58	63	70	78	89	99	104	102	94	81	67	57
(°C)	14	17	21	26	32	37	40	39	35	27	19	14
Low Temp. (°F)	39	44	49	56	66	75	81	79	71	59	47	39
(°C)	4	7	9	13	19	24	27	26	22	15	8	4
Rainfall (in.)	0.6	0.8	0.4	0.2	0.1	0.1	0.4	0.3	0.3	0.3	0.4	0.5

wild **WEATHER**

Las Vegas rests in the middle of a desert, so how wacky can the weather possibly get? A lot crazier than you think. Although the city's location results in broiling-hot temperatures in the summer, many people tend to forget that deserts get cold and rainy, while wind is also a potential hazard.

Winter temperatures in Las Vegas have been known to dip below 30°F (–1°C), and when you toss in 40 mph winds, that adds up to a very chilly stroll on the Strip. Snow is not an unheard-of occurrence. Most years see a flurry or two falling on Las Vegas, and since 1949, a total of 12 "storms" have resulted in accumulations of 2 inches or greater, with the largest storm dropping 9 inches on the Strip in January 1949. In December 2003, parts of Las Vegas got 6 inches of the white stuff, and although it didn't stick around too long on the Strip, the sight of the famous "Welcome to Fabulous Las Vegas" sign in the middle of a driving blizzard was quite a spectacle. In the winter of 2008–09, Vegas received nearly 3 inches of snow on the Strip itself, with nearly 10 inches accumulating in other areas of town. Locals usually find the snow a charming addition to the city (and the stuff melts completely in a day or two, so they don't have to shovel it—lucky them). In 2017, Vegas saw snow flurries for Christmas, while February 2019 saw not one but two unseasonal snowstorms in one week.

Though snow is a novel quirk that many Vegas residents and visitors welcome, rain isn't always as well received.

The soil in Las Vegas is parched most of the year, making it difficult for the land to absorb large amounts of water coming down in a short time. Between June and August, when most of the area's rainfall takes place due to the Southwest's monsoon season, there is a good possibility of flash flooding.

At times, the skies just open up, resulting in flooding that wreaks havoc. On July 9, 1999, Mother Nature unleashed more than 3 inches of rain *in just a few hours* on a city that averages about 4 inches of rain a year. The deluge killed two people, swamped cars, and destroyed millions of dollars in property. A 2013 storm caused havoc up and down the Strip with collapsed ceilings in the Mirage, a flooded casino at Caesars Palace, and a waterfall inside Gilley's at Treasure Island. This kind of storm (and rain in general) is rare, but even a light shower can make things treacherous on the roads, the sidewalks, and the slippery marble walkways that front almost every casino in town.

The topography of the Las Vegas region also makes it prone to high, often damaging winds. Situated at the bottom of a bowl ringed by mountains, 15 to 20 mph steady winds are not uncommon, and gusts of 70 to 80 mph have been recorded. In 1994, a brief windstorm knocked down the massive sign at the Las Vegas Hilton, and in 2010 a storm tore apart the Cloud 9 balloon, billed as the largest tethered helium balloon in the world.

biting wind of up to 40 mph or more. And so there are entire portions of the year when you won't be using that hotel pool at all, even if you want to. Most of the hotels close huge chunks of those pool areas for "the season," which can be as long as the period from Labor Day to Memorial Day. If you aren't traveling in the height of summer, bring a jacket. Also, remember sunscreen and a hat—even if it's not all that hot, you can burn very easily and very fast.

MAJOR convention DATES FOR 2020

Listed below are Las Vegas's major annual conventions, with projected attendance figures for 2020; believe us, unless you're coming for one of them, you probably want to avoid these biggies. Because convention schedules frequently change, contact the **Las Vegas Convention and Visitors Authority** (www.vegasmeansbusiness.com) to double-check the latest info before you commit to your travel dates.

Event	Dates	Attendance
Consumer Electronics Show	Jan 7–10	182,000
International Builders Show	Jan 21–23	60,000
Shooting, Hunting & Outdoor Trade Show	Jan 21–24	61,000
AVN Adult Entertainment Expo	Jan 22–25	50,000
Las Vegas Market Furniture Show	Jan 26–30	50,000
National Association of Broadcasters	Apr 18–22	103,000
National Hardware Show	May 5–7	37,000
Int'l Esthetics Cosmetic and Spa Conference	June 15–17	25,000
Las Vegas Market Furniture Show	July 26–30	50,000
SEMA/Automotive Aftermarket Industry Week	Nov 3–6	130,000

Holidays

Banks, government offices, post offices, and many stores, restaurants, and museums are closed on the following legal national holidays: January 1 (New Year's Day), the third Monday in January (Martin Luther King, Jr., Day), the third Monday in February (Presidents' Day), the last Monday in May (Memorial Day), July 4 (Independence Day), the first Monday in September (Labor Day), the second Monday in October (Columbus Day), November 11 (Veterans Day/Armistice Day), the fourth Thursday in November (Thanksgiving Day), and December 25 (Christmas).

Any holiday, especially ones that involve a day off work for most people, will mean big crowds in Vegas. This includes "holidays" like St. Patrick's Day, Cinco de Mayo, and Spring Break.

Las Vegas Calendar of Events

You may be surprised that Las Vegas does not offer as many annual events as most other tourist cities. The reason is the city's *raison d'être*: the gaming industry. This town wants its visitors spending their money in the casinos, not at Renaissance fairs and parades.

When in Vegas, check the local paper and contact the **Las Vegas Convention and Visitors Authority** (www.visitlasvegas.com; ✆ **877/847-4858** or 702/892-7575) or the **Las Vegas Chamber of Commerce** (www.lvchamber.com; ✆ **702/735-1616**) to find out about other events scheduled during your visit.

FEBRUARY

The Super Bowl. Granted, the actual game is not held in Las Vegas, but the numbers of

people it brings to the city rival those that go to wherever the big game is being held. Sports fans and sports bettors come out in droves to watch the action on the big screens around town and to lay down a wager or two on the outcome. It usually takes place on the first Sunday in February.

Valentine's Day. This is the marriage (and possibly divorce) capital of the world, so the betrothed line up to exchange their vows all across town on Cupid's day. As on other days of the year, the city's Marriage Bureau stays open until midnight, and some chapels perform dozens of weddings. February 14.

MARCH

USA Sevens. Not a rugby fan? No matter, a day at the Sevens tourney is an experience. The largest attended rugby event in the country welcomes some 75,000 visitors to the **Sam Boyd Stadium,** 7000 E. Russell Rd. (samboydstadium.com; ✆ **702/895-3761**), located about 20 minutes from the Strip. Teams from 16 countries compete in some 45 matches, and fans travel from all around the world to cheer on their home countries or teams, dressed in jerseys, war paint, and outlandish costumes. Though the games are on the weekend, leading up to the tournament is a full week of events, including pep rallies, a beer festival, and a Parade of Nations. Held in early March. For more information, visit www.usasevens.com.

NASCAR. The **Las Vegas Motor Speedway,** 7000 Las Vegas Blvd. N. (www.lvms. com; ✆ **800/644-4444**), has become one of the premier facilities in the country, attracting races and racers of all stripes and colors. The biggest races of the year are the Boyd Gaming 300 and the Kobalt Tools 400, held in early March.

March Madness. Remember everything we just said about the Super Bowl? Apply it here for the NCAA college basketball championship games throughout the second half of the month.

MAY

Vegas Uncork'd. Once Las Vegas was crowned as a dining destination, it didn't take long for the city to capitalize on having so much gourmet talent packed into a few square miles. The long food and celebrity chef–filled weekend lets the most discerning gourmands get a little closer to the culinary gods whose names grace the doors. When and where else can you rub elbows with Guy Savoy at the Grand Tasting, get to see Gordon Ramsay in action at a Master Series dinner, or drink margaritas with Too Hot Tamales Mary Sue Milliken and Susan Feniger over a 4-day span? If you don't leave this weekend with a huge food hangover, you're doing it wrong. For more information, visit www.vegasuncorked.com.

Electric Daisy Carnival. One of the biggest annual Electronic Dance Music (EDM) events in the world draws upward of 400,000 people to the city with a multiday series of concerts from the biggest DJs and club music stars in the business. Past festivals saw EDM megastars like Tiesto, Afrojack, Eric Prydz, Richie Hawtin, Carl Cox, and Adam Beyer in front of the dancing mobs. If you don't know who any of those acts are, it's probably best to consider a different weekend, as rooms are scarce. Usually held the third weekend in May at the Las Vegas Motor Speedway. For more information, visit www.electricdaisy carnival.com.

JUNE

World Series of Poker. When Harrah's Entertainment bought the legendary Binion's Horseshoe in Downtown Vegas out of bankruptcy, it quickly turned around and sold the hotel, but kept the hosting rights to this famed event, moving its location and place on the calendar. Now held at the **Rio All-Suite Hotel and Casino,** 3700 W. Flamingo Rd. (✆ **800/752-9746**), in June and July (with the final table held in Nov for some incomprehensible reason), the event features high-stakes gamblers and showbiz personalities competing for six-figure purses. There are daily events, with entry stakes ranging from $125 to $5,000. To enter the World Championship Event, players must pony up $10,000 but could win a fortune: The 2018 top prize was $9.5 million. It costs nothing to crowd around the tables and watch the action, but if you want to avoid the throngs, you can catch a lot of it on TV. For more information, visit www.wsop. com.

SEPTEMBER

Life Is Beautiful Festival. This festival takes over a huge chunk of Downtown Las Vegas with music from bands both big (Beck, Imagine Dragons, Janelle Monae) and small; food and cooking demonstrations from celebrity chefs; art projects and displays; a speaker series; performances from Vegas shows including Cirque du Soleil; and more. The friendly neighborhood vibe, terrific organization (at least so far), and endless array of things to see, do, and eat make this a favorite for more than 65,000 people.

OCTOBER

Halloween. Las Vegas gets scarier than normal on and around Halloween, with "spooky" twists to many of the major attractions (Adventuredome becomes "Fright Dome," with haunted houses and more), debauched costume parties at the nightclubs, and a parade and festivities in Downtown Las Vegas. October 31.

DECEMBER

National Finals Rodeo. This is the Super Bowl of rodeos, attended by about 200,000 people each year and offering more than $6 million in prize money. Male and female rodeo stars compete in everything from calf roping to steer wrestling, bull riding, team roping, saddle bronc riding, bareback riding, and barrel racing. In connection with this event, hotels book country stars into their showrooms, and a cowboy shopping spree—the **NFR Cowboy Christmas Gift Show,** a trade show for Western gear—is held at the convention center. The NFR runs for 10 days, during the first 2 weeks of December, at the 17,000-seat Thomas & Mack Center of the University of Nevada, Las Vegas (UNLV). Order tickets as far in advance as possible (© **866/388-3267**). For more information, see www.nfrexperience.com.

New Year's Eve. Between 300,000 and 400,000 people descend on Las Vegas to ring in the New Year, making it one of the largest gatherings for the holiday outside of New York's Times Square. Fireworks are the dominant entertainment, with pyrotechnics launched from the roofs of many hotels on the Strip and under the canopy at Fremont Street in Downtown Las Vegas. The Strip is closed to vehicles for the night, so traffic and parking are a nightmare, as is booking a room (expect to pay a hefty premium), which should be done well in advance. December 31.

WHERE TO STAY

There are about 150,000 hotel rooms in Las Vegas. If you stayed in a different room every night, it would take you 411 years to get through them all. You could give one to every single resident of Dayton, Ohio, and still have enough left over for you and about 10,000 of your closest friends.

The point is, finding a hotel room in Las Vegas is not hard; it's finding the right one for *you* that can be challenging. Do you want a luxurious suite where you can lounge in bed and order room service, or basic accommodations where you'll dump your luggage and then not see the room again until you stumble back to it as the sun is coming up the next morning? Do you want classic Glitter Gulch glitz or contemporary Sin City glamour? High tech or low cost? Las Vegas has all the above and just about everything in between.

PRACTICAL INFORMATION
The Big Picture

With a few exceptions in the very expensive category, most hotel rooms in Las Vegas are pretty much the same. After you factor in location and price, there isn't that much difference between rooms, except perhaps for size and the quality of their surprisingly similar furnishings.

Hotel prices in Vegas are anything but fixed, so you will notice wild price fluctuations. The same room can routinely go for anywhere from $60 to $250, depending on demand. So, use our price categories with a grain of salt and don't rule out a hotel just because it's listed as "Expensive"—it's very common to get great deals on pricey hotels. On the negative side, some hotels start with their most typical lowest rate, adding "and up." Don't be surprised if "up" turns out to be way up. Just look online or call and ask.

Yes, if you pay more, you'll probably, but not certainly, get a "nicer" establishment and clientele to match (perhaps not so many loud drunks in the elevators). On the other hand, if a convention is in town, the drunks will be there no matter how upscale the hotel—they'll just be wearing business suits and/or funny hats. And frankly, the big hotels, no matter how fine, have mass-produced rooms; at 3,000 rooms or more, they are the equivalent of '60s tract housing. Consequently, even in the nicest hotels, you can (and probably will) encounter plumbing noises, notice scratch marks on the walls or furniture, overhear conversations from other rooms, or be woken by the housekeeping staff as they knock on the doors that don't have the DO NOT DISTURB sign up.

Cancellation policies vary hotel to hotel, but generally speaking, you can usually back out of your booking anywhere from 24 to 48 hours ahead of your check-in date without penalty. Exceptions to both of these general rules are often found on major holidays like New Year's Eve, or during big event weekends like the Super Bowl.

Getting the Best Deal

Here are some tips for landing a low rate:

o **Remember the law of supply and demand.** Las Vegas hotels are most crowded and therefore most expensive on weekends. So, the best deals are offered midweek, when prices can drop dramatically. If possible, go then. You should also check the convention calendar run by the **Las Vegas Convention and Visitors Authority** (www.vegasmeansbusiness.com; © **877/847-4858**) to find out whether a big trade show is scheduled at the time of your planned visit. If more than 50,000 conventioneers are descending on Vegas, *change your dates,* as one-third or more of the beds will be booked and prices will soar. The most popular conventions are listed under "When to Go" on p. 38; use it as a guide for when to avoid the city. Remember also that planning to take your vacation just a week before or after official peak season can mean big savings.

o **Book online.** This is such a smart way to book that we've devoted an entire box to it. See p. 44.

o **Be social.** Almost every major resort in town has some presence in the social media world, including Facebook pages, Twitter feeds, and smartphone apps. Connect with them and you may find yourself getting exclusive offers that the Luddites out there won't be hearing about.

o **Don't be afraid to bargain.** Get in the habit of asking for a lower price than the first one quoted. Always ask politely whether a less expensive room is available than the first one mentioned, or whether any special rates apply to you. If you belong to the players' club at the hotel-casino, you may be able to secure a better deal. Of course, you will also be expected to spend a certain amount of time and money gambling there.

o **Beware of fees.** So-called "resort fees" are *de rigueur* on the Strip, and common elsewhere. They can add up, ranging anywhere from $15 to $45 per night. Although the specifics vary from property to property, they usually cover amenities like Internet service, health club access, newspapers, printing of boarding passes, maybe a bottle of water or two, and the like. So, what if you're not going to use any of that? Too bad—you still have to pay (at most hotels). Many hotels include this in their totals when you book your room, but a few wait and sock it to you at checkout. Be sure to ask ahead. (We have noted those hotels with resort fees in the listings, but do note that they change often.)

o **Beware of hidden extras.** The hotels that don't charge resort fees (which are few and far between these days) charge extra for things that are always free in other destinations, such as health-club privileges. Expect to pay anywhere from $15 to $35 to use almost any hotel spa/health club. Wi-Fi also doesn't come free; usually there is a $12-to-$20 charge per 24-hour period. (We've noted when there is a fee in the listings so that you won't be taken by surprise.)

o **Consider a suite.** If you are traveling with your family or another couple, you can pack more people into a suite (which usually comes with a sofa bed) and thereby reduce your per-person rate. Remember that some places charge for extra guests and some don't.

What Am I Looking for in a Hotel?

If gambling is not your priority, what are you doing in Vegas? Just kidding. But not 100% kidding. Vegas's current identity as a luxury, and very adult, resort destination means there are several hotels that promise to offer you all sorts of alternatives to gambling—lush pool areas, fabulous spas, incredible restaurants, lavish shopping. But if you look closely, much of this is Vegas bait-and-switch: The pools are often chilly (and often closed during non-summer months), and it will be years before there is more foliage than concrete in these newly landscaped environments; the spas cost extra (sometimes a whole lot extra); the best restaurants can require a small bank loan; and the stores are often the kinds of places where average mortals can't even afford the oxygen. So, what does that leave you with? Why, that's right—gambling.

The other problem with these self-proclaimed luxury hotels is their size. True luxury hotels do not have 3,000 rooms—they have a couple of hundred, at best, because you simply can't provide first-class service and Egyptian-cotton sheets in mass quantity. But while hotels on the upper end of the price spectrum (Wynn, Encore, Bellagio, the Venetian, and so on) have done their best to offer sterling service and to make their rooms more luxurious than those at other Vegas hotels, there's only so much that any place that big can do. Don't get us wrong—these places are absolutely several steps up in quality from other large hotels, and compared to them, even the better older hotels really look shabby. But they are still sprawling, frequently noisy complexes.

If the hubbub of a casino makes you itch, there are a few non-gaming hotels and even non-gaming towers within casino hotels that could help reduce your stress level. Check out Vdara or Waldorf Astoria next to Aria, or the Delano at Mandalay Bay.

Casino hotels, by the way, are not always a nice place for children. It used to be that the casino was a separate section in the hotel, and children were not allowed inside. (We have fond memories of standing just outside the casino line, watching Dad put quarters in a slot machine "for us.") But in almost all

TURNING TO THE internet or apps FOR A HOTEL DISCOUNT

Before going online, it's important that you know what "flavor" of discount you're seeking. Currently, there are three types of online reductions:

1. **Extreme discounts on sites where you bid for lodgings without knowing which hotel you'll get.** You'll find these on such sites as **Priceline.com** and **Hotwire.com**, and they can be money-savers, particularly if you're booking within a week of travel (that's when the hotels resort to deep discounts to get beds filled). As these companies use only major chains, you can rest assured that you won't be put up in a dump. For more reassurance, visit the website **BiddingTraveler.com**. On it, actual travelers spill the beans about what they bid on Priceline.com and which hotels they got. I think you'll be pleasantly surprised by the quality of many of the hotels that are offering these "secret" discounts.

2. **Discounts on chain hotel websites.** In 2016, all the major chains announced they'd be reserving special discounts for travelers who booked directly through the hotels' websites (usually in the portion of the site reserved for loyalty members). They weren't lying: These are always the lowest rates at the hotels in question, though discounts can range widely, from as little as $1 to as much as $50 lower than the best prices found elsewhere. Our advice:

Search for a hotel that's in your price range and ideal location (see below for where to do that) and then, if it is a chain property, book directly through the online loyalty portal.

3. **Use the right hotel search engine.** They're not all equal, as we at Frommers.com learned in 2018 after putting the top 20 sites to the test in 20 cities (including Las Vegas) around the globe. We discovered that **Booking.com** listed the lowest rates for hotels on the Strip, and in the under $200 range, 16 out of 20 times—the best record, by far, of all the sites we tested. And Booking.com includes all taxes and fees in its results (not all do, which can make for a frustrating shopping experience). For top-end properties, again in the city center only, both Priceline.com and HotelsCombined.com came up with the best rates, tying at 14 wins each.

4. **Last-minute discounts.** Last-minute booking can be a great savings strategy, as prices sometimes drop in the week before travel as hoteliers scramble to fill their rooms. But you won't necessarily find the best savings through companies that claim to specialize in last-minute bookings. Instead, use the sites recommended in point 3 of this list.

It's a lot of surfing, I know, but in the hothouse world of Sin City hotel pricing, this sort of diligence can pay off.

the new hotels, you must walk through the casino to get anywhere—the lobby, the restaurants, the outside world. This makes sense from the hotel's point of view; it gives you many opportunities to stop and drop $1 or $100 into a slot. But this often long, crowded trek gets wearying for adults—and it's far worse for kids. The rule is that kids can walk through the casinos, but they can't stop, even to gawk for a second at someone hitting a jackpot nearby. The casino officials who will immediately hustle the child away are just doing their job—but, boy, it's annoying.

So, take this (and what a hotel offers that kids might *like*) into consideration when booking a room. Again, please note that those gorgeous hotel pools are often cold (and again, sometimes closed altogether) and not very deep. They look like places you would want to linger, but often (from a kid's point of view) they are not. Plus, the pools close early. Hotels want you inside gambling, not outside swimming.

Finally, the thing that bothers me the most about this latest Vegas phase: It used to be that I could differentiate between rooms, but that's becoming harder and harder. Nearly every major hotel has changed to more or less the same effect; gone is any thematic detailing, and in its place is a series of disappointingly similar (if contemporary and sleek) looks. Expect clean-lined wood furniture, plump white beds, and monochromes everywhere you go. All that may distinguish one from another is the size of the room or the quality of the furnishings.

Ultimately, though, if it's a busy time, you'll have to nab any room you can, especially if you get a price you like. How much time are you going to spend in the room anyway?

SOUTH STRIP

The southern third of the Strip, from roughly Russell Road to Harmon Avenue, is home to some of the biggest and most extravagant hotels in the world.

Best for: First-time visitors who want to experience all the Vegas insanity they have read about and seen on TV.

Drawbacks: Prices are higher here than in non-Strip locations; the sheer number of people can cause major traffic jams (and we're not just talking about on the street).

Expensive

Aria Las Vegas ★★★　The first time I drove into this megaresort complex at night, it was so dazzling, with its Gehry-esque jagged front (of the Shops at Crystals), sleek skyscrapers towering over the Strip, and bulletlike tram coasting between the buildings, that I distinctly remember thinking, "So this is what the future is like." And to this extent, Aria, at the center of this faux urban block, exemplifies the future of Las Vegas: imposing and on the cutting edge of design.

Though its glass and steel exterior may seem sterile from afar, once you get up close and personal with Aria, you'll see that it's actually quite a vibrant space. The entire property is awash with imaginative visual details, even near the

Price Categories	
Expensive	$150 and up
Moderate	$100–$150
Inexpensive	Under $100

entrance, where a waterfall quietly cascades down a ridged wall on the outside of the building. Obviously, gaming is the main focus of the 150,000-square-foot casino, but there are plenty of other elements to catch your eye, whether it's a hand-carved wooden mural, Maya Lin's *Silver River* installation "flowing" behind the front desk, or the array of enormous, colorful butterflies suspended from the ceiling in the lobby. One of my favorite artworks is a series of smoky prints by actor Christopher Walken that lines a corridor of the casino. If that doesn't make this hotel cool, I don't know what does.

The resort is enormous, with some 4,000 rooms, all with their own distinct character. The "standard" rooms are hardly standard, starting out at 520 square feet, with rich, warm tones and floor-to-ceiling windows that bathe the room in abundant sunlight. Should you want to shut out the sun without getting out of bed, that isn't a problem—the blackout curtains, along with pretty much everything electronic in your room, can be controlled by the in-room tablet on the nightstand next to the bed. I love the spacious bathrooms with their plush robes (to keep guests warm amid all the cold granite). Some might consider it a design flaw that getting to the deep-soaking tub means you have to first pass through the frosted-glass shower, but a few extra steps won't kill you.

Aria also offers an even more VIP experience in its Sky Suites, where the smallest accommodation is a one-bedroom at 1,050 square feet. Suite guests enjoy such niceties as a private entrance and elevator, a pool exclusively for Sky Suites guests, and a lounge with a daily wine and cheese reception, not to mention front-of-line passes for the buffet.

Aria's restaurants on the main and second floors feature cuisine from some of the best chefs in the country—when was the last time you had a James Beard Award–winner make your pizza? Venture out of the hotel to see the rest of the complex, which includes more hotels, shopping, and more dining options at Crystals.

If Aria is any indication of what Vegas is going to be like for the next 50 years, we're happy to jump on board.

3730 Las Vegas Blvd. S. www.arialasvegas.com. ⓒ **866/359-7757** or 702/590-7757. 4,004 units. $149 and up double; $289 and up suite. Resort fee $39. Extra person $50. No discount for children. Parking 1 hr. free, self-parking $9–$18, valet $21–$30; hotel guest 24-hour parking fees allow same-day in-and-out parking privileges at other MGM Resorts; prices vary during special events. **Amenities:** 15 restaurants; casino; concierge; executive-level rooms; health club; heated outdoor pools; room service; spa; showroom; free property-wide and in-room Wi-Fi (included in resort fee).

Four Seasons Hotel Las Vegas ★★★ Before Nobu and the Cromwell, if you wanted a true boutique hotel in Las Vegas, your only option was the Four Seasons. Not that this was a bad thing—Four Seasons' reputation for luxury and attentive service is unrivaled worldwide. Except now there are a few more rivals on the Strip. Even with the increasingly crowded market, the Four Seasons has stayed on point in the luxury game, from its picturesque lobby to all 424 rooms located on the top five floors of Mandalay Bay.

Las Vegas Hotels

Aria Las Vegas **39**
Bally's Las Vegas **27**
Bellagio **31**
Caesars Palace **30**
California Hotel & Casino **4**
Circus Circus Hotel & Casino **17**
The Cosmopolitan of Las Vegas **32**
The Cromwell **26**
The D Las Vegas Casino Hotel **9**
The Downtown Grand **6**
El Cortez Hotel & Casino **8**
Excalibur **44**
Flamingo Las Vegas **25**
Four Queens **10**
Four Seasons Hotel Las Vegas **48**
Fremont Hotel & Casino **5**

The Gold Coast **34**
The Golden Gate **12**
Golden Nugget **11**
Green Valley Ranch Resort, Spa & Casino **51**
Hard Rock Hotel & Casino **38**
Harrah's Las Vegas **23**
JW Marriott **1**
The LINQ **24**
Luxor Las Vegas **46**
M Resort **50**
Main Street Station **3**

Mandalay Bay/ Delano Las Vegas **47**
MGM Grand Hotel & Casino **43**
The Mirage **22**
New York–New York Hotel & Casino **42**
Oasis at Gold Spike **7**
The Orleans **41**
Palace Station **14**
Palms Casino Resort **35**
Paris Las Vegas Casino Resort **28**
Park MGM/NoMad Las Vegas **40**
Planet Hollywood Resort & Casino **29**
The Plaza Hotel & Casino **2**
Red Rock Resort **13**
Rio All-Suite Hotel & Casino **33**
Sahara Hotel & Casino **16**
Silver Sevens **37**
South Point **49**
The Strat **15**
Treasure Island **20**
Tropicana Las Vegas **45**
Tuscany Suites & Casino **36**
The Venetian/ Palazzo Las Vegas **21**
Westgate Las Vegas Resort and Casino **18**
Wynn/Encore **19**

4

WHERE TO STAY | South Strip

Cool, mod-style patterns on the walls plus well-placed mirrors make the standard rooms feel bigger than their allotted 500 square feet, while retro lamps and jacquard-patterned footstools at the end of the bed provide contrasting industrial and lush textures. And the bathrooms! Shiny chrome finishes, backlit mirrors, and a lack of frame around the shower glass make the space feel seamless, and therefore bigger. Somehow the beauty of the space rubs off: I don't know how they do it, but the lighting in them makes every guest look 10 years younger. The hotel's high perch allows for sweeping views; those rooms directly overlooking the Strip command a steeper price.

One of the best things about Four Seasons is that, despite its connection to the massive resort next door, it's as secluded as they come, perfect for its discerning, often celebrity guests. It has its own pool, two restaurants (the Verandah serves afternoon tea), and an excellent bar in the lobby. The private driveway and cul-de-sac are surrounded by palm trees and other tropical foliage, shielding guests from the typical Vegas loudness (in volume and garishness). This sense of calm carries throughout the entire resort, from the pleasant check-in until you arrive in your beautiful room. But if guests want to leave this serene space to immerse themselves in the true Vegas experience, they can simply bop next door to the Mandalay Bay.

3960 Las Vegas Blvd. S. www.fourseasons.com. ☎ **877/632-5000** or 702/632-5000. 424 units. $224 and up double; $399 and up suite. Resort fee $39 per night. Extra person $35. Children 17 and under stay free in parent's room. Valet parking $22; no self-parking. Pets under 25 lb. accepted. **Amenities:** 2 restaurants; concierge; executive-level rooms; fitness center; heated outdoor pool; room service; spa; free Wi-Fi.

Mandalay Bay/Delano Las Vegas ★★★ Mandalay Bay has anchored its end of Las Vegas Boulevard since 1999 and has managed to stay fresh and relevant by undergoing a series of facelifts. First it revamped the casino floor to make it less campy and more modern. Then it added a new nightclub, as well as a couple of new restaurants and upgrades to existing ones, followed by the addition of a resident Cirque du Soleil show in 2013. You'll be hard-pressed to find a resort this large that's as upscale and exciting, with as many amenities.

The original Mandalay Bay Tower boasts 3,211 rooms, which, thanks to the building's height, offer great views of the Valley. (Request one of the 550 "DR View Rooms" to ensure you've got the lights of the Strip outside your window, not the highway). In 2016 the resort completed its $100-million remodel of its suites, taking the spacious rooms into the 21st century with new color palettes. Resort Kings are now decked out in white and cobalt, while Resort Queens stay warm with combinations of either rich ruby and latte shades or lavender and mocha. Both feature onyx-print murals as accent walls behind the headboards, and cushy seats right against the window are a nice touch. Bathrooms are large, with shower and tub separated by lots of cold marble, but that's a first-world problem.

The adjoining Delano has taken the place of THEhotel and infused it with South Beach spirit, a welcome change. The Miami touch has lightened everything up, though it includes nods to Las Vegas's natural landscape. In the now neutral-colored foyer between valet and the lobby is an impressive 126,000-pound, 150-million-year-old, split metaquartzite boulder hauled in from the surrounding Nevada desert. Pass between the smoothed halves to enter the lobby, where you'll encounter several smaller rocks before registration. A piece by Korean artist Jaehyo Lee features hundreds of them strung along pieces of wire stretched from the tall ceiling to the ground. The hotel presents changing art installations; one showcased works derived completely from wood and other natural materials from the Mojave.

All the hotel's 1,117 suites were redone as well, with lots of white and neutral tones and touches of gold. Ultra-plush beds with white tufted headboards can be difficult to part with in the morning, while gigantic bathrooms feature black marble around the separate tub and the glass-enclosed shower. And there are cute touches, like postcards left on the bed with cheeky sayings like "My life has a superb cast. I just can't figure out the plot."

A little less secluded than the Four Seasons, there's still a sense of exclusivity at Delano, with its own beach club, reserved for guests, right off Mandalay Beach. Also, the addition is non-gaming, but it's just a quick walk down the hallway to the Mandalay Bay's loud, 135,000-square-foot casino, one of the largest on the Strip.

As a whole, Mandalay Bay hosts some of the finest restaurants on the Strip, including **Strip Steak, Aureole, Border Grill,** and more (see chapter 5). Beer aficionados take note: The resort's beverage director is the first female *cicerone* (the beer equivalent of a sommelier) in the country, and she has made sure that craft beers are featured prominently on many menus.

The resort has managed to maintain a good balance of grown-up and family fun by including in its arsenal a massive arena for live performances; **Shark Reef** aquarium (p. 154); and **Mandalay Beach,** an impressive pool complex that features a wave pool, lazy river, and bona fide sand on a beach that sometimes hosts live concerts. **Light** nightclub (p. 233) has its own pool component, **Daylight,** set to an electronic music soundtrack.

Mandalay Place, the retail-lined walkway that connects Mandalay Bay and neighbor Luxor, is a convenient way to traverse the two indoors (and to shop).

3950 Las Vegas Blvd. S. (at Hacienda Ave.). www.mandalaybay.com. © **877/632-7800** or 702/632-7108. 4,429 units (including Delano). $60 and up double; $225 and up suite. Resort fee $37. Extra person $40. Children 14 and under stay free in parent's room. Parking 1 hr. free, self-parking $9–$15, valet $16–$24; hotel guest 24-hour parking fees allow same-day in-and-out parking privileges at other MGM Resorts; prices vary during special events. **Amenities:** 24 restaurants; aquarium; casino; concierge; 12,000-seat events center; executive-level rooms; health club; showroom; 5 outdoor pools w/lazy river and wave pool; room service; sauna; spa; watersports equipment/rentals; free Wi-Fi.

MGM Grand Hotel & Casino ★★ MGM Grand is a big green monster. When you combine this megaresort with its two auxiliary accommodation towers, Signature Suites and Skylofts, it's the third-largest hotel in the

Even though Las Vegas is back on its economic upswing, room rates have stayed a tad lower than in other cities in order to stay competitive. Hotels, however, have found new ways to increase their bottom line, mainly through the addition of nefarious "resort fees." These extra charges are tacked on top of the nightly room rate and variously include things like Internet access, entry to the fitness center, printing of boarding passes, local and toll-free phone calls, and the like. Some hotels throw in extra goodies like bottles of water, discounted cocktails or meals, and credits for future stays. So, try to take advantage of all the fee covers, because even if you don't, you still have to pay the fee. We indicate which hotels charge resort fees in the listings in this chapter and include their current prices, but do note that the amount, and what they include, changes *often;* ask when booking your room or take some time to read the fine print if making arrangements online.

4

WHERE TO STAY | South Strip

world and the second-largest hotel on the Strip. You might think a property this enormous would feel like it's too big for its own britches, treating visitors like they're numbers rather than guests. But MGM Grand has a surprisingly high standard for customer service on all levels.

It helps that a $160-million renovation in 2012 updated all the rooms with bold strokes, placing pleasantly contrasting geometric patterns on everything from the padded headboards to carpets, while jewel tones on the accessories add nice pops of color.

Except for the West Wing, rooms tend to be oversized; standard king and queen rooms are even large enough to have a couch in a seating area, plus a writing desk and chair. Modern touches include 40-inch flatscreens and media hubs brimming with electrical outlets. If you want to start getting into real space, there are the residential spots at the Signature, the tall white buildings behind the MGM. If you've got the money to burn and need a palace, there's always the Skylofts, the mind-blowing, multi-bedroom villas that feature their own Strip-view balconies with hot tubs, 24-hour butler service, and other spiffy amenities. A final room category is the "Stay Well" rooms dedicated to the health-conscious Vegas visitor (yes, there is such a thing) and designed in conjunction with Cleveland Clinic and Deepak Chopra. Set on one entire floor, they feature vitamin C–infused showers, specialized lighting to suppress melatonin and fight jetlag, and welcome HEPA air filtration to rid your atmosphere of the very Vegas toxins of smoke, allergens, and pollen.

Getting from your room to most anywhere else in the hotel is relatively easy, unless you're headed to megaclub and restaurant **Hakkasan** (p. 100). Then, you must navigate most of the mazelike 170,000 square feet of casino—but follow the path (and the crowds) and you will be at one of the biggest nightlife hot spots in town. The club has a day party at the pool known as Wet Republic, where you get to hear the DJs you usually see at night in broad daylight.

If being crammed into the club isn't your scene, resident Cirque du Soleil show *KÀ* (p. 208) is one of the most breathtaking on the Strip, and the other non-party pools have a lazy river running through them.

MGM boasts one of the more exciting restaurant lineups on the Strip, including two from the restaurant group started by the late, highly acclaimed French chef Joël Robuchon; Emeril's **New Orleans Fish House;** and Iron Chef-helmed **Morimoto.** All are reviewed in chapter 5.

3799 Las Vegas Blvd. S. (at Tropicana Ave.). www.mgmgrand.com. © **800/929-1111** or 702/891-7777. 5,044 units. $165 and up double; $265 and up suite. Resort fee $37. Extra person $40. Children 13 and under stay free in parent's room. Parking 1 hr. free, self-parking $9–$15, valet $16–$24; hotel guest 24-hour parking fees allow same-day in-and-out parking privileges at other MGM Resorts; prices vary during special events. **Amenities:** 23 restaurants; nightclub; cabaret theater; casino; concierge; events arena; executive-level rooms; large health club; Jacuzzi; 5 outdoor pools w/lazy river; room service; salon; shopping arcade; spa; wedding chapel; free Wi-Fi.

Moderate

Excalibur ★ Kitsch is still king at this elaborate castle on the Strip. Excalibur fulfills that "adult Disney" mentality that the city was trying to go after in the early '90s. It's enormous, it's loud, and it's often crowded, but despite a few updates to the decor, it still doesn't take itself too seriously.

If you're on a budget, the standard rooms should suit you just fine; they're comfortable, if a bit outdated. The Contemporary Tower rooms are worth the extra price upgrade for more modern (as the name implies) touches and decor, as well as nicer bathrooms. Both come with 21st-century amenities like flatscreen TVs, Internet, and cable access. Come prepared with earplugs, however, as the walls are woefully thin, so you can hear exactly what your neighbors are saying and doing (and vice versa). For the price though, you won't find any better location on the Strip.

A medieval wedding isn't a rare request these days, and should you decide at the last minute you want to do a themed wedding, you can rent your own Guinevere and Lancelot—or Arthur, whoever fits—attire from the Canterbury Wedding Chapel (though one representative told us that requests lately have been more *Game of Thrones* than Arthurian legend).

For those fair maidens who aren't getting married just yet, the hunky Aussies from *Thunder From Down Under* are ready to show you what the fuss is all about. A totally different group of Aussies, the Australian Bee Gees, is a surprisingly accurate tribute act that puts on a fun, disco-filled, nostalgic show.

Excalibur is still one of the only kid-friendly resorts on the Strip. (We suppose it's hard to get away from that reputation when you're in the shape of a giant castle.) The **Fun Dungeon** arcade features more than 150 carnival and arcade games and is perfect for those bored kids and teens who have nothing else to do in town.

Following the trend of buffets being reborn, Excalibur's underwent its own overhaul in 2015. The remodel included transforming the dining room to more modern digs—all traces of the old Round Table theme have been erased—and updating the menu so that you and your knights have more international choices.

3850 Las Vegas Blvd. S. (at Tropicana Ave.). www.excalibur.com. ✆ **800/937-7777** or 702/597-7700. 3,981 units. $45 and up double. Daily resort fee $35. Extra person $25. No discount for children. Parking 1 hr. free, self-parking $6–$10, valet $12–$16; hotel guest 24-hour parking fees allow same-day in-and-out parking privileges at other MGM Resorts. **Amenities:** 5 restaurants; buffet; food court; casino; concierge; outdoor pools; room service; showrooms; wedding chapel; free Wi-Fi.

Luxor Las Vegas ★ Though it was never as grand as the ruins at Giza, the black, bold Luxor pyramid that punctuates the Strip has lost its original kitschy glory. Sure, the exterior hasn't changed, and the 315,000-watt beam of light that shoots from the top of the Luxor is still powerful and impressive. But inside, the dynasty has definitely fallen. Gone are the once-unavoidable faux-Egyptian monuments (except for Cleopatra's Needle and the Sphinx in the front, as well as the ominous Ramses statues still guarding the main entrance) in favor of a toned-down environment. It's a shame, really. The little details were what made Luxor so fun to explore. Today it's known only for its reasonable room rates and connection to Mandalay Bay.

Most believe that the Pyramid Rooms are the best to stay in, if only for the inclinator (not an elevator) ride that guests must take to get to their abode. It's a jolting, not-smooth ride at a 39-degree angle up the side of the building, but a novel way to change floors. But beyond that elevator ride, I don't recommend the Pyramid for stays; the angled windows in it make the rooms in that tower feel smaller than they are. And if you need a tub, you're out of luck in the pyramid. Bottom line: Request a room in one of the other twin, 22-story cubes, which upgraded out of the garish ancient Egypt phase with a more natural color palette and streamlined décor.

The casino feels enormous even by Las Vegas standards at 120,000 square feet, but its Egyptian kitsch is long gone, making it pretty banal. Maybe the artifacts were too distracting from the clanging of more than 2,000 slot machines.

Luxor's 5-acre pool is divided into four sections. An oasis of faux Egyptian decor, it boasts one of the largest pool decks on the Strip. During the summer, there's an LGBT-friendly pool party (one of the few on the Strip) called Temptation Sundays, with a live DJ and lots of hot, sculpted eye candy.

What Luxor lacks in personality these days, it makes up for in entertainment options. Prop comedian **Carrot Top**'s (p. 220) long-running show is still a hit, while **Blue Man Group** (p. 206) is always a fun night out. The departure of Criss Angel's show in 2018 left a Cirque-sized gap in the offerings, but Cirque du Soleil has announced that its newest spectacle, *R.U.N,* touted as its "first live action thriller," will open in late 2019. Things can get educational as well, with visits to the popular *Bodies* and well-regarded *Titanic* exhibits, both of which are reviewed in chapter 6.

Though the restaurant collection is more diverse at neighbor Mandalay Bay, Luxor has a few of its own gems, such as modern Diablo's Cantina, and game meat–oriented **Tender Steakhouse,** covered in chapter 5.

3900 Las Vegas Blvd. S. (btw. Reno and Hacienda aves.). www.luxor.com. ℂ **888/777-0188** or 702/262-4000. 4,400 units. $63 and up double; $150 and up whirlpool suite; $249–$800 other suites. Resort fee $35. Extra person $35. No discount for children. Parking 1 hr. free, self-parking $6–$10, valet $12–$16; hotel guest 24-hour parking fees allow same-day in-and-out parking privileges at other MGM Resorts. **Amenities:** 6 restaurants; buffet; food court; nightclub; casino; concierge; executive-level rooms; health club; 5 outdoor pools; room service; showrooms; spa; free Wi-Fi.

New York–New York Hotel & Casino ★★   The hotel that's so-nice-they-named-it-twice is really good at detail (at least on the exterior). Even though the one-third-size replica of the New York skyline seems crammed into the facade, it covers it all in 2.4 million square feet: the 150-foot Statue of Liberty, the 300-foot-long Brooklyn Bridge, the Chrysler Building, the Empire State Building. It's like looking at a live-action cartoon postcard. And it's these aesthetic touches that make this one of the quintessential Las Vegas resorts. People still want a hotel that has a roller coaster wrapped around it.

Along with Park MGM (p. 55), New York–New York has been pushing its offerings more to its front on the Strip, adding busy restaurants such as **Shake Shack** (there's always a line, but worth it; p. 108) and **Tom's Urban,** along with candy-land **Hershey's Chocolate World** (p. 195). Follow the restaurants around the corner to see that they anchor the south side of the Park, the outdoor entertainment space that leads to T-Mobile Arena.

While the outside of New York–New York is still exciting, the inside has been toned down, with less "New York–ness" to the casino floor and the rooms. Sure, the rooms are sleek, with plush padded headboards, 40-inch flatscreen TVs, and marble in the bathrooms, but we miss the Chrysler Building–like Art Deco pizzazz they once had. Call it gentrification.

family-friendly HOTELS

We've said it before and we'll say it again: Vegas is simply not a good place to bring kids. Most of the major hotels no longer offer babysitting, and fewer offer discounts for children staying in a parent's room (many others have lowered the age for children who can stay for free). But if you must bring them, you'll be best served at the hotels below or in a non-casino hotel, particularly a reliable chain, and a place with kitchenettes.

- **Circus Circus Hotel & Casino** (p. 71) Centrally located on the Strip, this is our first choice if you're traveling with the kids. The hotel's mezzanine level offers ongoing circus acts daily from 11am to midnight, dozens of carnival games, and an arcade. And behind the hotel is a full amusement park.

- **Excalibur** (p. 51) Though the sword-and-sorcery theme has been considerably toned down, Excalibur features an entire floor of midway games and a large video-game arcade. It also has some child-oriented eateries and shows, but there's a heavily promoted male-stripper show, too, so it's not perfect.

- **Four Seasons** (p. 46) For free goodies, service, and general child pampering, the costly Four Seasons is probably worth the dough. Your kids will be spoiled!

- **Mandalay Bay** (p. 48) This hotel certainly looks grown up, but it has a number of factors that make it family-friendly, including good-size rooms that you do not have to cross a casino to access; a variety of restaurants; a big ol' shark attraction; and, best of all, the swimming area— wave pool, sandy beach, lazy river, lots of other pools—fun in the Vegas sun!

- **The Orleans** (p. 85) Proximity to the Strip makes the Orleans, considered a "local" hotel, a viable alternative, especially for families seeking to take advantage of its plus-size pool area, kids' activity area, bowling, and movie theaters.

- **The Strat** (p. 72) For families looking for reasonably priced, if not particularly exciting, digs, this is a good choice. Plus, it's not in the middle of the Strip action, so you and your kids can avoid that. Thus far, it's not moving in the "adult entertainment" direction, and it has thrill rides at the top.

One thing that hasn't changed? It's a long, looooonng slog from registration to your room, no matter which tower you're in. But if you can make it there, you'll make it anywhere . . . else in the hotel. (I'm sorry.)

The risqué resident Cirque du Soleil show *Zumanity* (p. 212) is adult-oriented, best for those who are really comfortable with the sensuality of the human body.

3790 Las Vegas Blvd. S. (at Tropicana Ave.). www.newyorknewyork.com. ℂ **800/693-6763** or 702/740-6969. 2,024 units. $79 and up double. Daily resort fee $37. Extra person $35. No discount for children. Parking 1 hr. free, self-parking $9–$15, valet

$16–$24; hotel guest 24-hour parking fees allow same-day in-and-out parking privileges at other MGM Resorts; prices vary during special events. **Amenities:** 13 restaurants; food court; buffet; casino; executive-level rooms; fitness center; Jacuzzi; outdoor pool; room service; showroom; spa; free Wi-Fi.

Park MGM/NoMad Las Vegas ★ "Bland" is a dirty word in Las Vegas. And it was often lobbed at the Monte Carlo, the name of this property before it was given a $550-million makeover and reemerged as Park MGM in 2018. Was that massive outlay worth it? Well, the hotel now fits in far better with its surroundings, which include the Park outdoor entertainment space and T-Mobile Arena. The contemporary guest lobby added an enormous sculpture of tree roots emerging from the center of the ceiling; that artwork, along with fresh flowers and lots of bright, natural light, brings the park indoors. Gone is the standard walk-up registration, replaced by kiosks with touchscreen tablets so you can check in with minimal human interaction, if you so choose.

Going all in on the park theme, the newly renovated rooms are named after birds—Skylark, Nightingale, and Nighthawk—and are done in either rich red or warm green tones. Walls are adorned with lovely little details such as smaller pieces of framed art, photos, and knickknacks rather than the standard giant-frame hotel art that you'll usually find over the bed. It's meant to evoke city apartment living, and you wouldn't be faulted for feeling like you're staying at an Airbnb rather than a mega resort, even in the standard 400-square-foot rooms.

The renos also brought in more cosmopolitan choices for on-site eateries, such as pretty breakfast-and-lunch spot **Primrose,** as well as Chicago favorite **Bavette's Steakhouse.** Perhaps most intriguingly, Las Vegas finally got its own **Eataly** on the Strip side of the property, as well as Los Angeles wunderkind Roy Choi with his fun **Best Friend.**

The final piece of the puzzle was the boutique, hotel-in-a-hotel addition, **NoMad Las Vegas,** whose 293 rooms sit in the top floors of the towers. This outpost is as beautifully appointed as the brand's New York property, with carefully curated art pieces and bespoke furniture, and curious additions like the freestanding tub next to the bed in the Atelier suite. Oak flooring in the room is a nice, homey touch, though New Yorkers may feel a bit of size envy; some guest rooms are larger than plenty of East Village apartments, even if they're decorated with the same artful sensibility.

3770 Las Vegas Blvd. S. (btw. Flamingo Rd. and Tropicana Ave.). www.parkmgm.com. ℂ **888/529-4828** or 702/730-7777. 3,002 units (including NoMad). $69 and up double; $145 and up suite. Daily resort fee $37. Extra person $37. No discount for children. Parking 1 hr. free, self-parking $9–$15, valet $16–$24; hotel guest 24-hour parking fees allow same-day in-and-out parking privileges at other MGM Resorts. **Amenities:** 3 restaurants; casino; concierge; executive-level rooms; fitness center; Jacuzzi; outdoor pool; room service; showroom; spa; watersports equipment/rentals; wedding chapel; free Wi-Fi.

Tropicana Las Vegas ★   Sadly, the Tropicana has lost its soul and its way. A number of restaurants and attractions have come and gone as the resort's owners (Doubletree by Hilton, believe it or not, since 2013) have attempted to define the iconic resort's new identity. Luxurious? Sure. But there isn't much memorable about it anymore, which is a bummer. They attempted to transport the Miami feel to its dining and pool parties, to minimal success, so the powers that be have kept things at status quo (reasonable rates, middle-of-the-road dining, active casino) until they discover the magic formula to make this once legendary property relevant again. It maintains its spectacular location, right on the corner of Las Vegas Boulevard and Tropicana, offering great value to guests, and that remains its saving grace.

The $200 million spent on renovations transformed the main floor from a dark, dingy casino into a bright, white gambling palace. The rooms, which were completely gutted, follow suit in terms of brightness. Plantation-style shutters on the windows allow just the right amount of light in to highlight the bleach-white, high thread count linens; bamboo and rattan furniture makes you feel like you've checked into a beach house rather than a Strip hotel room. Our favorites are the Bungalow Deluxe Rooms, located just off the pool in two-story buildings, which feel very exclusive and offer potent eye candy from their private balconies.

Restaurant: Impossible host and buff chef Robert Irvine first announced his **Public House** by rappelling 22 stories down the outside of the building. A little cheesy, sure, but his brand of TV magic and energy has pumped a bit more oomph into this once-legendary resort.

3801 Las Vegas Blvd. S. (at Tropicana Ave.). www.troplv.com. 🕻 **888/826-8767** or 702/739-2222. 1,375 units. $89 and up double. Resort fee $37. Extra person $25. No discount for children. Free self- and valet parking. **Amenities:** 3 restaurants; food court; casino; executive-level rooms; health club; 3 outdoor pools; showroom; wedding chapel; free Wi-Fi.

MID-STRIP

The middle of the Strip is from Harmon Avenue to Spring Mountain/Sands Road and features many of the grand Vegas gambling destinations you have seen in the movies.

Best for: People without transportation who want to be able to walk to everything they want to see.

Drawbacks: Peak times bring out massive crowds and higher prices.

Expensive

Bellagio ★★★   The Bellagio has come to exemplify everything that's recognized as luxury in Las Vegas. It was opened in 1989 by Steve Wynn (along with the Mirage), setting the standard for Las Vegas elegance. Decades later and now part of MGM Resorts, the Lake Como–inspired resort is still at the top of its game.

Just walking into the Bellagio is a thrill. First you pass the aquatic spectacle of the **Fountains of Bellagio** (p. 160) outside, and then you enter the lobby under a stunning ceiling garden of artist Dale Chihuly's hand-blown flowers. Follow your nose to the wafting scents from the lush **Conservatory** (p. 160) and botanical garden, which changes its displays seasonally five times a year (the fifth, in case you're wondering, is in celebration of Chinese New Year).

The handsome accommodations are available in two different color palettes, inspired by the attractions downstairs. The blue and platinum scheme, contemporary and relaxing, is meant to evoke the Fountains of Bellagio; while the serene green and plum pairing offers the earthy warmth of the Conservatory. The decor straddles the line between funky and elegant. Bathrooms are larger than most Brooklyn apartments, with marble vanities and large soaking tubs.

Many of the upscale restaurants that were part of the opening team are still here, including **Michael Mina, Fix,** and **Le Cirque,** with a few newcomers that reflect Las Vegas's changing appetites, like **Yellowtail** and **Lago,** which are all reviewed in chapter 5. Nightlife beats on at lounges such as Hyde Bellagio and Lily. Resident Cirque du Soleil show *O* (p. 211) is still an aquatic and acrobatic masterpiece.

The price points are pretty steep all around the hotel, and not just at the gaming tables. Weekend cabana rentals next to one of the six pools in its Mediterranean oasis are $300; head to the more-exclusive Cypress Pool, and just sitting in a chair will cost you a whopping $50—or more.

3600 Las Vegas Blvd. S. (at the corner of Flamingo Rd.). www.bellagio.com. © **888/987-6667** or 702/693-7111. 3,933 units. $169 and up double; $450 and up suite. Resort fee $39. Extra person $50. No discount for children. Parking 1 hr. free, self-parking $9–$18, valet $21–$30; hotel guest 24-hour parking fees allow same-day in-and-out parking privileges at other MGM Resorts. prices vary during special events. **Amenities:** 14 restaurants; buffet; nightclubs; casino; concierge; executive-level rooms; large health club; 6 outdoor pools; room service; showrooms; spa; wedding chapel; free Wi-Fi.

Caesars Palace ★★★ Caesars dips its toes into old Vegas and new Vegas, maintaining that kitschy, over-the-top cheesiness that was associated with the city for a long time (Roman columns and statues), while at the same time embracing all the modern elegance that's become expected.

There are six towers of varying degrees of luxury, and each has its own personality. The most basic rooms are in the Roman and Forum towers, which are the oldest, but these rooms, like most of the others at this expansive hotel, have been renovated with modern touches like mirrored headboards, sleeker lines, and in-mirror TVs in the bathroom. As the name implies, Palace Tower rooms (the closest to the convention space) are decidedly more regal, and larger, with wood and gold finishes. The Laurel Connection is a boutique hotel experience comprised of the Augustus and Octavius Towers, which not only have their own line of luxury amenities but also a private valet on Flamingo, so guests don't have to navigate the casino floor to get to their rooms.

Floor-to-ceiling windows admit plenty of light into the big sleeping areas, which come complete with plush sofas that hug the corner of the room.

And yes, you can even book the Hangover Suite. The one in the film *The Hangover,* however, isn't an actual suite in the hotel, but a set modeled after the Emperor's Suite in the Forum Tower. Just don't end up on the roof.

The old Centurion Tower took on a new identity in 2013 as the **Nobu Hotel Las Vegas,** named for the restaurants by modern Japanese pioneer Nobu Matsuhisa. Everything about it departs from the Caesars aesthetic: It's appointed with contemporary and traditional Japanese decor such as mini-teak stools and black stone tile in the open showers. Exclusive amenities include sleep oils, Nobu's own brand of tea in the mini-bar, and priority seating in the Nobu restaurant downstairs. Since the hotel-within-the-hotel essentially operates as its own entity, the smaller guest-to-staff ratio allows for more personalized service.

There are almost as many pools at the **Garden of the Gods** complex as there are hotel towers. Named for various Roman gods, each caters to its own niche of clientele based on its moniker. The Venus pool is European style (as in bikini-top optional) and often has a DJ soundtrack, while you can play swim-up blackjack at Fortuna. Tucked away in the corner, Jupiter pool is the most secluded and quiet, but Bacchus is secluded in its own way, reserved for the high rollers, invited guests, and celebrities.

Dining options at Caesars Palace are diverse and renowned, including Italian favorite **Rao's,** French gastronomic temple **Restaurant Guy Savoy,** and Bobby Flay's **Mesa Grill,** as well as others reviewed in chapter 5.

Shoppers love wandering around the massive **Forum Shops** (p. 198) for high end retail. The **Colosseum** (p. 214) hosts resident acts such as Mariah Carey and Rod Stewart. Head outdoors to the big tent for *Absinthe* (p. 206), the most outrageous show on the Strip.

3570 Las Vegas Blvd. S. (just north of Flamingo Rd.). www.caesarspalace.com. ✆ **877/427-7243** or 702/731-7110. 3,960 units. $119 and up double; $440 and up suite. Resort fee $39. Extra person $30. No discount for children. Parking 1 hr. free, self-parking $12–$18, valet $21–$30; hotel guest 24-hour parking fees allow same-day in-and-out parking privileges at other Caesars Entertainment properties. **Amenities:** 11 restaurants; buffet; food court; nightclubs; casino; concierge; executive-level rooms; health club; 8 outdoor pools; room service; spa; 3 wedding chapels; free Wi-Fi.

The Cosmopolitan of Las Vegas ★★★   When the Cosmopolitan opened in 2010, it was the start of a brand-new era in Las Vegas. The town was slowly climbing out of the recession, and this was likely to be the last new resort to be built from the ground up for a long time. So, it broke the mold.

What you'll notice first about the Cosmopolitan is that there are so many things to notice. Crisp LED screens on the columns near check-in display fluid, moving graphics that keep guests entranced. At one point, Liberace's Rhinestone Roadster was even parked near the Strip entrance. There's no shortage of visual stimulation in the 100,000-square-foot casino or the floors above, and that's even without the frenetic slot machines.

Chandeliers are big—literally—at the Cosmopolitan. The three-story specimen in the middle of the casino floor is made of 2 million crystals and houses the multilevel Chandelier Bar. It joins the more subdued Vesper Bar near registration (a spot where you might find casino execs having a drink). Each has its own dedicated cocktail program to match the vibe.

The most basic rooms are quite swank, done up in relaxing blues and metallics, and start at around 500 square feet. Each features a giant, marble-tiled bathroom. The direct view from the bed right into the shower is . . . cool? (If you're not feeling modest.) If it's reasonable, upgrade to at least the terrace studio. In these, you also get the benefit of 200 more square feet and a kitchenette, plus a private terrace, a rarity on the Strip. The one-bedroom suites have even better amenities, like deep Japanese soaking tubs that look out the window, separate seating areas that can be closed off from the bedroom, and terraces that wrap around the corner of the building.

The Cosmopolitan's restaurant collection also ushered in a new era for Vegas's culinary scene. It helped move appetites away from celebrity chef–driven spots to more urban, real-food-city fare. Its **Wicked Spoon** buffet reset the bar for the all-you-can-eat-experience (it, along with some of the other dozen restaurants at Cosmo, are reviewed in chapter 5). Even more foodie cred was earned when they added David Chang's hipster Asian restaurant **Momofuku** and acclaimed dessert spot **Milk Bar.**

Entertainment-wise, Cosmopolitan has made a name for itself as a stop for indie bands and big-name artists. Sometimes they play the intimate **Chelsea** showroom; sometimes they'll play outdoors to standing room only at the

Boulevard Pool. The pool also serves as the day life part of **Marquee,** one of the biggest nightclubs on the Strip. In winter, the pool gets covered, faux snow gets piped into the air, and the space becomes a skating rink.

The clientele here, whether they're guests or not, tend to run on the younger side. This isn't a quiet hotel, that's for sure, nor does it ever aim to be.

3708 Las Vegas Blvd. S. www.cosmopolitanlasvegas.com. ℂ **877/551-7778** or 702/698-7000. 2,995 units. $140 and up double. Resort fee $44. Extra person $35. Children under 17 stay free in parent's room. Complimentary self- and valet-parking for registered hotel guests. For visitors, parking 1 hr. free, self-parking $10–$15, valet $15–$20. **Amenities:** 13 restaurants; buffet; casino; concierge; executive-level rooms; health club; heated outdoor pools; room service; spa; free Wi-Fi.

The Cromwell ★★

At 188 rooms, this is probably the only Strip hotel that can truly call itself "boutique," which is exactly what the Cromwell was going for when it transformed the old, tired Bill's Gamblin' Hall into this handsome newbie in 2014.

Yes, the casino is still pretty dark inside, but now it's the kind of sophisticated dark that you want to be caught in. Warm, sultry colors and textures decorate the casino floor, starting at the modern vintage (if there is such a thing) **Bound Bar** at the front, which allows guests to have a drink in the lobby without feeling overwhelmed by the casino. They kept the original red chandeliers of Bill's, which fit in perfectly with the new, sexy digs.

The rooms tend to run a little smaller but make up for it in luxurious appointments. Influenced by modern Paris (down to the French phrases elegantly scrawled on the carpets in the hallways), the accommodations feature dark, hardwood floors (practically unheard of in Las Vegas), antique trunks as furniture, tufted leather headboards, and deep, luscious berry hues. Bathrooms are definitely small but pack a visual punch, with tall showers, handheld showerheads, and readable tile that offers more life coaching quotes. On the tech front, you no longer need a key to open your room. Opt for the eKey app that allows you to wave your iPhone over the pad on the door, *et voi*là*!* Access granted. Perfect for those of us who have a habit of misplacing keycards.

While it's dark in the casino, **Giada** (p. 118) De Laurentiis's namesake restaurant on the second floor is a bright, airy space awash in natural light. We review her first eatery in chapter 5.

The Cromwell is definitely aiming at a younger demographic—but those with disposable incomes; guests also receive admission to the party scene of the hotel. Nightclub mainstay **Drai's** (p. 232) emerged from its basement lair to take over the rooftop and its pool for a nightlife and daylife component. Drai's Afterhours, though, still operates 'til the wee hours of the morning down in the depths of the hotel.

3595 Las Vegas Blvd. S. www.thecromwell.com. ℂ **844/426-2766** or 702/777-3777. 188 units. $99 and up double. Resort fee $37. Extra person $35. No discount for children. Parking 1 hr. free, self-parking $9–$15, valet $15–$24; hotel guest 24-hour parking fees allow same-day in-and-out parking privileges at other Caesars Entertainment properties. **Amenities:** Restaurant; nightclubs; casino; concierge; heated outdoor pool; room service; free Wi-Fi.

The Venetian/Palazzo Las Vegas ★★ When Las Vegas was going through its period of building hotels in homage to other cities (New York–New York, Luxor, Paris Las Vegas), there was a tendency to create these hotels as more of a caricature of the real deal. Somehow, Venetian managed to escape that campy, kitschy feel; it is, without a doubt, one of the most beautiful and luxurious properties to come out of that trend.

The exterior, much like Paris Las Vegas, crams a lot of the actual city's landmarks into one small footprint. There are the canals and Campanile right at the front, and the Doge's Palace facade—where the plaza sometimes gets shut down for private, hoity-toity events. Indoors, right at Venetian's registration, guests are treated to Michelangelo's work on the ceiling of the Sistine Chapel, recreated in the type of gorgeous detail that carries through the rest of the property.

St. Mark's Square is another masterful fake, an actual square within the **Grand Canal Shoppes** (p. 199), ringed by retailers and restaurants with "patio" seating. Wandering minstrels treat crowds to live performances. It's a nice nod to the city, with less worry about pickpockets.

Both Venetian and Palazzo are proper all-suite hotels, with the smallest rooms starting at a generous 650 square feet. The suites are bi-level, with sunken living rooms that have full-size sleeper sofas on request, and even enough room to fit in two more comfortable chairs and a dining table with three seats. Colors are rich and royal, and the entire space has a warm, relaxing glow, perfect for when you fall into one of the plush beds tucked with soft, high thread count sheets. Bathrooms are downright palatial, complete with deep, marble-encased Roman tubs, separate enclosed shower, and double vanities. Three TVs—one each in the bedroom and living rooms, and of course one in the bath—make sure that you're always entertained.

The Venetian also has boasting rights in the culinary realm: Its celebrity chef arsenal of restaurants includes a brasserie by the legendary Thomas Keller, a steakhouse and sports bar by Emeril Lagasse, and desserts by Buddy Valastro. See chapter 5 for a more detailed discussion.

The Grand Canal Shoppes meander between the Venetian and Palazzo, featuring faux canals that snake through them, complete with singing gondoliers. The Palazzo's atrium features seasonal floral displays, as well as a waterfall. The Chinese New Year display is often one of the most elaborate on the Strip (the year of the dragon featured a giant, mechanical, fire-breathing one). The display is created with feng shui in mind, and guests are encouraged to walk around it three times, clockwise, in order to bring good luck for the lunar new year.

3355 Las Vegas Blvd. S. www.venetian.com. ✆ **888/283-6423** or 702/414-1000. 7,093 units. $159 and up double. Resort fee $45. Extra person $35. Children 12 and under stay free in parent's room. Free self- and valet parking. **Amenities:** 39 restaurants; casino; concierge; executive-level rooms; health club; outdoor pools; 24-hr. room service; extensive shopping mall; showrooms; spa; wedding chapels; free Wi-Fi.

Moderate

Bally's Las Vegas ★   The obvious reason to stay at Bally's: its prime, center-Strip location. The less-obvious reason? Some of its suites are darn nice (something that few visitors know).

What was originally the MGM Grand when it opened in 1973, Bally's has pretty much stayed the same, as the rest of the Strip grew bigger and more opulent. It's only since 2014 that we've been seeing more grand changes throughout the property, first inside, then out.

The Jubilee Tower rooms were the first to be completely renovated and are worth spending an extra $20 above the price of the standard rooms. If Bally's feels a little dated on the outside, these spaces say otherwise, with polished wood furnishings, tufted headboards, pillow-top beds, and lots of marble in the bathrooms. The colors are a little tame, but everything feels clean and swanky. Should you decide to go a little bigger—and you should—a suite here will run at least $100 less per night than you'll find at Bellagio right across the street. The Jubilee Grand Suites will surprise you; they're twice the size of the regular rooms, with lots of red, more amenities, and why, yes, that *is* a whirlpool right in the middle of your room. The other non–Jubilee Tower rooms and suites are serviceable, but if you can afford to stay somewhere prettier, why not?

Most visitors who aren't bedding down here stop by for the famed **Sterling Brunch,** which runs nearly $100 a pop. **BLT Steak** replaced Bally's Steakhouse in 2014 but retained the brunch, so now you get to eat your endless caviar and lobster tails in a much more contemporary setting. It's only a quick walk through the corridor connecting Bally's and Paris Las Vegas next door to get to more dining options.

Finally, the front of Bally's is the **Grand Bazaar Shops** (p. 199), an outdoor retail and dining experience with lots of tiny boutiques you won't find elsewhere in Las Vegas.

3645 Las Vegas Blvd. S. (at Flamingo Rd.). www.ballyslv.com. ☎ **800/634-3434** or 702/739-4111. 2,814 units. $39 and up double; $199 and up suite. Resort fee $35. Extra person $30. No discount for children. Parking 1 hr. free, self-parking $9–$15, valet $15–$24; hotel guest 24-hour parking fees allow same-day in-and-out parking privileges at other Caesars Entertainment properties. **Amenities:** 4 restaurants; buffet; food court; casino; concierge; health club; outdoor pool; room service; showrooms; spa; 8 night-lit tennis courts; free Wi-Fi.

Flamingo Las Vegas ★   Aside from the Tropicana, Flamingo is probably the most recognizable hotel name in Las Vegas, mainly because it's the longest survivor on the Strip. Bugsy Siegel opened the 105-room (it would be considered "boutique" today) Flamingo in 1946, and 7 decades later, even though the original bones are completely gone, he'd probably still recognize the place.

The pink neon that has been burned into our collective memories still streams through the hotel, especially when you check into the FAB rooms and

Flamingo rooms. The main difference between the two? The Flamingo rooms are prettier to look at, having been more recently renovated, and come with showers only (FAB rooms do have tubs). The Flamingo embraces its Rat Pack history, with the Flamingo rooms attempting to throw you back into all its mod glory, with vinyl padded headboards, black-and-white photos of Vegas days of yore, and pops of color on the striped wallpaper. There are modern amenities like electronic window treatments, and TVs built into the mirrors. Try to score a room in the Habitat tower for easy access to the LINQ Promenade so you don't have to navigate the casino floor to leave the building.

For those in search of nostalgia, **Donny and Marie** will take a bow at the end of 2019, and Paula Abdul will set up shop, while **Legends in Concert** (p. 216) continues to chug along to sold-out crowds. Irreverent magician **Piff The Magic Dragon** (p. 217) has become a favorite as well.

The pool is one of the hotel's biggest draws. Lush foliage adorns 15 acres of lagoons, waterfalls, and streams, as well as five pools and whirlpools. The GO pool features DJ-driven pool time, but the other swimming spots are more family-friendly. You can find the flocks of the namesake bird on Flamingo Island, part of the property's famed **Wildlife Habitat,** as well as other animals such as ducks, ibis, and turtles, all part of this carefully maintained ecosystem. These species might not be native to Nevada, but they're definitely a part of the Las Vegas landscape.

3555 Las Vegas Blvd. S. (btw. Sands Ave. and Flamingo Rd.). www.flamingolv.com. © **800/732-2111** or 702/733-3111. 3,517 units. $85 and up double; $122 and up suite. Resort fee $35. Extra person $30. No discount for children. Timeshare suites available. Parking 1 hr. free, self-parking $9–$15, valet $15–$24; hotel guest 24-hour parking fees allow same-day in-and-out parking privileges at other Caesars Entertainment properties. **Amenities:** 4 restaurants; buffet; food court; casino; executive-level rooms; health club; 5 outdoor pools; room service; showrooms; spa; wedding chapels; free Wi-Fi.

Harrah's Las Vegas ★ What Harrah's lacks in panache, it makes up for in location, and for the nonstop action on its casino floor. It's not exactly the most luxurious or sophisticated place on the Strip, but it is smack dab in the middle of it, and for that it's worth a stay if you're planning on a) doing stuff at lots of other hotels or b) gambling here the whole time.

Accommodations are forgettable looking, with the expected amenities, but roomier than other hotels you'll find at this price point. In a word, they're just fine, except for a handful of basic rooms that haven't been updated yet—don't be afraid to ask for more modern digs in the Carnaval South tower if you get stuck with one of them.

The casino is a gambler's paradise, with more than 80 table games and 1,200 slot machines hungry for your money. Entertainment options are about right for the demographic: There's the long-running **Menopause The Musical,** as well as headliners the **Righteous Brothers** and afternoon-favorite **Mac King** (p. 216) comedy show.

Restaurant-wise, **Ruth's Chris** is a good standby for steak, with a primo view of the Strip, while **Fulton Street Food Hall** (p. 124) is an easy, casual

option. It's not a food court, but you know those big marketlike eating emporiums popping up around the country? This is Las Vegas's version.

3475 Las Vegas Blvd. S. (btw. Flamingo and Spring Mountain rds.). www.harrahs
lasvegas.com. © **800/427-7247** or 702/369-5000. 2,526 units. $65 and up double; $270
and up suite. Resort fee $35. Extra person $30. No discount for children. Parking 1 hr.
free, self-parking $9–$15, valet $15–$24; hotel guest 24-hour parking fees allow same-
day in-and-out parking privileges at other Caesars Entertainment properties. **Amenities:** 5 restaurants; buffet; casino; concierge; executive-level rooms; health club;
outdoor pool; room service; showroom; spa; free Wi-Fi.

The LINQ ★ Formerly the pseudo-Asian-themed Imperial Palace, it took
a few name changes before the powers that be settled on the LINQ in 2014—if
only so it wouldn't be confusing when people were talking about the LINQ
Promenade, a shopping and retail space that extends straight from the Strip
between the LINQ and Flamingo hotels.

The rebirth of IP into the LINQ meant a total overhaul of the property:
brand spankin' new casino floor, total gutting of the rooms, and a beautiful
new facade to match. The rooms are small, starting at 250 square feet (the
47-inch flatscreen TVs seem almost comically large in such a tiny space), but
pack a punch visually. Deluxe rooms feature white linens, natural wood fur-
nishing, and Vegas-oriented wallpaper behind the beds, from mod patterns to
huge macro images of old Las Vegas signs. Poolside rooms double as cabanas,
with patio access direct to the pool, if you're interested in creating your own
dayclub experience. Or do you and your squad need to be together at all
times? The Bunk Bed Rooms (with two queens and one twin bunk bed) channel that sleep-away-camp-meets-cool-European-hostel feeling, except these
rooms are at grown-up prices. If you're lucky, you'll have a great view of the
High Roller (p. 157), the observation wheel that now marks the center of the
Vegas skyline.

The pool now matches all the other beautiful pools on the Strip; you'll find
it on the second floor of tower 3. It's 21-and-over, which obviously makes this
not suitable for families, but ideal for young adults who are looking for a good
time during the day.

There are plenty of dining options in the LINQ Promenade next door, but
you can get your own celebrity chef fix at **Guy Fieri's Vegas Kitchen & Bar**
(p. 120) right at the front of the hotel.

3535 Las Vegas Blvd. S. www.caesars.com/linq. © **800/634-6441** or 702/794-3366.
2,553 units. $61 and up double; $193 and up suite. Resort fee $35. Extra person $30.
No discount for children. Parking 1 hr. free, self-parking $9–$15, valet $15–$24; hotel
guest 24-hour parking fees allow same-day in-and-out parking privileges at other Caesars Entertainment properties. **Amenities:** 8 restaurants; casino; concierge; health
club; heated outdoor pool; room service; spa; showrooms; salon; auto museum; wedding chapel; free Wi-Fi.

The Mirage ★★ What we know of Las Vegas today—the over-the-top
offerings, the temples of excess, all with the notion that luxury can be
attainable even by regular folks—all started with the Mirage when it

opened in 1989. Since then, hotels have only been getting bigger and more extravagant.

But not all of them have an exploding volcano in front.

It's not just the volcano that's set to explode every hour to music: The lush foliage in the domed atrium, the 20,000-gallon aquarium behind the check-in desk, and **Siegfried and Roy's** (yes, they're still around) **Secret Garden & Dolphin Habitat** all help keep the Mirage top-of-mind to would-be visitors. Even if you've never been here before, you know that volcano. You know Siegfried and Roy.

And beyond the fake lava, this is a darn nice place to stay. Accommodations are downright luxurious for the price point, with clean lines, bold colors, and natural wood furnishings surrounding a great pillow-top mattress on the bed. Neutral-colored marble in the bathroom is a nice touch, and the hotel is vocal about its ADA-accessible rooms.

Dining options have gotten on par with the rest of the Strip: Tom Colicchio's **Heritage Steak** focuses on good, properly sourced meat cooked over an open fire; the **Pantry** serves as the 24-hour coffee shop but feels more like you're eating in your mom's kitchen; **Carnegie Deli** still serves some of the best football-sized, New York–style pastrami sandwiches in town.

The pool, open and heated all year, is considered one of the best on the Strip thanks to a lagoonlike setting, waterfalls, and waterslides. The adult-oriented Bare Pool Lounge allows for European-style sunbathing (read: topless) and is a nice oasis in its own right.

3400 Las Vegas Blvd. S. (btw. Flamingo and Spring Mountain rds.). www.mirage.com. ✆ **800/627-6667** or 702/791-7111. 3,044 units. $99 and up double; $160 and up suite. Resort fee $37. Extra person $35. No discount for children. Parking 1 hr. free, self-parking $9–$15, valet $16–$24; hotel guest 24-hour parking fees allow same-day in-and-out parking privileges at other MGM Resorts; prices vary during special events. **Amenities:** 14 restaurants; buffet; casino; concierge; executive-level rooms; health club; outdoor pools; room service; showrooms; spa; free Wi-Fi.

Paris Las Vegas Casino Resort ★★★   If visiting Paris, France is at the top of your bucket list, the Vegas version won't let you cross it off—but it *will* give you a snapshot of what you'll encounter in the real deal. The Eiffel Tower in front is half the size of the original but is exact in detail, right down to the number of rivets that hold it all together and the glass elevator that takes you to the top observation deck.

Inside, you're transported to Vegas's idea of the City of Light, with the legs of the Eiffel Tower coming through the ceiling—painted with clouds—to give you the illusion that you are directly under it. The rooms are clean, efficient, and larger than most standard accommodations, and after completing their $92-million renovation in 2019, they finally have some *joie de vivre* breathed back into all 2,900 of them. To get the full experience, make sure you specify that you'd like a view of the Eiffel Tower if you opt for one of the freshly remodeled Burgundy Rooms. Considering you're basically center-Strip, you're getting ample space for a decent price.

SO YOUR TRIP GOES swimmingly . . .

Part of the delight of the Vegas resort complexes is the gorgeous pools—what could be better for beating the summer heat? But there are pools and there are *pools,* so you'll need to keep several things in mind when searching for the right one for you.

During the winter, it's often too cold or windy to do much lounging, and even if the weather is amenable, the hotels often close part of their pool areas during winter and early spring. Also, the pools are not heated for the most part, but in fairness, they largely don't need to be.

Most hotel pools are shallow, chest-high at best, only about 3 feet deep in many spots (the hotels want you gambling, not swimming). Diving is impossible—not that a single pool allows it anyway.

Although the stories about the "Death Ray" at the Vdara hotel were overblown (where the sun reflecting off the mirrored hotel exterior reportedly caused plastic to melt), be warned that sitting by pools that offer scant shade requires diligent application of sunscreen.

At any of the pools, you can rent a cabana (which often includes a TV, special lounge chairs, and—even better—poolside service), but these should be reserved as far in advance as possible, and most cost a hefty fee. If you are staying at a chain hotel, you will most likely find an average pool. If you want to spend some time at a better one, be aware that most of the casino-hotel pool attendants will ask to see your room key. If they are busy, you might be able to sneak in, or at least blend in with a group ahead of you.

When it comes to our favorites, we tend to throw our support to those that offer luxurious landscaping, plenty of places to lounge, multiple dipping options, and some shade for those times when the desert sun gets to be too much. This is a good description of the pools at both the **Mirage** and the **Flamingo,** which offer acres of veritable tropical paradises for you to enjoy. Ditto the renovated pool area at the **Tropicana,** serving up a sunny Miami Beach vibe among lush grounds.

If you're looking for something a little more adventurous, try the epic facility at **Mandalay Bay,** complete with a wave pool, a lazy-river ride, and good old-fashioned swimming holes, along with a sandy beach. **MGM Grand** has a similar facility, although not as big and without the waves.

Partying is not confined to the nightclubs these days. Many of the hotels offer pool-club experiences (p. 234), but even when they aren't in full-on party mode, the pools at **Hard Rock** (sandy beaches, swim-up blackjack), the **Palms** (multilevel, high-end cabanas), **Aria Las Vegas** (acres of sexy modernity), and the **Cosmopolitan of Las Vegas** (not one but two party pools overlooking the Strip) serve up high-energy frolicking.

The **Eiffel Tower Restaurant** is still one of the most romantic spots in town. A meal at **Gordon Ramsay Steak** (p. 111) will set you back a bit but is the best of his five Vegas restaurants; make a reservation as soon as you can. French bistro **Mon Ami Gabi** (p. 122) seats you right in the front terrace of the hotel, offering some of the best people-watching and a killer view of the Bellagio Fountains, but there's better French food to be had in town, and all of this is covered in chapter 5.

Nightclub **Chateau's** rooftop perch makes it one of the few clubs in town that lets you hang outdoors while celebrity hosts have parties indoors. Or if the club isn't your thing, there's always pre- or post-game at *Napoleon's Dueling Pianos* for fun, live music, and cocktails.

3655 Las Vegas Blvd. S. www.parislv.com. ✆ **888/266-5687** or 702/946-7000. 2,916 units. $75 and up double; $170 and up suite. Resort fee $37. Extra person $30. No discount for children. Parking 1 hr. free, self-parking $9–$15, valet $15–$24; hotel guest 24-hour parking fees allow same-day in-and-out parking privileges at other Caesars Entertainment properties. **Amenities:** 12 restaurants; buffet; casino; concierge; executive-level rooms; health club; outdoor pool; room service; showrooms; spa; 2 wedding chapels; free Wi-Fi.

Planet Hollywood Resort & Casino ★★

The giant, continuous LED screens that lead down to the corner of Las Vegas Boulevard and Harmon Avenue might evoke the frenetic video boards of Times Square; they're definitely just as bright! That amazing stretch of signage is one of the most dazzling on the Strip and reminds us that this truly is still one of the most electrifying (if not electrified) places on Earth.

Once inside, your senses get a break from the constant flash—the interior is modern and elegant, and even the usually frenetic casino floor feels glamorous. Renovations in 2017 touched every room, casting them in the same color palette of stark white accented with grays and crimson. The Resort Rooms are standard, but for a few more dollars put yourself up in an Ultra Hip Room, where the beds are slightly comfier and there's a convenient mini-fridge and coffeemaker. One of our favorite things about PH is the placement of their soaking tubs. The 570-square-foot Vista Rooms, as the name suggests, offer five Strip-view windows to gaze from, one of those perches being the tub. If you're staying in one of the tony Panorama Suites, corner rooms with sweeping views of the Strip, your oversize tub is basically in the middle of the room, so you can enjoy the view from your bubbles.

Other upgrades to the Panorama Suites put you in that Hollywood-star frame of mind, including cool decor like suspended sofas, round beds, and macro (close-up photography) artwork. Celebrities! They like weird furniture!

In addition to the PH rooms proper, we're also including in this review a few thousand more from the adjoining Elara, a timeshare/hotel by Hilton Grand Vacations that you have to book through Hilton directly, though you don't need to own a timeshare to stay there. But that type of property means that all units have kitchens, whether they're in studios or four-room suites, making Elara quite kid-friendly.

Check-in tip: For some reason, valet parking is always full here, even if you're a guest. Unfortunately, this means you have to self-park in the garage at the Miracle Mile Shops, then schlep your gear through the mall, which is a giant circle—so whether you go right or left from the garage doesn't really matter.

Planet Hollywood has numerous dining options including **Gordon Ramsay Burger** and the vegetarian-friendly **Spice Market Buffet** (discussed in chapter 5) and serious shopping opportunities (covered in chapter 7). For entertainment, Gwen Stefani headlines the 4,000-seat **Zappos Theater** a few times a month. The venue also draws performers including Christina Aguilera.

3667 Las Vegas Blvd. S. www.planethollywoodresort.com. ℂ **877/333-9474** or 702/785-5555. 3,768 units. $79 and up double. Resort fee $37. Extra person $30. No discount for children. Free self-parking, valet $15–$24; hotel guest 24-hour parking fees allow same-day in-and-out parking privileges at other Caesars Entertainment properties. **Amenities:** 11 restaurants; buffet; bars/lounges; casino; concierge; executive-level rooms; health club; 2 Jacuzzis; performing arts center; 2 outdoor pools; room service; showroom; spa; wedding chapel; free Wi-Fi.

Treasure Island ★★ Though it's called Treasure Island (TI to locals), the pirate theme that gave this hotel its name is no longer as obvious. Renovations have toned down the property almost to a fault. Gone from the front is the swashbuckling Sirens of TI ship, once home to an innuendo-laden (and pretty stupid) show, and now all you walk past is the giant red façade of a Señor Frog's and the docked pirate ship that reminds you of the show that once was. The hideous brown building that anchors the hotel at the corners of Spring Mountain and Las Vegas Boulevard houses a CVS and looks out of place, appearing more like a medical center than what should be a welcoming first sight for the formerly fun property.

TI rooms, while pleasant enough, aren't too exciting to look at. That being said, they're cozy, with warm, earthy tones, but the TI-branded ("SensaTIonal") pillow-top mattresses are probably the best part of the deal.

Mystère (p. 210) is the longest-running Cirque du Soleil show in town (since 1993) and is still considered one of the best.

3300 Las Vegas Blvd. S. (at Spring Mountain Rd.). www.treasureisland.com. ℂ **800/944-7444** or 702/894-7111. 2,885 units. $57 and up double; $112 and up suite. Resort fee $37. Extra person $30. Free for children 14 and under in parent's room. Free self- and valet parking. **Amenities:** 9 restaurants; buffet; casino; concierge; executive-level rooms; health club; outdoor pool; room service; showroom; spa; wedding chapels; free Wi-Fi.

NORTH STRIP

The northern end of the Strip, from Spring Mountain/Sands Road to Charleston Avenue, is not quite as densely populated with major casinos, but still has enough Vegas flair to make it worth your while.

Best for: Visitors who want to be on the Strip but want a slightly more manageable experience from a crowd-and-congestion perspective.

Drawbacks: It's a longer walk to most of what you'll want to see; in addition, some of the hotels here are past their prime.

Expensive

Wynn/Encore ★★ You can't get away from Steve Wynn when you vacation in Las Vegas. He's the guy who invented the notion that Las Vegas could become a luxury destination. And then he proved it, opening the Mirage and Bellagio (both now owned by MGM Resorts) and transforming Las Vegas into the high-service capital we know it as today. He's also the guy whose name is up on top of the hotel; and, sadly, he was featured in one of the ugliest #MeToo scandals of 2018. The allegations against him of sexual misconduct were so serious that he was forced to step down as CEO of his hotel company. (As of press time Wynn still denies any wrongdoing).

So, should one still stay here? We say yes, mostly for the efforts of the superb staff here. It seems a shame to punish them for the founder's transgressions. And these hotels are among the swankiest on the Strip. Breathe in the lovely (quite possibly pumped in, but we don't care) floral scent as you walk through the doors, and appreciate the lush red, gold, and green hues that accent the decor: You'll see what we mean. It's like walking through one big manufactured garden. These resorts are also humongous. No matter if you walk into Wynn or Encore, it's a winding road through and around the casino floor, wherever you need to go. But there's so much to visually take in, you won't mind the trek.

The Wynn Tower features the hotel's standard rooms, but they're far from ordinary. Floor-to-ceiling windows let in lots of light, and, with a nice touch of feng shui, the beds face the windows as opposed to the walls, so you can wake up to a gorgeous view of the mountains or the valley. In fact, you won't even have to get out of the ultra-plush bed to open the curtains in the morning. With a touch of a button on the panel on the bedside table, you can cast them open and say, "Hello, Las Vegas!" Rooms are awash in creamy tones, and the gorgeously appointed bathrooms are encased in plenty of marble, including the oversize bathtub next to the gloriously powerful shower. Soak it up; this is as glamorous as it gets.

Wynn Tower Suites offer slightly larger accommodations and have the benefit of a private entrance for check-in. It's a higher price point, but the rate includes breakfast for two daily at the hoity-toity Tableau, and the hotel also kicks in access to the Tower Suites' own pool.

The rooms of younger sister Encore next door are comparatively elegant and luxurious, following the same calming aesthetic, but with a few subtle, chic differences. Encore is all suites, with separate sitting and sleeping areas divided by a half wall. The black upholstery also makes the rooms seem far more contemporary. The pillow-top Wynn Dream Bed lives up to its name (I had one of most restful sleeps I've ever had on the Strip on one). Bathrooms are downright palatial, with a giant tub next to the glass-enclosed shower, dual sinks, and a 13-inch flatscreen TV, because feeling like you're rich means having a TV in your bathroom.

The Moroccan hammam that is Encore's spa is one of the most opulent on the Strip. The ornate mosaic tile in the lobby alone had me so entranced that it felt like the massage treatment was simply a nice bonus.

"Daylife" is a major component to Wynn and Encore, centered around three different pool areas, plus the clandestine digs of the Tower Suites pool. The Wynn and Encore pools are both calm and low-key, each with multiple bodies of water, Jacuzzis, and cabanas. The Encore European pool allows for topless sunbathing. **Encore Beach Club,** however, is another animal entirely: a daytime party on the weekends for guests more concerned with the live DJ than they are with their tans.

Eating at both these hotels will run up a bill, but high-end culinary options such as **Costa di Mare** (p. 126), **Sinatra** (p. 126), and **Wing Lei** are totally worth the splurge.

3131 Las Vegas Blvd. S. (corner of Spring Mountain Rd.). www.wynnlasvegas.com. ✆ **888/320-9966** or 702/770-7100. 4,750 units. $179 and up double. Resort fee $39. Extra person $50. No discount for children. Free self-parking, free valet when you spend $50 or more in the resort. **Amenities:** 19 restaurants; buffet; casino; concierge; executive-level rooms; health club; outdoor pools; room service; showrooms; spa; wedding chapels; free Wi-Fi.

Moderate

Sahara Hotel and Casino ★ What's old becomes new again in Las Vegas. The iconic Sahara Hotel shuttered in 2011, one of the last outward vestiges of vintage Vegas. In its place, the sleek, sophisticated SLS ushered in the new guard of Vegas resorts in 2014. It also made everyone take notice of the new things happening north of Wynn. And now, in the midst of another multimillion-dollar renovation, it's back to being the Sahara. The relaunch is scheduled for fall 2019.

For SLS, power designer Philippe Starck transformed the formerly kitschy Sahara into a temple of modern aesthetics, with edgy design, ornate chandeliers, and metallic colors throughout the casino floor. But what they didn't take into account is the hotel's location. Sure, if you build it, they will come, but the visitors SLS wanted to come—the hip L.A. weekenders, millennials with disposable income—weren't filling the place up as fast as management liked. The hotel's nearest neighbors are Circus Circus, the Strat, the World's Largest Gift Shop, and the slowly resurrecting Drew Las Vegas hotel (from the old abandoned Fontainbleu bones). A new developer acquired the property in 2018, and for now, the renamed, swanky Sahara still offers rooms at nearbudget prices.

The remodeled (2019) World Tower is a millennial's dream, starting right when you walk to its golden, mirrored elevator bank (and ceilings too!) in the lobby, perfect for those "#VegasReady" squad selfies. The 325-square-foot rooms—small for the Strip, but average for the area—are as hip as those in any modern boutique hotel. Platform beds give the illusion that sleepers are floating off the ground, while wall-size mirrors with soft border lighting make the room feel bigger. Cold metal and white bathroom features make good use of little space, with infinity sinks and dual-head, glass-enclosed showers. Dressers are gone from these rooms, perplexing for those who, like me, unpack their suitcases to feel orderly. But it's an efficient way to create more space, and most people don't mind living out of their suitcases, anyway.

The Grand Tower offers guests of those rooms exclusive amenities such as a dedicated valet entrance and private check-in, plus a private rooftop pool deck with European-style (topless) sunbathing.

Bazaar Meat (p. 125), one of the most talked-about restaurants in town, will expand and is the only original SLS restaurant to remain, but new dining options will certainly abound.

At press time renovations are still in full swing, and the hotel removed the casino center bar with a 3-D ceiling installation. An original Sahara hot spot, the Casbar Lounge, has opened, ushering in the legendary hotel's next incarnation.

2535 Las Vegas Blvd. S. (corner of Sahara Ave.). www.slslasvegas.com. (℘) **888/991-0887** or 702/761-7757. 1,600 units. $78 and up double; $200 and up suites. Resort fee $38. Extra person $35. Children 17 and under stay free in parent's room. Free self- and valet parking. **Amenities:** 8 restaurants; executive-level rooms; fitness center; outdoor pools; room service; free Wi-Fi.

Inexpensive

Circus Circus Hotel & Casino ★   Cheap? Check. Cheesy? Check. The last-standing reminder of when Vegas tried to go family-friendly? You betcha and thank goodness. This is one of the few places in Vegas where cash-strapped families can come without worry, knowing they won't mortgage the house for a vacation, and that they can let their kids loose to be entertained (or entertain themselves). They do the latter on the midway level, with its hundreds of carnival games and nonstop performers. There is a permanent circus with serious athletes, from jaw-dropping trapeze artists and high-wire acts, to acrobats, magicians, and yes, even some truly fantastic jugglers. It's this free, delightful spectacle that keeps Circus Circus the best option for traveling families.

Sure, Circus Circus is a budget resort/casino in the sense that it's way cheaper than anything new on the Strip, but you'll be hard-pressed to find another that's as massive and accommodating to all ages. There are almost 4,000 rooms over the three towers and five low-rise, motel-like Circus Manor buildings that sit on the property's 68 acres. Circus Circus is also home to the only RV park on the Strip. If you're going to be a stickler for modern appointments, the West and Casino towers are the most recently remodeled, with flatscreen TVs, Wi-Fi, and comfy pillow-top mattresses. Standard room sizes are all comparable, averaging about 360 square feet, so the only thing that sets these two towers apart from the Skyrise Tower is that the former feels slightly less blah and dated.

The enormous hotel also sports a casino to match its size, clocking in at 101,000 square feet, for when parents want to play a few games of their own.

The dining options are mostly kid-friendly, with pizza, sandwiches, and a buffet to satisfy everyone's taste. The **Steakhouse** (p. 127) is the hotel's culinary diamond in the rough, a bona fide classic Vegas red meat joint with white tablecloths, good cuts of dry-aged beef, and stellar service.

We did say this place was family-friendly, right? Indoor amusement park **Adventuredome** (p. 159) pleases kids of all ages—even the grown-up ones.

2880 Las Vegas Blvd. S. (btw. Circus Circus and Convention Center drives). www.circus circus.com. Ⓒ **877/434-9175** or 702/734-0410. 3,767 units. $79 and up double. Resort fee $32. Extra person $20. Children 17 and under stay free in parent's room. Self-parking free, valet $12–$16. **Amenities:** 7 restaurants; buffet; several fast-food outlets; casino; circus acts and midway-style carnival games; executive-level rooms; outdoor pools; room service; wedding chapel; free Wi-Fi.

The Strat Hotel, Casino and SkyPod ★

One of the best ways to get your bearings when you're in Las Vegas: Look for the Strat. It's at the very north tip of the Strip, and whatever you do, don't call it the Space Needle (this tower, the tallest freestanding tower in the United States, is twice the size, dammit!).

Known for its size and the whiz-bang rides at the top, the former Stratosphere Las Vegas Hotel has rebranded. It now calls itself "the Strat," has renamed the observation deck the SkyPod, and has revamped its food and beverage and gaming offerings, hoping to be recognized as much more than a no-fuss, no-muss budget accommodation.

Heaven knows there's an army of budget-conscious visitors just looking for a clean, inexpensive place to sleep, but now they also want it with a bit more polish. The Strat fits that bill. The exterior is still a bit dated, but the rooms remodeled in 2018 make you forget all about that. These new "Elevate" rooms and the "Select" category digs, both at an impressively reasonable price (usually) are surprisingly contemporary. The former are done in calming blues and the latter with a warm color palette of red and brown, and all have such essentials as flatscreen TVs and alarm clocks with MP3 docks. Bathrooms run small, but at these rates, who's complaining?

And you'll be within spitting distance of the best perch from which to see the entire Las Vegas Valley. At the top of the tower, the elegant continental restaurant, **Top of the World** (p. 128), is in motion, giving guests a 360-degree view of the surrounding area, making one full revolution every 80 minutes. Thrill seekers climb up even higher to hang out (literally) on crazy rides that are discussed more on p. 160.

The big downside to staying here? The immediate area surrounding the hotel is a little shady. At night, take a cab or car if you're leaving the hotel.

2000 Las Vegas Blvd. S. (btw. St. Louis and Baltimore aves.). stratrising.com. Ⓒ **800/998-6937** or 702/380-7777. 2,444 units. $48 and up double; $107 and up suite. Resort fee $33. Extra person $15. Children 12 and under stay free in parent's room. Free self- and valet parking. **Amenities:** 8 restaurants; buffet; several fast-food outlets; arcade; casino; concierge; executive-level rooms; large pool area w/great views of the Strip; room service; showrooms; wedding chapel; fitness center; Wi-Fi.

coming ATTRACTIONS

The D Las Vegas owners Derek and Greg Stevens are gambling on another hotel set to open by December 2020. **Circa** will be a 777-room property along the Fremont Street Experience, the first ground-up resort development in Downtown since 1980. It's a nod to its vintage Vegas locale (the classic Vegas Vickie neon sign will figure prominently in the lobby) combined with modern amenities, including a stadium-style sports book.

Heavily themed hotels faded away in the 1990s but may make a return with the proposed **Resorts World Las Vegas.** The Asian-inspired, $7-billion project from Malaysia-based gambling giant Genting Gaming will have at least 3,500 rooms, a 175,000-square-foot casino (the biggest in Vegas), a 4,000-seat showroom, an indoor waterpark, a panda habitat, and replicas of the Great Wall of China and the Terra Cotta Warriors. It will be located on the North Strip in place of the old Stardust and should open by late 2020.

Across the street, the towering property that was to be the Fontainebleu is slowly being brought to life. Set to open by late 2022, the **Drew** will be a 4,000-room casino resort managed by Marriott International, making this the Strip's first JW Marriott. Details are light as this goes to press, but overseeing the launch of the property is hotelier and former Cosmopolitan CEO John Unwin. He brought a wow factor to the Cosmo, and we think he can recreate that excitement on the Strip again.

DOWNTOWN

The original Las Vegas, with classic and historic hotels, is Downtown; the glare of Glitter Gulch has become the must-see tourist destination of the Fremont Street Experience.

Best for: Budget-minded tourists; those looking for a friendlier atmosphere than the snooty Strip.

Drawbacks: Harder-to-find upscale experiences; the surrounding neighborhoods can be a bit rough.

Moderate

The D Las Vegas Casino Hotel ★ Why is this place called "the D"? Well, it's a nod to Detroit, the hometown of the property owners; or it could reference the nickname of CEO Derek Stevens. Final guess: an homage to the neighborhood of Downtown Las Vegas. Nah, scratch that. With all the Detroit references, this may well be the only hotel in the United States, outside of those in Detroit itself, that uses Motor City as its inspiration. (Non-Detroit related, but just as quirky, a large-scale, bronze replica of Brussels' Mannekin Pis statue also greets guests outside the main valet, an homage to the Stevens family's Belgian roots.)

And you know what? That downright-weird homage works. The two-level casino floor is far more airy than when it had its Irish theme (under the old management, before 2012). The 629 rooms all got a nice refresher too, with bold red and black accents throughout. They're not the fanciest hotel rooms in town, but for Downtown, and for the price, these are veritable sanctuaries.

The aptly named Longbar—the longest bar in Nevada, naturally—is one of the few bars left in Vegas where flair bartenders whip bottles about their heads before they make you a drink. Detroit exports **American Coney Island** (open 24 hr., like the original) and **Joe Vicari's Andiamo Steakhouse** make the D a favorite stop for Motor City natives, but both are tasty enough to warrant a trip even if you've never been there.

Final fun (or perhaps odd fact): The D is one of two hotels in town (the other is Golden Gate, p. 77) to accept cryptocurrency Bitcoin as payment at its front desk, restaurants, and retail shop.

301 Fremont St. (at 3rd St.). www.thed.com. ✆ **800/274-5825** or 702/388-2400. 629 units. $27 and up double. Resort fee $28. Extra person $20. Children 11 and under stay free in parent's room. Free self-parking and valet parking for registered guests. **Amenities:** 3 restaurants; lounge; casino; concierge; unheated outdoor pool; room service; free Wi-Fi.

The Downtown Grand ★★ Lady Luck Casino said farewell and became the Downtown Grand in 2013, and to be fair, we think Lady Luck was okay with it. She's been reborn as a hipster hotel with a trendy, industrial aesthetic. Reclaimed factory space? Exposed brick walls? Funky chandeliers and framed artwork on the ceilings? Are we still in Vegas? The 25,000-square-foot casino floor reminds us, of course, yes.

There are five different room types to choose from, the smallest a respectable 350 square feet, which is fine if you don't want to move around a whole lot. The next level up, Premium, are usually corner rooms at 450 square feet, with room for extra seats. All come equipped with conventional and USB plugs near the beds, have 46-inch flatscreens, and are decorated straight out of Crate & Barrel's CB2 catalog.

The Downtown Grand has four eateries, though three are across the street from the hotel proper: **Freedom Beat,** its 24-hour restaurant, plus **Pizza Rock** (p. 131) and old-timer **Triple George Grill,** all of which serve Downtown Grand guests.

The pool on the roof is a nice touch. It's big enough that it doesn't feel jam-packed, even when nonguest locals hang out on a Sunday afternoon, which happens often. The scene here has a definite cool-neighborhood feel; guests enjoy meeting the locals and vice versa.

206 N. 3rd St. (btw. Stewart and Ogden aves.). www.downtowngrand.com. ✆ **888/384-7263.** 680 units. $40 and up double. Resort fee $30. Free self- and valet parking for registered hotel guests. **Amenities:** 4 restaurants; 6 bars; rooftop pool; fitness center; casino; room service; free Wi-Fi.

Golden Nugget ★★ One of the most iconic facades of Downtown, the white and gold sparkling face of the Golden Nugget may seem like it's a throwback, but the interior is light-years ahead. The Golden Nugget has spent $300 million on upgrades to keep the hotel in step with Las Vegas's ever-changing zeitgeist. The Carson and Gold Towers boast lots of gold and black mod decor, while the Rush Tower rooms are just as comfortable and plush, but bigger, and with a more sedate color palette. All offer cloudlike pillow-top mattresses, 42-inch plasma TVs, and excellent views.

For the light sleepers out there, make sure you request a room that's not overlooking the loud action of the Fremont Street Experience. Free earplugs are an amenity in the rooms for a reason.

But why are we talking rooms? It's the pool area that's made this place justly famous. At the **Tank,** you can swim (kind of literally) with sharks, or at the very least, go screaming down a tube that cuts through the live shark aquarium. The three-story pool complex also features waterfalls and a bar that stays open year-round, even when the pool isn't.

The Hand of Faith, the world's largest gold nugget, is on display near the North Tower lobby.

129 E. Fremont St. (at Casino Center Blvd.). www.goldennugget.com. (℃) **800/846-5336** or 702/385-7111. 2,419 units. $69 and up double; $259 and up suite. Resort fee $32. Extra person $30. No discount for children. Free self- and valet parking (with validation). **Amenities:** 8 restaurants; buffet; bars, lounges, and nightclub; casino; executive-level rooms; health club; outdoor pool; room service; showroom; spa; Wi-Fi (for a fee).

Inexpensive

California Hotel & Casino ★   Las Vegas is sometimes referred to as the "Ninth Island," in that so many people from Hawaii end up here. And those trading in their own paradise for ours, just for a visit, like to stay at the California, which has manufactured its own brand of aloha. A Hawaiian theme touches all the public areas of the hotel, from casino dealers decked out in bright Hawaiian shirts to restaurant menus heavy with such Island faves as saimin, moco loco, and the ever-popular oxtail soup.

Guest rooms depart from "island style" (thankfully, I'd say). As at sister properties the Downtown Fremont Hotel and Main Street Station, rooms are understated but comfortable (to be honest, they appear to be cookie-cutter versions of each other), with standard amenities at decent prices. Other than the Hawaiian theme, staying at one of these hotels is just like staying at any of the others in the same family. But for the value, and if you really need to get your spam sushi fix, the California does in a pinch.

12 Ogden Ave. (at 1st St.). www.thecal.com. (℃) **800/634-6255** or 702/385-1222. 781 units. $55 and up double. Resort fee $17. Extra person $10. Children 13 and under stay free in parent's room. Parking first 30 minutes free, self-parking $8–$24. **Amenities:** 5 restaurants; casino; small rooftop pool; Wi-Fi (for a fee).

El Cortez Hotel & Casino ★   With the revitalization of the Fremont East Entertainment District (that's at the other end of the Fremont Street Experience tunnel), El Cortez managed to dust itself off and revamp and renew with the area, which is now teeming with trendy bars and restaurants. Touting itself as the "longest continuously operating hotel-casino in Las Vegas," El Cortez has a rich history that began in 1941; it's peppered with names like Meyer Lansky and Bugsy Siegel (two of the "businessmen" who purchased it in 1945), and Jackie Gaughan (who bought it in 1963, selling it to corporate interests in 2008). The hotel is now on the National Register of Historic Places, and the sign that sits atop the corner of Fremont and Seventh streets has been the same since the 1940s.

Ten Designer Suites are the result of collaboration between the hotel and Las Vegas Design Center, where four talented designers showcased their take on the city's iconic aesthetic: Live out your Sin City fantasy in a mob-themed suite, in 1950s glam chic, or in digs reminiscent of vintage Vegas, among others. The tony Cabana Suites are in a separate tower entirely, a batch of 64 boutique rooms that straddle both vintage decor and ultra-contemporary design. The original rooms may pale in comparison to all the additions. They're vintage as in "traditional," not "hipster," but run larger than plenty of other rooms Downtown and are usually priced quite affordably.

During Downtown's home-grown autumn music, food, and arts festival, Life Is Beautiful, El Cortez is smack dab in the middle of it all. If you're planning on attending, staying here is a fantastic idea. But thanks to a location in the heart of the now-gentrifying Downtown, it's still one of the coolest places to stay, even when there's not a festival going on.

600 Fremont St. (btw. 6th and 7th sts.). www.elcortezhotelcasino.com. © **800/634-6703** or 702/385-5200. 428 units. $28 and up double; $55 and up suite. Resort fee $17. Extra person $10. No discount for children. Free self- and valet parking. **Amenities:** 2 restaurants; casino; free Wi-Fi.

Four Queens ★   Old-school Vegas is alive and well at Four Queens, open since 1966. It's a popular spot for those serious about gambling, but who don't need all the frills of a Strip casino and are fine with camping out in one spot as their stacks of chips rise and fall.

The rooms won't be winning interior design awards anytime soon, thanks to the garishly striped drapes and nondescript, standard hotel art, but they serve their purpose as a clean, comfortable place to rest your head and gather yourself for a night of braving the Fremont Street Experience, which is right outside Four Queens' door. The South Tower's rooms are bigger, but the North Tower offers views of the hubbub of FSE, so choose wisely.

In-house Chicago Brewing Company serves a satisfying bar menu, as well as a selection of its own microbrews, which you can get in a 64-ounce to-go jug known as a growler, though it may be cumbersome to tote around as you walk Downtown. Local prom favorite **Hugo's Cellar** (p. 130) is one of the last examples you can find of vintage Vegas dining, a proficient gourmet room that still greets ladies with long-stemmed red roses.

202 Fremont St. (at Casino Center Blvd.). www.fourqueens.com. © **800/634-6045** or 702/385-4011. 690 units. $39 and up double; $110 and up suite. No resort fee. Extra person $15. Children 11 and under stay free in parent's room. Free self- and valet parking. **Amenities:** 3 restaurants; 2 bars; casino; room service; Wi-Fi (for a fee).

Fremont Hotel & Casino ★ You know those Vegas movie montages where the camera gives a 360-spinning view from the overwhelmed traveler who is visually assaulted by the flashing lights and activity of old Vegas? That's usually filmed right in front of the Fremont Hotel, under the $70 million LED canopy that is the Fremont Street Experience. The Fremont is pretty much Ground Zero if you plan on spending the majority of your time in the area. With rooms that start at around 280 square feet, you're paying (not a lot) for location here. Rooms are clean, comfortable, and decorated with serene, low-key, and modern furnishings to give your mind a rest from the constant activity that's just outside.

Food isn't a focus here, with a couple of chain restaurants and obligatory buffet (though we'd hardly call eight stations a decent buffet by Vegas standards), but you're close enough to all the culinary delights now open Downtown that it won't matter. Also, those looking for a day at the pool will be disappointed; you'll have to go across the street to sister hotel California if you want to catch some pool time.

200 E. Fremont St. (btw. Casino Center Blvd. and 3rd St.). www.fremontcasino.com. ℂ **800/634-6182** or 702/385-3232. 447 units. $48 and up double. No resort fee. Extra person $10. No discount for children. Free valet parking; no self-parking. **Amenities:** 3 restaurants; buffet; casino; access to outdoor pool at nearby California Hotel; Wi-Fi (for a fee).

The Golden Gate ★ Las Vegas celebrated its sesquicentennial in 2014, and the only spot that's been around nearly as long is the Golden Gate, formerly known as the Nevada Hotel, which opened in 1906. Even then it was at the forefront of modern technology. The hotel was the site of the first telephone in the state in 1907. Its number was 1.

The hotel survived all attempts to outlaw fun in Nevada—gambling from 1910 to 1931, and Prohibition from 1920 to 1933—and became a mainstay in Las Vegas lore, through the roaring '20s, the Rat Pack era, and the whispered days of the Vegas mob. Frank Sinatra used to sit at the Casino Bar before and after performances. The bar still serves his signature Frankie Two Fingers: two fingers of Jack Daniels, splash of water, and four ice cubes.

Golden Gate finally underwent a much-needed renovation in 2012, remodeling 106 of the rooms that had been there since 1906, and adding a five-story luxury tower, including two showgirl-inspired penthouses, complete with giant feather motifs in the carpet, vintage photographs on the walls of beautiful girls in ornate headdresses, and black-and-whites of Marilyn Monroe. These suites take over the entire fifth floor. The pretty fab, non-suite rooms give a nod to the design aesthetic of *Mad Men:* some swinging '60s mod patterns on the curtains and furnishings; black, brown, and red leather touches and Art Deco accents, plus requisite vintage photos of Vegas celebrities who frequented the hotel in its heyday. The rooms and bathrooms are tiny but well-appointed, with queen beds and 32-inch flatscreen TVs; suites have wet bars and sectional couches.

Golden Gate's longevity also means it embraces the trappings of the 21st century. This, along with the D, is one of the first hotels to accept cryptocurrency Bitcoin as payment (though you still can't gamble with Bitcoin—they're not that progressive).

1 Fremont St. www.goldengatecasino.com. ℂ **800/426-1906** or 702/385-1906. 120 units. $89 and up for up to 4 people. Resort fee $29. Free self- and valet parking. **Amenities:** 2 restaurants; casino; bars; free Wi-Fi.

Main Street Station ★★
The Victorian-themed Main Street Station is an underrated hotel and one of the great bargains in the city.

Taking a walk through the casino is like being in a well-organized, less-dusty antiques shop: The chandeliers come from the Coca-Cola building in Austin and the Figaro Opera House in Paris, France, and the ornate hammered-tin ceilings are also vintage. Men get a more modern glimpse of history in the restroom off the casino floor, where there's a bona fide chunk of the Berlin Wall on display.

The rooms run a little small at 400 square feet but are adequate for a Downtown stay. Sadly, their contemporary decor is a departure from all the historical artifacts downstairs. Suites are slightly larger, but their color schemes and furnishings are more dated than in the rooms. The amenities are all up to date, though, including flatscreen TVs, cable TV, Internet for purchase, and refrigerators. *Tip:* The noisier part of the tower is the north side, nearer the freeway, so light sleepers should opt for the south side.

You can head right over to Fremont Street Experience for a full-on Vegas experience, but if you crave something more low-key, **Triple 7 Brewery** is right inside the hotel. Its catchall menu (steaks, seafood, pizza, and even sushi) is fine, but the surprise comes from the decent selection of microbrews. There's a seasonal selection, including a rotating IPA on draft. The **Garden Court Buffet** remains a favorite in town and is described in chapter 5.

200 N. Main St. (btw. Fremont St. and I-95). www.mainstreetcasino.com. ℂ **800/465-0711** or 702/387-1896. 406 units. $36 and up double. No resort fee. Extra person $10. No discount for children. Free self- and valet parking. **Amenities:** 2 restaurants; buffet; casino; access to outdoor pool at nearby California Hotel; free shuttle to Strip and sister properties; Wi-Fi $9.99 for 24 hr.

Oasis at Gold Spike ★★
In 2013, when Zappos CEO Tony Hsieh moved his company into Las Vegas's old town hall and invested $350 million of his own money into buying properties and backing small businesses who promised to move into Downtown, it looked like the area was on the verge of a total turnaround. That initiative, called the Downtown Project, hasn't yet created the promised Las Vegas utopia (in fact, the success of the endeavor is still being hotly debated), but one of the results is that the "Project" went into the hotel business. Oasis is the hotel portion of Gold Spike, a formerly sketchy hotel and casino that was transformed into a trendy bar and playground (the **Living Room** offers pool tables and shuffleboard, while the **Backyard** features giant Jenga blocks and boards to play cornhole).

I have to say: The Oasis lives up to its name. It's a serene, 44-room getaway from all the millennial-oriented fun downstairs. Look past the fact that the rooms are referred to as "crash pads" and appreciate that they're custom designed with beautiful minimalist art, comfy furnishings, and solid walls to keep them quiet. Ultra-contemporary touches include co-working space in the lobby, bike rentals, and turntables with a selection of vinyl. The bathrooms are more spacious than is usual, with spa showers but no tubs. The pool courtyard is a bit on the small side, but not too small for a hotel with fewer than 50 rooms. Its latest claim to fame is that the Oasis was home to the 31st (!) season of MTV's *The Real World* in 2016 (yes, that show is still running, now on Facebook Watch). Should you want to start being "real" yourself, the decked-out, 5,000-square-foot, three-bedroom penthouse is available for a stay.

Note: This place is so modern, it doesn't have in-room phones or alarm clocks (since most guests simply use smartphones). But they will furnish them upon request.

217 Las Vegas Blvd. www.oasisatgoldspike.com. © **702/768-9823.** 44 units. $39 and up double; $69 and up suite. Resort fee $22. No discount for children. Free self- and valet parking. **Amenities:** Restaurant; room service; fitness center; business center; pets welcome (for a fee); outdoor pool; free Wi-Fi.

The Plaza Hotel & Casino ★★ How the Plaza, which has stood on Main Street since 1971, got so darn nice-looking is one of those only-in-Vegas tales. We can thank the Fontainebleu, a luxury property that was supposed to go up on the north end of the Strip, for going bankrupt halfway through construction. When it couldn't be finished, all of its "soft goods"—furniture, upholstery, carpets, beddings—had to go, and it all went to pretty-up the Plaza as part of its $35 million renovation in 2017.

And with the Fontainebleu's furnishings (cushy beds and sheets, fab vintage photos for the walls, Keurig coffeemakers in the suites), you'd never guess that the Plaza had once been one of Downtown's dingiest properties. Today, guests feel they've snagged a luxurious Strip experience at rock-bottom Downtown prices.

The hotel anchors the Fremont Street Experience, so you can walk right out the front door under the neon canopy, but make it a night at **Oscar's Steakhouse** (p. 130)—the namesake restaurant of former Las Vegas mayor Oscar Goodman—or gorge yourself on the obscenely large plates of food from **Hash House a Go Go** (p. 120).

The notion of "you get what you pay for" doesn't apply at the Plaza; you'll get so much more than you expect.

1 Main St. www.plazahotelcasino.com. © **800/634-6575** or 702/386-2110. 1,003 units. $29 and up double. Resort fee $25. Extra person $15. No discount for children. Free parking for hotel guests; nonguests first 90 minutes free, $5–$10 self-parking. **Amenities:** 4 restaurants; food court; casino; showrooms; bars and lounges; wedding chapel; salon; fitness center; outdoor pool; tennis courts; free Wi-Fi.

JUST OFF THE STRIP

Within about a mile east, west, and south of the Strip are dozens of hotels, many of which offer the same kind of casino-resort experience but usually at significantly cheaper rates.

Best for: People with a car at their disposal; those who want to be near the action but not in the thick of it.

Drawbacks: Traffic to and from the Strip can be a nightmare, even if you are only driving a mile.

Expensive

Hard Rock Hotel & Casino ★★ For visitors seeking to achieve a certain level of "cool," the Hard Rock is the place. The off-Strip hotel advertises itself as where celebrities party when they're in town (and to be fair, sometimes they do), selling the notion that if you stay here, you'll be as groovy as the stars whose memorabilia decorates the casino floor and walls.

Even if you haven't had your 15 minutes of fame, the rooms will make you feel like a big shot. Original Casino Tower rooms boast ultramodern furnishings, a steely color palette, and French doors that fully open onto a railing, but no balcony (just don't channel your inner Keith Richards and throw anything out the window). Paradise Tower rooms run slightly larger and are warmer in color, but have the same amenities, including fully stocked minibars, 40-inch TVs, and extra-large showers. The newest, HRH Tower features all suites, but departs from the color scheme and goes with clean white all around, from the linen and furnishings to the TV hutch that separates the sleeping and living rooms. Open-minded guests might be interested in the fetish-themed Provocateur Penthouse, enhanced with furniture custom made for more risqué activities.

Notorious weekend pool party **Rehab** closed in 2018, so you'll just have to settle for a plain old regular 21-and-over pool party at the Breathe Pool Lounge, though there are still plenty of hard, barely clad bodies to gawk at. At night, the **Joint** welcomes huge-named rock acts, and the nightclubs are a steady stream of hip-hop and EDM acts each weekend. There are enough levels of cool here that everyone can leave feeling like they're the rock star.

Enjoy it while you can, as gazillionaire Richard Branson snapped up the property and will transform it into one of his Virgin Hotels. At press time, work was slated to start in February 2020. Hard Rock will close around then, with the metamorphosis taking around 8 months. There is already some construction happening, so check the website, and the social media scuttlebutt, before booking.

4455 Paradise Rd. (at Harmon Ave.). www.hardrockhotel.com. ⓒ **800/473-7625** or 702/693-5000. 1,489 units. $48 and up double; $177 and up suite. Resort fee $36. Extra person $35. Children 12 and under stay free in parent's room. Free self- and valet parking. **Amenities:** 6 restaurants; casino; concert venues; concierge; fitness center; spa; executive-level rooms; outdoor pools w/lazy river and sandy-beach bottom; room service; free Wi-Fi.

Palms Casino Resort ★★   The Palms first planted its stake in pop culture as the home to seven strangers in the first installment of *Real World: Las Vegas,* then as a constant backdrop on E! reality show *The Girls Next Door* when Hugh Hefner–mates visited the Playboy-branded tower, now known as the Fantasy Tower. These days, Palms has maintained its cool factor without needing any camera time and is in the midst of a $620-million head-to-toe renovation that includes the Fantasy Tower, the casino floor, nightclubs, and new restaurants. But you won't be walking into an obvious construction zone. They've already completed work on the casino floor, four restaurants, and several nightlife options, not to mention the marquee and exterior of the hotel itself. (And we must say the addition of art by Damien Hirst, Basquiat, and Andy Warhol, on loan from the personal collections of Palms' owners Frank and Lorenzo Fertitta, raise the entire aesthetic of the property.)

The rooms are being worked on as we go to press, but the hotel is promising no impact on guest stays. You've got to be a serious high roller to even think about staying in the insane suites of the Fantasy Tower, like the two-floor Hardwood Suite, complete with basketball court, or the coyly named Make Good Choices Suite, which clocks in at 1,470 square feet with two bedrooms and a sleek living-room area accented by a long onyx wet bar. The real stunner is the Damien Hirst-designed Empathy Suite, which goes for something like $200,000 for two nights. Over-the-top does not begin to describe this 9,000-square-foot homage to excess, which includes massage tables, a salt relaxation room, and a hot tub that juts out from the side of the building, all with Hirst's signature touches. His artwork features prominently as well, such as a shark in formaldehyde (similar to the one on the casino floor).

While the construction is still going on, there's the already-renovated Ivory Tower (home of the still-pimped-out Real World Suite). The original building of the Palms, with its 428 guest rooms, is still super swank, even at 440 square feet. Warm wood furnishings nicely play off the fuchsia, teal, and silver of the throw blanket and chaise lounge. A stark-white bathroom is meant to evoke being in the spa, and it's pretty close, with open showers (no tubs, sorry), frosted glass, and lots of marble. If you really need to stretch out, upgrade to a Superior Room with a Jacuzzi, or if you're feeling especially fancy, a 1,200-square-foot one-bedroom at Palms Place with a state-of-the-art whirlpool bathtub.

The nightlife scene is going through a little facelift; now the top of the hotel has **Apex Social Club,** which removed the DJ aspect of going out and built an atmosphere where guests can have fun and talk to each other (imagine that!). But if you still need your club fix, there's a 29,000 square-foot venue in the works. The Palms overhauled its restaurant portfolio, revamping both their buffets, calling it all **A.Y.C.E,** and steakhouse, now known as **Scotch 80 Prime** (p. 136). More celebrity chef names have also been added to the roster. Michael Symon opened his fun **Mabel's BBQ** (p. 140), while Bobby Flay surprised us with **Shark,** his Mexican/South American/Mediterranean-influenced seafood restaurant.

4321 W. Flamingo Rd. (just west of I-15). www.palms.com. ℂ **866/942-7777** or 702/942-7777. 1,300 units. $85 and up double. Resort fee $39. Extra person $30. No discount for children. Free self- and valet parking. **Amenities:** 9 restaurants; buffet; food court; casino; concierge; executive-level rooms; movie theaters; nightclubs and bars; showroom; outdoor pool; room service; spa; fitness center; free Wi-Fi.

Moderate

Rio All-Suite Hotel & Casino ★★   The multi-towered Rio stands in all its purple- and red-striped glory just off the main drag of the Strip on Flamingo. Though it's technically off-Strip, it's got all the excitement of the storied Boulevard. This is definitely a rowdy spot geared toward revelers; if you're looking for a quiet getaway, the Rio might not be your cup of tea.

The other selling point here is the (usually) moderate price of the digs, but I must insert one warning: Though it's a self-billed "all-suite" hotel, don't be misled. Instead of separate sleeping and living spaces, the rooms are merely bigger, clocking in starting at 600 square feet, with couches and coffee tables across from the beds. The Samba Suites add a much-needed splash of teal to the otherwise neutral colors of the original rooms, as well as upgraded, dark-wood furniture and chrome finishes.

No matter which room you go with, floor-to-ceiling windows and a high floor choice offer spectacular views of the area.

There's a vast array of entertainment options at the Rio, from long-running magicians **Penn & Teller** to eye candy performances by the **Chippendales,** not to mention rooftop nightclub and lounge **VooDoo.** You won't go hungry either, with its sprawling **Carnival World Buffet,** Chinese favorite **KJ Kitchen and Dimsum,** and Guy Fieri's Mexican spot, **El Burro Burracho.** Just make sure you wait a spell after you eat if you're going to take a ride on the **VooDoo Zipline** that suspends you 490 feet in the air and, well, zips you back and forth between the two towers. If a few rounds of golf are on your agenda, the Rio features access to tee times at **Rio Secco** and **Cascata Golf** courses.

3700 W. Flamingo Rd. (just west of I-15). www.riolasvegas.com. ℂ **888/752-9746** or 702/777-7777. 2,582 units. $69 and up suite. Resort fee $32. Extra person $30. No discount for children. **Amenities:** 11 restaurants; multiple fast-food outlets; casino; concierge; executive-level rooms; golf course; health club; spa; outdoor pools; showrooms; room service; free Wi-Fi.

Tuscany Suites & Casino ★   While you're not exactly transported to Italy when you're at Tuscany Suites, you're definitely transplanted to a more laid-back Sin City (and one that's less costly than a Strip hotel).

The all-suite hotel offers a high level of customer service and generous rooms that start at 650 square feet of space. They're nothing to write home about in the looks department, though they do boast separate dining areas and come equipped with refrigerators and wet bars, which make this a family-friendly option. Each has either two queens or one king bed alongside a living room with full-size couch and chair. A small casino is also on-site.

RELIABLE CHAIN alternatives

Most people who come to Las Vegas want to stay in one of the big megaresorts on the Strip. But sometimes budget, timing, or having points usable for a free stay may steer you to a more traditional lodging. Just about every hotel chain has at least one outlet in the city, and all offer the kind of reliable, comfortable, and often affordable accommodations that they are known for. Here are some examples, all of which are located within a mile or two of the Strip, so you can have the best of both worlds.

Best Western Mardi Gras, 3500 Paradise Rd.; mardigrasinn.com; ✆ 800/634-6501

Best Western McCarran, 4970 Paradise Rd.; bwvegas.com; ✆ 800/275-4743

Candlewood Suites, 4034 Paradise Rd.; ihg.com/candlewood; ✆ 877/226-3539

Clarion Hotel, 305 Convention Center Dr.; choicehotels.com; ✆ 702/952-8000

Courtyard by Marriott, 3275 Paradise Rd.; marriott.com; ✆ 800/661-1064

Courtyard by Marriott, 5845 Dean Martin Dr.; marriott.com; ✆ 800/321-2211

Embassy Suites, 3600 Paradise Rd.; lasvegasembassysuites.com ✆ 800/362-2779

Embassy Suites, 4315 Swenson St.; embassysuites.com; ✆ 800/362-2779

Fairfield Inn by Marriott, 3850 S. Paradise Rd.; marriott.com; ✆ 702/791-0899

Fairfield Inn Suites, 5775 Dean Martin Dr.; marriott.com; ✆ 702/895-9810

Hampton Inn, 4975 S. Dean Martin Dr.; hamptoninn3.hilton.com; ✆ 702/948-8100

Holiday Inn Express, 5760 Polaris Ave.; hiexpress.com/lasvegas; ✆ 888/465-4329

Hyatt Place, 4520 Paradise Rd.; lasvegas.place.hyatt.com; ✆ 702/369-3366

La Quinta Inn and Suites, 3970 Paradise Rd.; laquintalasvegasairportnorth. com; ✆ 800/753-3757

Las Vegas Marriott, 325 Convention Center Dr.; marriott.com; ✆ 702/650-2000

Renaissance Las Vegas, 3400 Paradise Rd.; renaissancelasvegas.com; ✆ 702/784-5700

Residence Inn, 3225 Paradise Rd.; marriott.com; ✆ 800/677-8328

Residence Inn, 370 Hughes Center Dr.; marriott.com; ✆ 702/650-5510

Staybridge Suites, 5735 Dean Martin Dr.; staybridge.com/lasvegas; ✆ 800/238-8889

Super 8, 4250 Koval Lane; super8.com; ✆ 800/454-3213

Travelodge, 3735 Las Vegas Blvd. S.; travelodgevegasstrip.com; ✆ 800/525-4055

The immense conference and banquet space brings in most of Tuscany Suites' clientele, so many revelers carry on their event from their hall straight to the Piazza Lounge for after-parties before retiring to their rooms. The lounge is often bumping with great live entertainment and packed with guests having a fantastic time.

255 E. Flamingo Rd. www.tuscanylv.com. ✆ **877/887-2261** or 702/893-8933. 700 units. $79 and up suite. Resort fee $29. Extra person $20. Children 12 and under stay free in parent's room. **Amenities:** 4 restaurants; lounge; casino; concierge; fitness center; outdoor pool; room service; free Wi-Fi.

Westgate Las Vegas Resort and Casino ★   Formerly the Las Vegas Hilton—and briefly, LVH—Westgate is the hotel most convenient to the

Convention Center. The developers are best known for their timeshare properties around the country. They treated the hotel and casino built in 1969 to a multimillion-dollar facelift, hoping to make the iconic property near the north of the Strip relevant once again. Though they converted some of the rooms into timeshares while they were at it, it still operates primarily as a hotel. You may get a quick pitch to "stop in for a quick presentation" while you're there, which is code for a timeshare sales pitch. But the few folks I talked to who experienced this said it was low-pressure, and they never felt obligated to actually go.

The premium rooms are still efficient, but try to stay in one of the updated rooms or 300 suites. The Signature Rooms reveal some much-needed color and pizzazz, with Hollywood-inspired touches like black tufted-leather headboards and red-leather pullout sofas in the king suites. Marble floors, Keurig coffeemakers, 60-inch TVs, and sateen linens have guests relaxing in style.

The hotel has a lot of dining options, including the country's largest **Benihana,** Park City, Utah transplant the **Edge Steakhouse,** and a 24-hour American comfort food spot, **Sid's Café,** named for Westgate Las Vegas owner David Siegel's father, Sid Siegel.

Close proximity to the Las Vegas Convention Center makes this an easy choice if you're attending a show there (comedian George Wallace has a residency, and Barry Manilow will hopefully extend his), but a convenient Monorail stop on-property also makes the rest of the Strip just as accessible.

There's 95,000 square feet of gaming space, so this isn't the biggest casino floor in town, but nearly 5,000 square feet of it constitutes the world's largest race and sportsbook, the "SuperBook" (bonus: It's totally nonsmoking).

3000 Paradise Rd. (at Riviera Blvd.). www.westgatelasvegasresort.com. © **800/732-7117** or 702/732-5111. 3,000 units. $60 and up double. Resort fee $39. Extra person $35. Children 17 and under stay free in parent's room. Free self- and valet parking. **Amenities:** 12 restaurants; buffet; food court; casino; executive-level rooms; health club; spa; outdoor pool; room service; showrooms; 6 tennis courts; free Wi-Fi.

Inexpensive

The Gold Coast ★ Close proximity to the Strip, as well as having the more upscale Rio and Palms within throwing distance, makes this budget-friendly hotel a contender for those who want to be near the action without necessarily paying for it. Definitely a local favorite thanks to well-prepared, well-priced drinks and meals, Gold Coast isn't the most glamorous of hotels, but it gets the job done.

The rooms start on the small side, at about 320 square feet, but they're appointed as nicely as anywhere else. What they lack in space they make up for in style, with contemporary furniture and textures throughout a space that won't for a second make you think you've opted for a second-rate hotel room. Flatscreen TVs, in-room coffeemakers, hair dryers, and ironing boards are among the amenities; bathrooms are a little tight but are efficient with the space available, and spotless.

The 86,000-square-foot casino is always teeming with locals who know the right places to make their bets, with nearly 2,000 slot and video poker machines at the ready. There's also a 70-lane bowling alley should you want to throw a few rocks, and **Ping Pang Pong** (p. 140), long considered one of the best Chinese restaurants in Las Vegas.

Shuttle service takes you where you want to go on the Strip, as well as to sister property the Orleans (see below).

4000 W. Flamingo Rd. www.goldcoastcasino.com. Ⓒ **800/331-5334** or 702/367-7111. 711 units. $48 and up double. Resort fee $21. Extra person $21. Children under 15 stay free in parent's room. Free self- and valet parking. **Amenities:** 4 restaurants; buffet; fast-food outlets; bowling alley; casino; executive-level rooms; fitness center; heated outdoor pool; room service; barber shop; free Wi-Fi.

The Orleans ★   Unless you're really into faux New Orleans decor, the Orleans probably hasn't hit your radar. But in all fairness, it's a reasonably priced, if oddly placed, hotel and casino that serves its purpose. Set on Tropicana Avenue a non-walkable distance from the Strip (though shuttles run continuously between it and sister properties Gold Coast near the Strip, Sam's Town to the far east, and Suncoast on the west side of town), the Orleans is a self-contained resort with an 18-screen movie theater, bowling alley, massive arena, and a showroom that hosts well-established comedians and throwback artists that make you think, "Oh. Air Supply still tours."

The Orleans has updated the hotel using warm tones and more upscale decor. They've played up the all-suite moniker they've given themselves, keeping the separate sitting areas set off from the sleeping space. The second phase of the upgrade includes dining options, including the sleek **Alder & Birch** (p. 137), a modern steakhouse whose clean lines stick out like a sore (but pretty) thumb off of the Orleans' Mardi Gras–laden casino floor and **Ondori Asian Kitchen,** with more to come.

If you've rented a car or don't mind cabbing it down to Las Vegas Boulevard, you'll be satisfied with your choice to stay here. What it lacks in authenticity, it definitely makes up for in value.

4500 W. Tropicana Ave. (west of the Strip and I-15). www.orleanscasino.com. Ⓒ **800/675-3267** or 702/365-7111. 1,886 units. $53 and up double; $185 and up suite. Resort fee $23. Extra person $20. Children 15 and under stay free in parent's room. Free self- and valet parking. **Amenities:** 8 restaurants; buffet; food court; 9,000-seat arena; 70-lane bowling center; casino; children's center offering amusements and day care for kids 3–12; concierge; executive-level rooms; health club; 18-screen movie theater; outdoor pools; room service; showroom; spa; free Wi-Fi.

Palace Station ★   When the Fertitta family started their chain of casinos dedicated to locals, they opened the first, interestingly enough, as close as possible to the Strip. In business since 1976, but known then as simply "the Casino," Palace Station has stood proud over I-15 near Sahara as a reminder to those hotels on Las Vegas Boulevard that the locals have a stake in this town, too. And we're happy to announce that a 2018 facelift has brought the hotel's style into the 21st century. Before, the rooms were simply adequate,

locals' HOTELS

Most residents of Las Vegas—the locals—never go anywhere near the Strip. They prefer to play, eat, be entertained, and occasionally stay at casino-hotels in their own neighborhoods, partly because of convenience, but mostly because it usually costs a lot less money. All the following hotels are, admittedly, located away from the main tourist areas, but if you have a car at your disposal, you can save yourself some dough by trying them. Several offer free shuttles to other sister properties.

Just south of the Strip along I-15 is **Silverton** ★★, 3333 Blue Diamond Rd. (www.silvertoncasino.com; ✆ **866/946-4373** or 702/263-7777), a delightful ski lodge–themed hotel and casino with a warm casino, surprisingly stylish rooms (considering how cheap they usually are; figure in the $40–$75 range), and several affordable restaurants. The sports-minded may want to stop here just for the massive Bass Pro Shops attached to the complex, offering everything from skis to the boats with which to pull people wearing the skis.

About 5 miles west of the Strip along Boulder Highway are several locals' hotel options. The biggest and best known is **Sam's Town** ★, 5111 Boulder Hwy. (www.samstownlv.com; ✆ **866/897-8696** or 702/456-7777). In addition to the second-biggest casino in town (behind only MGM Grand), the Western-themed property has a 56-lane bowling alley, an 18-screen movie theater, more than a dozen restaurants, bars and lounges, and a big indoor atrium with a silly light-and-laser show. The rooms are nothing to write home about, but they are fine, especially for the bargain-basement prices they go for. Another favorite is **Boulder Station** ★, 4111 Boulder Hwy. (www.boulderstation.com; ✆ **800/683-7777** or 702/432-7777), which has more than 300 guest rooms, a 75,000-square-foot casino, movie theaters, restaurants, bars, and a concert venue. Rates usually run from $75 to $125 a night, but rooms can be had for as little as $49 per night. **Arizona Charlie's East** ★, 4575 Boulder Hwy. (www.arizonacharlies.com; ✆ **888/236-9066** or 702/951-5900) features 300 minisuites, a 37,000-square-foot casino, several restaurants, and a casino lounge. It's only a step or two above budget accommodations, but priced similarly, and still very well maintained. Lastly, the **Eastside Cannery** ★, 5255 Boulder Hwy. (www.eastside cannery.com; ✆ **866/999-4899** or

clean, and comfortable; now they're worthy of using #highroller as a hashtag on your selfies. The upgraded rooms, in the 21-floor Luxury Tower, are done in earth tones and feature leather-padded headboards, pillow-top mattresses, 55-inch flatscreen TVs, and great views of the Strip.

Palace Station is a required stop for serious players who want to get their money's worth out of a night of gambling, with lower limits than those a few blocks away on the Strip. More than 100,000 square feet of casino hold the most baccarat and pai gow tile games off the Strip, and an always-busy Asian gaming section. There are more than 1,700 one-armed bandits and video poker machines to chunk your change into (just kidding, machines don't take or give coins anymore), 44 table games, and a 307-seat bingo hall—the closest to the Strip—that runs from 9am to 11pm 7 days a week.

702/856-5300) has a casino, several restaurants, bars and lounges, and 300 very stylish rooms that rival the Strip for amenities and decor but are miles away in terms of price.

Just down the street, you'll find locals' favorite **Sunset Station ★**, 1301 W. Sunset Rd., Henderson (www.sunsetstation.com; ℂ **888/786-7389** or 702/547-7777), with 450 fairly basic hotel rooms but a host of amenities like a bowling alley; movie theaters; an outdoor amphitheater; a really nice, low-limits casino; lots of restaurants; a very good buffet; and more. Meanwhile, nearby **Fiesta Henderson ★**, 777 W. Lake Mead Dr., Henderson (www.fiestahenderson lasvegas.com; ℂ **888/899-7770** or 702/558-7000) is a Southwestern-themed joint with basic yet comfortable lodgings, plus plenty of gaming options, restaurants, bars, movie theaters, and more. Things are cheap here, with rooms going for as low as $30 a night during the week.

On the north and west sides of town are several smaller properties popular with locals. **Fiesta Rancho ★**, 2400 N. Rancho Rd. (www.fiestarancholasvegas.com; ℂ **888/899-7770** or 702/631-7000) is similar in concept and execution to its

sister property mentioned above. In addition to the 100 rooms, there is a big casino and a regulation-size ice-skating rink, complete with equipment rentals and lessons (p. 186). Prices go as low as $40 a night. Right across the street is **Texas Station ★**, 2101 Texas Star Lane, North Las Vegas (texasstationsclv.com; ℂ **800/654-8888** or 702/631-1000), which (unsurprisingly, owing to its name) has a "Yeehaw!" theme covering its basic motel rooms, bowling alley, movie theaters, big casino, and one of the best steakhouses in town, **Austins.** If you continue north—about as far north as you can go without running into a mountain—you'll find **Aliante Casino and Hotel ★★**, 7300 Aliante Pkwy., North Las Vegas (www.aliantecasinohotel.com; ℂ **877/477-7627** or 702/692-7777), a beautifully done resort with smallish rooms that are gorgeously decorated with all of the latest amenities. The facility boasts several restaurants, bars and lounges, a Strip-worthy pool, and a big casino, all wrapped up in warm design elements. It's a solid 25-minute drive from the Strip without traffic, but with prices as low as $29 a night for rooms this nice, it might just be worth it.

Restaurant newcomer **bBd's Burgers, Beers, Desserts** (p. 138) has become a destination for both burger and beer lovers. The beloved the **Oyster Bar** remains. In fact, it seems that everything else in the casino shifted around the popular eatery. The 10-seat bar still has long lines of hungry regulars who are there for dozens of raw, plump oysters and giant, seafood-filled pan roasts. This spot, like the rest of Palace Station, is no-frills Las Vegas, but will fill you up.

2411 W. Sahara Ave. www.palacestation.com. ℂ **800/678-2846** or 702/367-2411. 576 units. $39 and up for up to 4 people. $34 resort fee. Free self- and valet parking. **Amenities:** 5 restaurants; buffet; food court; airport and Strip shuttle; arcade; casino; executive-level rooms; fitness center; outdoor pools; room service; free Wi-Fi.

Silver Sevens ★   When this low-slung hotel near the airport was called Terrible's—after a local chain of gas stations—a common question arose: "Why would I go someplace called Terrible?" To be fair, it never really lived up to its unfortunate moniker, and since its name and management change in 2013, things have certainly taken a turn for the better. It's the ultimate in budget Vegas vacation properties—low-limit gaming, easy-on-the-wallet accommodations and dining—without any hint of sketchiness.

The rooms in the newer tower feature calm blue and brown decor, and perfunctory amenities: flatscreen TVs, decent beds, and a smaller-than-average bathroom, but you get what you pay for. One bonus is that all the rooms are non-smoking, so you don't have to deal with the scent of the last guest's habit. And while you may not like the idea of the daily resort fee, this one includes access to the fitness center, free Wi-Fi both in the rooms and at the Corona Cantina, and transportation to and from the Strip and McCarran International Airport.

The pool is nice little surprise in the middle of the hotel's courtyard, an oasis away from the loud traffic from the surrounding Paradise and Flamingo Roads. Plus Tower Patio rooms do have a door adjacent to the pool deck, with private seating areas for you to lounge. If you're really watching your pennies, there's also a buffet and 24-hour coffee shop, but you're close enough to the Strip that you can eat better if you just take a little walk.

4100 Paradise Rd. (at Flamingo Rd.). www.silversevenscasino.com. © **877/773-4596** or 702/733-7000. 330 units. $47 and up double. Resort fee $26. Extra person $12. Children 17 and under stay free in parent's room. Free self- and valet parking. Pets under 50 lb. accepted with fee and deposit. **Amenities:** 3 restaurants; buffet; outdoor pool; fitness center; room service; free Wi-Fi.

SOUTH & EAST OF THE STRIP

The main areas worth knowing about are the Boulder Highway strip on the far east side of town, the bedroom community of Henderson, and Lake Las Vegas (see box p. 91)—all of which offer a range of casino and non-casino hotels that can save you money and/or provide a unique Vegas experience.

Best for: Repeat visitors who want to try something new; value hunters.

Drawbacks: You'll have to drive to get to most of the major tourist attractions; upper-end restaurants and shows are harder to find.

Expensive

Green Valley Ranch Resort, Spa & Casino ★★★   Green Valley claimed its title as the posh side east of the Strip when this opulent hotel opened its doors in 2005. Part of the Stations Casinos family of properties dedicated to giving locals the same luxurious experience as its Strip counterparts, Green Valley Ranch set the ever-raising bar for amenities and restaurants that we see today in spots such as Red Rock in Summerlin and Aliante on the north side, at incredibly reasonable prices. And it's only 15 minutes from the Strip.

The tiled eaves, exposed stone walls, vaulted ceilings, and mosaic stone walls of the registration and lobby area that scream Mediterranean decor continue into the expansive, 95,000-square-foot casino floor that's jam-packed with locals and visitors alike. Lower limits and a bingo room draw in plenty of habitual players, but there isn't that sense of desperation that you might catch a whiff of at other off-Strip slot factories.

Casino guests and locals get to take full advantage of the lagoonlike pool and 17 private cabanas, as well as one of the poshest spas off the Strip, complete with 22 treatment rooms, co-ed steam rooms, Jacuzzis, and a private outdoor lap pool.

The 495 guest rooms are as nice as the public areas, starting at 500 square feet—generous for an off-Strip hotel. And when you upgrade to one of 80 luxury suites, your square footage increases immensely, from 695 square feet to the behemoth 4,000-square-foot Penthouse. All suites have ultra-comfortable beds, marble bathrooms, and in-room martini bars.

The caliber of dining has improved over the years. **Hank's Fine Steak and Martinis** has held strong since opening, with great cuts of meat and ice-cold martinis. On Fridays at **Feast Buffet,** ask for the buffet's best-kept secret, New Orleans–style crab legs seasoned to order. Just look for the long line of in-the-know guests.

Green Valley Ranch is a perfect spot to become a regular. They know the true meaning of customer service.

2300 Paseo Verde Pkwy. (at I-215). www.greenvalleyranchresort.com. © **866/782-9487** or 702/617-7777. 495 units. $149 and up double. Resort fee $45. Extra person $35. Children 17 and under stay free in parent's room. Free self- and valet parking. **Amenities:** 8 restaurants; buffet; food court; casino; concierge; executive-level rooms; spa; health club; lounge; movie theaters; outdoor pools; room service; free shuttle service to the airport and the Strip; free Wi-Fi.

Moderate

M Resort ★★   If you're making the trek from California on I-15, the M Resort is your first indication that you're about to enter Sin City proper, but your last chance if you want the Las Vegas experience without being inundated with the Vegas *experience.* About 10 miles south of Mandalay Bay, M Resort has the luxury, sophistication, and swank design that are hallmarks of many of today's Vegas properties; but with much better value, a low-key clientele of locals, and a lower threshold for sensory overload from throngs of visitors.

Built by the Marnell family (the "M" in M Resort), who are also responsible for such iconic hotels as the Mirage, Caesars Palace, and Wynn, the hotel's casino relies on its natural surroundings to accent its beauty. Skylights above the casino floor allow abundant light in, so there's no casino-cave feeling; decor is in natural materials such as wood, crystal, stone, and mother-of-pearl.

In each of the nearly 400 rooms, dark wood paneling combined with ample natural light makes everything seem airy, and contemporary touches abound. Foreign travelers will be familiar with inserting the key in the holder next to the door to power up the room; remove it and everything shuts down. Windows from the bedroom into the bathroom might make you feel exposed, but once you're soaking in the tub, with a killer view of the desert, you won't even notice (and no, they probably can't see you from outside the hotel).

Some 30,000 square feet of the hotel is kitchen space devoted to food and beverage, including **Anthony's Prime Steak and Seafood** (named for M Resort president Anthony Marnell) and his namesake Gourmet Burgers and Brews, as well as the hugely popular **Studio B Buffet,** which puts out a legendary seafood spread on weekends.

Oenophiles can spend time in the property's wine cellar, or you can catch some rays on the glorious pool deck, where most of the restaurants also have patio seating. On weekends, **Daydream Pool** is a DJ-driven pool party where locals who have worked hard all week take some leisure time without having to deal with overzealous partiers from the Strip.

It might be a good hike from the Strip, but the vibe and value make this a serious contender for a relaxing getaway.

12300 Las Vegas Blvd. S. (at St. Rose Pkwy.). www.themresort.com. ✆ **877/673-7678** or 702/797-1000. 390 units. $95 and up double. Resort fee $25. Extra person $30. Children 17 and under stay free in parent's room. Free self- and valet parking. **Amenities:** 8 restaurants; buffet; casino; concierge; executive-level rooms; health club; spa; salon; heated outdoor pool; room service; shuttle service to the airport and Strip; Wi-Fi (for a fee).

Inexpensive

South Point ★★   The gold, gleaming towers that stand apart from the Strip are bound to catch your eye, making you wonder, who stays all the way out there when the main attraction is close enough to touch? The answer: budget-conscious travelers who still fulfill their need for expensive-feeling accommodations. And they also probably like horses.

Similar in caliber to the Orleans and Gold Coast, South Point offers decent rooms at reasonable prices. You can spend what you save on lodgings right at South Point, either on the sprawling casino floor or at its myriad entertainment options, such as the bowling alley, cinema, or, during the right time of year, at the 500,000-square-foot Arena and Equestrian Center.

Super old-school continental restaurant **Michael's Gourmet Room** is alive and well at South Point, after being transported there from Barbary Coast years ago—stained-glass dome and all. There's a perfunctory steak house, traditional oyster bar, and a Mexican spot, but one of the most pleasant surprises is finding Midwestern favorite **Steak 'n Shake** flipping burgers until late at night.

The rooms are spacious for the area, starting at about 500 square feet, with all the amenities you'd find in rooms farther north on Las Vegas Boulevard:

should you stay AT LAKE LAS VEGAS?

Originally created as a playground for the rich and famous (Céline Dion had a house here), Lake Las Vegas is a man-made reservoir created in a formerly dry, dusty valley about 20 miles east of the city on the way to Lake Mead. Surrounded by multimillion-dollar houses and rambling upscale condominium complexes, the bulk of the area is privately owned; but curving gracefully around the western lip of the lake is Monte Lago Village, an homage to an Italian seaside community. It's got luxury accommodations, dining, shopping, entertainment, and recreation options for those who want a taste of Las Vegas, but in a more tranquil setting. Many locals choose the area for their own "stay-caytions."

Since 2013 the former Ritz-Carlton has operated as the **Hilton Lake Las Vegas Resort & Spa,** 1610 Lake Las Vegas Pkwy. (www.hilton.com;

℗ 702/567-4700). Though not much changed in the rooms and amenities, a focus on the business traveler has diminished some of the personal touches. Still, the immaculate gardens are serene, the pool is a blissful retreat, and rooms are gorgeous, especially those on the re-creation of the Ponte Vecchio bridge over the lake.

On the other side of the lake, the **Westin Lake Las Vegas,** 101 MonteLago Blvd. (www.westinlakelasvegas.com; ℗ 702/567-6000) was a Loews until 2012, and before that a Hyatt. Westin's ownership brought with it the trademark Heavenly beds and some toning down of the Moroccan-themed decor. There are more than 500 rooms, a spa, several pools, restaurants, recreation programs, kids' programs, and more, so you won't be lacking in things to do here or in ways to be pampered.

42-inch plasma screen TVs and comfy beds, and decor in a subdued color palette. And let's face it, for those who just want a place to store their stuff and lay their head at night (or morning), the price at South Point—often a whole $100 less than its Strip counterparts on any given night—is always right.

9777 Las Vegas Blvd. S. www.southpointcasino.com. ℗ **866/796-7111** or 702/796-7111. 2,163 units. $79 and up double. Resort fee $21. Extra person $20. Children 16 and under stay free in parent's room. Free self- and valet parking. **Amenities:** 11 restaurants; buffet; several fast-food outlets; 70-lane bowling center; casino; concierge; 4,400-seat equestrian and events center; 16-screen movie theater; outdoor pool; room service; spa; fitness center; free Wi-Fi.

NORTH & WEST OF THE STRIP

Summerlin, on the far west side of town, and North Las Vegas (north of the city, appropriately enough) are suburbs that have pockets of casino-hotel options ranging from budget to luxury, as well as lots of outdoor opportunities from golf to hiking and beyond.

Best for: The recreation-minded; people who want a more relaxing Vegas vacation.

Drawbacks: Long drives to the Strip and fewer entertainment options.

Expensive

JW Marriott ★★   If the whole point of staying off the Strip is so you can feel like you're not in Las Vegas, then JW Marriott has your name written all over it. A mere 15 minutes from Las Vegas Boulevard, through the cul-de-sacs and fancy plaza shopping of Summerlin, JW Marriott sits on 54 acres of pristinely landscaped grounds. A lot of the resorts that go up in town seem to be all steel and glass, but this 500-room hotel stays very West Coast with its Spanish mission–style buildings.

Part of JW Marriott's charm is that it's literally an oasis away from the Strip's madness. A large, resort-style pool features waterfalls, and **Spa Aquae** allows guests to tune out in serene lounges, cold dipping pools, and soothing steam rooms. Yet while you're away from the Strip, you're not missing out on any of its luxurious appointments. JW Marriott's rooms are stacked with visually bland but plush furnishings, big-screen TVs, rainfall showers, and marble throughout the bathrooms. Ground-floor rooms offer outdoor patios—something relatively unheard of for standard rooms—and a nice perch when the weather permits.

This may be a non-gaming hotel, but most visitors aren't here to put their money on red. Rather, they come to see how they do on the greens. The **TPC Las Vegas** course is one of the most prestigious golf courses in the state, complete with babbling brooks and quaint footbridges over 18 holes, making this one of the few hotels in town where you can actually enjoy the grounds.

In the event you decide you do want that casino experience, the adjacent **Rampart Casino** will bring you right back.

221 N. Rampart Blvd. www.jwlasvegasresort.com. (℃) **877/869-8777** or 702/869-7777. 500 units. $119 and up for up to 4 people. Resort fee $30. Free self- and valet parking. **Amenities:** 7 restaurants; buffet; casino; concierge; fitness center; outdoor pool; room service; spa; free Wi-Fi.

Red Rock Resort ★★★   When the far-west property opened in 2006, many assumed it would be a close facsimile of sister property Green Valley Ranch, which is pretty tony in its own right. The 800-room hotel and casino Red Rock Resort proved to be the swankier sister, even giving Strip contenders a run for their money.

Set right against the **Red Rock Canyon National Conservation Area** (see chapter 9), it's one of the most picturesque places you can stay, with red-tinged mountains just to the west and the lights of the Strip about 10 miles away to the east. Whichever side you decide to stay on, there's no such thing as a bad view.

It's perfect for those who want the Vegas experience without the craziness of the Strip, complete with an 80,000-square-foot casino that is like a maze through the subdued, gorgeous main floor, with 3,000 slot and video poker machines. And unlike many of the Strip casinos, Red Rock's bingo hall is popular with visitors and locals alike—of all ages. A lot of locals come through Red Rock Resort and many bring their families, as it's not just for gambling, with options such as a luxury bowling alley and even a day care center. Pool-wise, there's a 3-acre water feature, complete with beach, Jacuzzis, and even a stage for outdoor concerts by big-name acts. Downtown Summerlin, a shopping mecca, is next door.

The Red Rock has had a renaissance in its dining offerings, going beyond the standard proficient buffet, coffee shop, and food court typical of locals' casinos. Its stellar steakhouse, **T-Bones,** chugs along nicely, but there's also **Blue Ribbon Sushi** for those who don't want to go to the Strip outpost, and **Hearthstone,** the hotel's attempt at a trendy, neighborhood comfort-food eatery—which they manage to pull off with success. Lovely outdoor patio seating is available at all these spots, a nice option for those who want to get away from the casino.

The rooms take their cue from the natural landscape surrounding the resort and are done in earthy colors, with such niceties as 42-inch plasma TVs, sound systems you can jack your phone into, and enormous bathrooms. Pair all that with the views and you might just forget that you're in Sin City.

11011 W. Charleston Rd. www.redrocklasvegas.com. ℂ **866/767-7773** or 702/797-7777. 816 units. $132 and up (up to 4 people). Resort fee $44. Extra person $35. Children 15 and under stay free in parent's room. **Amenities:** 10 restaurants; buffet; food court; bars and lounges; casino; concierge; day-care center; health club; 72-lane bowling alley; 16-screen movie theater; outdoor pools and beach area; room service; spa; free Wi-Fi.

WHERE TO EAT

For a long time, Vegas was considered an epicurean wasteland, a place where prime rib that cost more than $4.99 was considered haute cuisine, and all-you-can-eat buffets dominated the landscape. Then the pendulum swung in the opposite direction. It got to the point where you couldn't swing a delicately seasoned roast leg of lamb with a honey-mint jus without hitting a celebrity chef and their fancy, very expensive restaurants. Wolfgang Puck, Emeril Lagasse, Joël Robuchon (who passed, sadly, in 2018), Thomas Keller, Julian Serrano, Gordon Ramsay, Alain Ducasse, Charlie Palmer . . . the list goes on and on, and so did the bills that came at the end of the meals.

Now, things have sort of settled in the middle. Fine dining continues to be more than fine in Vegas, but the good news for folks with less adventurous palates, or less extravagant budgets, is that there is plenty to eat here for everyone. All-you-can-eat buffets still abound, cheap eats can still be found if you know where to look, and moderately priced restaurants are making a big comeback. We hope you're hungry!

5

RESTAURANTS BY CUISINE

AMERICAN
Carson Kitchen ★★, p. 132
Dick's Last Resort ★, p. 104
Eat ★★, p. 133
Guy Fieri's Vegas Kitchen ★,
  p. 120
Hash House a Go Go ★★,
  p. 120
The Kitchen at Atomic ★★,
  p. 130
Lagasse's Stadium ★, p. 121
Spago ★★★, p. 114

ASIAN
Flock & Fowl ★★★, p. 134
Momofuku ★★, p. 122
Other Mama ★★★, p. 142
Red 8 ★★, p. 128

BARBECUE
Big Ern's BBQ ★★, p. 132
Gilley's ★★, p. 119
Mabel's BBQ ★★, p. 140

BISTRO
Bardot Brasserie ★★, p. 96
Blue Ribbon Brasserie ★★,
  p. 108
Bouchon ★★, p. 110
Mon Ami Gabi ★★, p. 122

BUFFETS
Bacchanal Buffet ★★★, p. 147
The Buffet at Aria ★★, p. 145
The Buffet at Bellagio ★★★,
  p. 147
The Buffet at Excalibur ★, p. 146

The Buffet at Luxor ★, p. 146
Carnival World Buffet ★★, p. 150
Corner Market Buffet ★, p. 148
Flavors Buffet ★, p. 148
Garden Court Buffet ★★★, p. 150
Le Village Buffet ★★, p. 149
Mandalay Bay's Bayside Buffet ★★, p. 146
Mirage Cravings Buffet ★★, p. 149
Ports O' Call ★, p. 151
Spice Market Buffet ★★, p. 149
Wicked Spoon Buffet ★★★, p. 147
Wynn Las Vegas Buffet ★★★, p. 150

BURGER
bBd's Burgers, Beers, Desserts ★★, p. 138
Black Tap ★★, p. 116
Bobby's Burger Palace ★, p. 107
Gordon Ramsay Burger ★★, p. 124
Heart Attack Grill, p. 133
Holstein's Shakes & Buns ★★, p. 120
Shake Shack ★, p. 108

CHINESE
China Poblano ★, p. 118
Hakkasan ★★★, p. 100
Ping Pang Pong ★★, p. 140

CONTINENTAL
Crush ★★, p. 99
Hell's Kitchen ★, p. 111
Hugo's Cellar ★, p. 130
Red Square ★★, p. 102
Rose.Rabbit.Lie ★, p. 114
Top of the World ★, p. 128

DELI
American Coney Island ★, p. 132

DINER
Burger Bar ★, p. 107
Sadelle's ★★, p. 122

ECLECTIC
Best Friend ★★, p. 98
Brooklyn Bowl ★★, p. 117
Greene St. Kitchen ★★, p. 139
Sparrow + Wolf ★★★, p. 143
Yardbird ★★, p. 123

FOOD HALL
Block 16 Urban Food Hall ★★, p. 116
Eataly ★★, p. 104

Forum Food Court ★★, p. 124
Fulton Street Food Court ★★, p. 124

FRENCH
Fleur by Hubert Keller ★★★, p. 99
Joël Robuchon ★★★, p. 100
L'Atelier de Joël Robuchon ★★★, p. 101
Pamplemousse ★, p. 135
Picasso ★★, p. 113
Restaurant Guy Savoy ★★★, p. 113

GERMAN
Hofbrauhaus ★, p. 139

IRISH
Rí Rá Irish Pub ★★, p. 107

ITALIAN
Buddy V's Ristorante ★★, p. 117
Costa di Mare ★★★, p. 126
Carmine's ★, p. 118
Giada ★★★, p. 118
Piero's ★★, p. 136
Rao's ★★★, p. 113
Sinatra ★★, p. 126

JAPANESE
Morimoto ★★★, p. 101
Raku Grill ★★★, p. 143
Zuma ★★, p. 115

MEXICAN/LATIN
Border Grill ★★, p. 103
Cabo Wabo Cantina ★, p. 117
Doña María Tamales ★, p. 133
La Comida ★★, p. 131
Nacho Daddy ★★, p. 125

NEW AMERICAN
Aureole ★★, p. 96
Herringbone ★★, p. 104
Sage ★★★, p. 102

PIZZA
Naked City Pizza ★, p. 141
Pizza Rock ★★, p. 131

PUB
Gordon Ramsay Pub & Grill ★, p. 119
Pub 1842 ★★, p. 105

SANDWICHES
Capriotti's ★, p. 140
Egg Slut ★★★, p. 123
Goodwich ★, p. 134

SEAFOOD

Emeril's New Orleans Fish House ★, p. 99

Estiatorio Milos ★★★, p. 110

Gordon Ramsay Fish & Chips ★, p. 125

Mercato della Pescheria ★★, p. 121

SOUL FOOD

M&M Soul Food ★★, p. 142

SOUTHWESTERN

Mesa Grill ★★, p. 112

SPANISH

EDO Gastro Tapas & Wine ★, p. 138

Julian Serrano Tapas ★★, p. 101

STEAK

Alder & Birch ★★, p. 137

Andiamo Steakhouse ★★, p. 128

Bavette's Steakhouse ★★, p. 98

Bazaar Meat ★★★, p. 125

Delmonico Steakhouse ★★, p. 110

Gordon Ramsay Steak ★★★, p. 111

MB Steak ★★, p. 135

Old Homestead Steakhouse ★★★, p. 112

Oscar's Steakhouse ★★, p. 130

Scotch 80 Prime ★★, p. 136

The Steakhouse ★★, p. 127

Strip House ★, p. 115

THAI

Lotus of Siam ★★★, p. 141

VENEZUELAN

Viva Las Arepas ★★, p. 134

SOUTH STRIP

Expensive

Aureole ★★★ NEW AMERICAN Even if you have no idea what kind of food Aureole serves, you definitely know about its wine tower. The four-story, gleaming glass and steel structure in the middle of the main dining room not only houses one of the best wine collections in the city, but also has an added bonus of stunning, well-dressed "Wine Angels" who gracefully rappel up and down the wine racks on wires to secure your bottle of wine from the 50,000 available. After witnessing this very Vegas spectacle, you get to enjoy one of the city's great fine-dining experiences. The seasonal menu focuses on American, responsibly sourced ingredients treated with the most delicate of touches. Mainstays such as a rib eye or filet mignon can be had everywhere else on the Strip, so I'd rather opt for more interesting bites like young rabbit saddle and asparagus risotto. The best seats in the house are by the Swan Court, where you can observe the resident paired swans through the floor-to-ceiling windows. Though Chef Charlie Palmer only stops in every once in a while, his kitchen is as exacting as it would be if Palmer were running service himself.

In Mandalay Bay, 3950 Las Vegas Blvd. S. www.mandalaybay.com. © **877/632-1766.** Main courses $22–$110. Mon–Sat 5:30–10:30pm.

Bardot Brasserie ★★ FRENCH Chef Michael Mina's take on a bistro is as classic as they come, down to the dark wood paneling, brass railings, and low lighting. If you've encountered a dish in

Price Categories	
Main courses	
Expensive	$30 and up
Moderate	$15–$30
Inexpensive	under $15

South Strip Restaurants

Map legend:
- Las Vegas Monorail
- Free monorail
- Pedestrian bridge

0 — 0.25 mi
0 — 0.25 km

RESTAURANTS

Aureole **8**
Bardot Brasserie **1**
Bavette's
  Steakhouse **3**
Best Friend **3**
Bobby's Burger
  Palace **2**
Border Grill **8**
Burger Bar **8**
Crush **5**
Dick's Last Resort **6**
Eataly **3**
Emeril's New Orleans
  Fish House **5**
Fleur by Hubert
  Keller **8**
Hakkasan **5**
Herringbone **1**

Joël Robuchon **5**
Julian Serrano
  Tapas **1**
L'Atelier de Joël
  Robuchon **5**
Morimoto **5**
Pub 1842 **5**
Red Square **8**
Rí Rá Irish Pub **8**
Sage **1**
Shake Shack **4**

BUFFETS

The Buffet at Aria **1**
The Buffet at
  Excalibur **6**
The Buffet
  at Luxor **7**
Mandalay Bay's
  Bayside Buffet **8**

a Paris neighborhood bistro, it's on the menu here. Charcuterie and pâté are popular ways to begin dinner, as are buttery escargots Bardot-style, served in puff pastry. Other traditional offerings, such as steak frites, mussels in white wine, and roasted bone marrow feature rustic presentations in copper pans or on plain white plates, so you can feel like you're eating real food rather than a piece of art.

Weekend brunch is one of the most popular meals here, thanks to well-executed preparations of *croque madame* and ample eggs Benedict served on croissants rather than boring English muffins—not to mention a reasonably priced, bottomless glass of rosé. The concise, French-heavy wine list is meant to pair with the dishes, while a really strong cocktail program encourages guests to hang out at the bar and make a night of it there.

In Aria Las Vegas, 3730 Las Vegas Blvd. S. www.arialasvegas.com. © **877/230-2742.** Brunch courses $18–$35, main courses $36–$165. Mon–Fri 5:30–10:30pm; Sat–Sun 9:30am–10:30pm.

on RESERVE

Bavette's Steakhouse ★★ STEAK   One thing you need to know about Bavette's: It's dark. When you come straight from the slot machines of the Park MGM casino floor into the library-esque foyer of the steakhouse, your eyes need to adjust. This is by design, in homage to the original Chicago flagship where, legend has it, the power went out one night during their first year, and service went on by candlelight. The grand dining room evokes a quintessential Chicago steakhouse, with lots of rich, dark woods and red banquettes. Prime-grade beef is all prepared to the standard you'd expect from either a Chicago—or Las Vegas—steakhouse, and all steaks are served with béarnaise sauce. I'm a fan of the candied sweet potato, topped with a brûléed bourbon glaze for a little extra crunch. The centerpiece brass rail bar is a seductive spot for a drink, but insiders know that the place to be is way in the back, past the dining rooms. The secluded bar offers the full menu, but with its low-slung seating and vintage artwork, this has more of a "let's retire to the drawing room" atmosphere. It's an ideal spot for a nightcap, or even simply make a night out of it and sample your way through the excellent martinis.

At Park MGM, 3770 Las Vegas Blvd. S. www.bavettessteakhouse.com. ✆ **702/730-6700**. Main courses $24–$91. Sun–Thurs 5–10pm; Fri–Sat 5–11pm.

Best Friend ★★ ECLECTIC   Roy Choi gave us the world's first Korean barbecue tacos, and for that I would gladly call him my best friend. This Korean and Mexican mash-up is a product of his Los Angeles upbringing, where he built his culinary fortune on wares from his taco trucks. Here Choi showcases his greatest hits, fused with some Las Vegas style. The entry to the restaurant is modeled after a corner liquor store, with lots of neon and hip-hop posters—except here you're welcome to hang out at the bar, or pick up an adult slushie. But come back later with a reservation, and through the back of the bodega is the promised land. There's a nostalgic '90s vibe to the 9,000-square-foot space, with servers donning Adidas tracksuits; a hip-hop soundtrack is provided by live DJs. The eclectic menu includes Choi's humble

Kogi short rib tacos, and there are playful L.A.-inspired bites like *elotes* (a street corn treat) slathered with Japanese Kewpie mayo. But Choi knows that in Las Vegas, you gotta go big. Dynamite uni fried rice is that ideal mix of Sin City opulence with comfort food, and as for tostadas extravagantly topped with caviar, sure, why not? Shared pots of Korean classics like the pork belly–filled kimchi *jjigae* stew evoke a classic sentiment: Your best friend should always feel like home.

At Park MGM, 3770 Las Vegas Blvd. S. www.parkmgm.com. © **888/769-2404.** Main courses $12–$89. Daily 5pm–midnight.

Crush ★★ CONTINENTAL   This long and narrow eatery from local restaurateurs Michael and Jenna Morton—who also own **La Comida** (p. 131) Downtown—is always busy, especially when there's an event at the MGM Grand Garden Arena. Large steel doors (with text from the epic of Gilgamesh etched into them) separate the rustic front from the more private dining areas and another bar in the back. If you want to be where the action is, though, sit near the front bar. Keep it casual and share a couple of apps or a pizza or two over some creative cocktails. For bigger appetites, I'd recommend the hearty ricotta gnocchi or shrimp risotto. There are also options for those with dietary restrictions, including vegan, gluten-free, dairy-free, and shellfish-free foods.

At MGM Grand, 3799 Las Vegas Blvd. S. www.crushmgm.com. © **702/891-3222.** Small plates $11–$17, main courses $18–$52. Mon–Thurs, Sun 5:30–10pm; Fri–Sat 5–10pm.

Emeril's New Orleans Fish House ★ CREOLE/SEAFOOD   Few names in the American culinary world are as recognizable as Emeril Lagasse, thanks to his many shows in the early days of the Food Network. Before TV stardom, his original Fish House in New Orleans was his claim to fame. This outpost at the MGM Grand isn't as good as the original, but it's still one of the best representations of Crescent City cuisine on the Strip. Grab a seat at the raw bar to watch as your oysters are shucked just for you, or go for the full monty in the dining room and order all the Creole classics: barbecue shrimp, shrimp *etouffée,* and the tastiest gumbo in town. To get the full "bam!" effect, Emeril's signature banana cream pie is a must for dessert.

In MGM Grand, 3799 Las Vegas Blvd. S. www.emerils.com. © **702/891-7374.** Main courses lunch $16–$37, dinner $24–$55 (more for lobster). Daily 11:30am–10pm.

Fleur by Hubert Keller ★★★ FRENCH   Chef Hubert Keller goes full bistro at this relaxed establishment, revealing his French roots in impeccable versions of classics such as steak frites, *coq au vin,* and duck confit. Earth tones, leather chairs, and stone walls help set the mood. Brunch is perfunctory but does offer craft beer pairings to go with your carnitas hash or braised short rib Benedict. You can get a burger from Keller's Burger Bar, also located in Mandalay Bay, or you can order a Fleur Burger here, made of Wagyu beef with caramelized onions and mushrooms, served on toasted brioche. Just be sure you're not ordering the Fleur Burger 5000, which is pretty much the same thing, except topped with more extravagant ingredients like truffles and foie gras and served with a bottle of 1995 Petrus to wash it down. Oh, and that one costs $5,000.

In Mandalay Bay, 3950 Las Vegas Blvd. S. www.hubertkeller.com. © **702/632-9400.** Main courses lunch $19–$22, dinner main courses $34–$70. Sun–Thurs 11am–10pm; Fri–Sun 11am–10:30pm.

Hakkasan ★★★ CHINESE   All those bright, hole-in-the-wall Chinese restaurants you've been to? This is the complete opposite of them. Hakkasan's first floor (above it is a dance club) is all about cutting-edge design: High ceilings and tall black lacquer lattices evoke the feeling of walking in a maze. The meals are as pleasantly puzzling. While you'll encounter familiar dishes like dim sum, Mongolian beef, and crispy chicken in lemon sauce, they're elevated with elegant presentation and delicate flavors and ingredients (the prices are elevated in turn). The Peking duck, for example, is served with traditional accoutrements of thin crepes, scallions, and cucumbers, but also with a healthy dose of reserve caviar. Less familiar Chinese dishes on the menu are aimed at the high-roller Asian clientele, but adventurous diners will find them exciting.

Hakkasan first served its brand of haute Chinese cuisine in London, where Chef Ho Chee Boon won a Michelin star before expanding the empire here and adding the nightclub that has become one of the MGM's biggest draws.

In MGM Grand, 3799 Las Vegas Blvd. S. www.hakkasannightclub.com. © **702/891-3838.** Main courses $18–$255. Mon–Wed 6–10:30pm; Thurs–Sun 6pm–midnight.

Joël Robuchon ★★★ FRENCH   There are fancy French meals in Las Vegas, and then there are meals at Joël Robuchon. Nearly every culinary accolade in the world has been bestowed on the late, great Robuchon (he passed away in 2018): He had 28 Michelin stars under his toque—more than any other chef in the world. He won the *Meilleur Ouvrier de France* for culinary arts, the highest honor given to French craftspeople. European guidebook Gault-Millau named him Chef of the Century. All this is to say that your meal here will be worth the sticker shock.

The jewel box of a dining room features plenty of regal purple, fresh flowers, and a stunning crystal chandelier. It's so formal that it can feel like eating at church, but once you get started on the exquisite, 18-course tasting menu, the over-the-top decor begins to feel appropriate. Each dish is a study in pristine ingredients and impeccable technique, combining flavors and textures in ways that only chefs of this caliber can imagine. Where else would you even consider eating a crab *gelée* or foie gras carpaccio? Having witnessed the kitchen during service, I can tell you that the chefs are working silently, paying attention to the most painstaking details. This is how this chef earned three Michelin stars over and over again.

In MGM Grand, 3799 Las Vegas Blvd. S. www.joel-robuchon.com. © **702/891-7925.** Reservations strongly recommended. Jacket recommended. Prix-fixe tasting menus $127–$250, 18-course tasting menu $445, a la carte main courses $85–$235. Daily 5:30–10pm.

Julian Serrano Tapas ★★ SPANISH   After years of being known as one of the first fine-dining titans in Las Vegas (thanks to his restaurant Picasso at Bellagio), Serrano went back to his Spanish roots when he opened this restaurant at Aria. Definitely more relaxed and casual than its haute cuisine French sister, it offers Spanish fare in the form of tapas, to be shared with others over lots of sangria. While it's definitely a Vegas version of what you'd find in Barcelona, it's as authentic as possible, with dishes like a classic tortilla (like an omelet) with eggs and potatoes, crusty tomato bread topped with thin slices of Serrano *jamón* (no relation to the chef), and fried chicken *croquetas,* crunchy on the outside, creamy with béchamel inside. There is also a selection of traditional paella, the Spanish rice dish cooked with meats and seafood until a *soccarat* (crunchy, charred brown crust) forms at the bottom of the pan. While the tapas are all reasonably priced on their own, you might be ordering quite a few of them to get a full meal, which can get pricey.

In Aria Las Vegas, 3730 Las Vegas Blvd. S. www.arialasvegas.com. ℭ **702/590-8520.** Reservations recommended. Main courses lunch $12–$50, $38–$50, tapas $8–$39. Sun–Thurs 11:30am–10:30pm; Fri-Sat 11:30am–11pm.

L'Atelier de Joël Robuchon ★★★ FRENCH   Compared to its buttoned-up sister restaurant next door, *l'atelier* (French for "the workshop") of Chef Robuchon is downright casual. Make no mistake, it's still very much a fine-dining experience, but one where you're not afraid to use the wrong fork or laugh really loud. The best seats are at the counter around the open kitchen, where you can watch the choreography of the chefs preparing your meal on a black box stage, and chat with fellow patrons.

The food here is as meticulously constructed at the big Robuchon, but approaches the realm of comfort food, if your idea of comfort includes the fancy Spanish ham *jamón ibérico* sliced right off the leg and placed onto tomato toast. The signature foie gras–stuffed quail is tiny, but rich and satisfying, especially when accompanied by the famed *pommes purée*—the silkiest, creamiest mashed potatoes you'll ever eat, reportedly made with a pound of butter for each pound of potatoes. The multicourse seasonal discovery menu will set you back (but not nearly as much as Robuchon next door), though there are a couple of three-course prix fixe menus at around $100 pop, and one pre-theater offering of $55, so it's possible to experience a meal here without breaking the bank.

In MGM Grand, 3799 Las Vegas Blvd. S. www.joel-robuchon.com. ℭ **702/891-7358.** Reservations strongly recommended. Main courses $29–$90, prix-fixe tasting menus $85–$142, 9-course discovery menu $195, small plates $28–$40. Daily 5–10pm.

Morimoto ★★★ JAPANESE   If you're keeping track, you can cross another Iron Chef off your culinary bucket list. Masaharu Morimoto settled into the former Shibuya space at MGM in 2016, wisely keeping most of its minimalist design aesthetic. The celebrity chef enhanced an already legendary sake collection with the addition of shochu and Japanese whiskies and brought with him his own style of contemporary Asian cuisine, highlighting beautiful sushi and sashimi. There's also pure decadence, like the oyster topped with warm foie gras, uni, and teriyaki. I'm not embarrassed to say I closed my eyes when I ate it so that I could tune everything else out. A little less over the top are approachable dishes such as duck meatball soup or the sizzling *ishi yaki buri bop,* which features a yellowtail cooked at your table in a hot stone bowl. Who are we kidding: This is Iron Chef cuisine in Las Vegas—the more over the top, the better, and in this regard, Morimoto is a winner.

In MGM Grand, 3799 Las Vegas Blvd. S. www.mgmgrand.com. ⓒ **702/891-3001.** Reservations strongly recommended. Main courses $32–$170. Sun–Thurs 5–10pm; Fri–Sat 5–10:30pm.

Red Square ★★ CONTINENTAL/RUSSIAN The headless statue of Stalin outside the restaurant is a little misleading, because Red Square is dedicated to more than just Russian delicacies (though there is plenty of vodka and caviar to go around). It also happens to be one of the few restaurants where you'll find actual Eastern European food on the Strip (okay, it's the only one). But they've been kind enough to translate the dishes to help us Americans out. What would be called *ajarski khachapuri* in its native tongue gets softened to Georgian cheese bread, a hearty bread boat with melted cheese and a soft egg in the middle. The classic Chicken Kiev is miniaturized, taking the butter splatter out of the equation. There are even three types of traditional dumplings—*pelmeni, pierogi,* and *vareniki*—because dumplings are the universal food group. The caviar service is of fine domestic varieties (that happily won't break the bank), with proper accompaniments of egg whites, shallots, and crème fraîche, to be piled extravagantly on blini or toast points. This all may seem beside the point if you decide to go full fantasy here, donning a (loaner) fur coat and Cossack's hat to dine in the vodka locker, an icy chamber near the front of the bar where one can drink vodka and shiver at the same time— like they do in the old country.

In Mandalay Bay, 3950 Las Vegas Blvd. S. www.mandalaybay.com. ⓒ **702/632-7407.** Main courses $33–$55. Mon–Sun 4–11pm.

Sage ★★★ NEW AMERICAN This restaurant, from Chef Shawn McClain, often flies under the radar because, while McClain has won James Beard Awards and owned a number of successful restaurants in Chicago, outside of culinary circles, he's not a household name. As such, this is one of the most underrated restaurants in the city, but one that serious food lovers need to discover for themselves. You could do so at the bar, which not only offers innovative cocktails but also features one of the few absinthe programs in the city. But I'd recommend heading into the dining room for a more relaxing meal of eclectic dishes like Wagyu beef tartare, prepared with a crushed caper aioli and topped with a poached egg and little chocolate bits that create texture and bitterness. Sage's signature foie gras custard brûlée is a savory take on the creamy dessert. The menu changes seasonally, with emphasis on organic, sustainable ingredients, often foraged for Sage itself. Dishes that stay

SHHHHHH . . . half-price meals, **ON THE STRIP & OFF**

Cut-price meals at some of the city's top eateries are being sold by Tix4Tonight, the same people who peddle theater tickets. Either stop by a booth, call ✆ **800/269-8499,** or visit www.tix4d. com. Request a reservation from their list of partner restaurants (which vary often but can include gourmet options such as Hugo's Cellar to all-you-can-eat like the Buffet at TI), pay a small fee, and get discounts of up to 50% off. Reservations must be made in person at a Tix4Tonight booth.

Booths can be found at the following locations:

- In the Fashion Show mall (across from the Wynn)
- In the Hawaiian Marketplace (near Harmon St.)
- In Bally's Grand Bazaar Shops (at Flamingo Rd.)
- In front of Planet Hollywood Resort & Casino (at Harmon St.)
- In the Showcase Mall (at the base of the giant Coca-Cola bottle)
- In the Casino Royale (across from the Mirage)
- At the Town Square shopping center (across from Claim Jumper)

on the menu, like a Wagyu short rib braised for 36 hours, only change in accompaniment; you might have white asparagus one month, or horseradish-smoked potatoes another. Lighter options include pan-roasted halibut or butter-poached salmon, and a vegan tasting menu.

Shawn McClain's other Vegas restaurants, **Five50 Pizza Bar,** also at Aria, and the small plates–driven **Libertine Social** at Mandalay Bay, showcase a more casual side to the award-winning chef.

In Aria Las Vegas, 3730 Las Vegas Blvd. S. www.aria.com. ✆ **877/230-2742.** Main courses $42–$62. Mon–Fri 6–10pm, Sat 6–10:30pm

Moderate

Border Grill ★★ MEXICAN   The Food Network made chefs Susan Feniger and Mary Sue Milliken into household names in the '90s as the *Two Hot Tamales* with a contemporary take on authentic Mexican fare. Outside of Chicago chef Rick Bayless, there are few other gringos who understand the soul and flavors of the cuisine as well as they do. I'm talking home-cooked, regional Mexican dishes, all executed with modern flair. Yucatan-style pork is slow-roasted with crimson *achiote* and in banana leaves; simple grilled skirt steak needs nothing more than charred corn relish and a warm, house-made flour tortilla as a vehicle to your mouth. Yes, they have tacos too, but here you want them filled with Wagyu beef and grilled pineapple salsa, or shredded brisket with a zesty, crunchy slaw. Border Brunch, offered on weekends, is an all-you-can eat extravaganza that is not a buffet. Rather, items are cooked to order for optimum freshness. This is a Mexican restaurant after all, so *cervezas* are cold, and margaritas, in flavors like pineapple vanilla or mango cilantro, are strong. ***Warning:*** Be prepared for a hike. This border is deep into Mandalay Bay, on the way to the Shark Reef, far away from the casino.

In Mandalay Bay, 3950 Las Vegas Blvd. S. www.bordergrill.com. ✆ **702/632-7403.** Main courses lunch $17–$28, dinner $21–$53, Border Brunch $43. Mon–Fri 11am–close; Sat–Sun 10am–close.

Dick's Last Resort ★ AMERICAN   A frat bro's paradise, Dick's is beer- and beef-fueled, and it doesn't pretend to be anything else, which is refreshing for those who don't want to think too hard about dinner. You'll be hard-pressed to find any other restaurant serving mains like barbecue half-racks of ribs and honey-glazed chicken from a bucket, among other artery-clogging (but totally worth it) specialties like chicken-fried steak and beer-battered fish-and-chips. Servers are deliberately rude to customers (it's part of the schtick here); they can get a little vulgar at times but tend to be good at reading how far they can push people's buttons. Plus, they can take it as well as they can dish it out, so feel free to sass back.

In Excalibur, 3850 Las Vegas Blvd. S. www.dickslastresort.com. ✆ **702/597-7791.** Main courses $18–$29. Mon–Thurs, Sun 11am–11pm; Fri–Sat 11am–midnight.

Eataly ★★ ITALIAN   In pretty much any other major city with a serious food scene, there's an Eataly. This 40,000-square-foot Italian market-cum-food hall sits at the front of Park MGM and is intended to look like a rail station. It bustles like one, especially before or after Vegas Golden Knights' games or concerts at T-Mobile Arena next door. Vegas's version doesn't differ much from other Eatalys—fresh seafood counter, cured meat kiosk, and giant bags of flour to show that, yes, they're making all that pasta in house! But unlike cities where you buy charcuterie, cheese, and crusty bread for a picnic in a nearby park, Vegas doesn't have quite the same vibe. Here, you're more likely to walk up to one of the counters for (not inexpensive) ready-made or made-to-order items, like Roman-style pizza from the bakery, and post up at a high-top table in the center or at the Gran Caffé Milano wine bar. Sweets are plentiful at stands on the lower level, whether it's small-batch gelato or can-noli filled to order—or the only Nutella bar in town.

For a more structured meal, try the intimate and rustic steakhouse Manzo or the airy La Pizza e La Pasta. When you find the mosaic bull—a replica of one in Milan's Galleria Vittorio Emanuele II—at the entrance between the market and the casino, take a spin around it three times. It's supposed to bring you luck, handy if you head back to the casino floor.

At Park MGM, 3770 Las Vegas Blvd. S. www.eataly.com. ✆ **702/730-7617.** Main courses $24–$91. Market open daily 9am–11pm, but restaurant and counter hours vary.

Herringbone ★★ NEW AMERICAN   *Top Chef* alum Brian Malarkey opened Herringbone as his second restaurant on the Strip (the first was Sear-sucker at Caesars Palace, but we like this one better). The restaurant, which has original outposts in La Jolla and San Diego, specializes in what he calls "Southern California coastal cuisine." What that means is a lot of small

South Strip

WHERE TO EAT

quick BITES

Food courts are a dime a dozen in Vegas, but the one in **New York–New York,** 3790 Las Vegas Blvd. S. (© **702/740-6969**), deserves a mention for two reasons. First, it's the nicest setting for this sort of thing on the Strip, sitting in the Greenwich Village section of New York–New York, which means scaled replica tenement buildings, steam rising from the manhole covers, and more than a little (faux, naturally) greenery, a nice change from unrelentingly shrill and plastic mall decor. Second, the selections are better-than-average food court, with a deli and pizza (as befitting an ode to NYC), and excellent if expensive (for this situation) double-decker burgers, plus **Ben & Jerry's** ice cream. Hours vary by outlet.

The food court at **Flamingo Las Vegas,** 3555 Las Vegas Blvd. S. (© **702/733-3111**), has a couple of interesting outlets like **Pan Asian Express** and **Johnny Rockets** hamburgers, among others. Hours vary, but it's usually open from 8am until 2am.

If you head farther down the Strip, to the **Grand Canal Shoppes** at the Venetian, 3355 Las Vegas Blvd. S. ((© **702/414-4500**), you can find another decent food court, with a **Panda Express,** a good pizza place (despite the confusing name of **LA Italian Kitchen**), and more. Plus, it's right by the canals of this faux Venice, one of our favorite places in Vegas. Hours are Sunday through Thursday from 10am until 11pm, and Friday and Saturday from 10am until midnight.

And of course, it should come as no surprise that the biggest mall in Vegas has the biggest food court as well. The **Fashion Show Mall,** 3200 Las Vegas Blvd. S. (© **702/369-8382**), has more than a dozen outlets from **KFC Express, Nathan's Famous, Subway, Wendy's,** and more. Hours are Monday through Saturday from 10am until 9pm, and Sunday from 11am until 7pm.

shareable, seafood-heavy plates. Classic raw bites like a ceviche tostada and the tuna poke will have you wishing that you were at the beach. Entrée options have a little more global flavor, such as the Asian-nuanced dayboat halibut with tamarind broth. Cocktails are fun and innovative, so they might take a few minutes to make, but are worth the wait. You could even conceivably get away with just ordering a dozen oysters and a few glasses of wine and still get the full Herringbone experience. There is indoor lounge seating with large windows, but the best seats are on the outdoor patio overlooking the Aria's pool. Umbrellas and pergolas over the tables offer much-needed shade from the sun during the day, especially during the popular all-you-can-eat weekend brunch.

In Aria Las Vegas, 3730 Las Vegas Blvd. S. www.herringboneeats.com. © **702/590-9898.** Brunch $59, main courses $34–$51. Mon–Thurs 11am–10pm; Fri 11am–11pm; Sat 10am–11pm, Sun 10am–10pm.

Pub 1842 ★★ PUB FARE   Chef Michael Mina has three other spots in town, and this is his most casual, not to mention the most affordable. The 1842 in the name refers to the year that the pilsner was invented, and so Mina built this restaurant as a gastropub, where the brews are as important as the food.

YOU GOTTA HAVE A theme

It shouldn't be too surprising to learn that a town devoted to gimmicks has just about every gimmick restaurant there is. No matter your interest, there is probably a theme restaurant here for you, from sports to pop culture and back again. Fans should have a good time checking out the stuff on the walls, but for the most part the memorabilia are usually more interesting than the food. Here are some of the best of the bunch.

The **House of Blues ★★**, in Mandalay Bay, 3950 Las Vegas Blvd. S. (www.hob.com; © **702/632-7600;** Sun–Thurs 7am–11pm, Fri–Sat 7am–midnight), has a Mississippi Delta blues theme complete with frequent concerts and a gospel brunch. The food is down-home Southern, and there is lots of it for pretty decent prices.

Southern staples are also on tap at the **Harley-Davidson Café ★**, 3725 Las Vegas Blvd. S., at Harmon Avenue (www.harley-davidsoncafe.com; © **702/740-4555;** Sun–Thurs 8:30am–11pm, Fri–Sat 9am–midnight), alongside shrines to the easy-rider lifestyle evoked by the motorcycle brand.

The **Hard Rock Cafe ★**, 3771 Las Vegas Blvd. S. (www.hardrock.com; © **702/733-7625;** daily 8:30am–11pm), has decent burgers and all of the requisite music memorabilia you have come to expect packed in a massive, 42,000-square-foot, three-level behemoth with a gigantic gift shop, a 1,000-seat concert

venue, and more. **Note:** There is a second Hard Rock Cafe at the Hard Rock Hotel, 4475 Paradise Rd., at Harmon Avenue (© **702/733-8400**).

Parrot Heads, as fans of Jimmy Buffet refer to themselves, like to party it up at **Margaritaville ★**, at the Flamingo, 3555 Las Vegas Blvd. S. (www.margaritavillelasvegas.com; © **702/733-3302;** Sun–Thurs 11am–1am, Fri–Sat 11am–2am), the singer's tropical-themed cafe/bar/club. The menu runs a range from Mexican to something sort-of-Caribbean-themed to basic American, and it's not all that bad, considering. Partaking in lots of fruity tropical drinks doesn't hurt, either.

If the rodeo is more your style, the Pro Bull Riding organization has its own place at the **PBR Rock Bar & Grill ★** at Planet Hollywood, 3663 Las Vegas Blvd. S. (www.pbrrockbar.com; © **702/750-1685;** daily 8am–late). It serves up down-home American food in a country-western environment complete with a mechanical bull and tire swings above the tables.

You would think the celebrity shrine and memorabilia factory that is the **Planet Hollywood ★** restaurant would be in the Planet Hollywood Resort. But you'd be wrong. Instead, it's at Caesars Palace in the Forum Shops, 3500 Las Vegas Blvd. S. (www.planethollywood.com; © **702/791-7827;** Sun–Thurs 11am–11pm, Fri–Sat 11am–midnight).

Which is fantastic, because the menu includes foodie-friendly items like thick-cut smoked pork belly with a chipotle coffee glaze, and burgers topped with peanut butter, bacon jam, and potato chips (it works—really!). Each dish looks as beautiful as it tastes. In addition to more than 30 craft and imported beers on tap, there's a section of the bar menu dedicated to variations of the Moscow Mule. Mina's wine programs in all his other restaurants are exceptional—that rings true here as well, including wines by the glass.

In MGM Grand, 3799 Las Vegas Blvd. S. www.pub1842.com © **702/891-3922.** Main courses $18–$39. Thurs–Mon 11:30am–10pm.

Rí Rá Irish Pub ★★ IRISH How authentic is this Irish pub? It was imported piece by piece from West Cork in Ireland, along with a number of servers and bartenders (you can't fake a brogue that thick) who've lucked out on a great work exchange program. The Guinness flows freely—not to mention properly, and at the right temperature—to accompany traditional Irish pub fare like bangers and mash, fish and chips, and shepherd's pie. The menu also encompasses contemporary Irish fusion cuisine, like the potato cake starter topped with sour cream and balsamic oil, and a fantastic meatloaf made with pork, veal, and beef, and served with Guinness ketchup, cheddar, and onion rings. Take a tour of the space; it looks narrow from the front but goes much deeper than you expect, to include three more bars—one Victorian-themed bar watched over by a 500-pound statue of St. Patrick, a whiskey room, and a live music venue that hosts bands direct from, where else, Ireland.

At Mandalay Place, 3930 Las Vegas Blvd. S. www.rira.com. © **702/632-7771.** Main courses lunch $12–$20, dinner $12–$28. Mon–Fri 8am–3am; Sat–Sun 9am–3am.

Inexpensive

Bobby's Burger Palace ★ BURGERS Though he's best known for Southwest flavors (like those at his Mesa Grill at Caesars Palace), Food Network old guard Bobby Flay decided to go the more pan-American route for his second restaurant in town. Though the menu at the walk-up counter is almost exclusively stuff that goes between two buns, he's maintained his reputation for big, bold flavors in just about every version. Flay takes a regional approach to the burger, which you can build on standard beef, turkey, or chicken breast. He offers varieties like the Philadelphia, which is a play on its native cheese steak, with grilled onions, provolone cheese, and hot peppers; and the Miami, served Cubano-style, pressed with ham, Swiss cheese, mustard, and pickles. He's also a fan of putting potato chips in his sandwiches, like the Crunchburger with double American cheese and house-made chips. Shakes are fun, with out-of-the-ordinary flavors like pistachio and blueberry pomegranate, but you can't beat the classic dark chocolate.

At Crystals, 3750 Las Vegas Blvd. S. www.bobbysburgerpalace.com. © **702/598-0191.** Main courses $10–$12. Daily 11am–midnight.

Burger Bar ★ DINER At the original fancy burger restaurant on the Strip, chef Hubert Keller encourages diners to get creative. Everyone starts with patty options that range from Angus beef to lamb to buffalo, then diners pile on toppings, from the usual bacon and cheddar cheese to the extravagant, like foie gras, truffle mayo, or jalapeño bacon. Be careful: Enough high-ticket items, plus a side of fries, and you might be wondering why you didn't just go out for a steak. If you feel like leaving it up to the experts, there are "predetermined" burgers, like the Keller special made with buffalo, caramelized onions, baby spinach, and blue cheese, or the Hangover Burger. The latter will

We've already alluded to the rock-bottom budget meals and graveyard specials available at casino hotel restaurants, quality not assured and Pepto-Bismol not provided. As prices and deals can change without notice, we don't want to list examples, but finding a full prime-rib dinner for around $10 is not rare (pun definitely intended).

Your best bet is to keep your eyes open as you travel through town, as hotels tend to advertise their specials on their marquees. Or you can go to www.vegas.com and click on **"Restaurant"** and then **"Las Vegas Restaurant Deals."** Note that the tips and prices may change frequently. Following are two examples of options for late-night munchies: **Coronado Café** at the South Point offers a $6 steak-and-eggs meal, while that same $6 gets you a slice of pizza bigger than your head at **Pin-Up Pizza** at Planet Hollywood.

remind you of a certain fast food burger that also has special sauce, lettuce, and cheese on a sesame seed bun—but this one is way better.

In Mandalay Place, 3930 Las Vegas Blvd. S. www.burgerbarlv.com. ℂ **702/632-9364.** Main courses $10–$65 (burgers start at $10, depending on kind of meat; toppings start at 45¢ and go way up). Sun–Thurs 11am–11pm; Fri–Sat 11am–midnight.

Shake Shack ★ BURGERS As the first West Coast outpost of the New York burger institution, Shake Shack opened up back in 2014 with great fanfare outside, appropriately, New York–New York Hotel and Casino. At heart, it's a simple burger joint, but the line for service shows it's more than that. All the Angus beef burgers are cooked to medium, and if you get the most-plain iteration, it would simply be tucked into the soft brioche bun with lettuce, tomato, cheese, and the secret Shack Sauce. And in a town where you can get a burger topped with foie gras and truffles and a side of Chateau Petrus, sometimes all you want is a plain, but really good, burger. A couple of only-in-Vegas bites that might interest you are the ShackMeister burger, topped with ale-marinated onion rings, cheese, and Shack Sauce, and the Shack-a-palooza, a sundae monstrosity with three scoops of each frozen custard flavor, made to be split between four to six people (or just two if you're feeling gluttonous).

In New York–New York, 3790 Las Vegas Blvd. S. www.shakeshack.com. ℂ **725/222-6730.** Main courses $5–$10. Daily 11am–2am.

MID-STRIP

Expensive

Blue Ribbon Brasserie ★★ BISTRO When Cosmo added two new Japanese-heavy restaurants to their portfolios (Zuma and Momofuku), it made sense that the former Blue Ribbon Sushi Bar and Grill should change its focus. Not that they didn't make great sushi, but Blue Ribbon has never been a one-trick pony. The New York favorite went back to its bistro roots and

Mid-Strip Restaurants

NORTH STRIP

Wynn Las Vegas

Spring Mountain Rd.

Sands Ave.

Sammy Davis Jr Dr

••▸ ◼ ◂•• Las Vegas Monorail
••▸ ◼ ◂•• Free monorail
▰▰▰▰ Pedestrian bridge

1 Treasure Island

2 The Palazzo

3 The Venetian

Mirage **4**

Casino Royale

5 Harrah's

Forum Shops **6**

Harrah's/ The Linq

7 The Linq

Caesars Palace **8**

(THE STRIP)

Flamingo

Flamingo/ Caesars Palace

9 The Cromwell

Flamingo Rd.

Bally's

Bally's/ Paris

Bellagio **10**

LAS VEGAS BLVD.

11 Paris

The Cosmopolitan of Las Vegas **12**

Audrie St.

13 Planet Hollywood

Ave.

Harmon

Aria

The Shops at Crystals

Harmon Ave.

Waldorf Astoria

SOUTH STRIP

Park MGM

0   0.25 mi
0   0.25 km

RESTAURANTS

Black Tap **3**
Block 16 Urban
  Food Hall **12**
Blue Ribbon
  Brasserie **12**
Bouchon **3**
Brooklyn Bowl **7**
Buddy V's
  Ristorante **2**
Cabo Wabo
  Cantina **13**
Carmine's **6**
China Poblano **12**
Delmonico
  Steakhouse **3**
Egg Slut **12**
Estiatorio Milos **12**
Forum Food Court **8**
Fulton Street
  Food Court **5**
Giada **9**
Gilley's **1**
Gordon Ramsay
  Burger **13**
Gordon Ramsay
  Fish & Chips **7**
Gordon Ramsay
  Hell's Kitchen **8**
Gordon Ramsay
  Pub & Grill **8**
Gordon Ramsay
  Steak **11**
Guy Fieri's Vegas
  Kitchen **7**
Hash House
  a Go Go **7**

Holstein's Shakes
  & Buns **12**
Lagasse's Stadium **2**
Mercato della
  Pescheria **2**
Mesa Grill **8**
Momofuku **12**
Mon Ami Gabi **11**
Nacho Daddy **13**
Old Homestead
  Steakhouse **8**
Picasso **10**
Public House **3**
Rao's **8**
Restaurant
  Guy Savoy **8**
Rose.Rabbit.Lie. **12**
Sadelle's **10**
Spago **10**
Strip House **13**
Yardbird **3**
Zuma **12**

BUFFETS

Bacchanal Buffet **8**
The Buffet at
  Bellagio **10**
Corner Market
  Buffet **1**
Flavors Buffet **5**
Le Village Buffet **11**
Mirage Cravings
  Buffet **4**
Spice Market
  Buffet **13**
Wicked Spoon
  Buffet **12**

5

WHERE TO EAT | Mid-Strip

reemerged as Blue Ribbon Brasserie, with a redesigned space with a "vintage cool" look. The menu puts a lot of emphasis on dishes that put Blue Ribbon on the map, including bone marrow with oxtail jam, their famed fried chicken, and the festive pupu platter meant to share. If you're there for a late-night bite, steer toward the "bucket" of fried chicken wings served with wasabi honey, which offers the impressive fried chicken flavor in a smaller portion, at about half the price. And if you really need a raw fish fix, you can still find sashimi and sushi on the menu.

At the Cosmopolitan of Las Vegas, 3708 Las Vegas Blvd. S. www.blueribbonrestaurants. com. ✆ **702/698-7880.** Main courses $31–$145. Daily 5pm–midnight.

Bouchon ★★ BISTRO   When Thomas Keller, one of the greatest chefs in the American pantheon, decided to open a restaurant in Las Vegas, rather than try to replicate his famed French Laundry in Napa Valley in a field already crowded with 4-hour fine-dining experiences, he brought this relaxed bistro instead. "Relaxed" is a term we use loosely, as there are still white tablecloths and impeccable service to go along with the stellar food. The classic French brasserie setting, with brass rails and dark woods, is lightened up by sunlight that streams in through the windows that open to a courtyard. Set in the exclusive Venezia tower, it's one of the few places where you can eat on the Strip and not feel like you're eating on the Strip. The fare is traditional French bistro dishes, like roasted chicken with seasonal vegetables, steak frites with herbed hotel butter, and trout amandine. But you don't have to necessarily go big to enjoy a meal. Grab a seat at the raw bar to slurp down some of the most pristine oysters in the city, or dive into a selection of hors d'oeuvres like the lovely salmon rillettes. Though the food is seemingly simple, you're paying for the attention to detail that goes into making the most humble dishes taste divine.

In the Venetian, 3355 Las Vegas Blvd. S. www.bouchonbistro.com. ℭ **702/414-6200.** Reservations strongly recommended. Main courses dinner $19–$59, brunch $12–$34. Mon–Thurs 7am–1pm, 5–10pm; Fri–Sun 8am–2pm (brunch), 5–10pm; Oyster bar daily 3–10pm.

Delmonico Steakhouse ★★ CREOLE/STEAK   Though Emeril Lagasse is best known for his Creole fare at the original Delmonico in New Orleans, he's fine-tuned the menu here to focus on meat. (If you want to sample his NOLA fare exclusively, you're better off heading to the New Orleans Fish House at MGM Grand.) The front lounge is a popular place to grab a pre-dinner or pre-show drink, though you can order most of the dining room menu here, like the potato chips dressed with Parmesan cheese and truffle sauce, or his famed gumbo. But guests at Delmonico's are far more likely to go for meat, and rightly so; we're big fans of the dry-aged, bone-in rib eye for its deep flavor, the fine chateaubriand for two, and the double-cut Kurobuta pork chop. Sides are ample, like the enormous twice-baked potato, or the Southern-inspired grits with cheddar and bacon. An extensive whiskey library is worth a gander; they have one of those sliding ladders found in real libraries to pull down some of the interesting vintages from the top shelf.

In the Venetian, 3355 Las Vegas Blvd. S. www.emerils.com. ℭ **702/414-3737.** Main courses lunch $17–$55, dinner $40–$140. Daily 11:30am–2pm; Sun–Thurs 5–10pm; Fri–Sat 5–10:30pm.

Estiatorio Milos ★★★ GREEK/SEAFOOD   Those who have been to an actual fish market in Greece or Tokyo might be familiar with this sight as your server gives you a tour past the kitchen: varying species and sizes of fish and shellfish all waiting on ice to be plucked and cooked. As at those markets, the fish here have only been out of the water about 24 hours, having been caught in the Mediterranean specifically for Milos before catching the first flight to Vegas. If words like *lavraki, fagri,* and *barbouni* are literally all Greek to you, your server will explain each fish—from where they came from, down to their flavor profiles. Pick the one that sounds good, and they're grilled with nothing more than olive oil and a bit of lemon juice. If you are a non–seafood lover, there are options like grilled lamb chops and a filet mignon, both served with fried Greek potatoes. You'll both enjoy a starter of the Milos special: a pile of light, deep-fried zucchini and eggplant.

Dinner is insanely expensive (flying fish in from the Mediterranean every day ain't cheap!), but the lunch special is one of the best deals on the Strip, hands down. For $29, you can taste your way through three courses of Milos's most popular dishes, with choices that include Greek meze of various yogurt-based dips, whole-grilled Mediterranean sea bass, and dessert.

In the Cosmopolitan of Las Vegas, 3708 Las Vegas Blvd. S. www.milos.ca. ℂ **702/698-7930.** Lunch 3-course prix fixe $29, dinner main courses $53–$141. Daily 11:30am–3pm; Sun–Thurs 5–10:30pm; Fri–Sat 5pm–11:30pm.

Gordon Ramsay Steak ★★★ STEAK/SEAFOOD   Though his TV persona on shows like *Hell's Kitchen* and *Kitchen Nightmares* make chef Gordon Ramsay seem like a terror, in reality he's a passionate chef who earned many accolades before he ever became famous. Out of his five restaurants in town, this is his finest. Enter via the tubelike "Chunnel" structure, which is meant to "transport" guests from "Paris" to "London." On the ceiling are a Union Jack and a neon sculpture that looks like a bunch of random squiggles, but the lines actually represent Ramsay's hand motions when he's making beef Wellington. The Wellington, one of the dishes feared most by contestants on *Hell's Kitchen,* is done superbly here, in the classic manner, with a filet wrapped in prosciutto and cooked with a mushroom *duxelles* inside pastry dough. Steaks are a must, and they're presented to guests on a multitiered mirrored cart, so you can choose between the 28-day dry-aged cuts or the more marbled American Wagyu. The Wagyu rib cap is pricey, but luscious and tender. The other Gordon Ramsay restaurants on the Strip have a version of the sticky toffee pudding, but it's best at the steakhouse. The traditional English dessert cake comes soaked in brown sugar toffee sauce, with a side that looks like a stick of butter but is really brown butter ice cream.

In Paris Las Vegas, 3655 Las Vegas Blvd. S. www.gordonramsay.com. ℂ **877/346-4642.** Main courses $36–$117. Daily 4:30–10:30pm.

Hell's Kitchen ★ CONTINENTAL   Slowly but surely, Gordon Ramsay has taken over the Strip, but this time he's done it literally. His newest restaurant, Hell's Kitchen, sits as close to Las Vegas Boulevard as a restaurant can without actually being in the street, standing proud and apart from its parent hotel, Caesars Palace. For his fifth endeavor after his acclaimed steakhouse, burger joint, pub, and fish-and-chips spots, Ramsay came back full circle to upscale dining with a restaurant in the image of his hit reality cooking competition. Fans of the show get giddy when they're greeted not only by the trademark bronze HK and pitchfork, but also by a life-size video of Ramsay hurling some of his best insults from the show.

Inside, the open kitchen is the stage at the front of the 300-seat room, and the cooks on the line, donning red or blue bandanas, are the performers. Except the plot is not about Red vs Blue Team, but rather everyone works together for a seamless dinner service. Dishes from the show figure prominently, including lobster risotto, seared scallops, and beef Wellington, all of which require notable technical proficiency. The $80, three-course tasting menu will let you taste your way through the show's greatest hits.

The cocktails are just as dramatic, with a favorite being Notes from Gordon, a peachy, gin-based cocktail that comes with a little note from the man himself. Smoke on the Blvd arrives in a cherrywood smoke-filled glass cabinet, and the heady smoke escapes when you open the door.

You don't have to be a fan of the show Hell's Kitchen to like the restaurant Hell's Kitchen, but hardcore fans will get way more enjoyment out of it.

In Caesars Palace, 3570 Las Vegas Blvd. S. www.gordonramsay.com. (C) **702/731-7373.** Main courses $32–$125. Daily 11am–midnight.

Mesa Grill ★★ SOUTHWESTERN   One of the first Food Network chefs (after Emeril) to set up shop in Vegas, Bobby Flay has proved that his reputation, and his Mesa Grill, has some longevity. He's known for creating strong Southwestern flavors, but with a delicate touch. The tiger shrimp tamale is a mainstay at all his restaurants, a combination of sweet shrimp and mildly pungent garlic. While I'd normally never put anything on a steak besides salt and pepper, the chipotle glaze on the rib eye works like gangbusters. The rest of the menu features dishes that are "ancho-chile glazed" or "New Mexico spice-rubbed," but in each, the spice is applied with great balance so that flavors never become overwhelming.

In Caesars Palace, 3570 Las Vegas Blvd. S. www.mesagrill.com. (C) **877/346-4642.** Main courses brunch and lunch $18–$52, dinner $29–$60. Mon–Fri 11am–2:30pm, 5–11pm; Sat–Sun 10:30am–3pm, 5–11pm.

Old Homestead Steakhouse ★★★ STEAK   Though the steakhouse is a mainstay of Las Vegas dining, New York has been doing steak waaaay longer. Case in point: Old Homestead, which opened in 1868 in the Big Apple. When Old Homestead finally made it out West, they knew they didn't have to mess with what's been working for the past 150 years. The same giant steaks, direct from famed butcher Pat LaFrieda, are here: the New York Strip, a porterhouse for two, and even the Gotham rib eye, a cut so big that the bone that remains in it makes you feel like Fred Flintstone. Homestead does well by veggies, too, especially the Kitchen Sink Salad, chock-full of shrimp, salami, bacon, avocado, and hearts of palm. The rest of the menu is classic steakhouse fare with insane upgrades, such as shrimp cocktail with some of the biggest shrimp we've ever seen, lobster mac and cheese, and duck fat fries.

In Caesars Palace, 3570 Las Vegas Blvd. S. www.theoldhomesteadsteakhouse.com. (C) **877/346-4642.** Main courses $35–$145. Sun–Thurs 4:30–10pm; Fri–Sat 4:30–10:30pm.

Picasso ★★ FRENCH   As one of the original fine-dining restaurants in Las Vegas when Bellagio opened in 1989, Picasso, like the priceless artwork that hangs in it, is timeless. Chef Julian Serrano has been in command since the beginning, and he's still spinning haute French fare like no one else. There are several prix-fixe menus, though they change often, reflecting the season and whatever looks best that day. Does Serrano's artful cuisine complement the millions of dollars of artwork or is it the other way around? With dishes like warm quail salad with sautéed artichokes and pine nuts, roasted milk-fed veal chops, or pigeon and torchon of foie gras, all beautifully arranged by nimble hands in the kitchen, it's a toss-up. Though we feel that you can see Picasso's paintings in Vegas more often than you can experience a meal this exceptional.

In Bellagio, 3600 Las Vegas Blvd. S. www.bellagio.com. ✆ **866/259-7111.** Reservations required. Prix-fixe 4-course dinner $122, 5-course degustation $132. Daily 5:30–9:30pm.

Rao's ★★★ ITALIAN   The original Rao's in Harlem, New York City is purportedly the hardest reservation in the world to get. With only 13 tables, all of which are claimed with standing reservations, you've got to know some-body who knows somebody to eat there. When Rao's finally decided to expand to Las Vegas in 2006, lovers of classic Southern Italian cuisine rejoiced. The Caesars Palace outpost is an exact replica of the original, com-plete with Christmas decorations hung up over the bar year-round, portraits of celebrities who have joined them for dinner all along the walls, and the work-ing Wurlitzer jukebox, except *this* space has the good fortune of having an outdoor patio and being three times the size. The food is essentially the same as it has been for decades, and no one would want that to change. Meatballs are the thing here, made from "Aunt Anna" Rao's original recipe of pork, beef, and veal, tender and swimming in tangy marinara sauce. Uncle Vincent's Lemon Chicken, with the right amount of char on the skin to soak up the tart lemon vinaigrette, is mandatory as well. The seafood salad, full of calamari, shrimp, crab, and lobster, is tossed in an acidic citronette dressing so bright, we contemplated drinking it right from the plate. For dessert, the tiramisu is one of the most satisfying in the city.

In Caesars Palace, 3570 Las Vegas Blvd. S. www.caesarspalace.com. ✆ **702/731-7267.** Main courses $26–$53. Sun–Thurs 5–10pm; Fri–Sat 5–10:30pm.

Restaurant Guy Savoy ★★★ FRENCH   In 2006, at the height of the dining revolution in Las Vegas, there was an influx of French chefs to the Strip. Guy Savoy, a star in Paris, was recruited by the president of Caesars Palace based on one dish: the artichoke black truffle soup. Once you've tasted it yourself, you can understand why. The soup, and Savoy's other signature dishes, are far from the ultra-modern, deconstructed dishes that come from other French chefs in town. Instead, this is French fare elevated to its most elegant form. Colors of Caviar is a shot-glass parfait of expensive roe in layers of black and green, topped tableside with white vinaigrette sabayon. Feeling extra fancy? There's a prix-fixe menu that revolves just around caviar and the many ways the French have mastered the delicacy. In the fall, during white truffle season, the restaurant creates an entire menu around the expensive tuber—the one we like best is a simple risotto with a few shavings of the truffle. These dishes, along with a roaming bread cart (to pair bread with each course, naturally) and dessert cart (the chocolate mousse is Savoy's own grandmother's recipe) are ideal introductions for those who want to leap into fine French dining, without being completely lost.

In Caesars Palace, 3570 Las Vegas Blvd. S. www.caesars.com. © **702/731-7286.** Reservations required. Prestige Menu $385; Caviar Tasting $170; main courses $110–$250. Wed–Sun 5:30–9:30pm.

Rose.Rabbit.Lie ★ CONTINENTAL Billing itself as a supper club, this haphazardly punctuated restaurant does a good job of straddling the lines between fancy dining room, weird entertainment space, and speakeasy. So, if you're eating in the main room or drinking in the library bar, you'll get treated to random lounge musicians with performances just avant-garde enough to pique your interest. The focus is small plates that are small in size but not in price. Though with dishes like caviar "tacos" on Yukon gold potato shells, duck confit pasta, and crispy oysters Rockefeller, Rose.Rabbit.Lie can be forgiven. For dessert, don't miss the chocolate terrarium, a garden served under a glass cloche with chocolate "dirt" and other cocoa-enhanced delights.

At the Cosmopolitan of Las Vegas, 3708 Las Vegas Blvd. S. www.cosmopolitanlasvegas. com. © **877/667-0585.** Small plates $15–$25, main courses $26–$85. Wed–Sat 5:30pm–midnight.

Spago ★★★ AMERICAN Before the French chefs, Emeril, or Gordon Ramsay ever set foot in Las Vegas, there was Wolfgang Puck. One of the first celebrity chefs—before celebrity chefs were even a thing—to see the future of dining in Las Vegas, Puck opened Spago at the Forum Shops in 1992. Now he has a wide assortment of restaurants bearing his name all over Las Vegas. On the Strip alone, there's his Italian Lupo at Mandalay Bay, his namesake Bar & Grill at MGM Grand, and his casual pizza and wine spot at the Shops at Crystals. But if you're going to do Puck, you might as well go to the original, even if it's not in its original location. After 26 years surrounded by the marble of Caesars Palace, Spago made the move to the Bellagio, in a space with a full view of the Strip and the iconic fountains through giant floor-to-ceiling windows. Outdoor patio seating makes this an exclusive perch as you watch the fountain shows. Some things do remain the same, such as the seasonal American menu with everything from seafood to beef, and we're not complaining. Classic Puck inventions, such as pizza topped with smoked salmon and crème fraîche (pay extra for osetra caviar if you want to be super-luxurious), and the fresh, crisp, and summery chinois chicken salad, have stood the test of time and are as popular and delicious as ever.

In Bellagio, 3600 Las Vegas Blvd. S. www.bellagio.com. © **702/693-8181.** Reservations recommended. Main courses $22–$129. Lunch daily 11:30am–2:45pm. Dinner Sun–Thurs 5–10:30pm; Fri–Sat 5–11pm.

kid-friendly DINING STRATEGIES

Buffets   Cheap meals for the whole family. The kids can choose what they like, and there are sometimes make-your-own sundae machines. See "Buffets" (p. 144) for reviews. Those with reduced prices for kids are noted.

Food Courts   Yes, you can get a Subway sandwich at home, but there is something comforting about the safe array of choices that kids will recognize and probably not complain about. In addition to those listed in the Quick

Bites box on p. 105, check out Forum Food Court (p. 124) at Caesars, which has few recognizable names but better quality.

Theme Restaurants   Although the cuisine usually won't win any awards, theme restaurants are often great places to take kids because of their wide-ranging menus and plenty of distractions to keep them entertained. See "You Gotta Have a Theme" (p. 106).

Strip House ★ STEAK   Tucked away into the mezzanine of Planet Hollywood, Strip House is dark and definitely romantic, though the low lighting isn't the only thing contributing to the intimate atmosphere. The red-flocked walls are dressed with vintage burlesque and borderline naughty photos of barely clad girls (by today's standards, they seem tame). Talk your way into one of the corner booths so you have a view of the rest of the room; the close seating allows you and your dining companion to whisper sweet nothings in each other's ears. The meat program is concise, offering favorite cuts like a New York Strip and dry-aged rib eyes, all served with a bulb of roasted garlic so mild it won't put a damper on your evening. A side of potatoes crisped up in goose fat is small but packed with flavor and crunch, while creamed spinach offers a hint of black truffles. And if chocolate is your aphrodisiac, the towering 24-layer chocolate cake should be your sweet finish.

In Planet Hollywood Resort & Casino, 3667 Las Vegas Blvd. S. www.striphouse.com. ⓒ **702/737-5200.** Main courses $31–$105. Sun–Wed 5–10pm; Thurs–Sat 5–11pm.

Zuma ★★ JAPANESE   Plenty of restaurants opening on the Strip have focused on Asian cuisine; the only problem is telling them all apart. Zuma is the visually stunning one, with a view of the Las Vegas Strip to match. The variety of textures, both natural and synthetic, make almost every inch of the space interesting to look at. The robata and sushi bar counters are hewn from massive slabs of ancient Thai wood, while there's a rice paper "statement wall" in the lounge. There's a drink that is literally smoked for guests at the bar (they heat a piece of wood and trap the smoke in your glass; you don't inhale anything), and another features cute plastic bags served in a small, square bamboo box. This creative presentation, called "Fish in the Bag," is inspired by the Asian street-food method of the to-go beverage: served in a plastic bag and sipped through a straw. And no, there's not an actual fish in there, just a killer gin and tonic with dehydrated orange and green tea tonic water. The dishes from this *izakaya* are just as photogenic, with shareable

5

WHERE TO EAT | Mid-Strip

small plates that blend traditional Japanese bar fare and modern ingredients, such as thin-sliced sea bass with yuzu, salmon roe and black truffle, or skewers of Kurobuta pork belly with mustard miso. Between this and the pristine sushi selection, don't get overwhelmed with choices; you can go with the flow through a prix-fixe *omakase* (the chef chooses for you) tasting starting at $128 per person. However you order, you'll remember it as one of the best-looking meals you've had in a long time.

At the Cosmopolitan of Las Vegas, 3708 Las Vegas Blvd. S. www.zumarestaurant.com. ✆ **702/698-2199.** Small plates $8–$27, main courses $29–$190. Sun–Thurs 5:30–10:30pm; Fri–Sat 5:30–11pm.

Moderate

Black Tap ★★ BURGERS   If there were awards for most Instagrammable restaurant, Black Tap would take the cake—er, shake. From the graffiti-covered decor to the over-the-top shakes and burgers, it's all photogenic, and servers actively encourage guests to share their experience on their social medium of choice. This New York native first became known for its ridiculous, towering milkshakes with so much more than just sprinkles and a cherry on top. The cold concoctions are piled high with full-size cookies, candy, ice cream sandwiches… and why yes, that is a whole piece of cake atop the Birthday Cake Shake. The Brooklyn Blackout is as chocolicious as it sounds, topped with a whole chocolate brownie immersed in a glass whose rim is coated with chocolate chips. I loved pairing it with the cremini mushroom and Swiss-cheese-laden Old-Fashioned burger, an intimidating burger on its own. And the flamboyant shakes and burgers aren't just for show; they actually taste good too.

In the Venetian, 3355 Las Vegas Blvd S. www.blacktapnyc.com. ✆ **702/607-2355.** Main courses $15–$22. Sun–Thurs 11am–midnight; Fri–Sat 11am–2am.

Block 16 Urban Food Hall ★★ FOOD HALL   The Cosmopolitan collected some of the country's best hot spots and planted them together in a corner of the second floor. Neon lights and high barstools at counters build an Asian night market vibe, where you can eat and drink your way through the various stalls—a *bao* (steamed dumpling) here, a sake there—and make a night of it. Pok Pok Wing features the greatest hits from the original Portland Pok Pok menu, including the spicy papaya salad that goes so well with the famous Vietnamese fish sauce sticky, crispy sweet wings. The other Portland native is Lardo with its stacked sandwiches, like the Sancho grilled cheese with brisket burnt ends. From the South comes Hattie B's Hot Chicken, best enjoyed in sandwich form, tossed in varying degrees of hot sauce. Be forewarned: "Shut the Cluck Up" left me literally speechless from the searing heat. Once you come to your senses, duck into the charming Ghost Donkey in the back, a cozy speakeasy that focuses on mezcal. Stake your claim early if you can; seats fill up fast and tend to stay occupied for the night.

At the Cosmopolitan of Las Vegas, 3708 Las Vegas Blvd. S. www.cosmopolitanlasvegas. com. ✆ **702/698-7880.** Main courses $6–$19. Open daily 11am, closing hours vary by restaurant.

Brooklyn Bowl ★★ ECLECTIC   You get one-stop shopping at this multipurpose venue: a two-story concert hall at the LINQ, a 32-lane bowling alley, and a restaurant that serves fantastic comfort food. Start on one floor and head to the rest in any order you like. The menu alone might just keep you in the restaurant all night, though, thanks to a huge selection that includes hummus, pork rinds, French bread pizzas, and barbecue. For having such a diverse menu, Brooklyn Bowl does a surprisingly good job with all of it. The fried chicken is stellar—it can even be prepared gluten-free. Oh, and if you do decide to go bowling, definitely keep that separate from eating, as fingers greasy from fried chicken don't belong in bowling balls.

In the LINQ, 3545 Las Vegas Blvd. S., Ste. 22. www.brooklynbowl.com. ℂ **702/862-2695.** Main courses $14–$28. Daily 5pm–close.

Buddy V's Ristorante ★★ ITALIAN   Though he's best known as the *Cake Boss* on TLC and Discovery Family, Buddy Valastro has a savory side too, which he shares at this restaurant at the front of the Shoppes at Palazzo. The menu is rooted in his family's original recipes, with favorites like a hearty lasagna, steak pizzaiola, and his mother-in-law's shrimp scampi with angel-hair pasta. It doesn't have to be Sunday to enjoy the gravy—a rich, chunky red sauce chock full of sausage, lamb, and meatballs—that tastes like it's been simmering on the stove all day, served in a bowl over rigatoni. Go full on family-style for brunch, for an all-you-can-eat extravaganza that includes salumi, frittatas, eggs *al forno,* carbonara, and traditional chicken Parmesan. As you can imagine, desserts are strong here, with bites like warm Nutella cake, and traditional cannoli filled with sweet pastry cream. But half the fun of the showcase bakery across the hall is the windows into the pastry kitchen, where crowds watch cooks make and fill Valastro's signature "lobster tail" puff pastry cone with custard cream and fruit.

In the Grand Canal Shoppes at the Palazzo, 3325 Las Vegas Blvd S. www.buddyv lasvegas.com. ℂ **702/607-2355.** Main courses lunch $14–26, dinner $14–$46. Mon–Thurs 11:30am–10pm; Fri–Sat 11:30am–11pm; Sat 10:30am–11pm; Sun 10:30am–10pm.

Cabo Wabo Cantina ★ MEXICAN   Sammy Hagar not only has his own brand of tequila, but a Mexican restaurant in which to serve it. Celebrity backer notwithstanding, Cabo Wabo has a fun party atmosphere that's amplified when it spills out on the Strip-front patio. An offshoot of the original Cabo San Lucas location in Mexico, it's spring break year-round here, fueled, naturally, with margaritas laden with Hagar's tequila, which can be slammed by the glass or by the pitcher. Watch out for the "Can't Drive 55," a mind-eraser with tequila, Sammy's Beach Bar rum, vodka, gin, and a couple of mixers—you shouldn't be driving anything after this. The menu features perfunctory Mexican fare. Though no one's really expecting it to be Border Grill caliber, it does the job, with tacos, burritos, and enchiladas laying the base for a long night of drinking. The Red Rocker has a residence in Las Vegas, so chances are good you might actually run into him here.

In Planet Hollywood Resort & Casino, 3663 Las Vegas Blvd. S. www.cabowabocantina. com/vegas. ✆ **702/385-2226.** Main courses $15–$39. Mon–Thurs 8am–1am; Fri–Sat 8am–2am; kitchen closes at 11pm.

Carmine's ★ ITALIAN The menu for this family-style Italian restaurant is plastered against the wall, and when you look at the prices—averaging $40 a pop for entrees—you will experience some sticker shock. But the blow is softened when you realize that each order is meant for at least four people (or two really gluttonous ones). With high ceilings and two stories, it feels like a banquet hall, but the servers have a knack for making you feel like you're the only people there. The chicken wings Scarpariello-style, with hot and sweet peppers, are a great starter before you get into plate-sized veal scaloppini and enough pasta to feed an Italian army. Whether you're in a big group or a four top (seriously, you want to go with at least three other people), these massive dishes still taste like they were made in a home kitchen. And there's no shame in asking for a doggy bag.

In the Forum Shops at Caesars Palace, 3500 Las Vegas Blvd. S. www.carminesnyc.com. ✆ **702/473-9700.** Family-style main courses $38–$50. Sun–Thurs 11am–11pm; Fri–Sat 11am–midnight.

China Poblano ★ CHINESE/MEXICAN Pronounced "CHEEna poBLAno," this is chef José Andrés' unlikely mash-up of two popular cuisines. The menu explains that they are related thanks to the Spanish galleons that brought Asian spices and fruits to Mexico and chilies to China. The best part? It's not really fusion fare, as evidenced by the two different walk-up windows in front: one for tacos, one for dumplings. Ultimately China Poblano is a study in regional street food, which you are welcome to mix and match as you please. From the Chinese section (where all the prices end in 88¢ for good luck), we're fans of the *har gow,* a standard on dim sum menus; the *rou jia mo,* the Chinese version of a hamburger with braised red pork on a sesame bun; and When Pigs Fly, steamed barbecue pork buns. Speaking of pigs flying, Andrés is the only chef we'd allow to charge us $6 to $7 for one taco, reasonable for fillings like *nopales* with seared *queso fresco* and slow-cooked Yucatan-style barbecue pork. Also noteworthy are the super-cheesy *chilaquiles* in a bright green tomatillo salsa.

In the Cosmopolitan of Las Vegas, 3708 Las Vegas Blvd. S. www.chinapoblano.com. ✆ **702/698-7900.** Small plates $6–$29. Sun–Thurs 11:30am–11pm; Fri–Sat 11:30am–11:30pm.

Giada ★★★ ITALIAN Chefs usually have a restaurant or two under their belts before they are elevated to "celebrity chef" status, but Food Network staple Giada de Laurentiis did it the other way around. After finding success through showcasing her easy-breezy, California Italian cuisine on TV for many years, she added a brick-and-mortar in 2014. And her name is everywhere in this bright, airy restaurant at the Cromwell that overlooks the

Strip—embroidered on the napkins, embossed on the plates, stitched into backs of the chairs. Giada wants you to know you're in *Giada's* house. Antipasti platters are a great way to start, mixing and matching bites like eggplant caponata, bacon-wrapped dates, cheese and salumi from the market-style deli in the front. Not in the mood for a full-on Italian feast? Skip the dining room, take a seat at the bar, and make a meal of the antipasti. You'll save a little money too. Whatever you do, try at least one of her signature dishes—the lemon spaghetti, or the chicken cacciatore for two. A cute footnote: When Giada refers to Italian dishes on her show, she turns on her Italian accent, enunciating words like "spah-GEH-ti" and "ree-gah-TOH-ne." For guests to channel her, the menu includes phonetic spellings of how she says them aloud. We told you she wants you to know where you're eating.

In the Cromwell, 3595 Las Vegas Blvd. S. www.thecromwell.com. (✆ **702/777-3777.** Main courses $26–$83. Mon–Thurs 5–10:30pm; Fri–Sun brunch 9am–3pm; Fri–Sun 5–10:45pm.

Gilley's ★★ BARBECUE   There's really only one spot serving real barbecue on the Strip, and it's this honky-tonk at Treasure Island. Don't be discouraged if you don't know how to two-step or are lacking cowboy boots, Gilley's 'cue is loved by all. There's a namesake beef and bean chili on the menu, but it was the award-winning green chili that had us wanting another bowl. A rich tomatillo sauce enhanced with Hatch and poblano chilies that make it tangy and only slightly spicy, it is studded with big chunks of pork, topped with Mexican sour cream, and served with fresh tortillas. Barbecue is done properly here, smoked over a mesquite pit. St. Louis spareribs get finished with a Southern Comfort barbecue sauce glaze, while the baby back ribs also take a glaze at the end, though you're more than welcome to order them naked if all you need for flavor is smoke. The combos are the best way to go here, with choices of two to six meats, so you can sample everything. Should you want to ride the mechanical bull, do it before you eat, or wait a good period after—it's definitely not fun when you're as stuffed as you'll get here. Line dancing to help digest is always a good idea.

At Treasure Island, 3300 Las Vegas Blvd. S. www.gilleyslasvegas.com. (✆ **702/894-7111.** Main courses $18–$49. Daily 11am–midnight.

Gordon Ramsay Pub & Grill ★ PUB/BRITISH   If you want to leave Vegas being able to brag you ate at one of Gordon Ramsay's restaurants, yet aren't into paying an arm and a leg for it (as you would at his steakhouse at Paris), somehow aren't a fan of his show (as in Hell's Kitchen), and want more than just a burger to show for it (as you'd get from his Burger at Planet Hollywood), then this is your best compromise. During the day it's a casual pub, comfortable enough to down a few pints from the 36 beers on tap, and perhaps a Scotch egg (traditionally this bar snack would be a hard-boiled egg encased in sausage, but this one is delicate, silky, and soft-boiled). At night, when the lights dim in the dining room, the mood shifts and the vibe becomes (slightly) more elegant. I'm particularly fond of the fish-and-chips: flaky cod dressed in a crunchy Yorkshire ale batter with thick-cut chips and mushy peas. A suggested pairing of Innis & Gunn is right on, and also happens to be one of Ramsay's favorite pints. The front of the bar and dining room are open to the casino floor, which is great for people-watching, terrible for intimate conversations.

In Caesars Palace, 3570 Las Vegas Blvd. S. www.gordonramsay.com. ✆ **877/346-4642.** Main courses $21–$67. Sun–Thurs 11am–11pm; Fri–Sat 11am–midnight.

Guy Fieri's Vegas Kitchen ★ AMERICAN   Even if his name wasn't emblazoned (literally, with flames on the sign, much like the flames often found on his shirts) on the front of the restaurant, when dishes have names like Tatted-up turkey burger, and Dragon's Breath chili cheese fries, it's obvious that this restaurant belongs to Food Network favorite Guy Fieri. He's made his reputation showcasing outrageous dishes that fit his ebullient personality. While the food may sometimes feel overwrought (Does a burger really need bacon AND mac and cheese on it? Is this crudité just for show?), you can't deny that some of his Franken-flavor combinations work. Like the tempura-battered lobster lollipops served with Old Bay and cheese-smothered fries and garlic aioli, which is at once comforting and upscale. And I'll admit that the bacon mac and cheese burger is freaking good. Fieri's second Vegas restaurant, El Burro Burracho, is at the Rio and features his take on Mexican fare, which means lots more flare but *en español.*

In the LINQ, 3535 Las Vegas Blvd. S. www.guyfieri.com. ✆ **702/734-3139.** Main courses $19–$35. Daily 8am–midnight.

Hash House a Go Go ★★ AMERICAN   If you're going to get up early to enjoy breakfast, please don't do it at a buffet (brunch is another story, though). Your first meal of the day deserves to be a good one. This is Vegas, after all; you need to be properly fueled. Enter Hash House a Go Go (either at the LINQ, Plaza, Rio, or its original location on the West side), known for (1) "twisted farm food" and (2) obscenely large portions. For example, the crispy pork tenderloin (used in a sandwich) is pounded out to the size of a Frisbee. When it arrives, eclipsing a tiny bun, it's comical. Farm Scrambles are served not on plates, but platters, with a thick foundation of griddled mashed or crispy potatoes. The omelets have salmon, tomato, pesto, and brie, or ham, spinach, and cheddar, folded in. One of the biggest hits is the fried chicken Benedict, dressed with a reduction of sweet maple syrup, and two eggs on bacon-studded mashed potatoes . . . and there's a split biscuit somewhere underneath all of that. Lunch and dinner feature more of the same home-style fare, from meatloaf to 1-pound burgers, all way bigger than most can finish. *Note:* Check the website for other locations.

In the LINQ, 3535 Las Vegas Blvd. S. www.hashhouseagogo.com. ✆ **702/254-4646.** Main courses $12–$35. Open daily 24 hrs.

Holstein's Shakes & Buns ★★ BURGERS   Who knew pigs dressed as cows could be this cute? That's the motif at Holstein's, created by local artist

Juan Muniz, and it's part of the appeal of this fancy burger joint, obviously meant to draw in a younger crowd, perhaps even luring in those waiting in line for Marquee outside. Vegas has many gourmet burger spots, but Holstein's is my favorite; they kept it classy, yet funky and cool, which is great when you've got burgers like the Gold Standard, made with dry-aged beef sirloin and topped with aged goat cheddar, tomato confit, and garlic-chive aioli. The Steakhouse Burger, a black peppercorn–crusted patty with steak sauce, onion jam, wild mushrooms, and Swiss, is also primo. There are plainer options, like the classic with the usual toppings; or the Fatty Patty, which, while built on a grass-fed beef patty, is dressed with Swiss cheese and Thousand Island dressing and served on Hawaiian bread. For shakes, the grown-up Bamboozled varieties are fun (drink more than one of these and you'll definitely feel it later).

In the Cosmopolitan of Las Vegas, 3708 Las Vegas Blvd. S. www.holsteinsburgers.com. ⓒ **702/698-7940.** Main courses $17–$32. Sun–Thurs 11am–midnight; Fri–Sat 11am–1am.

Lagasse's Stadium ★ AMERICAN Emeril is a self-proclaimed sports guy, so he transformed this space (a former nightclub) into the best man cave ever. You can't look anywhere without having an HDTV in your line of sight, as about 100 of them broadcast every sport imaginable. The draw here is the stadium seating, all facing a wall of giant screens, that you have to reserve for big sporting events (table minimums can be hefty, but the comfy couches and personalized service are worth it for a large group). The Super Bowl, as you can imagine, is nuts, as is March Madness. But you'll also see grown men interested in women's college softball—a step forward (or maybe they had bets down). Friendly rivalries play out in the dining room, with the kitchen rolling out specials that relate to the teams at stake in big games. For the Patriot-Seahawks matchup during Super Bowl XLIX, for example, New England clam chowder and Fanny Bay oysters from Puget Sound were on the menu. The daily offerings are a mix of Emeril's classic NOLA cuisine, including a shrimp po' boy, gumbo, and his fantastic jambalaya; and pub fare like pizza, burgers, and sandwiches, all with the chef's special "bam."

In the Palazzo, 3325 Las Vegas Blvd. S. www.emerils.com. ⓒ **702/607-2665.** Main courses $15–$41. Daily 11am–10pm.

Mercato della Pescheria ★★ SEAFOOD Miami has been importing quite a few restaurants to Las Vegas recently, like **Yardbird** (p. 123) and Chica, and they've all landed at the Venetian. This addition has imported a lot of seafood with it. Tucked into the corner of St. Marks's Square in the Grand Canal Shoppes, the Mercato is designed true to its name, with some 12 different market stations devoted to various ingredients throughout the space. Take a gander at the fresh pasta made in-house or a cheese and salumi selection that made us weep. A starter of grilled octopus is a must, served with the classic confit fingerling potatoes and salsa verde. We got our carb fix via the linguine frutti di mare, thin strands of fresh pasta spun together with ample clams, mussels, and calamari in a white wine and tomato sauce. Dessert offers another show entirely with the tableside tiramisu, where your server will build your sweet, creamy treat from ladyfingers, coffee, mascarpone, and chocolate just for you. The dining room is massive, but we prefer to sit on the faux patio to people-watch on the Square (though it can get loud at times when the "streetmosphere" operatic voices start soaring).

In the Venetian, 3377 Las Vegas Blvd. S. www.mercatodellapescheria.com. ℰ **702/831-0309.** Main courses lunch $22–$55. Daily 11am–11pm.

Momofuku ★★ ASIAN   It took a long time for a resort to woo New York golden boy David Chang to Las Vegas. So, when he arrived in 2017, he was met with much fanfare—as well as high expectations. Like many headliners who pass through Vegas, he has whittled down his extensive catalog to his greatest hits. The melding of casual and decadent works well in this town, as in Chang's pork belly ramen with a silky, slow-poached egg. While small plates are king right now, along with his bao (that only come two to an order), he also goes big with shared large-format dishes such as his Korean Bo Ssäm, and the fried chicken and caviar, which is the fanciest fried chicken you will ever eat. Next door is partner and pastry chef Christina Tosi's **Milk Bar** walk-up counter for the full Big Apple Chang experience, but you can also order the desserts in the restaurant. If you've eaten at his spots in New York, you can probably take a pass (unless you're a real fangirl/boy). The only difference is this one is easier to get into.

In the Cosmopolitan of Las Vegas, 3708 Las Vegas Blvd. S. https://vegas.momofuku.com. ℰ **702/698-7930.** Small plates $9–$32, dinner main courses $16–$78, large-format dishes $180–$1,888. Daily 11am–3pm, 5:30–11pm.

Mon Ami Gabi ★★ BISTRO   In a town full of faux French bistros, it can be difficult to figure out how they differ from one another. They all serve roasted chicken and steak frites; they all have quiche and charcuterie boards as starters. While Mon Ami Gabi might not have the same caliber of chef behind it as **Bouchon** (p. 110) or **Bardot** (p. 96), what it lacks in celebrity affiliation, it makes up for in location. Occupying prime real estate center-Strip at Paris, under the shadow of the Eiffel Tower, with patio seating and a perfect view of the Bellagio Fountains, it offers what is possibly the best perch for people-watching in the city. So, what does it matter that the *frisée* salad with poached egg, the buttery escargots, and the delicate crepes aren't ground-breaking or original? They're all done exceptionally well, and this place charges lower prices than the other Strip bistros. At dinner the prices go up a dollar or two, but you're paying for bigger portions, as well as the view.

In Paris Las Vegas, 3655 Las Vegas Blvd. S. www.monamigabi.com. ℰ **702/944-4224.** Main courses $20–$44. Sun–Thurs 7am–11pm; Fri–Sat 7am–midnight.

Sadelle's ★ DINER   Tucked behind the Bellagio Conservatory, Sadelle's breathes new life into the all-day hotel cafe. The massive, airy dining room features muted blues and pinks for a serene setting, while natural light pours in through French windows, a rarity for Vegas restaurants. Breakfast is the meal of choice, and fans of New York–style delis are in smoked fish heaven here. You'll see many tables sporting multitiered towers of house-smoked lox, sable, and sturgeon, all served with proper accoutrements of sliced tomatoes, capers, cucumbers, and cream cheese. Bagels, made on-site, include gluten-free offerings so no one has to miss out. Because this is Bellagio, there's a dash of luxury on the caviar menu, which features soft scrambled eggs or latkes (crispy potato pancakes) with smoked salmon and crème fraiche, topped with a choice of varying calibers of roe. The roaming pastry cart won't let you forget about dessert, and it teems with classics such as black-and-white cookies, rugelach, and flaky pastries.

In Bellagio, 3600 Las Vegas Blvd. S. www.bellagio.com. ℭ **702/639-7075.** Main courses $17–$59. Daily 6am–midnight.

Yardbird ★★ ECLECTIC   Miami probably isn't the first place you'd think of for Southern comfort food, yet it's the birthplace of Yardbird, a spot that nails down-home cooking. At first glance, it's one of those trendy places with exposed filament lighting and reclaimed wood panels on the walls, but that pretension doesn't harm the food. (They also serve drinks in mason jars, but since they're from the South, we'll give them a pass.) The key dish here is the fried chicken, named for Llewelyn, one of the grandmothers of the original Yardbird owners, and it's purported to be her recipe. The chicken brines for about 27 hours before anybody even thinks about cooking it; then it gets covered in cayenne pepper and deep-fried. You can order the bird alone as a half chicken, or get the whole shebang; it's served with golden brown, cheddar cheese waffles, honey hot sauce, and chow-chow, a sweet and tangy Southern relish. Besides the chicken, they've got a fab version of shrimp and grits, topped with crispy ham. The perfect starter? A set of old school hors d'oeuvres like deviled eggs with smoked trout roe, and a fun BLT with thick-cut bacon and fried green tomatoes. For cocktails, they've created an ice program like no other, infusing cubes with herbs like rosemary and thyme, and freezing the sprigs inside; or adding mustard so that as the ice melts, it adds a savory flavor. It's weird, but I like it, even in a mason jar.

In the Venetian, 3355 Las Vegas Blvd. S. www.runchickenrun.com. ℭ **702/297-6541.** Main courses lunch $15–$36, dinner $18–$65. Daily 11am–11pm.

Inexpensive

Egg Slut ★★★ SANDWICHES   Cosmopolitan has always been good at collecting restaurants with just the right amount of buzz. And few have been buzzier than Egg Slut, the Downtown Los Angeles transplant notorious for its long lines at the Eastern Market. The lines unfortunately translate to Las Vegas, starting around the corner and down a long hallway from the walk-up diner with limited seating. And what are they lining up for? The namesake Egg Slut features a silky, coddled egg resting atop creamy potato puree in a jar (how hipster), served with toasted baguette slices meant for dipping into the jar or spreading. It's all so luscious, rich, and lusty that you can see what's so slutty about it. If you're feeling more demure, a concise menu of egg sandwiches is also worth the wait. The Fairfax features sriracha-tinged, creamy scrambled eggs, while the sausage, egg, and cheese offer just that, as herbed turkey sausage. Eating from jars, waiting in long lines, the constant Instagramming—it's all painfully yet deliciously on-trend.

In the Cosmopolitan of Las Vegas, 3708 Las Vegas Blvd. S. www.eggslut.com. ✆ **702/698-7000.** Main courses $7–$15. Mon–Fri 7am–7pm; Sat–Sun midnight–7pm.

Forum Food Court ★★ FOOD HALL   You might wonder why we'd include a food court in a Vegas guidebook when there are plenty of food courts in malls around the country. To put it mildly: decision fatigue. Sometimes you just want to eat and not think too hard about it, or you just have a taste for one thing but don't want to pay through the nose or sit through a whole experience to get it. Formerly the Cypress Street Marketplace, this assortment of casual eateries got a facelift and a name change and added a few nationally recognized brands: the Halal Guys, Smashburger, Di Fara Pizza from Brooklyn, even La Gloria all the way from San Antonio. Sure, it's fast food, but at least it's not your usual suspects.

In Caesars Palace, 3570 Las Vegas Blvd. S. www.caesarspalace.com. ✆ **702/731-7110.** Most items under $15. Mon, Wed 7am–1am; Tues, Thurs, Sun 7am–3am; Fri–Sat 7am–4:30am.

Fulton Street Food Hall ★★ FOOD HALL   This one *looks* like a food court at first glance, but it's not. And while you order and collect your food yourself, it's also not a buffet since you pay for each dish a la carte. This is Las Vegas's first food hall, one of those vast marketplaces popping up all over the country that focus on quality prepared food (rather than mass volume fare). Here, nine distinct stations specialize in sushi, pizza, noodles, and comfort food. If you're on the go, there are options prepared fresh daily, ready for hungry guests to eat and run. Or stay awhile and build your own meal, like custom pizzas and bento boxes, all made to order.

In Harrah's Las Vegas, 3475 Las Vegas Blvd. S. www.harrahs.com. ✆ **800/214-9110.** Most items start at $9. Daily 24 hrs.

Gordon Ramsay Burger ★★ BURGERS   Gordon Ramsay's got a high-priced steakhouse, a more casual (but still pricey) pub, and then there's Burger, his take on the classic American comfort food. It's set in a *Hell's Kitchen*–themed dining room, with colorful booths and a wall of glass-enclosed fire near the front. Large glossy shots of Ramsay loom over guests throughout the dining room, his arms crossed in the classic chef's pose, ready to judge you (be glad you're not in the kitchen!). The menu comprises more than a dozen burgers from the traditional, like the American, to the uber cheesy—topped with aged provolone, Dublin cheddar, and boursin. We're partial to the Hog Burger, with a patty made of sustainably raised pork, topped with more sharp cheddar, apple-braised pork shank, and cabbage-apple slaw. Shakes are layered concoctions of multiple flavors, like brown butter pecan caramel or crème brûlée. No matter what you think of Ramsay's persona on TV, this is as fun as his food gets.

In Planet Hollywood Resort & Casino, 3667 Las Vegas Blvd. S. www.gordonramsay.com. ✆ **702/785-5462.** Main courses $13–$26. Sun–Thurs 10:30am–midnight; Fri–Sat 10:30am–2am.

Gordon Ramsay Fish & Chips ★ SEAFOOD   His most casual (and smallest) concept so far, the Fish & Chips joint is straight out of the U.K., down to the newspaper wrap for crunchy fillets of fish and copious piles of chips (or French fries, on this side of the pond). Its LINQ location makes it a prime stop for a midday snack, so expect long lines to order at the walk-up counter. Seating is quite limited as well indoors, with some outdoor standing counter for street-side people-watching as you tuck into some of the lightest fish in town. Yes, you can get this same exact dish at his Pub across the street at Caesars Palace, but this version comes with a side of authentic English ambience, just fewer accents.

In the LINQ, 3545 Las Vegas Blvd. S. www.gordonramsay.com. ✆ **702/322-0529.** Entrees $15–$18. Daily 11am–11pm.

Nacho Daddy ★★ MEXICAN   Skip the ultra-touristy chain restaurants for a legit local spot: Nacho Daddy. The 6,000-square-foot restaurant promises as fun and rowdy a time as you'd get in those tourist traps, but this one's owned by bona fide born-and-raised Las Vegans. Nachos are my favorite food group, and Nacho Daddy goes way beyond the toppings on the standard Tex-Mex versions. Extravagant options include lobster and crab for seafood lovers, or Thai chicken or sloppy joes, all stacked properly on mounds of multicolored, crispy tortilla chips. Sports are meant to be enjoyed with nachos, so you won't miss a game thanks to 21 high-def TV screens around the room. There's a live scorpion tank near the front door where you can play "find the scorpion." Or you can cut to the chase and order a Scorpion Shot to your table, which contains one formerly live scorpion that has been marinating in tequila. (Disclaimer: Scorpions from the tank do not go into these shots.)

In Miracle Mile Shops at Planet Hollywood, 3663 Las Vegas Blvd. S. www.nachodaddy. com. ✆ **702/462-5000.** Main courses $14–$25. Sun–Wed 8am–2am; Thurs–Sat 8am–3am.

NORTH STRIP

Expensive

Bazaar Meat ★★★ STEAK   Chef José Andrés is one of the most avant-garde chefs of his generation, yet he manages to translate his whimsy into approachable food for anyone. Bazaar Meat, an offshoot of his Bazaar in Los Angeles, is his take on a Vegas steakhouse. The massive room feels like a hipster hunting lodge, with mounted animal heads on the wall and hanging tapestries. Seating is a mix and match of chairs and love seats, all leather, but not all the same. The centerpiece of the main dining room is an open kitchen with a wood-burning grill, where you can watch the cooks searing off big hunks of meat. At other counters, guests can dine and interact with chefs, like the charcuterie bar where whole legs of *jamón* hang from the window. Interaction is a big concept here—you don't just order oysters, for example. You request them, and a roving oyster server comes to you, pulls one out with a gloved hand, and shucks it for you. One of our favorite starters is the Wagyu beef carpaccio, served wrapped around a breadstick with Parmesan cheese and an onion dipping sauce. Andrés' meat menu focuses on sustainably sourced cuts, most of them from Angus or Wagyu cows, sold by the pound, which explains the exorbitant prices. But there are a few, like a flat iron or skirt steak, that won't break the bank.

In the Sahara, 2535 Las Vegas Blvd. S. www.slslasvegas.com. © **702/761-7757.** Main courses $22–$140. Sun–Thurs 5:30–10pm; Fri–Sat 5:30–11pm.

Costa di Mare ★★★ ITALIAN/SEAFOOD   People used to joke about being afraid to eat seafood in the desert until James Beard Award winner Paul Bartolotta proved there was nothing to laugh about. He left in 2015, and his namesake Bartolotta Ristorante di Mare was handed over to Chef Mark LoRusso; the biggest change was apparently only to the name. The seafood at this two-story restaurant is flown in daily from the Italian Mediterranean, caught by regional fishermen whom the chef has met and recruited himself. When the server swings the glass cart around to your table to show you what's available, you'll be introduced to specimens like dorado, purple snapper, and scorpion fish, all of which have been out of the water for only about 24 hours. Sweet, giant langoustines come from a very specific region near Italy that chefs will not divulge. If you choose one of the whole fish, or the langoustines, you can opt to have it grilled simply with olive oil and lemon, or have the fish baked under a salt crust. With the latter treatment, they bring the finished dish out to you on a cart and crack the hardened mound, releasing the fish. Don't be put off by all the sea salt; the cooking process results in a perfectly seasoned, perfectly cooked fish. Pastas are as divine as the bounty from the sea, and they aren't all dressed with seafood. The ravioli filled with sheep's-milk ricotta and served with pecorino and Marsala wine glaze, and the pappardelle, wide ribbons of pasta with earthy porcini mushrooms, are both eye-rolling good. The price for seafood this fresh and pristine is exorbitant. But if you're going to have one Las Vegas dining splurge in a gorgeous setting with impeccable service, this is one of those times where "you get what you pay for" applies.

In Wynn Las Vegas, 3131 Las Vegas Blvd. S. www.wynnlasvegas.com. © **888/352-3463** or 702/248-3463. Main courses $41–$150. Daily 5:30–10pm.

Sinatra ★★ ITALIAN   As the name suggests, this restaurant is an homage to Ol' Blue Eyes, with giant portraits of him on the wall, and other memorabilia, like his Grammy and his Academy Award for *From Here to Eternity.* (Interestingly, Sinatra himself was an avid home cook. He'd often toil all day on Sundays for a large family dinner, offering dishes like the ones you'd find here.) The fare is homey, with dishes like veal Milanese (crusted and panfried, topped with arugula) and simple pastas like lasagna Bolognese taking

North Strip Restaurants

RESTAURANTS

Bazaar Meat **2**

Costa di Mare **5**

Red 8 **5**

Sinatra **4**

The Steakhouse
at Circus Circus **3**

Top of the World **1**

BUFFETS

Wynn Las Vegas
Buffet **5**

center stage. Should you want to eat "his way," Frank's personal favorites were spaghetti and clams in a fragrant tomato broth, and *osso buco* with creamy risotto Milanese. The soundtrack here, as you'd expect, comes exclusively from the crooner's catalog, but with contemporary covers here and there; you can even purchase a CD of the piped-in music.

In Encore Las Vegas, 3121 Las Vegas Blvd. S. www.wynnlasvegas.com. © **702/248-3463.** Main courses $36–$148. Daily 5:30–10:30pm.

The Steakhouse ★★ STEAK   Despite the unimaginative name, this mainstay at Circus Circus is one of the most underrated steakhouses on the Strip. Open since 1982, this place is about as retro as they come—no renovations here, we're guessing. Probably the only difference between now and when this place opened is that you can't smoke in the dim dining room anymore. As you enter, you're greeted by the dry-aging lockers, where you can peer into the windows to see big hunks of meat aging, creating intensely flavored beef. While many steakhouses on the Strip have a wide variety of options as far as appetizers, starters, and sides—at this classic spot you don't have to make many decisions. You pick your cut of meat, how you want it prepared on the mesquite grill, and you get a choice of potato, and soup or salad. If you feel like you'll want more, there are other starters available, like the hearty French onion soup or the shellfish tower. The prices, unfortunately, didn't stay in the '80s, but dropping around $100 on a full steak dinner for two is one of the best deals you'll find on the Strip these days.

In Circus Circus, 2880 Las Vegas Blvd. S. www.circuscircus.com. ✆ **702/794-3767.** Main courses $40–$82. Sun–Fri 4–10pm; Sat 4–11pm.

Top of the World ★ CONTINENTAL   At nearly 850 feet above the Las Vegas Strip, this revolving restaurant is one of the best perches from which to see the city. The food used to come second but has caught up with the lures of the view. Top of the World has fully embraced being a steakhouse, with ample cuts of meat to choose from, like Wagyu skirt steak or the 60-day-aged bone-in Kansas City strip. It takes nearly 90 minutes for one full revolution of the restaurant. Try to score a table right next to the window so you get the full experience and can watch the daring souls drop off from the Sky Jump platform above.

In the Strat, 2000 Las Vegas Blvd. S. www.topoftheworldlv.com. ✆ **702/380-7777.** Main courses lunch $19–$66, dinner $30–$69. Daily 11am–11pm.

Moderate

Red 8 ★★ ASIAN   This Asian eatery at Wynn is much easier on the wallet than just about every other restaurant in the resort (including the other Chinese restaurant, upscale Wing Lei). Dressed in red, the luckiest color in Asian mythology, it's a funky, intimate spot overlooking the casino floor (undoubtedly with many players hoping the crimson luck reaches them). The menu is predominantly Chinese, with delicate dim sum, roasted ducks, barbecue, and hearty congee, but you can find other regions of Asia represented as well, with Thai-style vermicelli and Malaysian charred rice noodles also on offer. It's not fast food, but it is laid-back, casual, and quick, so you can have a satisfying meal before you head back to the tables.

In Wynn Las Vegas, 3131 Las Vegas Blvd. S. www.wynnlasvegas.com. ✆ **702/770-3380.** Main courses $17–$38. Sun–Thurs 11:30am–midnight; Fri–Sat 11:30am–1am.

DOWNTOWN

Expensive

Andiamo Steakhouse ★★ STEAK/SEAFOOD   When the Detroit-based chain arrived in 2013, it fit right in with the other steakhouses in town, perhaps because it "went native." The outposts in its hometown are more modern and chic; here, they went all-in on the old-school, but upscale, Vegas vibe. The brick-lined hallway evokes walking through a grotto, while tall, high-backed leather booths make cozy date spots. It's a place Dean and Frank would have headed to after a show, had this place been around. The focus is

Downtown Restaurants

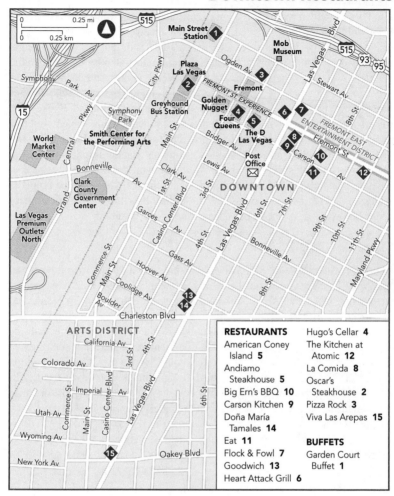

RESTAURANTS

American Coney Island **5**
Andiamo Steakhouse **5**
Big Ern's BBQ **10**
Carson Kitchen **9**
Doña María Tamales **14**
Eat **11**
Flock & Fowl **7**
Goodwich **13**
Heart Attack Grill **6**
Hugo's Cellar **4**
The Kitchen at Atomic **12**
La Comida **8**
Oscar's Steakhouse **2**
Pizza Rock **3**
Viva Las Arepas **15**

BUFFETS

Garden Court Buffet **1**

on steaks from butchers like Pat LaFrieda, each served with a selection of sauces. (I think the signature Zip Sauce, a tangy, herby butter whose exact ingredients the staff won't divulge, is the best choice to go with big cuts like the rib eye and the enormous 24-oz Tomahawk steak.) If you go Italian, you'll understand why this chain has been so popular in Detroit since 1989. With dishes like hearty veal ragù with wide ribbons of pappardelle, and potato gnocchi tossed with wild mushroom and Madeira wine sauce, Andiamo quickly became one of my favorites.

In the D Las Vegas, 301 E. Fremont St. www.thed.com. ✆ **702/388-2220.** Main courses $26–$69. Daily 5–11pm.

Hugo's Cellar ★ CONTINENTAL   Among Downtown restaurants, there are those that want to be cutting edge and cool . . . and then there are places like Hugo's, which will never change. Nor does anyone want it to. As they've been doing since they opened, all women receive a red rose when they descend into the below-street-level restaurant, and the rest of the night includes many other rituals, all of which are orchestrated by the affable and devoted waitstaff. Their duties extend beyond taking and bringing your orders; salads are prepared from a cart they roll up to your table, with choices like shrimp, marinated artichokes, hearts of palm, and chopped eggs, to be tossed with romaine lettuce. They'll also recommend mains, which aren't as exciting as the salad but come with grandiose names like "chicken *champignon*" and "duckling anise *flambé*"—continental standards of a bygone era that have somehow survived here. Desserts are included with your entree, so have the bananas Foster or cherries jubilee, either of which is also prepared tableside and set ablaze (hooray!). Considering how the Las Vegas culinary scene has evolved, it's not a bad idea to see where it started.

In the Four Queens, 202 Fremont St. www.hugoscellar.com. ✆ **702/385-4011.** Main courses $44–$175. Daily 5–10pm.

Oscar's Steakhouse ★★ STEAK   What does a former mob lawyer and mayor of Las Vegas do after he retires? Hizzoner Oscar Goodman opens a steakhouse, of course. And it's like a shrine built to a person who hasn't died yet, including memorabilia and photographs from the 12 years he ruled this city (for what it's worth, his wife, Carolyn, is now the mayor). It also has all the elements of a classic Vegas experience. The menu reads like Goodman's client list, with dishes such as Vinnie F's steakhouse wedge or Crazy Phil's onion soup. Cuts of meat like Joe C's filet and the Spilotro steak (nods to former clients when Goodman was a lawyer) are cooked over 600-degree grills for a nice crust on the outside. He's been called the "Happiest Mayor in the Universe," and we suspect that has to do with his love of martinis. Do as Oscar does and drink a cold, stiff one with dinner. If you're catching a show at the Smith Center nearby, the Plaza and Oscar's offer a shuttle to and from the hotel.

In the Plaza, 1 Main St. www.oscarslv.com. ✆ **702/386-7227.** Main courses $25–$64. Daily 5–10pm.

Moderate

The Kitchen at Atomic ★★ AMERICAN   As the oldest freestanding bar in Las Vegas, Atomic Liquors has managed to keep itself relevant, and that means going with the ebbs and flows of Downtown. Now that the area is on the upswing, it seemed like the perfect time to add a restaurant. But just because the bar is from 1945 doesn't mean the restaurant had to be. Salty little nibbles such as a charcuterie board with candied fruit, nuts, and pickles whet your appetite, but those more adventurous might dig the roasted bone marrow with pomegranate vinaigrette, or the fresh hamachi crudo hit with a little chili and lime juice, all of which are ideal with one of the craft beers on tap. The restaurant has a separate entrance from the bar itself, but it's become commonplace to start your evening at the Kitchen and end up at the bar for (more) drinks after.

927 Fremont St. (at 10th St.). www.kitchenatomic.vegas. ✆ **702/534-3223.** Reservations recommended. Main courses $14–$32. Wed and Sun 5–11pm; Thurs–Sat 5pm–midnight.

La Comida ★★ MEXICAN   After passing on ownership of N9NE Steakhouse at the Palms, in 2013 local restaurateurs Michael and Jenna Morton set their sights on Downtown and their first Mexican restaurant. It's a very Vegas sort of place, in that Downtown restaurants don't want to appear like they're in Las Vegas at all. The dim eatery opens to a rustic dining room, featuring dark woods, plaster, brick-exposed walls, and Day of the Dead, Santeria-inspired decor. A walk-up window outside allows bartenders to serve guests who don't have the time to stop in. The menu goes above and beyond what you'd expect from a neighborhood Mexican joint, including full-roasted sea bass prepared Veracruz-style with onions, olives, and chilies, and marinated beef steak with nopales, or prickly pear fruit, and roasted poblano peppers. Of course, there are also tacos on the menu, with toothsome fillings like chicken with salsa verde and avocado. The margarita list includes an impressive selection of tequilas on which to base the fresh fruit flavors.

100 Sixth Ave. (btw. Fremont St. and Carson Ave.). www.lacomidalv.com. ✆ **702/463-9900.** Main courses $15–$25. Mon–Thurs 11:30am–11pm; Fri–Sat 11:30am–2am.

Pizza Rock ★★ PIZZA   Las Vegas used to be a not-very-good pizza town, but that's slowly changing. When Tony Gemignani brought his California-based Pizza Rock to Las Vegas in 2013, he didn't just bring one style of pizza with him—he brought all of them. Gemignani, who is an 11-time World Pizza Champion, installed five different types of electric, gas, and wood-burning ovens to be able to prepare 10 different regional styles of pizza. There's the proper Napolitana-style pizza, with a chewy, blistered crust (this is the one that earned him a few awards); they only make a set amount of dough for this pizza each day, so when they're out, they're out. The rectangular Roman pies are long enough to warrant three different sections of toppings on them. New York pizza lovers are represented as well, along with Detroit and New Haven, CT. And we like that instead of trying to tackle Chicago deep dish, he went the opposite direction, making cracker-thin crust that can be topped with traditional ingredients like fennel-laced sausage. As for the ambience: The music is loud, and as the name suggests, rock-heavy, and there's a curious half-cab of a semi-truck that anchors one side of the dining room, which also serves as the DJ booth. A second Pizza Rock location opened at Green Valley Ranch, with Little Tony's at Palace Station for a closer slice.

201 N. Third St. (at Ogden Ave.). www.pizzarocklasvegas.com. ✆ **702/385-0838.** Main courses $10–$25. Mon–Thurs 11am–midnight; Fri–Sat 11am–2am; Sun 10am–midnight.

Inexpensive

American Coney Island ★ DELI/HOT DOGS   Despite its name, this legendary restaurant came from Detroit, not New York, though the hot dog–heavy menu does suggest boardwalk fare. The original was opened in 1917 by a Greek immigrant who put chili, onions, and mustard on a griddled link, thereby creating a regional style of hot dog. The descendants of this gentleman finally expanded their brand to Las Vegas and the hotel that is closely associated with its hometown. The menu is small, but so is the one in Detroit; it includes the namesake hot dog, topped with the classic, no-bean chili that has a hint of cinnamon, and a Midwestern-style lamb gyro, with proper, homemade tzatziki yogurt sauce as dressing. Being happily fed for under $10 makes the grub all that tastier.

In the D Las Vegas, 301 E. Fremont St. www.thed.com. ℂ **702/388-2400.** Main courses under $5. Daily 24 hr.

Big Ern's BBQ ★★ BARBECUE   Barbecue is such a divisive topic that true connoisseurs refuse to believe that it can be properly made outside of the South. Add to that the fact that Big Ern himself is from California, and 'cue aficionados grow even more skeptical. But once you smell the smoke from his brisket or pulled pork, you'll know this is the real deal. Ern's shop in Downtown Container Park is small, but packs 'em in. Diners clamor not only for the brisket here, but also for chicken, hot links, and ribs, all served with a sweet sauce that's more molasses than Kansas City. It's also rare to find a BBQ joint outside the Midwest that serves rib tips, but here they can be added on to any rib dinner. Complete your meal with classic sides like pork and beans, coleslaw, or a baked potato, make your way to a spot in the park, and enjoy a barbecue feast that won't make you miss the South. If you find yourself north of Downtown, Big Ern's has also set up shop at Fiesta Rancho.

In Downtown Container Park, 707 Fremont St. (at 7th St.). www.bigernsbbq.com. ℂ **702/834-7845.** Main courses $7–29. Sun–Thurs 11am–10pm; Fri–Sat 11am–11pm.

Carson Kitchen ★★ AMERICAN   The late chef Kerry Simon built his culinary empire all over Vegas, starting at Hard Rock, then the Palms, and a few other spots, but this is his crowning achievement. It's a two-story, relaxed, neighborhood restaurant—something that restaurateurs all over the city are desperately trying to replicate—serving up contemporary, seasonal, and addictive, comfort food. A starter of crispy chicken skins comes with a small dose of smoky honey, and you'll eat them like potato chips. The "butter burger" is just as fun, served with creamy boursin and cheddar, and yes, cooked in a healthy dose of butter. But don't worry, the menu's not all calorie bombs. One of the best dishes we've ever eaten was Carson Kitchen's spicy ragù of rabbit, served with spaghetti squash—something that healthy should never be that delicious. The cocktail program includes thoughtful, multifaceted drinks that run the gamut from clean and fruity to smoky. Grab a seat at

save YOURSELF

the counter and watch the chefs in the open kitchen, and keep an eye on the "swear jar" to see how they're doing.

124 S. 6th St. (at Carson Ave.). www.carsonkitchen.com. ✆ **702/473-9523.** Main courses $10–$19. Sun–Wed 11:30am–10pm; Thurs–Sat 11:30am–11pm.

Doña María Tamales ★ MEXICAN   For more than 30 years, this stand-alone restaurant has been the house that tamales built. Situated between the Strip and Downtown, it's a convenient location when you need a proper Mexican fix. Its expansive menu features all of Mexico's greatest hits: ample platters of tacos, burritos, enchiladas and, my favorite, handmade tamales (unwrap the corn husk to reveal packets of masa filled with pork, chicken, cheese, or beef, or in the dessert version, pineapples, and raisins). The chili rellenos are dauntingly big, but getting every bite down won't be a problem because they're so good. Dinners come as full-on meals, complete with rice, beans, soup or salad, and tortillas.

910 Las Vegas Blvd. S. (at Charleston Blvd.). www.donamariatamales.com. ✆ **702/382-6538.** Main courses breakfast and lunch $11–$18, dinner $10–$22. Daily 8am–10pm.

Eat ★★ AMERICAN   Eat was one of the first restaurants to open during the recent period of gentrification Downtown, and fortunately, has managed to stay open, unlike others in its class. Chef Natalie Young cut her teeth at restaurants on the Strip for many years before finding this opportunity in 2012. She created a restaurant she knew the area needed; a place that doesn't seem like it belongs in Las Vegas at all. The storefront features funky decor, local art, and an herb garden near the front, welcoming guests in to dine. Only open for breakfast and lunch, the place always seems to be bumping with guests there for her Southern-influenced fare. Shrimp and grits are outstanding, and hearty egg dishes like the flavorful truffled egg sandwich with chives, feta, and bacon are served all day. For lunch, I'm a huge fan of the classic Reuben sandwich, along with the shrimp po'boy with spicy kimchi slaw. Brunch is worth the wait, especially for the beignets blanketed in powdered sugar; but note that since Eat has live music and the space is small, you might be shouting to be heard by the person next to you.

707 Carson Ave. (at 7th Ave.). www.eatdtlv.com. ☎ **702/534-1515.** Main courses $11–$16. Mon–Fri 8am–3pm; Sat–Sun 8am–2pm.

Flock & Fowl ★★★ ASIAN   You may be wondering why I'm sending you to Downtown Las Vegas for boiled chicken and rice. What if I were to tell you this was the best chicken and rice you'll probably have in the United States? It's not just chicken and rice, of course, but Hainanese chicken and rice, an Asian comfort food that sounds simple but is far from easy to make and perfect when done correctly. Restaurants in Singapore have cult followings for this dish alone. Chef Sheridan Su, who cut his chops at Strip restaurants such as Joël Robuchon before striking out on his own (he also owns the fun Fat Choy in the Eureka casino), fell in love with the humble dish when he and his wife (who works behind the counter) were traveling in Asia, and decided to open a restaurant serving just that. Organic chicken is poached until cooked to the proper texture and temperature, and the broth is used to cook the fragrant rice. It's served with traditional condiments all made in-house, like garlic, ginger, and scallions minced in oil, sweet soy sauce, and spicy sambal. Everyone doctors their chicken and rice, sometimes customizing it with every bite. The restaurant has a full cocktail bar and other options such as a fine steak, but it's still not uncommon for them to sell out of the chicken. It's that good.

150 N. Las Vegas Blvd. (at Ogden Ave.). www.flockandfowl.com. ☎ **702/983-4880.** Entrees $10–$26. Sun–Thurs 11am–11pm; Fri–Sat 11am–midnight.

Goodwich ★ SANDWICHES   Originally housed in a weird little kiosk outside of a local dive bar, Dino's, Goodwich quickly made a name for itself with excellent, reasonably priced gourmet sandwiches. The brick-and-mortar space means prices have slightly gone up, but the sandwiches are just as fantastic. Starting at $6.50, Goodwich offers bites like the thick-cut ham, cheddar, and greens with a tangy mostarda, or an egg salad sammie with crispy chorizo. A nice innovation is the BTLG (bacon, tomato, lettuce, and pimento cheese grits). The Reuben-ish features house-made corned beef that's stacked with Swiss and fennel sauerkraut, dressed with a luscious Thousand Island sauce.

900 Las Vegas Blvd. S. www.thegoodwich.com. ☎ **702/910-8681.** Sandwiches $6.50–$12. Mon–Sat 11am–6pm.

Viva Las Arepas ★★ VENEZUELAN   Las Vegas strip malls are home to some of the best holes-in-the-wall we've got. Take Viva Las Arepas, which began in the kiosk now occupied by Goodwich and gained such a following it needed a bigger kitchen and a dining room. If you've never eaten the

Venezuelan street snack, arepas are savory, griddled cornmeal cakes stuffed with a wide variety of ingredients. I prefer them chock-full, as in the *Reina Pepiada,* which has chicken breast, avocados, mayo, and cilantro. Vegetarians can opt for vegetables, black beans, or cheese, or all three. Other than the arepas, the roasted, marinated chicken is a big seller here, cooked over mesquite wood for nice char and flavor. Add in a few authentic sides, like fried yucca or plantain, for a tasty but inexpensive, meal.

1616 Las Vegas Blvd. S. (at Oakey Blvd.). www.vivalasarepas.com. ℂ **702/366-9696.** Main courses $4–$15. Sun–Thurs 8am–10pm, Fri–Sat 8am–midnight.

JUST OFF THE STRIP

Expensive

MB Steak ★★ STEAKHOUSE This spot from Morton Hospitality, which has other hits such as Crush at MGM and La Comida Downtown, marks the first time that the Morton brothers, David and Michael, have actually done a restaurant together, the MB standing for "My Brothers." It's sexy and cool, a great fit for Hard Rock. And it's massive. At 7,800 square feet, the restaurant spans two floors, with not only a private dining room upstairs but also a fantastic view of the Stip. On the main floor, try to score one of the round corner booths so you have the full view of the room; this seat also happens to help you look like a high roller. The menu also makes you feel pretty rich, especially with starters such as charred Spanish octopus, or caviar, stacked atop three blinis and crème fraîche like a mini slider. Steaks are prepared only with salt, pepper, and a bit of oil before they take a turn under a 1200-degree broiler for the perfect crust—you don't need much more when the beef is this good. If you have the good fortune of meeting longtime Morton Group host John O'Donnell when you're there—he's the Irish guy with the light brogue who is greeting everyone like he's the mayor—it's going to be a good night. He'll not only steer you toward what he thinks are the best options are for the evening cocktail- and food-wise, but he also makes everyone he talks to feel like a VIP.

In the Hard Rock Hotel, 4455 Paradise Rd. (at Harmon Ave.). www.mbsteaklv.com. ℂ **702/483-4888.** Main courses $28–$160. Nightly 5pm–close.

Pamplemousse ★ FRENCH It doesn't get a lot of play in the press these days, but Pamplemousse is still very much a part of the Las Vegas landscape. Set in a low-slung building on East Sahara, the restaurant has been around since 1976, and was once the epitome of fine dining in town. Outside, it looks like something you might find in the French countryside. Inside, it's as though time has stood still, and you're transported to Vegas in the late 1970s: low ceilings, round red booths, and a domed Tiffany ceiling above the main dining room. Although the building and interiors have seen better days, the food is as elegant as ever, starting with a mandatory starter of *crudités* (raw vegetables), with the house-made vinaigrette. Most of the menu derives from Provence, like the rack of spring lamb with crusted pistachios, served with a light rosemary sauce. In an era when many chefs are creating their presentations with tweezers and microgreens, Pamplemousse plates each dish in the continental style, with its sauce and a simple side garnish. The food doesn't need more than that. Plus it's dark, so you can't see much anyway.

400 E. Sahara Ave. (btw. Santa Paula and Santa Rita drives, just east of Paradise Rd.). www.pamplemousselerestaurant.com. ☎ **702/733-2066.** Main courses $24–$42. Tues–Sun 5–10:30pm.

Piero's Italian Cuisine ★★ ITALIAN
A beloved Las Vegas institution, Piero's has been a longtime hangout for Vegas bigwigs from every industry—Rat Packers, hotel bosses, performers, and even folks they refer to as "casino industry businessmen," which is a nice way of not calling them mob guys. On any given night, you can still see local execs and politicians having dinner around the tables with their families. The rule of the house: Everybody gets to eat in peace, so even if you see a celebrity, play it cool. You might recognize the dining room from the 1995 film *Casino,* which shot several scenes with Joe Pesci, Robert De Niro, and Sharon Stone in the low, leather booths here. To encourage a convivial atmosphere, bartenders are heavy-handed with what they call a "stiff pour." The menu has stayed essentially the same since Piero's first opened in 1982, if only because the Glusman family who runs it has a very "if it ain't broke, don't fix it" attitude. Favorites include the chef's special veal scaloppini, pounded thin and tender, then battered and covered with prosciutto and cheese, and linguine *alla vongole,* or with clams, a favorite of Sinatra's whenever he came in. If guests who have been coming in for 35 years don't need a change, neither do we.

355 Convention Center Dr. www.pieroscuisine.com. ☎ **702/369-2305.** Main courses $32–$49. Daily 5:30–10pm.

Scotch 80 Prime ★★ STEAK
As part of the Palms' nearly $700-million renovation, the hotel did away with beloved N9NE Steakhouse and transformed it into Scotch 80 Prime, a place that basks in its 21st century aesthetic. The gold-accented, dark-wood room is at once intimate yet opulent, surrounding you with works by Damien Hirst, Basquiat, and Andy Warhol, though Scott Hove's frosted cake–inspired art installation will catch you by surprise when you stumble upon it. (Hint: It's not in the dining room.) Many steakhouse classics are done exceptionally well, but as far as beef goes, the chef-recommended cap of rib eye is where it's at. As for drink, this place *is* called Scotch 80 Prime, so whisky is a must. If you don't take it neat, then try it from the cocktail cart, where your custom Manhattan or old-fashioned is made tableside, with whichever luxurious brown spirit moves you.

In the Palms, 4321 W. Flamingo Rd. (at Arville St.). www.palms.com. ☎ **702/942-7777.** Reservations recommended. Main courses $29–$168. Sun–Thurs 5–10pm; Fri–Sat 5pm–midnight.

Restaurants Beyond the Strip

RESTAURANTS

Alder & Birch **9**	Lotus of Siam **13**	Pamplemousse **3**	**BUFFETS**
Capriotti's **2**	M&M Soul Food **1**	Piero's Italian Cuisine **4**	Carnival World &
EDO Gourmet	Mabel's BBQ **10**	Ping Pang Pong **11**	Seafood Buffet **12**
Tapas **5**	MB Steak **14**	Raku Grill **7**	Ports O'Call **11**
Greene St.	Naked City Pizza **16**	Scotch 80 Prime **10**	
Kitchen **10**	Other Mama **6**	Sparrow + Wolf **8**	
Hofbräuhaus **15**			

Moderate

Alder & Birch ★★ STEAK   As you're navigating your way through the Mardi Gras–themed Orleans casino to find this steakhouse, it might help to know that Alder & Birch looks completely out of place. In stark contrast to the garish holiday decor, the restaurant has a modern facade and floor-to-ceiling windows separated by tall wooden panels. Inside, away from the madness of the casino floor, the surprise continues, with a downright sleek dining room in a mix of neutral colors and natural and industrial finishes. The menu is classic for a contemporary Vegas steakhouse, with intriguing selections such as watermelon salad with goat cheese and sea salt, and beef carpaccio with arugula, mustard, and capers. I was pleased to learn that the raw oysters came from New Orleans, as sort of proof that Alder & Birch knows exactly where it is. The dry-aged Wagyu sirloin looks tempting, but for more bang for your buck (which you can get quite a lot of here), the rib eye makes more sense for serious carnivores. The other nice touch is the craft beer selection on tap—several from local brewery Joseph James—plus a thoughtful cocktail list.

In the Orleans, 4500 W. Tropicana Ave. (at Arville St.). www.orleanscasino.com. ℂ **702/365-7111.** Reservations recommended. Main courses $26–$70. Sun–Thurs 5–9pm; Fri–Sat 5–10pm.

bBd's Burgers, Beers, Desserts ★★ BURGER

One of the best things to come out of the Palace Station renovation in 2018 is the addition of this burger joint, decked out with an open kitchen, high, arched ceilings, and black-and-tan leather decor. Chef Ralph Perazzo cut his teeth in Vegas as a pastry chef at the venerated Bradley Ogden and was named a Rising Star Pastry Chef in 2005. When he opened the original bBd's in New York, he proved he's got the savory skills to match. bBd's gets their prime beef in large format, butchering and grinding it to make all the patties in-house. (You can watch this process as you walk in past the glass windows of the butchering room.) This way they can control the fat-to-meat ratio to ensure that every burger is up to their juicy, flavorful standard. You choose one of three cooking methods—grilled over cherrywood and charcoal flames, griddled on a flat top like at In-N-Out, or steamed over chopped onions and pickles à la White Castle. And though there's no "W" in the name, the wings are not to be missed, as they're cooked confit in chicken fat and tossed with Buffalo sauce. Non-carnivores appreciate the extensive vegan and vegetarian options, including those Impossible burger patties that are all the rage.

Now back to the first B: beers. A custom, high-tech draft system shuttles 26 beers to the taps on the long, imposing bar, including some nitro and cask brews. There's a big focus on sours, as well as vintage and rare finds, and the list is constantly rotating. Desserts were Perazzo's first passion, and he hasn't let that go. Classic finishes like peanut butter or chocolate chip cookies keep things casual, but a gooey Cinnabomb topped with house-made coffee ice cream is the real winner.

In Palace Station, 2411 W. Sahara Ave. (at Harmon Ave.). www.eatbbds.com. ℂ **702/221-6513.** Main courses $12–$39. Sun–Thurs 11am–10pm; Fri–Sat 11am–11pm.

EDO Gastro Tapas & Wine ★ SPANISH

José Andrés may get all the buzz for Spanish cuisine with his Jaleo on the Strip, but that comes with all the glitz and glamour of the Boulevard. Anyone who's ever eaten in Spain will be much more familiar with the vibe at EDO, about a 10-minute drive from Andrés' palace. EDO—which stands for Extra Day Off in hospitality speak—has made a name for itself among the restaurant industry elite. It's a hot spot for chefs to duck into for small bites and a gin and tonic or three after their shifts on the Strip, so you know it has to be good. Classic Spanish tapas get touches of elevated and Asian flair, such as familiar *croquetas* served with a kimchi aioli, or the smoked salmon *montadito,* adorned with truffled cream cheese and honey. There's also a playfulness to this food: tweezers to pick up paper-thin slices of *jamón iberico;* paella that finishes sizzling its soccarat (the caramelized bottom crust) at the table, timed by a sand hourglass. If this whimsy seems familiar, you can thank the general manager, who came from Bazaar Meat, another well-known, playful Andrés joint. Gin and tonics, a staple of the Spanish tapas hour, are prepared with aromatic infused gins made in-house, and served from a classic cart.

3400 S. Jones Blvd., Ste. 11A. www.edotapascom. © **702/641-1345.** Reservations recommended. Tapas $6–$14; paella $23–$25. Sun–Thurs 5–11pm; Fri–Sat 5pm–1am.

Greene St. Kitchen ★★ ECLECTIC   If you don't know that you're looking for Greene St. Kitchen, chances are you probably won't even know it's here. The entrance is disguised as an '80s video arcade with actual working games, but are those splits of Moët et Chandon sparkling rosé stocked in a vending machine? (Indeed, yes.) Right next to it is the hidden entrance to the restaurant, disguised as an industrial refrigerator door. The art inside is worth a tour, but the food actually lives up to the excitement of the decor. You'll walk through a hallway reminiscent of New York subway street art before you even get to the Banksy on the wall. Most of the art was commissioned for the restaurant, including colorful murals by such pop artists as Kenny Scharf and DabsMyla, a three-dimensional wall installation etched by Portuguese street artist Vhils, and a golden birdcage surrounding the lounge bar. And about that menu: It's an eclectic mix of small plates, handheld bites, and cutesy entrées, all appealing to the young, good-looking crowd of snap-happy diners. Sliders, mini lobster rolls, and sushi hand rolls are fine, and there are a few thoughtful vegan options. Decadent items hit all the right notes, such as the Legs and Eggs, a starter of butter-poached king crab legs topped with caviar, or the Big Ass! Stuffed Lobster (their name, not ours), a contemporary take on a thermidor, with lump crab and Ritz crackers. Because that's how you top a meal after a champagne vending machine, a giant golden birdcage, and a Banksy on the wall.

In the Palms, 4321 W. Flamingo Rd. (at Arville St.). www.palms.com. © **702/942-7777.** Reservations recommended. Main courses $22–$78. Mon–Wed 5–10pm; Thurs–Sun 5–11pm.

Hofbräuhaus ★ GERMAN   If the name—and the looks—of this restaurant are familiar, that's because it's a Madame Tussauds–worthy replica of the famed beer hall in Munich (the one that's been around for 4 centuries). The food is *sehr* German, including schnitzel, strudel, and wurst, but the real treats are from the *schmankerl* (which means "treat") section. Sauerbraten cooked in red wine is the Bavarian equivalent of pot roast, *jägerschnitzel* is a hunter's dish of a pork cutlet topped with mushrooms, bacon, onion, and *spaetzle* (dumplings). It's all hearty, all meaty, and all meant to be eaten with a cold brew while listening to live polka and oompah bands. The beer, it turns out, tastes this authentic because it's brewed at the original site and imported here, so even the Dunkel and Hefeweizen are the real deal. In case you can't make it to Germany, the Oktoberfest here, like in Munich, starts in September, with parties every week featuring local Vegas celebrities in keg-tapping ceremonies.

4150 Paradise Rd. (at Harmon Ave.). www.hofbrauhauslasvegas.com. © **702/853-2337.** Main courses $10–$25. Sun–Thurs 11am–11pm; Fri–Sat 11am–midnight.

Mabel's BBQ ★★ BARBECUE   Though the multilevel dining room of chef Michael Symon's restaurant feels cavernous, the BBQ feels quite cozy and down-home. Symon respects his meat, using humanely raised animals and smoking them all in-house as different styles of American 'cue. Pork spareribs are dressed with Memphis-style dry rub with sauce on the side, or sauced as they do in Kansas City, using the chef's own blend of sweetish barbecue sauce. Slabs of pork belly are cured with pastrami spices, while kielbasa can be had as a traditional sausage or flavored with spicy cheddar. Order your meats by the half-pound so that your inner carnivore doesn't feel like you're missing out. Salt and vinegar cracklings are a savory, crunchy way to wake up your palate before the onslaught of meat. As so many restaurants are doing now, meats are served on utilitarian metal half-sheet trays, while stiff, bottle-aged cocktails are poured tableside and meant to be shared by two thirsty patrons. Sara's, the fine-dining speakeasy within Mabel's, features classic continental dishes served with a touch of vintage Vegas glamour.

In the Palms, 4321 W. Flamingo Rd. (at Arville St.). www.palms.com. © **702/944-5931.** Reservations recommended. Main courses $12–$50. Mon–Wed 11:30am–10pm; Thurs–Sat 11:30am–midnight; Sun 11:30am–2pm.

Ping Pang Pong ★★ CHINESE   When high rollers jet in from Asia, this is usually the first place they head for a meal. In fact, the vast majority of the clientele is from that corner of the globe, because it's nearly impossible to find Chinese fare this authentic elsewhere in Las Vegas. A lot of the menu is Cantonese—noodle soups, barbecue meats, roasted duck, and clay pots stuffed with rice and other meaty bits—but other regions are represented as well. One of our favorite times to go is for dim sum brunch, when the steam carts piled high with bamboo and metal containers are pushed around the room. The caliber of dim sum here is close to what I've eaten in Hong Kong, especially the fresh *har gow* (shrimp dumplings with translucent wrappers), the long rolls of rice noodles, and the dense, steamed meatballs with cilantro. It's also a popular late-night dining spot.

In the Gold Coast Hotel & Casino, 4000 W. Flamingo Rd. www.goldcoastcasino.com. © **702/367-7111.** Reservations recommended. Main courses $12–$22. Daily 10am–3pm, 5pm–3am.

Inexpensive

Capriotti's ★ SANDWICHES   Originally from Delaware, this smallish chain (only in about 15 other states, so it's no Subway, thankfully) has had a hold on Las Vegas ever since it opened here in 1993. The storefront isn't much to look at, but that's okay when you've got enormous sandwiches to dig into. Most popular is "the Bobbie," with its combination of thick-cut turkey, stuffing, and cranberry sauce, reminiscent of your favorite Thanksgiving leftovers. I'm more partial to the Capistrami, a pseudo-Reuben made with hot pastrami, Swiss cheese, Russian dressing, and coleslaw. If that's too much stuff on a sandwich for you, the submarine options have more classic combinations, like Italian deli meats, or ham and cheese. The turkey and beef are all roasted in-house. The perfect bread—nice and soft, but with the proper integrity so that it doesn't disintegrate under the weight of multiple toppings—is also made in-house. There are several outposts throughout the Valley, but this is the closest to the Strip.

322 W. Sahara Ave. (at Las Vegas Blvd. S.). www.capriottis.com. © **702/474-0229.** Most regular sandwiches under $10. Mon–Sat 10am–8pm; Sun 11am–7pm.

Lotus of Siam ★★★ THAI   The grand pooh-bah of the city's international restaurants, once named the "Single Best Thai Restaurant in North America" (by the late, great *Gourmet* magazine), and winner of the James Beard "Best Chef in the Southwest" award in 2011, the venerable Lotus of Siam remains one of the city's best-reviewed, best-loved restaurants. Its digs since 2017 have high ceilings, more natural tones, and artistic nods to Thai culture, a modern upgrade this beloved restaurant deserved. If you come late at lunchtime, you'll likely be upset that the buffet is one of diminishing returns, as it doesn't get refilled when the food runs out. But to really get why foodies drive over from L.A. regularly just to dine here (and I know a couple who do), put yourself in your capable server's hands—or even better, ask for Penny, Chutima's daughter. They will know what's best that day, and likely steer you towards the Saipin (Northern) Thai specialties that really make this place unique. As an example: *Nua Dad Deaw,* a dry fried beef, almost like a lime-infused beef jerky, is so addictive, I save the leftovers to munch in my car the next day. Or the *Nam Kao Tod,* a wonderfully tart sausage, dry in texture, nutty, minty, and sided by crispy deep-fried rice. Or the jackfruit curry with smoked fish. Really, ignore what I'm writing here, and go with what the family recommends. Just be sure to tell them how much spice you can take, and don't overestimate your tolerance; the kitchen will sear your tongue off if you ask for it hot. Lotus is constantly adding to its stellar wine program, heavy on Rieslings and other vintages that pair well with spicy cuisine.

620 E Flamingo Rd. www.lotusofsiamlv.com. © **702/735-3033.** Main courses $10–$29. Mon–Fri 11am–2:30pm, 5:30–10pm; Sat–Sun 5:30–10pm.

Naked City Pizza ★ PIZZA   It turns out Buffalo isn't just known for its chicken wings. The chef here, who started out at a casino on the Strip before breaking out on his own, was born and raised in upstate New York, and he's introduced Las Vegas to his regional pie, made in rectangular pans like Sicilian-style, but with a thinner crust. Yes, you can order it by the slice (which are pretty sizable), but a slice of cheese can be had anywhere on the Strip. What you're going for at Naked City are the specialty pizzas, like the Stinger, topped with chicken fingers, steak, mozzarella, and cheddar and bleu cheese, plus sweet and hot peppers. Or the Fat Boy, a red sauce meat-lover's dream with salami, pepperoni, ham, and Italian sausage. If you're going big, know that they come in three sizes: Wee, Not So Wee, and Frickin' Huge (translated from Buffalo, New York, parlance, that's a quarter sheet pan, a half sheet pan, and a full sheet pan, respectively). And yes, they've got wings, too.

4608 Paradise Rd. (at E. Naples Dr.). www.nakedcitylv.com. © **702/722-2241.** Pizzas $15–$38. Sun–Thurs 11am–11pm; Fri–Sat 11am–1am.

NORTH & WEST OF THE STRIP
Moderate

M&M Soul Food ★★ SOUL FOOD   Despite all the famous chefs who are trying to recreate their versions of comfort food, finding true soul food in Las Vegas isn't easy. Especially when you have to trek off the Strip to get it. Originally, you had to head to a potentially sketchy neighborhood, but M&M added a second location just behind the Strat. Admittedly, this area is only marginally nicer, but at least it's closer. M&M looks like a greasy spoon diner from the outside, but inside there's a menu of no-nonsense, stick-to-your-ribs fare that begins with an order of mini–cornbread pancakes delivered to every table. The smothered chicken will make you rethink your cholesterol levels, but with gravy like that you can't say no. Finding oxtails not in a soup in Las Vegas is hard, but here they're also covered with luscious gravy instead of broth. Collard greens, fried okra, and mac and cheese are mandatory as sides if you want the full experience. Dishes like liver and onions and chitterlings are other faves, and as well-prepared as they are south of the Mason-Dixon line.

3923 W. Charleston. www.mmsoulfoodcafe.net. © **702/453-7685.** 2211 Las Vegas Blvd. S. © **702/478-5767.** Main courses $9–$19. Daily Sun–Thurs 8am–9pm; Fri–Sat 8am–10pm.

Other Mama ★★★ ASIAN   Part of the allure of Other Mama was that its innovative chef, Dan Krohmer, had never even cooked in town before. Unlike the handful of other Strip-chefs-turned-local-favorites, Krohmer was an alum of the original Morimoto in Philly before making his mark in Vegas on his own. But boy, he made a great first impression. The Japanese-influenced menu features a lot from the raw bar, such as fresh crudo of amberjack accented with ponzu salsa, or a crazy good spicy tuna tartare served with waffle fries. He tops his deviled eggs with fried oysters, and masters comfort food like kimchi fried rice loaded up with pork belly and fried egg. The cocktail program is worth the trip alone, and bellying up to the bar for well-prepared drinks paired with a small plate or two is common. His eatery has become one of the cool, low-key spots hardcore local food lovers will drive across town for, a big indicator that you should, too.

3655 S. Durango. www.othermamalv.com. © **702/463-8382.** Small plates $9–$16 main courses $15–$28. Daily 5–11pm.

Raku Grill ★★★ JAPANESE   If you're one of those travelers who insist on knowing where chefs go to eat in their own towns, look no further than Raku. This tiny restaurant in an unassuming strip mall in Chinatown has earned a reputation for being one of the best restaurants in Las Vegas under the care of Chef Mitsuo Endo. He was a semifinalist in both 2014 and 2015 for the James Beard "Best Chef in the Southwest" award and has also earned plaudits from a number of outlets. Because Raku is so small and popular, reservations (which you can only make by calling) are mandatory, although if you're lucky you can catch a seat at the bar in front of the kitchen. While there are some raw options, this isn't a sushi joint, but rather a *robata* grill, where most items are cooked over clean-burning *binchotan* charcoal on skewers. There are conventional bites, like Kobe beef filet and duck glazed with balsamic soy sauce, but more adventurous eaters will love the Kurobuta pork cheek, beef tendon, and foie gras with a soy glaze. One of our favorites is the bacon-wrapped enoki mushrooms, crunchy fungi held together by a thin, nicely rendered piece of salty pork belly. Raku also make its own tofu, best enjoyed cold and dressed at the table with soy sauce. Individually, the skewers—which come one or two to an order—are inexpensive, but order enough of them and it can add up. There are exceptional desserts, like a green tea crème brûlée and the weird, but tasty, custardlike bubbling brown sugar. For Endo's take on the end to the meal, head across the way to Raku Sweets, which offers a full tasting menu solely of confections.

5030 W. Spring Mountain Rd., no. 2 (at Decatur). www.raku-grill.com. ⓒ **702/367-3511.** Reservations required. *Robata* grill items $3–$18. Mon–Sat 6pm–3am.

Sparrow + Wolf ★★★ ECLECTIC   A quick Uber ride down Spring Mountain Road brings you to this dining darling that has both visitors and locals vying for a table. The sleek, but intimate restaurant has earned itself a reputation as not only one of the hottest restaurants in town, but also as an after-hours clubhouse for the restaurant industry elite. Go late enough and you may find yourself rubbing elbows and sipping a cocktail next to chefs who have just finished their own shifts on the Strip. Chef Brian Howard's almost manic menu straddles varying cuisines that have influenced his culinary style. Chinatown Clams Casino sports Chinese sausage with uni hollandaise in homage to the classic Vegas dish, plus the restaurant's neighborhood. Beef cheek and bone marrow dumplings offer an elevated taste of Howard's Midwestern roots. The cuisine may come across as complicated if words like "salted plum crème fraîche" or "barbecue salsify" don't excite you, but I assure you the dishes are as approachable as they are surprising.

4480 W. Spring Mountain Rd., Ste. 100 (at Arville). www.sparrowandwolflv.com. ⓒ **702/790-2147.** Reservations required. Entrees $15–$42. Nightly 5–11pm.

sweet SENSATIONS

Plenty of opportunities exist in Vegas for satisfying your sweet tooth, but for the discriminating, here are five spots you may have to make a detour for.

Bellagio Patisserie ★★★ in Bellagio, 3600 Las Vegas Blvd. S. (www.bellagio.com; ✆ **702/693-8788**), makes me swoon, mostly because I am always still mesmerized by the world's largest chocolate fountain. (It's 20 ft. high! Though only 11 ft. are on view, and they won't let us drink from it. Darn!) From perfect gourmet chocolates, to ice cream, to diet-conscious sorbets, to the eponymous pastries, each of which is a little work of art, I hit greed overload. For me, this is true Vegas decadence—if only "what happens in Vegas, stays in Vegas" applied to calories. The patisserie also serves some solidly good sandwiches, and some adequate savory crepes. It is open Monday through Thursday from 6am to 11pm and Friday through Sunday from 6am until midnight.

There's a second location inside Aria Las Vegas, but they don't have the chocolate fountain.

A local favorite for decades is **Freed's Bakery ★**, 9815 S. Eastern Ave., at Silverado Ranch Blvd. (www.freedsbakery.com; ✆ **702/456-7762**), open Monday through Thursday from 9am to 8pm, Friday and Saturday from 8am to 8pm, and Sunday from 9am to 6pm. Visiting here is like walking into Grandma's kitchen, provided you had an old-fashioned granny who felt pastries should be gooey, chocolaty, and buttery. Their signature wedding cakes will make you want to rush down the aisle, but you'll want to bring a basket for the fresh bread, napoleons, strawberry cheesecake, cream puffs, sweet rolls, danishes, and doughnuts, many of which are made with surprisingly fresh ingredients. Some may find the goodies too heavy and rich, but for those of us with a powerful sweet tooth, this place

BUFFETS

Like so much else that was Vegas tradition, buffets have evolved. Gone, mostly, are the days of trays and cafeteria-style lines serving mounds of blandness at bargain-basement prices. The modern buffet uses come-and-go serving areas, live-action cooking stations, and multiple ethnic and regional cuisines. A rise in quality puts many on par with traditional restaurants.

Of course, as the quality has gone up, so too have the prices, which now make buffets less of a bargain. But consider it this way: You would pay much more per person at one of the fancier restaurants in town, where you would order just one, potentially disappointing, item. At a buffet, there's more chance to find something you love. More variety per person means less likelihood for disappointment, so if you hate what you picked you can simply dump your plate and start all over. Buffets are, generally speaking, not nearly as atmospheric as a proper restaurant, but how else can you combine good barbecue with excellent Chinese and a cupcake or 10?

Buffets are extremely popular, and reservations are not taken, so be prepared for a long line at peak times. Eating at offbeat hours (lunch at 2pm, for hits the spot. There is no dining area, so everything is to go; do try to at least make it to your car before you start digging in.

Just down the street is the delightful the **Cupcakery ★**, 9680 S. Eastern Ave. (www.thecupcakery.com; _C_ **702/207-2253**). The delectable goodies here aren't large, but they pack a wallop of moist cake and creamy frosting. Clever combinations include Boston cream pie (filled with custardy cream), but even the basic chocolate-on-chocolate is a butter-cream pleasure. There are even sugar-free cupcakes. The Cupcakery is open Monday through Friday from 8am to 8pm, Saturday from 10am to 8pm, and Sunday from 10am to 6pm.

Hot Vegas days call for cool desserts, and frozen custard (softer than regular ice cream, but harder than soft serve) is a fine way to go. Head for **Luv-It Frozen Custard ★**, 505 E. Oakey (www.luvitfrozencustard.com;

_C_ **702/384-6452**), open Sunday through Thursday from 1 to 10pm and Friday and Saturday from 1 to 11pm. Because custard has less fat and sugar than premium ice cream, you can even fool yourself into thinking this is some-what healthful (ha!). Made every few hours using fresh cream and eggs, the custard is available in basic flavors for cup or cone. More exotic flavors (maple walnut, apple spice, and others) come in tubs.

If there is such as a thing as a milk-shake rut, **Black Tap ★★** (p. 116), in the Venetian, 3355 Las Vegas Blvd S. (www.blacktapnyc.com; _C_ **702/607-2355**), and its Crazyshakes will pull you right out of it. Each shake gets built on a base of really good ice cream, and then just keeps going from there until it's a pure sugar rush overflowing from your glass. Think whimsical additions like Rice Krispy Treats, Pop-Tarts, Fruity Pebbles—and that's just on the Bam Bam Shake.

example) will mean a shorter wait, as will some hotel/casino players' club cards, which can get you line cuts.

Money-saving tip: At press time, several hotels were offering all-you-can-eat all-day-long packages where you could pay one flat fee and come back to the buffets as many times as you like in a given day. Caesars Entertainment (Harrah's, Flamingo, Rio, and so on) is even offering a full-day pass to most of their buffets for as low as $50 so you can mix and match. Details and pricing on these change often, so visit the hotel's web-site or call ahead to see if they are offering any special deals when you're in town.

South Strip
EXPENSIVE

The Buffet at Aria ★★ BUFFET   Like everything else in Aria, its buffet is very pretty. Many stations are spread throughout the orange-tinted room, accented with brick and chrome. Unusually for Vegas, you can have your buf-fet food in the sunshine: Floor-to-ceiling windows let loads of natural light in. High-quality ingredients and international flavors abound here, including *naan* bread and roasted meats straight from a tandoor oven, fresh sushi from a sushi chef, and carving stations serving up nice slabs of tri-tip. The American game is strong as well, with a really tasty meatloaf that's almost like Mom's. Desserts are fantastic here, mixing such usual items as gelato and cookies with cream puffs and macarons.

In Aria Las Vegas, 3730 Las Vegas Blvd. S. www.arialasvegas.com. ☏ **702/590-7111.** Breakfast $26, Mon–Fri brunch $30, dinner $40. Sat–Sun brunch $35 (not including cocktails), all-day pass $60. Daily 7am–10pm.

MODERATE

The Buffet at Excalibur ★ BUFFET We get it: All buffets should keep up with the Joneses, but is there a way to do this without making everything look and sound alike? Renovation brought a bright, open, cheery space with sleek lines, as well as a noticeable upgrade to the food. Not bad, considering it's still one of the cheapest buffets on the Strip. But the food is still pretty standard fare: crepes and omelets at brunch, large mounds of peel-and-eat-shrimp, corn dogs and mac and cheese for the kiddies at other times. Best dishes include interesting bites like pork chile verde and garlic saffron butter mussels. Desserts are fun, with ice cream bars hand-dipped to order. The beverages are self-service, and there's a self-pay station in the front if you'd like to have an entire meal with no contact with another human being.

In Excalibur, 3850 Las Vegas Blvd. S. www.excalibur.com. ☏ **702/597-7777.** Breakfast $19, lunch $20, dinner $25–$28, brunch $23, all-day pass valid at both Excalibur and Luxor $40–$45. Daily 7am–10pm.

The Buffet at Luxor ★ BUFFET The mummies that used to rule this all-you-can-eat at Luxor fell victim to rebranding. Which is a shame, because now this buffet is really boring to look at. Fortunately, the food quality has remained as consistent as it was during pharaoh's reign. There's the 30-foot salad bar, and the international offerings, like Mexican and Chinese, are not authentic but are still tasty. This is all to say that it's not mind-blowing, but your kids will eat it.

In Luxor, 3900 Las Vegas Blvd. S. www.luxor.com. ☏ **702/262-4000.** Breakfast $19, lunch $21, dinner $25, weekend brunch $23, all-day pass valid at both Excalibur and Luxor $40–$45. Daily 7am–10pm.

Mandalay Bay's Bayside Buffet ★★ BUFFET The Asian bites are why I come here. Steamed barbecue pork buns are soft, sweet, and savory; shell-on salt and pepper shrimp are crunchy and eaten whole; and for whatever reason, I can't stop eating the pot stickers. I also like the off-the-beaten path Mexican selections, like shredded pork carnitas and Laredo beans with rice. Everything else is about average, but the setting is unusually pleasant, with a view of the pool (great people-watching) and lots of natural light (nothing is more uncomfortable than dozens of people binge eating in a stuffy space).

In Mandalay Bay, 3950 Las Vegas Blvd. S. www.mandalaybay.com. ☏ **702/632-7200.** Breakfast $19, lunch $22, dinner $33, Sun brunch $26. Daily 7am–2:30pm, 4:30–9:45pm.

Mid-Strip
EXPENSIVE

Bacchanal Buffet ★★★ BUFFET   Caesars Palace's beautiful Bacchanal Buffet is the crown jewel of the buffet empire. It isn't so much an all-you-can-eat buffet as it is nine restaurants in one massive area. The space is divided into different, and different-looking, sections (one is glass-enclosed, the back dining room uses reclaimed wood, and a gleaming all-metal space finishes the trio). More than 500 items are offered on any given day between the cold and raw bar, carving, Mexican, Asian, charcuterie, salad, and pizza stations. In addition, off-menu specials are based on the chef's whimsy. Each item we've eaten here, whether it was the little basket of fried chicken and waffles, delicate dim sum, red velvet pancakes, or the big hunks of Polish sausage cut just for us, has been prepared extremely well, as if it was made just for us. The desserts are some of our favorites in town, including Japanese mochi, macarons, and unusual gelatos (like brown butter gelato).

In Caesars Palace, 3570 Las Vegas Blvd. S. www.caesarspalace.com. ⓒ **702/731-7928.** Weekday breakfast $40, weekday brunch $45, weekday dinner $55, weekend breakfast $40, weekend brunch $60, weekend dinner $65. Mon–Fri 7:30am–10pm; Sat–Sun 8am–10pm.

The Buffet at Bellagio ★★ BUFFET   This is one of the most expensive buffets in town, but it was also the first to elevate the buffet experience by focusing on high-quality dishes and ingredients. The raw bar is a great place to start, with oysters, cocktail shrimp, crab legs, and smoked salmon, and while normally we eschew pizzas at buffets (we can get that at home!), their wood-fired oven works magic. Champagne brunch is one of the most popular meals here, but I prefer the Friday and Saturday dinner service, which includes caviar with all the proper accoutrements. High rollers may want to ante up for the so-called Chef's Table, where you and at least eight of your friends bypass the entire line and have a seat at a dedicated table near the buffet. Chefs come over, greet you, and pass hors d'oeuvres, before wheeling over carts to present meats like prime rib and chops. You are, of course, also welcome to eat from the buffet itself. At nearly $70 higher than the regular dinner prices, you're paying for the privilege, but we think it's almost worth the awkward "who is that?" stares from the regular guests.

In Bellagio, 3600 Las Vegas Blvd. S. www.bellagio.com. ⓒ **877/259-7111.** Breakfast $24, lunch $28, dinner $39–$45, weekend brunch $33 ($49 with champagne), chef's table experience add an additional $68. Daily 7am–10pm.

Wicked Spoon Buffet ★★★ BUFFET   When Cosmopolitan opened this buffet back in 2011, they set into motion a revolution that many other buffets would follow. Modeled after Asian food halls, Wicked Spoon began the trend of offering guests individual portions of dishes like eggs Benedict and short rib pasta in ramekins and small pots, rather than just placing food in a steam tray on the line. It allows for better turnover of the dishes, ensuring

The Southern Nevada Health District is the organization responsible for inspecting restaurants. Each is visited at least twice a year and then graded (A, B, or C), given demerits for infractions (improper food storage and handling, and the like), and, in extreme cases, shut down. You can now read the inspections online for every restaurant in town, although you may not want to if you ever feel like eating in Las Vegas again. If you think you and your stomach can handle it, visit www.southern nevadahealthdistrict.org.

that food is as fresh as possible. Gathering all these individual dishes on one plate can be challenging, but it also makes you aware of how much food you're eating, so they cut down on waste as well. Among the dishes are foodie-oriented finds like roasted bone marrow at dinner, and mac and cheese studded with ham hocks and truffled potato gratin. The selection of desserts has been lauded as some of the city's best, all in mini sizes so you can get a bite of everything without going into a coma afterward. While the other restaurants in the resort are in the East tower, this (along with Rose.Rabbit.Lie) is tucked into the West tower on the second floor. If you want to take the buffet back to your room, there's an express takeout option for $20.

In the Cosmopolitan of Las Vegas, 3708 Las Vegas Blvd. S. www.cosmopolitanlasvegas. com. (📞) **877/551-7772.** Weekday brunch $28, weekend brunch $36; dinner $42–$49. Brunch Mon–Fri 8am–5pm, Sat–Sun 8am–3pm; dinner Mon–Thurs 5–9pm, Fri–Sat 3–10pm, Sun 3–9pm.

MODERATE

Corner Market Buffet ★ BUFFET   The old-school buffet at TI finally got its much-needed upgrade in 2018, along with a different name. The dining room is much brighter and feels less stuffy than before, but it's the food that really needed the refresher. The updated menu hits on a lot of foodie trends, like the superfood "forbidden" rice, and protein bowls, as well as international flavors like Peruvian chicken and Korean beef bulgogi. Don't worry; there are still pizza and pasta for the rest of us. Daring to make soufflés en masse for a buffet is a big gamble, but it seems to pay off here.

In Treasure Island, 3300 Las Vegas Blvd. S. www.treasureisland.com. (📞) **702/894-7111.** Breakfast $23; lunch $26; dinner Mon–Thurs $30, Fri–Sun $35; Sat–Sun champagne brunch $30. Reduced prices for children 4–10; free for children 3 and under. Daily 7am–10pm.

Flavors Buffet ★ BUFFET   The meat section is the most laudable part of this buffet. In addition to an excellent carving station that includes gorgeous specimens of hams, turkey breasts, and prime ribs waiting to be sliced, Flavors also sometimes feature Brazilian barbecue known as *churrasco,* not a typical buffet offering. Since the other stations are average, fill up on meat and head to dessert. The selection of mini-cupcakes and cookies allows guests to sample many at once; kids and grown-ups alike love walking out of Flavors with cotton candy to-go.

In Harrah's, 3475 Las Vegas Blvd. S. www.harrahslv.com. © **702/369-5000.** Mon-Fri breakfast $21, lunch $25, dinner $31; Sat–Sun brunch $28, dinner $35. Daily 8am–9pm.

Le Village Buffet ★★ BUFFET   The French theme goes into overdrive at this buffet modeled after a countryside village, complete with faux outdoor patio seating and a painted sky on the ceiling above. The food is served at stations hailing five regions of France, offering recognizable dishes like charcuterie and pâté, a hearty onion soup, and even an ambitious bouillabaisse. As good as you'd find in Provence? Maybe not, but it's still flavorful and often teeming with seafood. Classics like custom-made crepes are hugely popular, as are desserts like macarons and crème brûlée, because, hey, if you're faking France, you should at least get the pastries right. There are, of course, American options here, like prime rib and snow crab legs, but we like the touches of truffles on the mac and cheese to remind us of why we're really here. This is still one of the most popular buffets in town, so on weekends long lines are *de rigueur.*

In Paris Las Vegas, 3655 Las Vegas Blvd. S. www.parislasvegas.com. © **702/946-7000.** Breakfast $22–$24, champagne brunch and dinner $31. Reduced prices for children 4–10. Daily 7am–10pm.

Mirage Cravings Buffet ★★ BUFFET   Mirage is one of those hotels that believe in the concept of under-promise, over-deliver. Visitors come to Las Vegas knowing about the Mirage, but they never have any idea of how good it is inside. The buffet is as underrated. It's a gorgeous, ultramodern space with familiar but top-notch fare. Delivered by 11 live-action stations, it includes juicy prime rib sliced to order, sushi as good as you'd get in your favorite Japanese restaurant, and Sunday brunch with such hangover-friendly items as pho and classic but pretty eggs Benedict (plus more champagne). Beverages are self-service from one of those new-fangled soda machines, so there's something like 150 different flavors of Coca-Cola to choose from. Unlimited beer and wine for those 21 and over is a nice touch.

In the Mirage, 3400 Las Vegas Blvd. S. www.mirage.com. © **702/791-7111.** Breakfast $19, lunch $24, dinner $30; Sat–Sun brunch $28. Mon–Fri 7am–9pm; Sat–Sun 8am–9pm.

Spice Market Buffet ★★ BUFFET   Out of all the buffets in the city, this is one of our underrated favorites. Planet Hollywood's former life as the Aladdin left the Middle Eastern cuisine of this buffet as its legacy. With well-prepared and flavorful options like a huge meze spread of hummus, baba ghanoush, and rice-stuffed grape leaves, it's a big hit with our vegetarian friends (who are happy to find more than just salad and pizza to eat). Never fear, carnivores, there's still stuff for you, like lamb skewers and chicken curry, plus a carving station with prime rib, and an impressive seafood selection with fish-and-chips and sushi.

3667 Las Vegas Blvd. S. www.planethollywoodresort.com. © **702/785-5555.** Breakfast $19, lunch $24, dinner $26, Sat–Sun brunch $24. Daily 7am–10pm.

North Strip
EXPENSIVE
Wynn Las Vegas Buffet ★★★ BUFFET   Bottom line: It's darn nice to stuff your faces in such lovely surroundings. Arched ceilings allow natural light to stream into the atrium, where pots and pots of flowers and plants give vibrant life to the otherwise neutral-colored decor. And for a mass-eating experience, much attention is paid to an individual guest's needs. There are 15 live-action stations, some of which allow guests to interact with chefs, as at the carving station, where they slice off your specific choice of prime rib or sausage. Some are self-service but swanky, like the pre-portioned salad station, where the greens are served in glasses that evoke the mason-jar salad craze that went around in the mid-2010s. Many bites feature premium ingredients like Wagyu beef and veal short ribs (does that justify the elevated prices? You decide). Desserts are a high point here, whether you choose made-to-order crepes, bon bons, excellent gelato . . . or all the above.

In Wynn Las Vegas, 3131 Las Vegas Blvd. S. www.wynnlasvegas.com. ℂ **702/248-3463.** Weekday brunch $28, dinner $44–$50, Sat–Sun brunch $38. Daily 7:30am–9:30pm.

Downtown
INEXPENSIVE
Garden Court Buffet ★★★ BUFFET   The buffet at Main Street Station is Downtown's prettiest and most extensive buffet—and a darn good deal at less than half what the Strip casinos are charging. Reminiscent of a Victorian train station, its ceilings are grandly arched, covered with white tile and small pinpoint lights, which glow daintily at dinnertime. At lunch, sunshine pours through the lovely stained-glass windows, one of the few in-casino eateries that allows sunlight to enter (blame Vegas's large vampire clientele, I guess). It may also be the most spacious buffet in town, with tables that are shouting distance apart and comfortable chairs. The buffet is a massive, well-staffed affair with nine live-action stations, each attended by a friendly chef popping pizzas into a brick oven, wokking up Chinese food, or running the Southern soul food station (which sometimes has chicken-fried steak with gravy). As a nod to the many Hawaiian visitors who come through, there are a lot of island options, like sweet Portuguese sausage for breakfast, sticky rice wrapped in banana leaves, and shredded kalua pork and cabbage.

At Main Street Station, 200 N. Main St. www.mainstreetcasino.com. ℂ **702/387-1896.** Breakfast $11, lunch $12, dinner $15–$30, Sat–Sun champagne brunch $16. Free for children 3 and under. Daily 7–10:30am breakfast; 11am–3pm lunch. Mon–Thurs 4–9pm dinner; Fri–Sun 4–10pm dinner.

Just Off the Strip
EXPENSIVE
Carnival World Buffet ★★ BUFFET   Locals love this all-you-can-eat in the Rio, as it was one of the first to offer a truly global dining experience that went beyond the standard Italian, Chinese, and American fare at other

5

Buffets

WHERE TO EAT

buffets. Plus, they loved the Village Seafood Buffet, which offered catches from the Pacific Rim, Mediterranean, and Baja. In 2015, the Rio consolidated the two into one mega buffet. The food court setting allows diners to navigate between the various cuisines—the meat-laden Brazilian grill and the Japanese *teppanyaki* station serve up just some of the more than 300 dishes on offer. On top of those are more than 70 desserts, with almost a dozen gelato flavors, pies, and cakes, all made on-site just for this restaurant.

In Rio All-Suite Hotel & Casino, 3700 W. Flamingo Rd. www.riolasvegas.com. *©* **702/252-7777.** Dinner $32–$35, Sat–Sun champagne brunch $29. Reduced prices for children 4–8; free for children 3 and under. Mon–Fri 4–9pm; Sat–Sun 10am–10pm.

INEXPENSIVE

Ports O' Call Buffet ★ BUFFET   There's nothing wrong with seeking out a cheaper buffet in the name of sustenance. While you won't find the myriad choices of buffets on the Strip, Ports o' Call in Gold Coast has a respectable seven cooking stations, and some genuine hits among its dishes, like the full rotisserie chickens at the carving station, the steak tacos from the Mexican line, and fried oysters from the seafood station. Fridays are seafood night, but I think the prime rib is a better choice. Gold Coast's buffet is clean, the food is decent, and the lines won't be insane; and sometimes that's all you need.

In Gold Coast, 4000 W. Flamingo Rd. www.goldcoastcasino.com. *©* **702/367-7111.** Breakfast $10, lunch $13, dinner $17–$22, Sun brunch $17. Mon–Sat 7–10am, 11am–3pm, 4–9pm; Sun 8am–3pm, 4–9pm.

EXPLORING LAS VEGAS

Y ou aren't going to lack for things to do in Las Vegas. Many of you have come here for the gambling, which should keep you pretty busy. But you can't sit at a slot machine forever. After all, you're going to have to get up to go to the bathroom at some point! When you do, maybe you should look around at some of the other things here that can keep you entertained.

Just walking on the Strip and gazing at the gaudy, garish, absurd wonder of it all can occupy quite a lot of time. This is the number-one activity we recommend in Vegas; at night, it is a mind-boggling sight. Beyond that, there are options galore, from popular bits of Vegas silliness like volcanoes and crooning gondoliers, to museums, thrill rides, spas, recreation, and more. And, of course, you can engage in those most iconic Vegas traditions, getting married and gambling. All of that and more is covered in this chapter. Don't forget there are shows and plenty of other nighttime entertainment, which you can read more about in chapter 8. There are also out-of-town sightseeing options, such as **Hoover Dam** (a major tourist destination), **Red Rock Canyon,** and excursions to the **Grand Canyon.** We've listed the best of these in chapter 9.

SEEING LAS VEGAS

ICONIC SIGHTS
Bellagio Conservatory ★★★, p. 160
Bellagio Fountains ★★★, p. 160
Eiffel Tower Light Show ★★★, p. 160
Fremont Street Experience ★★★, p. 163
Mirage Volcano ★★, p. 160
The Mob Museum ★★★, p. 163
The Neon Museum ★★★, p. 165
Stratosphere Tower & Thrill Rides ★★, p. 160
Welcome to Fabulous Las Vegas Sign ★★★, p. 161
Wynn Lake of Dreams ★, p. 161

ENTERTAINMENT COMPLEXES
Brooklyn Bowl ★, p. 185
Circus Circus Midway ★, p. 160
Dig This! ★★, p. 166
Fast Lap Indoor Kart Racing ★★, p. 167
KISS by Monster Mini Golf ★★, p. 167
Las Vegas Mini Gran Prix ★★, p. 171
Las Vegas Motor Speedway ★★, p. 172

Pole Position Raceway ★, p. 172
SkyZone ★, p. 171
SpeedVegas ★★★, p. 168
Topgolf ★★★, p. 168

EXHIBITS

Bodies . . . The Exhibition ★★, p. 154
Titanic: The Exhibition ★, p. 156

MUSEUMS & GALLERIES

Aria Fine Art Collection ★★, p. 153
The Arts Factory ★, p. 162
Bellagio Gallery of Fine Art ★★,
    p. 156
Cannabition Cannabis Museum ★★,
    p. 162
Clark County Museum ★★, p. 169
Discovery Children's Museum ★★★,
    p. 162
Las Vegas Natural History Museum ★,
    p. 163
Madame Tussauds Las Vegas ★★,
    p. 157
The Mob Museum ★★★, p. 163
National Atomic Testing
    Museum ★★★, p. 167
The Neon Museum ★★★, p. 165
Nevada State Museum ★, p. 172
Pinball Hall of Fame & Museum ★★★,
    p. 170
Shelby American Heritage Center ★,
    p. 170

THEME PARKS & RIDES

Adventuredome ★★, p. 159
Big Apple Coaster & Arcade ★★,
    p. 154
Eiffel Tower Experience ★, p. 156
High Roller Observation Wheel ★★,
    p. 157
SlotZilla ★★, p. 166
Stratosphere Tower & Thrill Rides ★★,
    p. 160
Wet 'n Wild ★, p. 173

ZOOS

Lion Habitat Ranch ★★★, p. 170
Shark Reef at Mandalay Bay ★, p. 154
Siegfried & Roy's Secret Garden & Dol-
    phin Habitat ★★★, p. 158

OTHER ATTRACTIONS

Downtown Container Park ★★★,
    p. 201
Ethel M Chocolates ★, p. 169
Fremont Street Experience ★★★,
    p. 163
The Park ★★, p. 158
The Smith Center for the Performing
    Arts ★★★, p. 218
Springs Preserve ★★★, p. 173
Wynn Conservatory ★, p. 161

SOUTH STRIP

Aria Fine Art Collection ★★ ART MUSEUM   Art in outdoor public spaces is a relatively new phenomenon in Las Vegas, mostly because the only time people spend outside is by the pool or hustling to get to another casino. But Aria wisely (I think) decided not to confine its works by 15 major artists to a stuffy museum within the resort, opting to make the entire hotel, and its neighbors, the gallery. A free app leads viewers through the casino to such works as the 250-foot LED wall by Jenny Holzer that scrolls "Vegas-isms" hidden at North Valet; or *Big Edge,* an installation of recycled aluminum canoes. There's also ephemeral art, like *Glacia* at the Shops at Crystals, which are ice columns that rise and melt each day; or the Lumia fountain that spouts color-infused water in the circular drive. Remember that the resort and its sur- roundings are huge—wear comfortable shoes to get you through the art hike.

Aria Las Vegas, 3730 Las Vegas Blvd. S. www.aria.com. ℂ **702/590-7111.** Free admis- sion. Most artworks are outdoors or in 24-hr. public spaces.

If you're planning on seeing Titanic: The Exhibition plus Bodies, both at Luxor, and Shark Reef next door at Mandalay Bay, you should purchase a combo pass for $57 for those, as well as other MGM Resorts attractions, at the box office. You'll save a good $30 that way.

Big Apple Coaster & Arcade ★★ THRILL RIDE As if the outside of New York–New York wasn't busy enough, someone decided to knock it up a few notches by having a roller coaster wind around the whole thing. The whimsically designed cars evoke Manhattan taxis and run at speeds up to 67 mph while going through drops of as much as 144 feet, a full loop, and the "heartline" twist, which simulates a jet-fighter barrel roll. And if this reality isn't enough for you, upgrade to the virtual reality experience. You'll don a fancy VR headset for the ride that immerses you into a vivid, 4-D world of chasing aliens while you fly high above the Las Vegas Strip. Adrenaline junkies may find it too tame, but the average thrill-seeker will do a lot of screaming. If your idea of fun is staying closer to the ground, try the amusements in the arcade that feature carnival and video games.

In New York–New York, 3790 Las Vegas Blvd. S. www.newyorknewyork.com. (**C**) **702/740-6616.** Single rides $15 adults, all-day pass $26. Virtual reality experience $20. Must be 54 in. tall to ride. Sun–Thurs 11am–11pm; Fri–Sat 10:30am–midnight. Closed during inclement weather.

Bodies . . . The Exhibition ★★ EXHIBIT Stunning and controversial, the exhibit features actual dead bodies, with over 200 full and partial specimens. (Some are possibly executed Chinese prisoners who may never have given permission for their bodies to be used in this way—hence the controversy.) Utilizing a patented freeze-dry operation, full bodies, artfully dissected body parts, and stripped cadavers are on display not for sensationalism—though it is pretty sensational in nearly all senses of the word—but for visitors to fully appreciate the wonder and mechanics that go into our transient flesh. When a body is positioned in an athletic pose, you can see how the muscles work, and when a cross section of a lung afflicted with cancer is right in front of you, you may be glad Vegas has passed stricter smoking laws. It's educational and bizarre, and not something you're likely to forget soon. It's surprisingly not grotesque, but it's not for the ultra-squeamish. Also, put your phones away, as photos are not allowed.

In the Luxor, 3900 Las Vegas Blvd. S. www.bodiestheexhibition.com/lasvegas. (**C**) **702/262-4000.** Admission $32 adults, $30 military, seniors 65 and over, $24 ages 4–12, free for children 3 and under, $29 Nevada residents. Daily 10am–10pm; last admission 9pm.

Shark Reef at Mandalay Bay ★ AQUARIUM Given that watching fish can lower your blood pressure, it's practically a public service for

0	0.5 mi
0	0.5 km

···🚋··· Las Vegas Monorail
···🚋··· Free monorail

Adventuredome **14**
Aria Fine Art Collection **25**
The Arts Factory **11**
Bellagio Conservatory **21**
Bellagio Fountains **21**
Bellagio Gallery
  of Fine Art **21**
Big Apple Coaster
  & Arcade **28**
Bodies...The Exhibition **30**
Brooklyn Bowl **18**
Cannabition Cannabis
  Museum **10**
Circus Circus Midway **14**
Clark County Museum **39**

Dig This! **13**
Discovery Children's Museum **7**
Eiffel Tower Experience **22**
Eiffel Tower Light Show **22**
Ethel M Chocolates **38**
Fast Lap Indoor Kart Racing **24**
Fremont Street Experience **8**
High Roller Observation Wheel **18**
KISS by Monster Mini Golf **20**
Las Vegas Mini Gran Prix **1**
Las Vegas Motor Speedway **3**
Las Vegas Natural History Museum **4**
Lion Habitat Ranch **37**
Madame Tussauds Las Vegas **17**
Mirage Volcano **16**
The Mob Museum **6**
National Atomic Testing Museum **23**
The Neon Museum **5**
Nevada State Museum **2**
The Park **27**
Pinball Hall of Fame & Museum **29**
Pole Position Raceway **19**
Shark Reef at Mandalay Bay **31**
Shelby American Heritage Center **36**
Siegfried & Roy's Secret Garden
  & Dolphin Habitat **16**
SkyZone **33**
SlotZilla **9**
The Smith Center for
  the Performing Arts **7**
SpeedVegas **34**
Springs Preserve **2**
Stratosphere Tower &
  Thrill Rides **12**
T-Mobile Arena **27**
Titanic: The Exhibition **30**
Topgolf **34**
Welcome to Fabulous
  Las Vegas Sign **35**
Wet 'n Wild **32**
Wynn Conservatory **15**
Wynn Lake of Dreams **15**

Mandalay Bay to provide this facility in a city where craps tables and jammed dance clubs can bring excitement levels to dangerous heights. Although I admire the style (it's built to look like a sunken temple), and standing in the all-glass tunnel surrounded by sharks is cool, it's just a giant aquarium, which is disappointing at these prices. Certified divers can get up close and personal with more than 30 sharks in the tank with a guide, if you dare. *Note:* It is *waaay* off in a remote part of Mandalay Bay, which might be a hassle for those with limited mobility.

In Mandalay Bay, 3950 Las Vegas Blvd. S. www.sharkreef.com. ☎ **702/632-4555.** Admission $25 adults, $23 seniors, $19 children 4–12, free for children 3 and under, $22 Nevada residents. Dive experience starts at $650. Sun–Thurs 10am–8pm; Fri–Sat 10am–10pm. Last admission 1 hr. before closing; hours vary seasonally.

Titanic: The Exhibition ★ EXHIBIT   It's too easy to say, "You've seen the movie, now see the exhibit." But that is sort of the case; if you were captivated by the Oscar-winning epic, you will definitely want to take in this exhibit on the unsinkable luxury liner that sank on its maiden voyage. While it's a can't-miss for buffs, it might still be of some interest for those with only marginal feelings about the massive 1912 disaster. It's a strangely somber subject for Vegas, featuring displays explaining the ship's ill-fated maiden voyage; relics salvaged from the sunken liner; and even re-creations of sample cabins from first, second, and third class, giving one a sense of how it felt to travel aboard what was an incredible vessel. There is even a large chunk of real ice standing in for the culprit berg.

In the Luxor, 3900 Las Vegas Blvd. S. www.luxor.com. ☎ **702/262-4400.** Admission $32 adults, $30 military, seniors 65 and over, $24 children 4–12, free for children 3 and under, $29 Nevada residents with ID. Daily 10am–10pm. Last admission 9pm.

MID-STRIP

Bellagio Gallery of Fine Art ★★ ART MUSEUM   As if there wasn't enough to look at in the rest of the resort! Should you tire of the thousands of glass flowers on the lobby ceiling or the real ones in the Conservatory, head here for actual art…in Las Vegas. The exhibits are small (alas, the price of admission isn't), but the artists showcased are of the highest caliber, running the gamut over the years, from Picasso to Fabergé to Warhol.

In Bellagio, 3600 Las Vegas Blvd. S. www.bellagio.com. ☎ **702/693-7871.** Admission $14 adults; $12 seniors, Nevada residents, teachers, students with ID, and military. Daily 10am–8pm. Last admission 7:30pm.

Eiffel Tower Experience ★ OBSERVATION TOWER   Whether this is worth the dough depends on how much you like views. The "ride" portion is a glass-enclosed elevator to the top as a guide delivers a few facts ("this is a half-size exact replica, down to the paint color of the original" and more). At the uppermost platform, viewers are welcome to stand around and look out for as long as they want, which probably isn't 2 hours, the length of the average movie, which costs about what this does. If you'd like a view that's just as spectacular but a little lower to the ground, opt instead for a cocktail in the lounge of the Eiffel Tower Restaurant, on the 11th floor of the structure. The price of a drink is about the same as the cost of the ride up to the top, but this is a much more relaxed way to enjoy the view. Plus, now you have a cocktail.

In Paris Las Vegas, 3655 Las Vegas Blvd. S. www.parislv.com. © **702/946-7000.** Admission $16 adults 10am–7pm, $22 7pm–close. Daily 10am–1am; weather permitting.

High Roller Observation Wheel ★★ THRILL RIDE The *if bigger is better, then biggest is best* ethos that Las Vegas loves so much continues here with the world's tallest observation wheel. Standing at nearly 550 feet high, the massive structure has fundamentally changed the skyline while also providing some of the best views of the Strip (and much of southern Nevada). The wheel has 28 fully enclosed, air-conditioned cabs, each capable of holding up to 40 people, although if you get stuck in one that full you will need to fight your way to good snapshot-worthy window space. One revolution takes about 30 minutes, so it's less of a thrill ride than a leisurely, albeit really high, walk in the park. Even those with height phobias may find this tolerable. Go at night for the best photo opportunities of the city in its fully lit-up glory—it's worth the extra few bucks. Or practice your sun salutations even closer to the sun at yoga classes three times a week in one of the spacious pods. A professional instructor leads you via wireless headphones through an hour of personalized poses and meditations. You'll be ready to face the Strip again in no time.

Prices are high for this relatively short experience—a pass to the top of the even-taller Stratosphere Tower (see below) is significantly less expensive for a similar kind of experience. The good news is that they not only allow drinking on board, they practically encourage it, with a bar on your way to the boarding area, or if you're willing to pony up a bit more, a cabin with an open bar. Of course, there are no bathrooms on the ride, so drink at your own peril. Note that lines can be long during peak periods, both to get tickets and to queue up for the cabs, so it's best to buy online beforehand and budget some extra time for standing in line.

3545 Las Vegas Blvd. S. www.thelinq.com. © **800/CAESARS.** High Roller admission $22 day, $32 night, $35–$47 Happy Half Hour cabins. Discounts for booking online. $75 and up for personalized yoga sessions. Daily 10am–2am.

Madame Tussauds Las Vegas ★★ MUSEUM Madame T's has outposts in nearly every major tourist city, and for 2 centuries it has been the best (borderline creepy) way to get close to celebrities. The figures themselves are quite impressive, both for their meticulous attention to detail and the eerie way they (often) reflect the personalities of their subjects.

The Vegas-specific exhibits are the star attractions, from the bedazzled, stuck-in-time Liberace to the "Hangover Experience" with Bradley Cooper (that stubble is so perfect) and Zach Galifianakis, complete with his mansatchel. You may have heard about the questionable poses visitors were holding with singer Nicki Minaj; not Vegas-specific, but hey, it fits in. Sadly, the

rambling THROUGH RESORTS

Las Vegas is unlike most every other place on Earth in that you don't necessarily leave your hotel to sightsee—the hotels themselves are attractions. So, when planning your daily itinerary, don't skip chapter 4, "Where to Stay." It will introduce you to all the glorious, and goofy, architectural elements of the Strip resorts (and off-Strip ones as well), their shopping opportunities and shows, the highlights of their casinos, their over-the-top restaurants, nightlife venues, and more. Who knew wandering through hotels could be this fun?

tuxedo-clad George Clooney, who visitors used to be able to "marry," has been replaced with a boring, regular suit-wearing, already-married Clooney. In homage to the popularity of electronic dance music in Las Vegas, the A-list heavy Club Tussauds exhibit unveiled the likeness of cake-throwing DJ Steve Aoki, and no, you can't throw cake at him.

In the Venetian, 3355 Las Vegas Blvd. S. www.madametussauds.com/lasvegas. *℃* **702/862-7800.** Admission $32 and up, free for children 2 and under. Discounts for booking online. Sun–Thurs 10am–8pm; Fri 10am–10pm; Sat 10am–9pm; hours vary seasonally.

The Park ★★ ENTERTAINMENT COMPLEX   The space between Park MGM and New York–New York has been developed into the very first outdoor gathering space on the Strip . . . that has nothing to do with a resort pool. There's certainly water, though, thanks to two welcoming 100-foot-long waterfalls near the Las Vegas Boulevard entrance of this bona fide park, complete with art installations, live entertainment, and restaurants. The Park combines natural and industrial design to create a comfortable oasis in the desert, including 16 75-foot-tall shade "trees" that line the area, blocking sun by day, casting cool shadows, and lighting up the paths by night. The 40-foot-tall *Bliss Dance* sculpture made her way from Burning Man to shimmy on the Strip, illuminated by 3,000 colored LED lights. Even if you're not headed to a show or a hockey game at the T-Mobile Arena, which sits behind the Park, there's plenty of reasons to take a stroll, including several restaurants that all offer indoor and outdoor space, such as the theatrical sushi spot Sake Rok and the waffle-driven Bruxie, which takes the Belgian specialty and uses it as a vehicle for excellent fried chicken sandwiches.

3784 Las Vegas Blvd. S. www.theparkvegas.com. *℃* **702/740-6969.** Free admission.

Siegfried & Roy's Secret Garden & Dolphin Habitat ★★★ ZOO   After more than 20 years, this engaging animal habitat remains one of the best antidotes to Las Vegas stress. Spend an hour watching dolphins and tigers and you won't care how much money you lost on the slots. The bulk of your time will most likely be spent in the well-regarded dolphin habitat, a 2.5-million-gallon home for bottlenose dolphins that were either rescued or born here. This is more than just a SeaWorld–style, sit in bleachers and watch the animals cavort kind of place (although they have that, too). Here you can get up close to the pools and sometimes interact with the dolphins (splashing is involved), which is a treat, especially for kids. Pay extra and you can get VIP, behind-the-scenes tours; spend an entire day as a trainer, complete with time in the pool; and even "paint" with them as you hold a canvas and the dolphin holds a special brush in its mouth. The latter is an unmitigated thrill that allows you to connect with these amazing animals, or at least pretend you are.

The Secret Garden part is a small zoo originally designed as an on-site home for the animals used in Siegfried & Roy's magic show, which ended in 2003 after a disagreement between Roy and a tiger. The animals that remain are mostly of the big cat variety, including some of the illusionists' famed white tigers. It's fine, but don't expect a lot of excitement. On hot Vegas days the animals mostly (and wisely) just lie in the shade or shallow pools, so don't expect them to be hunting elk or playing with big balls of yarn.

While it's easy to have a pang of environmentally conscious guilt over animals in captivity, the entire facility is well run and scrupulously maintained; the trainers are obviously passionate; and the animals seem to thrive here. A dolphin calf, Coco, was born here in 2017. Several of the dolphins are more than 30 years old, which is more than double their life expectancy in the wild.

In the Mirage, 3400 Las Vegas Blvd. S. www.miragehabitat.com. © **702/791-7188.** Admission $22 adults, $17 children 4–10, free for children 3 and under. Daily 10am–6:30pm; hours vary seasonally.

NORTH STRIP

Adventuredome ★★ AMUSEMENT PARK   This is a more than okay place to spend a hot afternoon, especially since it's one of the few family-friendly attractions in town. Plus, unlike most theme parks, it's indoors! The glass dome that towers overhead lets in natural light so you get the best of both worlds—sunlight and air-conditioning. The park has two roller coasters: a double-loop roller that careens around the simulated Grand Canyon, and the cutting-edge El Loco, which is one of only six of its kind in the world. Although El Loco is a short ride (a little longer than a minute), it's a scary one, with negative-g drops, reverse barrel rolls, and open cars that seem ready to tip you out. There's also a laser-tag area, some bouncy/twirly/stomach-churning rides, and a modest number of other, tamer rides for kids of all ages. Video games and a carnival-style arcade are separate from the attractions, though it all still feels pretty hectic.

2880 Las Vegas Blvd. S. (behind Circus Circus). www.adventuredome.com. © **702/794-3939.** Free admission; $6–$12 per ride; daily pass $33 adults, $19 children 33–47 in. tall. Mon–Thurs 11am–6pm; Fri–Sat 10am–midnight; Sun 10am–9pm; hours vary seasonally.

Vegas used to be the land of freebies— or at least, stuff so cheap it seemed free. Those days are an increasingly dim memory, but some hotels still offer free attractions designed to lure you into their casinos. Here's a handy list of the best of the free bait—er, sights:

Bellagio Conservatory (in Bellagio) ★★★ PARK/GARDEN A totally preposterous idea, a larger-than-life greenhouse atrium, filled with seasonal living foliage in riotous colors and styles, changed with meticulous regularity. From Easter to Chinese New Year, events are celebrated with carefully designed splashes of flowers, plants, and remarkable decorations—it's an incredible amount of labor for absolutely no immediate financial payoff. No wonder it's one of the most popular sights in Vegas. Open 24 hours.

Bellagio Fountains (outside Bellagio) ★★★ ICON Giant spouts of water shoot up and down and sideways and dance their little aquatic hearts out

to music ranging from show tunes to Chopin. When we tell people about this, they roll their eyes when they think we aren't looking, and then they go see it for themselves . . . and end up staying for several numbers. Shows are daily every half-hour, starting early afternoon, then every 15 minutes 7pm to midnight. Closed when it's windy; hours vary seasonally.

Eiffel Tower Light Show (outside Paris Las Vegas) ★★ ICON Similar to the nightly sparkly spectacular in Paris, France, this version has its own Vegas flair. The Eiffel Tower twinkles with more than 300 colored lights and 800 white strobe lights, all synchronized and choreographed to light up the Vegas skyline even more. Daily, every half-hour from sunset to midnight.

Mirage Volcano (outside the Mirage) ★★ ICON When it first opened with the hotel in 1989, this erupting "volcano" literally stopped traffic on the Strip. The fact that it's not

Circus Circus Midway ★ ENTERTAINMENT COMPLEX First inaugurated in 1968, the big-top action at this family-friendly hotel is billed as the largest permanent circus in the world. High-wire, trapeze, juggling, acrobatics, and more fill the top of the "tent" daily, while more than 200 carnival-style midway games get the young ones inured to the joys (and heartache) of risking money for questionable odds of a reward. Note that while the attractions here are definitely kid-friendly, you have to go through the casino to get to them. In Circus Circus, 2880 Las Vegas Blvd. S. www.circuscircus.com. © **702/734-0410.** Free admission. Mon–Thurs 11am–11pm; Fri, Sun 11am–midnight, Sat 11am–1am.

Stratosphere Tower & Thrill Rides ★★ THRILL RIDE Whether you come for the views or the scary rides, the Stratosphere Tower is a uniquely Vegas experience. Indoor and outdoor decks provide remarkable views of the city, southern Nevada, and perhaps even California on a clear day, from this, the tallest observation tower west of the Mississippi (more than 1,100 ft.). Obviously, acrophobics should avoid the tower at all costs.

Atop the tower are four marvelous thrill rides that will test your mettle and perhaps how strong your stomach is. The **Big Shot** is a breathtaking free-fall quite as spectacular these days—even after a 2008 makeover—says more about how jaded we've become than how cool it is. Get up close to feel the heat of the "lava" blasts and the rumble of the sound system. Eruptions are daily on the hour after dark until 11pm.

Welcome to Fabulous Las Vegas Sign ★★★ ICON Erected in 1959, this colorfully lit neon sign is probably the most iconic and most photographed attraction in Las Vegas. It's located in the median of Las Vegas Boulevard about a mile south of Mandalay Bay, but there is a parking lot. It has no formal address; GPS users should use 5200 Las Vegas Blvd. S. to get in the vicinity. The lot is open 24 hours, but go at night when it's lit for the best photo opportunities.

Wynn Conservatory (in Wynn Las Vegas) ★ PARK/GARDEN Although not as jaw-dropping as its spiritual cousin, the Bellagio Conservatory (see above), this indoor atrium of floral displays is still worth a gander, if for no other reason than it's on your way from the front door to the casino. The arrangements change regularly, though they may reflect the striking floral mosaics on the floor below. It's open 24 hours.

Wynn Lake of Dreams (in Wynn Las Vegas) ★ ICON Masked from the street by a 150-foot-tall "mountain," this light, laser, fog, and special-effect show can only be seen from select areas inside the hotel, mostly in bars requiring you to buy expensive drinks. Should you bother? Maybe. Twice an hour, a lake lights up with pretty colors, cued to tunes ranging from classical to Louis Armstrong, for "interludes." At the top of the hour are bigger extravaganzas of weird hologram erotic-psychedelic images, while shapes and puppets pop out for even more weird action, with some rather adult imagery. Shows are every 30 minutes, from 6pm to midnight.

ride that thrusts you 160 feet in the air along a 228-foot spire at the top of the tower, and then plummets back down again. Sitting in an open car, you seem to be dangling in space over Las Vegas. Amping up the terror factor is **X-Scream,** a giant teeter-totter-style device that propels you in an open car off the side of the 100-story tower and lets you dangle there weightlessly before returning you to relative safety. Then there's the aptly named **Insanity,** a spinning whirligig of a contraption that straps you into a seat and twirls you around 1,000 feet or so above terra firma. Insanity is right.

Finally, if whirling and twirling and spinning around at the top of the tower is just not rad enough for you, there's **SkyJump,** in which you get to leap off the top of the thing. We wish we were kidding. Jumpers are put into flight suits and harnesses, then taken up to the 108th floor where they get connected to a big cable/winch contraption. Then, they jump. It's a "controlled" descent, meaning that you don't just drop the roughly 830 feet to the landing pad, but you are flying down at speeds of up to 40 mph with nothing but a couple of metal wires keeping you in place. There are lots of safety features, and the three other SkyJumps around the world (in New Zealand, China, and South

Korea) have sterling safety records. Nevertheless, though the attraction calls the other ride Insanity, I think this one is the truly insane option. *Note:* The rides are shut down in inclement weather and high winds.

Atop the Strat, 2000 Las Vegas Blvd. S. www.stratospherehotel.com. ✆ **702/380-7777.** Tower: Admission $25 adults, $5 hotel guests; $16 Nevada residents and military with ID; $14 children 12 and under; prices higher on weekends. Rides: Big Shot $25, X-Scream $25, Insanity $25, SkyJump $120. Tower admission waived with ride purchase. Multi-ride and all-day packages available. Sun–Thurs 10am–1am; Fri–Sat 10am–2am; hours vary seasonally. Minimum height 48 in. for Big Shot, 52 in. for X-Scream and Insanity. Maximum weight 275 lb. for SkyJump.

DOWNTOWN

The Arts Factory ★ COMMERCIAL ART GALLERY   Believe it or not, Las Vegas has a pretty decent art scene (what some would consider soul-crushing is what others consider inspirational), and this complex, located in the 18b Arts District, is the place to find proof. It features several galleries, boutiques, and several workspaces for local artists, plus a bistro and bar.

107 E. Charleston Blvd. www.dtlvarts.com. ✆ **702/383-3133.** Free admission. Hours vary by gallery.

Cannabition Cannabis Museum ★★ MUSEUM   My tour guide's name is Blaze, and yes, that is his real name, along with his favorite pastime. A trip to the only interactive cannabis museum (not *that* kind of interactive, though) is full of these kinds of quirks and nods to Nevada's latest vice addition: recreational marijuana. Since pot became legal in 2016, dispensaries have popped up all over town, so it was only a matter of time before an enterprising soul figured out a way to celebrate Mary Jane out in the open (which, for the record, you definitely cannot do in Nevada). At this adults-only attraction, the tour begins outside of the museum to view a far-out, 170-foot mural that takes you through the origins of the plant and its uses in ancient cultures. Inside the 10,000-square-foot space, the guide leads you through several rooms with art installations dedicated to the various nuances of pot culture. One work uses LED lights to represent neurons leading into a giant brain (on drugs, get it?). You'll learn how marijuana is grown and cultivated and explore the types of environments and rituals in which people like to enjoy said marijuana. There's also Bongzilla, the World's Largest Bong, which stands 24 feet tall; its bowl holds (allegedly) a quarter of a pound of weed. If anything, this is a fun way to kill about 30 to 45 minutes and take some fun selfies with some really cool art. And it probably doesn't hurt to be stoned.

450 Fremont St. #140. www.cannabition.com. ✆ **702/909-0420.** Admission $24.20. Mon–Thurs 11am–9pm; Fri–Sun 11am–11pm. Ages 21 and over.

Discovery Children's Museum ★★★ MUSEUM   Bringing your little ones to Vegas isn't as taboo as it used to be, but it can be a drag for them to be dragged around to a bunch of overstimulating places where they can't do a thing. Thankfully, there's this lifesaver near the Smith Center of the

Performing Arts. It's filled with interactive exhibits, meaning the wee ones can touch and play, all the while learning about science, nutrition, and the environment (even if they might not realize it). There are three floors of hands-on fun where the kids storm a fantasy castle (Excalibur!), discover an ancient city (Luxor!), and scramble around on a 70-foot-tall science-filled jungle gym. You, and they, will definitely be tuckered out afterwards.

360 Promenade Place (at the Smith Center for the Performing Arts). www.discovery kidslv.org. © **702/382-5437.** Admission $14.50 ages 1–99. Tues–Fri 9am–4pm; Sat 10am–5pm; Sun noon–5pm. Hours vary by season.

Fremont Street Experience ★★★ ICON

The Fremont Street Experience is a 5-block, open-air, landscaped strip of outdoor snack shops, vendor carts, and colorful kiosks purveying food and merchandise. Overhead is a 90-foot-high steel-mesh "celestial vault" that at night becomes **Viva Vision,** a high-tech video-and-sound show (the canopy is equipped with more than 12.5 million lights), enhanced by a concert hall–quality sound system. There are a number of different shows, and there's music between the light performances as well. It's really cool, in the Vegas over-the-top way that we love so much. The addition of several hotel bars open to the pedestrian street has upped the "party" quotient, and frequent concerts and events have made it even more popular than ever. Oh, and look up to see people zooming by on a zip line! It's a great place where you can stroll, eat, or even dance to the music under the lights.

Fremont St. (btw. Main St. and Las Vegas Blvd.), Downtown. www.vegasexperience. com. Free admission. Shows nightly on the hour.

Las Vegas Natural History Museum ★ MUSEUM

Like many natural history museums, this one has its share of stuffed-and-posed animals. It's an often dusty, mangy collection of taxidermy, so I suggest breezing past it quickly to get to the museum's star attraction: the dinosaur exhibit. It showcases 35-foot-long *Jurassic World*–quality monsters that are able to growl and move (when you push the appropriate buttons). Instructive text next to the exhibits teaches children and adults about the creatures' habits and the theories surrounding their extinction. Along with the dinos are rooms with live lizards, sharks, and stingrays that guests can feed at certain times and days; and interactive displays that allow kids to dig for fossils as paleontologists or pretend they're marine biologists in a submarine. Old-fashioned? Maybe. An interesting, educational way to spend an afternoon? Absolutely.

900 Las Vegas Blvd. N. (at Washington Ave.). www.lvnhm.org. © **702/384-3466.** Admission $12 adults; $10 seniors, students, and military; $6 children 3–11; free for children 2 and under. Daily 9am–4pm. Closed Thanksgiving and Dec 25.

The Mob Museum ★★★ MUSEUM

This three-story former courthouse contains the actual courtroom where Senator Estes Kefauver held his famous syndicated crime hearings in 1950 and 1951. Watched by 30 million people, the most for any televised event of the time, the trials made it incontrovertibly clear that organized crime *did* exist in the U.S. In a town where it's easy to get caught up in the fantasy that's spoon-fed to visitors, this is a welcome, must-see attraction that will help you understand exactly what sins this city was built on. The famed, and beautifully restored, courtroom is the centerpiece of the museum and gives heft to the idea that a museum should open here, in a city where the majority of museums last no longer than mob stooges.

To avoid that fate, the designers and founders have added a healthy dose of razzmatazz to the proceedings: a fascinating 10-minute film on mob movies narrated by Nicholas Pileggi, slot machine–like displays of video testimonials, the opportunity to take part in a lineup, and fake machine guns to fire. Plan on spending around 2 or 3 hours to really explore.

The museum also makes a gripping case for the idea that mob history may actually be the truest history of the United States. "If you go deep enough, you can see the mob's fingerprints on everything," one bit of wall text grimly asserts. It's followed by exhibits on fixed elections, presidential assassinations, and labor disputes. This is a dark vision, enhanced by the unrelenting gore that assaults the visitor (this is NOT a museum for kids), with pictures of bloodsplattered crime scenes adorning at least half the walls in the place. (They start to look like grisly Rorschach tests after a while.) To its credit, the museum does not glorify crime. You'll learn about the battle for the soul of Las Vegas (and the country) not only from the mob side, but also from that of law enforcement.

The museum has expanded its scope to include modern organized crime, offering striking but educational exhibits covering human trafficking, money laundering, the international drug trade, and other rackets from around the world. Other additions include an interactive crime lab where you can match your fingerprints to famous criminals in history or perform an autopsy on a digital cadaver. (Warning: This gets a little graphic!) Also on the graphic side is the Use of Force Training Experience, which immerses visitors in situations from the perspective of law enforcement officers. Guests undergo a brief but intense training that was created with the guidance of local and national police officers. You are then given a CO_2 pistol and put into a simulation where you get to understand that split-second decision of when—and when not—to shoot. It's a timely yet touchy subject, but cops who have gone through the exhibit themselves have praised it as accurate and realistic.

Two notes: If all this crime talk has left you in desperate need of a drink, head down to the basement, where the museum has built its very own speakeasy, the **Underground,** with a full bar and distillery. You're transported back in time to Prohibition. Don't worry, this booze wasn't made in a bathtub, and you don't need to know the password to get in.

Second, you can get your full vintage Vegas experience for a little less scratch with ticket combos that get you into the Mob Museum and the Neon Museum or the Mob Museum and a ride on the High Roller.

300 Stewart Ave. www.themobmuseum.org. ✆ **702/229-2734.** Admission $27–$45 adults; $17 children 11–17 and students with ID; $21 seniors, military, law enforcement, and teachers; $17 NV residents with ID. Discounts for booking online. Sun–Wed 9am–10pm; Thurs–Sat 9am–midnight.

THE resurgence OF DOWNTOWN LAS VEGAS

For decades, the bulk of the attention, and development dollars, in Las Vegas has gone to the Strip, while the original part of Sin City, the Downtown area, languished and seemed on the verge of extinction.

Credit, at least in part, online retailer Zappos.com for changing all that. Its plan to move its headquarters and a couple of thousand employees into the former city hall building spurred a resurgence in Downtown Las Vegas, with major revamps to old hotels, new restaurants, fun and funky bars, attractions, street festivals, and more, all lending a new sense of life to the area.

The bulk of the action happens on the **Fremont Street Experience,** the pedestrian-only mall on Fremont Street between Main Street and Las Vegas Boulevard. That's where you'll find most of the casinos, shopping, and restaurants.

The **Fremont East Entertainment District** takes up several blocks of Fremont Street just east of Las Vegas Boulevard. It has several bars, lounges, and clubs all within a few feet of each other, so no matter how much you may be stumbling, you can probably still make it to the next one in your all-night pub crawl.

This is where you'll find the **Downtown Container Park** (p. 201), a shopping and dining complex made out of recycled shipping containers and prefabricated metal cubes. In addition to the retail and food options, there's a giant treehouse-style jungle gym inside for the kids, and a fire-breathing praying mantis sculpture out front for kids of all ages. Live entertainment adds more fun.

The **18b Arts District** is a few blocks south of Fremont Street, bounded, more or less, by Las Vegas Boulevard to the east, Commerce Street to the west, Hoover Avenue on the north, and Colorado Avenue on the south. Art galleries, antiques and collectible stores, and more than a few pawn shops and bail bonds offices (to give it color, we suppose) are scattered about the neighborhood, giving it a refreshingly bohemian feeling as it sits in the shadow of the overprocessed Strip.

The monthly **First Friday Las Vegas** street festival happens in the heart of the 18b Arts District on the blocks surrounding the intersection of Casino Center Drive and Colorado Avenue. Local artists hawk their wares while live bands and DJs keep the crowds moving, play areas (complete with a video game truck) keep the kids entertained, and food vendors and food trucks keep everyone fat and happy. It's one of the few places where there is a true sense of community in Vegas. It happens, appropriately enough, on the first Friday of every month from 5pm until 11pm. For more information, visit www.firstfriday lasvegas.com.

The area has even qualified for its own big-time music, arts, and food event with the **Life Is Beautiful Festival,** held in the fall. Last year the fest drew more than 130,000 people to it stages, and food tents had eats from local favorites such as Other Mama, Nacho Daddy, and STK. For more information, visit www. lifeisbeautiful.com.

The Neon Museum ★★★ MUSEUM   This is where old Las Vegas signs go to retire. Enter through the former La Concha Motel lobby, which was transplanted, then transformed, into a visitor center, then follow your guide out to a yard crammed full of fabulous old neon signs. But this experience isn't just about eye candy: The tour guides are freakishly knowledgeable about Las Vegas design history and have lots of great anecdotes to share about not just the neon signs, but also their creators and the city. Some of the 150 signs are familiar from iconic photos of Las Vegas, like those from the Stardust and Algiers casinos, while others are completely new to most visitors, like the splendidly curvaceous Silver Slipper sign and the funky Queen of Hearts. The Neon Museum has restored quite a few back to full function, so try to visit at night to get the full dazzle. Capitalizing on its unique collection, the Boneyard (as it's affectionately called by locals) lets individuals and professionals book time for private shoots, so the iconic signs have become the backdrop for many a wedding and engagement photo. Night tours are even more (forgive me) illuminating, especially if you shell out for Brilliant, a 40-minute choreographed show of the old signs lighting up to a soundtrack of Vegas standards. Tour groups are kept small and intimate, so you must book early, preferably online.

770 Las Vegas Blvd. N. (at McWilliams Ave.). www.neonmuseum.org. ℂ **702/387-6366.** Admission $19 daytime tours adults; $15 seniors, students, military, NV residents; $26 nighttime tours adults; $22 seniors, students, military, NV residents; children 6 and under free; $23 Brilliant tours adults; $15 seniors, students, military, NV residents; $42 Brilliant plus guided tour; $32 seniors, students, military, NV residents. No kids under 13 allowed on nighttime tours. Daily 9am–9pm; hours vary seasonally.

SlotZilla ★★ THRILL RIDE   Here it is, the Vegas attraction that deserves to take a place in the pantheon of iconic Sin City silliness alongside the Bellagio Fountains and the Welcome to Fabulous Las Vegas sign. Billed as, and shaped like, the world's tallest slot machine, it's really a launching platform for two sets of zip lines that run down Fremont Street. The lower four are traditional, seated lines running from about 6 stories up by Neonopolis to Binion's, or about 3 blocks. The top "zoom" lines feature an opportunity to fly superhero-style, facedown, from 12 stories up all the way to a platform next to Main Street some 5 blocks away. Compared to some zip lines in more adventurous settings, this one is pretty tame, but it's still not for the faint of heart, especially as you step out over the edge and then come in for the unexpectedly jerky landing. Go at night for the full effect of all the Glitter Gulch neon lights. This thing started out popular, so rides may be sold out and/or wait times could be epic. Consider booking in advance.

425 Fremont St. www.vegasexperience.com. ℂ **702/ZIPVEGAS.** Admission $25–$49. Must be over 60 lb. and under 300 lb. to ride. Sun–Thurs noon–1am; Fri–Sat 1pm–2am.

JUST OFF THE STRIP

Dig This! ★★ ENTERTAINMENT COMPLEX   Did you have a sandbox that you used to play in when you were a kid? Well, then you're going to love this: a big kid's sandbox where you get to play with real bulldozers and excavators. The program starts with classroom instruction that gives you an overview on how to operate the big machines. It's a lot more complicated than you'd think, requiring a level of hand-eye coordination far beyond that of piloting an SUV. Next, you get to climb into the machine out in a big dirt lot and get used to the controls. Then the real fun starts, with a series of games and challenges that include digging holes, moving rocks, and even playing a version of excavator basketball. It isn't cheap, but fantasy fulfillment rarely is.

3012 Rancho Dr. (btw. Meade and Sirius aves.). www.digthisvegas.com. © **888/344-8447** or 702/222-4344. Admission $169 and up. Daily; hours vary seasonally.

Fast Lap Indoor Kart Racing ★★ ENTERTAINMENT COMPLEX When NASCAR pro Kurt Busch is in Las Vegas, this is the place he comes to play. Tucked away on a dead-end street in a mostly industrial part of town near the Strip, this is a no-frills go-kart experience, with a short track filling a former warehouse space that still looks like a warehouse. The gasoline-powered karts are equipped with 200cc Honda motors, allowing you to push the little monsters up to 50 mph (if you dare) as you battle in 10-minute-long races (as many laps as you can get) against other drivers. While bumping and other unsportsmanlike contact is officially frowned upon, in reality this is a grown-up (mostly testosterone-driven) sport. So put your foot on the gas and see if you can be first to the checkered flag! *Note:* You must be at least 5 feet tall to participate, and children 17 and under must be accompanied by a guardian.

4288 Polaris Ave. www.fastlaplv.com. © **702/736-8113.** $26 per race or $65 for 3 races. Mon–Sat 10am–11pm.

KISS by Monster Mini Golf ★★ ENTERTAINMENT COMPLEX If they had stopped at the indoor, glow-in-the-dark, 18-hole miniature golf course themed to the classic rock band KISS, it probably would've been just mildly amusing. But then they went and added a gift shop, a cafe, a wedding chapel (where KISS impersonators will marry you), arcade games, a DJ playing nonstop KISS tunes, and more KISS memorabilia than the members of the band probably have in their garages. The entire package reaches an almost epic level of giddy, grin-worthy silliness. And yes, there is a hole where you have to putt the ball up a giant replica of Gene Simmons's tongue.

Rio Hotel and Casino, 3700 Flamingo Rd. www.kissminigolf.com. © **702/558-6256.** Free admission; 18 holes of mini-golf $12 ages 7 and up; free for children 6 and under. Daily 10am–midnight.

National Atomic Testing Museum ★★★ MUSEUM No thrill ride on the Strip will scare the wits out of you as effectively as the Atomic Testing Museum. That's not its purpose, of course. This is a science and history museum—an affiliate museum of the mighty Smithsonian Institution—covering the 50 years of atomic testing, from 1951 to 1992 (928 nuclear tests in all), that occurred in the desert outside Vegas. But there comes a moment when your heart will race, your stomach will drop down to your knees, and all at once the reality of the power of the nuclear bomb will hit you with the force of a nightmare. The moment comes early in the exhibit. After an effective and dramatic retelling of the history that led up to the invention of the bomb, you'll be ushered into a small room resembling a concrete bunker for a video about the testing, with shots of actual explosions. As the mushroom cloud rises in front of you, the lights flash a blinding white, subwoofers send vibrations to the center of your sternum, your bench shakes, and air cannons blast you with wind. It's intense.

After that wrenching start, the rest of the museum helps visitors put into context what they've seen. You'll learn about the physics behind the bomb; the myriad innovations, from high-speed photography to bigger drills, that emerged from the scientific work going on at the testing site; and the cultural "fallout," if you will, of the Cold War, from advertisements glamorizing the bomb to panic-provoking bomb shelters. Iconic items from the test site—a decoupler, a massive drill bit, a farm silo—are interspersed with news clips and state-of-the-art, truly whiz-bang, interactive exhibits. Pull your attention from these, however, if a docent happens by. Many of these volunteers are former employees of the Testing Site; no, they don't glow, but get one talking and they'll regale you with insider's tales of what it was like to wrestle with the bomb, live in its shadow, and work for the government.

755 E. Flamingo Rd. www.nationalatomictestingmuseum.org. ℂ **702/794-5151.** Admission $22 adults; $18 seniors, military, students with ID, and Nevada residents; $16 children 7–14; free for children 6 and under. Mon–Sat 10am–5pm; Sun noon–5pm.

SpeedVegas ★★★ RACECOURSE   Those who feel the need for speed don't necessarily need to haul themselves all the way out to the Las Vegas Motor Speedway anymore. Opened in 2016, this fast and furious addition to the Strip is 10 minutes from the Welcome to Las Vegas sign, with a full arsenal of exotic muscle and supercars ready to be taken around the track. After a quick peek around the 100-acre complex, which includes a 2-story welcome center, peel around the 1.5-mile Formula One–inspired racetrack (the longest in Las Vegas); it features 12 20-degree banked turns and a half-mile straight-away. The only thing more fun than driving the track is choosing which car you'll take for a spin: Feel flashy with the Lamborghini? Experience the German precision of the Porsche? Or ride the horsepower of American muscle with the Mustang? You're paying per lap, so why not all three?

14200 Las Vegas Blvd. S. www.speedvegas.com. ℂ **888/998-2505.** $39–$99 per lap. Sun–Fri 8am–6pm, Sat 7am–6pm.

Topgolf ★★★ ENTERTAINMENT COMPLEX   Some days you just want to hit a few balls, but a trip to Topgolf is a far cry from a day at the driving range. This four-level, 105,000-square-foot venue holds not only 102 hitting bays but also a live performance stage, multiple kitchens and bars, and VIP areas with water features and cabanas. Even if you consider yourself a "non-golfer," you'll find a way to work on your swing. Rent out a hitting bay with some friends and take your best shot, scoring points by hitting at targets located across the 215-yard outfield. Microchip technology in the balls and the targets lets you know how accurate and far (or not) you've launched that projectile with your club. Various games coded into the experience will help you with your competitive spirit.

4627 Koval Ln. www.topgolf.com/us/lasvegas. ℂ **702/933-8458.** Admission $5 one-time fee for membership card, $30–$75/hr. per bay, up to 6 players. Daily 9am–2am.

Clark County Museum ★★ MUSEUM   It's telling, I think, that the history of a doomed ocean liner is center stage on the Strip, but a history museum that details the story of Sin City itself is relegated to a site 10 miles southeast of the center. (This is a city with a penchant for bulldozing its history and for imploding anything that gets in the way of bigger profits.) Which is a shame because the museum is a real gem, chockablock with evocative artifacts and interactive exhibits detailing the story of the area, from Native Americans through gangsters through the pack of corporate thieves who control the Strip today. For a museum this far off the Strip, and so cheap to visit, it's startlingly high tech: Sensors turn on narration, sound effects, and even visual effects. Highlights are half a dozen actual houses that you wander through, hearing about the lives of the real people who lived in them, from a Paiute twig-hut village to a house lived in by men involved in the construction of the Hoover dam, to a gold miner's house and a 1960s abode from the Atomic Testing Site. The museum is also in the process of curating the October 1st Collection, amassing pieces that mourners left as memorials after the mass shooting at the Route 91 Festival in 2017, and the stories behind them. It's all part of the mission to preserve the city's history, and that includes its reaction after this tragedy. Back outside, there's a garden with native plants. *Note:* Because it is a good, long drive from the Strip, you'll need a rental car to get here. A rideshare or taxi really isn't practical.

1830 S. Boulder Hwy., Henderson. www.clarkcountynv.gov. © **702/455-7955.** Admission $2 adults, $1 seniors and children 3–15, free for children 2 and under. Daily 9am–4:30pm. Closed Thanksgiving, Dec 25, and Jan 1.

Ethel M Chocolates ★ FACTORY TOUR   Ethel Mars began making fine chocolates in a little candy kitchen in the early 20th century. Her small enterprise evolved to produce not only dozens of varieties of superb boxed chocolates, but also some of the world's most famous candies: M&Ms, Milky Way, 3 Musketeers, Snickers, and Mars bars. Alas, the tour lasts only about 10 minutes and consists entirely of viewing stations with an audiotape explaining the chocolate-baking process. Even more sadly, you get only one small chocolate as a sample. There is a fully stocked gift shop, or if you want to go nuts, chocolate-tasting classes are available hourly. *Note:* Come before 2:30pm, which is when the workers start to go home.

What's really worth seeing is outside: a lovely and extensive 4-acre garden displaying over 300 species of rare and exotic cacti with signs provided for self-guided tours. It's best appreciated in spring when the cacti are in full bloom, or in December when the garden is bedecked with holiday lights.

2 Cactus Garden Dr. (just off Mountain Vista and Sunset Way, in the Green Valley Business Park). www.ethelm.com. © **702/435-2655** or 702/435-2608. Free admission. Chocolate tasting classes $15 adults, $6 children. Daily 8am–8pm. Self-guided chocolate factory tours Mon–Thurs 8:30am–4:30pm. Holiday hours may vary.

Lion Habitat Ranch ★★★ ZOO   Longtime Vegas visitors roared with displeasure when the MGM Grand closed its signature lion habitat in 2012. The big secret, however, was that populating those casino-facing digs was merely the lions' day job, and their "main office" is now open for tours that are significantly more satisfying. More than two dozen lions, from infant to ancient, are in residence at the facility run by Keith and Bev Evans for more than 20 years. All the animals are either rescues or born here, and while it always gives one pause to see these majestic creatures in captivity instead of running wild, the digs are plush, and the animals are obviously well taken care of. Visitation programs vary from simple do-it-yourself tours to "Behind the Scenes" options where trainers take you a personal tour and explain their daily duties. How often can you say you fed a giraffe? *Note:* Finding the place can be challenging; it's in the middle of a scrub brush desert, close to the M Resort on the southernmost edge of Las Vegas. Consult a map or GPS before you go.

382 Bruner Ave. (near St. Rose Pkwy.). www.lionhabitatranch.com. © **702/595-6666.** Admission $25 and up adults; 1 child per adult free, $10 extra child, $20 seniors, military, and law enforcement with ID, $18 students. Fri–Mon 10am–2pm; hours vary seasonally.

Pinball Hall of Fame & Museum ★★★ MUSEUM   And you thought only children's museums could be interactive. Arguably the most fun museum in Las Vegas, this is 10,000 square feet of hands-on entertainment and history for a bargain. A nice departure from the slot machines in casinos, there are more than 150 pinball machines lined up wall-to-wall for visitors to play. Some of them go as far back as the 1940s and are still fully operational (though with the older ones, you may need a lighter touch) and are maintained daily. The games are actual works of art in themselves. Consider Elton John's costumes on the 1975 *Captain Fantastic* machine, or the campy cartoons of the *Star Trek* machine from 1979. You can even nerd-out on the non-pinball games, like when you sit in the cabin for the *Star Trek* arcade game direct from the '80s. You still have to pop in a quarter to play (two if the game is from 1990 or after), but it's money well spent, as proceeds go towards maintenance of the machines and to charity. In a modern twist, scan the QR bar code found on many of the machines with your smartphone to learn more about these old-school relics.

1610 E. Tropicana Ave. www.pinballmuseum.org. © **702/597-2627.** Free admission; game costs vary. Sun–Thurs 11am–11pm; Fri–Sat 11am–midnight.

Shelby American Heritage Center ★ MUSEUM   That's Shelby as in Carroll Shelby, who in the 1960s helped shape the American muscle car as we know it. In 2014, the museum moved from near the Las Vegas Motor Speedway to across from Town Square on Las Vegas Boulevard, so gear heads can easily get their Shelby fix. On display is the first Cobra roadster CSX2000 that Shelby ever built, along with cherry Mustangs and the Shelby Series 1 prototype, and about 20 more rides, all with spiffy racing stripes. The space also features the modification shop where fast cars become even faster, but you can't get near those. The guided tour takes about 90 minutes and is comprehensive, with anecdotes and a complete history of Shelby and his craft. Admission and tours are free, but consider donating to the Carroll Shelby Foundation, dedicated to organ transplant education, as Shelby was a heart transplant recipient in 1990.

6405 Ensworth St. (at Sunset Rd.). www.shelbyamerican.com. ⓒ **702/942-7325.** Free admission. Mon–Fri 9:30am–6pm, Sat 7am–6pm, Sun 10am–4pm; guided tours Mon–Fri 10:30am and 1:30pm, Sat 10:30am.

SkyZone ★ ENTERTAINMENT COMPLEX   So you brought the kids to Vegas and they're bouncing off the walls with boredom. How about giving them a chance to bounce off the walls with glee instead? This indoor facility features several trampoline arenas; some are used for organized games and activities such as dodgeball, and others are open for random bouncing. The kids are calling it "tramping" these days, but adults are catching on to this exhausting form of exercise. If you've wanted to practice your Cirque du Soleil skills, this might be the place—after you sign the waiver. There are other amusements here as well, including a foam-block pit that kids can jump into, games, and a small snack shop, plus a much-needed quiet area for parents.

7440 Dean Martin Dr. (at Warm Springs Rd.). www.skyzone.com/lasvegas. ⓒ **702/560-5900.** Admission $16–$26. Daily 3-11pm.

NORTH & WEST OF THE STRIP

Las Vegas Mini Gran Prix ★★ ENTERTAINMENT COMPLEX   After all our yammering about how Vegas isn't for families and how most of the kid-friendly options are overpriced tourist traps, we can wholeheartedly recommend a family-appropriate entertainment option. Part arcade, part go-kart racetrack, this is exactly what you want to help your kids (and maybe yourselves) work their ya-yas out. The arcade is well stocked, with a better quality of prizes than one often finds, but we suggest not spending too much time in there and instead hustling outside to the slide, the little roller coaster, and best of all, the four go-kart tracks. Each offers a different thrill, from the longest track in Vegas, full of twists and turns as you try to outrace other drivers, to a high-banked oval built just so you can try to make other drivers take spills onto the grass, to, best of all, a timed course. The last requires a driver's license, so it's for you rather than your kids (but the wee ones will find the fourth course is just for them). Here you can live out your Le Mans or police-chase fantasies as you blast through twisting runs one kart at a time, trying to beat your personal best. The staff is friendly, and the pizzas at the food court are triple the size and half the price of those found in your hotel. The one drawback: It's far from the Strip, so you'll need a rental car. *Note:* Kids have to be at least 36 inches tall to ride any of the attractions.

1401 N. Rainbow Rd. (just off U.S. 95 N.). www.lvmgp.com. ⓒ **702/500-1794.** Ride tickets $8 each, $7.50 each for 5 or more; ride wristbands $23 per hr. Mon–Fri 11am–9pm and Sat–Sun 10am–9pm; hours vary seasonally.

Las Vegas Motor Speedway ★★ RACECOURSE   This impressive facility is widely considered to be the premier racing venue in the Southwest United States, and rivals fabled speedways in Talladega, Charlotte, and Daytona for its scope and the deep catalog of year-round events. The main oval hosts a major NASCAR race weekend in March, packing pretty much every one of the 135,000 seats, but there are happenings on it and the other tracks more than 260 days a year. There is an NHRA-sanctioned drag strip that runs high-octane funny cars and motorcycles, two road courses, a dirt track, a short oval "bullring," and more.

Of the many unique features (how many raceways have a view of the Strip?), one of the most interesting for race fans is the Neon Garage, an infield facility where the drivers and their teams set up camp for the major races. Big windows and overhead galleries allow people to watch the cars being worked on and give up-close access to the men and women behind the wheel. You pay a premium, obviously, but true speed freaks should get their tickets early.

If watching the action is not enough for you, several programs are available to put you behind the wheel for some adrenaline junkie action. **The Richard Petty Driving Experience** (www.drivepetty.com; ✆ **800/237-3889**) offers both NASCAR-style vehicles and new American muscle cars (Camaro, Mustang, Challenger, and the like) that are raced on the superspeedway; **Dream Racing** (www.dreamracing.com; ✆ **702/605-3000**) has specially modified Ferrari race cars running the inside road track; and **Exotics Racing** (www.exoticsracing.com; ✆ **702/802-5662**) has a full fleet of Ferraris, Porsches, Lamborghinis, McLarens, and more that run on their proprietary 1.2-mile course. All give you classroom instruction and time behind the wheel, and while they are not cheap, there are few things more thrilling than going down the back straightaway in a race car doing 140 mph or trying to find the perfect path out of the tight curve you are taking in a 430 Scuderia at stupid, grinworthy speeds.

7000 Las Vegas Blvd. N. (directly across from Nellis Air Force Base). www.lvms.com. ✆ **702/644-4444.** Tickets $10–$75 (higher for major events), ride-along experiences $109 and up, drive experiences $199 and up. Race days vary. Take I-15 north to exit 54.

Nevada State Museum ★ MUSEUM   Part nature museum, part Native American museum, part Las Vegas museum: There's certainly a lot of history jam-packed into 13,000 square feet, though none of it is particularly in-depth. But it's worth a stop if you want to learn about the entire Silver State from soup to nuts, without committing much time. Sundays offer a few interactive activities geared toward kids. If your time is limited, skip this place in favor of the far more interesting **Springs Preserve** (p. 173).

309 S. Valley View Blvd. (at Meadows Lane). nvculture.org. ✆ **702/486-5205.** Tickets $20 adults, $10 NV residents, free for children 17 and under. Admission includes neighboring Springs Preserve. Tues–Sun 9am–5pm.

Pole Position Raceway ★ ENTERTAINMENT COMPLEX   Similar in concept to the **Fast Lap Indoor Kart Racing** facility (p. 167), Pole Position is a more polished go-kart racing venue with a sleek, modern facility and electric-powered racers. The indoor course is short but satisfying, and the lack of gas-powered engines doesn't mean you sacrifice any of the speed. You may retain your hearing longer, which is definitely a good thing. It's worth noting that the karts are small and the mandatory helmets are tight, so claustrophobics may want to seek alternative fun. The facility also has a small video and virtual-reality game arcade, and a gift shop.

4175 S. Arville Rd. www.polepositionraceway.com. ℂ **702/227-7223.** Adults 56 in. or taller $26, kids 17 and under or 48 in. and taller $22; multi-race packages available. Sun–Thurs 11am–11pm; Fri–Sat 11am–midnight.

Springs Preserve ★★★ NATURAL RESERVE By now, perhaps you've learned that *Las Vegas* is Spanish for "the meadows." This facility is set on the 180-acre site of the original springs that fed Las Vegas until it dried in the 1960s (we told you that Hoover Dam comes in handy). These days, Las Vegas is an environmental nightmare, along with much of the rest of the planet, and this remarkable attraction educates visitors about the possibilities of reversing some of the damage.

The preserve is set amid nature and hiking trails, plus man-made wetlands (an interesting concept). Its focal point is a large interpretive center that gives the history of Las Vegas from a land- and water-use perspective. The displays are creative and interactive, including a room with a reproduction flash flood that uses 5,000 gallons of water; and one with a simulation of the experience of working on Hoover Dam. The other buildings are all built according to standards that have the least environmental impact, using modern construction versions of adobe and other green concepts. Each building tackles an aspect of desert living and the environment, including one that instructs kids on the glories of recycling, complete with a compost tunnel to crawl through! Other displays focus on environmentally friendly kitchens and bathrooms, while the gardens demonstrate "green" gardening.

The outdoor kids' play area is made from recycled materials and has big fake animals to climb on and real live ones to look at, in case the kiddies have grown tired of learning responsible stuff. Given the care and knowledge with which these urgent issues are addressed, this is an extraordinary facility for any town, but particularly for this one.

Note: Admission includes entrance to the adjacent Nevada State Museum reviewed above.

333 S. Valley View Blvd. www.springspreserve.org. ℂ **702/822-8344.** Admission $19 adults, $17 seniors and students with ID, $11 children 5–17, free for children 4 and under, $10 Nevada residents. Free admission to trails and gardens. Daily 9am–5pm.

Wet 'n Wild ★ AMUSEMENT PARK This is the city's only (for now) water amusement park. A descendant of the Wet 'n Wild that was on the Strip for 2 decades, this state-of-the-art facility is on the far west side of town at the foothills of the famous Red Rock National Conservancy Area. It has more than 20 slides, rides, and attractions, from scary dropping, looping things to

ORGANIZED tours

Just about every hotel in town has a tour desk offering a seemingly infinite number of sightseeing opportunities in and around Las Vegas. You're sure to find a tour company that will take you where you want to go. For example, **Gray Line** (www.grayline.com; © **800/634-6579**) offers a rather comprehensive roster, including the following:

o A pair of 5- to 6-hour **city tours** (day or night) with various itineraries, including visits to **Ethel M**

Chocolates and the **Fremont Street Experience**

o Half-day excursions to **Hoover Dam** and **Red Rock Canyon**

o A half-day tour to **Lake Mead** and **Hoover Dam**

o Several full-day **Grand Canyon** excursions

Call for details or inquire at your hotel's tour desk, where you'll also find free magazines with coupons for discounts on these tours.

---

lazy, play-around-in-the-water–type features. Adrenaline junkies should try the Constrictor, featuring what are billed as the tightest, highest banked curves in the world; and the Tornado, a multi-person raft ride that shoots you 36 feet in the air before blasting you through a tunnel and into a whirlpool funnel. Shade is at a premium, and the crowds make the lines long, but if you want something fun to do with your kids, this is one of your few good Vegas options.

7055 S. Fort Apache Rd. (at Arby Ave.). wetnwildlasvegas.com. © **702/830-7975.** Admission $40 adults, $30 kids under 42 in. tall. Discounts available online. Season passes available. Sun–Thurs 10:30am–8pm; Fri–Sat 10:30am–10pm. Closed Oct–Mar; days and hrs. vary seasonally.

CASINO GAMBLING

Las Vegas is no longer the gambling capital of the world. That title belongs to Macau, China, where casinos with familiar names like MGM Grand, the Venetian, and Wynn pull in more money in 2 months than the casinos on the Strip generate all year. Even in the United States, the proliferation of legal gambling in other areas is eclipsing Las Vegas in terms of revenue and scope. As of this writing, there are more than two dozen states that have Native American or riverboat casinos, and nearly that many that have commercial casinos. Additionally, the 2018 Supreme Court ruling lifting the ban on sports betting will also likely take a big piece of the pie. And in Las Vegas, gambling is no longer the biggest revenue generator, earning less than half of most resorts' revenue. The rest comes from hotel rates, dining, nightclubs, and the like.

But strip away all the facts and figures, and what you are left with is the undeniable lure of Las Vegas as a gambling mecca. It is, in no small part, what built this city and what continues to drive it, as evidenced by the fact that you can find gaming almost everywhere. There are slot machines at the airport, waiting for you to get off the plane or giving you something to do while you wait for your baggage. Convenience stores and gas stations have video poker so you can play a few hands while filling up. And the average Strip casino has literally dozens of blackjack, craps, roulette, and other gaming tables.

People come here to play, and although they may lose more often than they win, it doesn't stop anyone from trying to win the Big One. You know, like that woman in 2010 who won $2.9 million on a "Wizard of Oz" penny slot (her name was Dorothy, by the way). That only a few ever do win big doesn't stop people from trying again and again and again. That's how the casinos make their money.

As you walk through the labyrinthine twists and turns of a casino floor, your attention will likely be dragged to the various games and, your interest piqued, your fingers may begin to twitch in anticipation of hitting it big. Before you put your money on the line, it's imperative to know the rules of the game you want to play. Most casinos offer **free gambling lessons** at scheduled times on weekdays and occasionally on weekends. This provides a risk-free environment for you to learn the games that tickle your fancy. Some casinos follow their lessons with low-stakes game play, enabling you to put your newfound knowledge to the test at small risk. During those instructional sessions, and even when playing on your own, dealers in most casinos will be more than happy to answer any questions you might have. Remember, the casino doesn't need to trick you into losing your money . . . the odds are already in their favor across the board; that's why it's called gambling. Another rule of thumb: Take a few minutes to watch a game being played in order to familiarize yourself with the motions and lingo.

Of course, the Internet has revolutionized gambling in more ways than one, not the least of which is that you can find a free, online version of just about every casino game imaginable. Spend a few hours online betting virtual bucks before you haul out your wallet to try the real deal.

If you are planning on gambling at all, it pays to join a **players' club.** These so-called clubs are designed to attract and keep customers in a given casino by providing incentives: meals, shows, discounts on rooms, gifts, tournament invitations, discounts at hotel shops, VIP treatment, and (more and more) cash rebates. Join a players' club (it doesn't cost a cent to sign up), and soon you too will be getting those great hotel-rate offers—$20-a-night rooms, affordable rooms at the luxury resorts, and even free rooms.

These days, players' clubs go beyond the casino as well. Many of them track your overall spending at participating casinos, including what you pay for meals, shopping, rooms, spa treatments, and more. This means you can earn points toward rewards pretty much anytime you pull out your wallet.

Baccarat

The ancient game of baccarat, or *chemin de fer,* is played with eight decks of cards. Firm rules apply, and there is no skill involved other than deciding whether to bet on the bank or the player. No, really—that's all you have to do.

The dealer does all the other work. You can essentially stop reading here. Oh, all right, carry on.

Any beginner can play, but check the betting minimum before you sit down, as baccarat tends to be a high-stakes game. The cards are shuffled by the croupier and then placed in a box called the "shoe." Players may wager on "bank" or "player" at any time. Two cards are dealt from the shoe and given to the player who has the largest wager against the bank, and two cards are dealt to the croupier, acting as banker. If the rules call for a third card, the player or banker, or both, must take the third card. In the event of a tie, the hand is dealt over. *Note:* The guidelines that determine whether a third card must be drawn (by the player or banker) are provided at the baccarat table upon request.

The object of the game is to come as close as possible to the number 9. To score the hands, the cards of each hand are totaled, and the *last digit* is used. All cards have face value. For example: 10 plus 5 equals 15 (score is 5); 10 plus 4 plus 9 equals 23 (score is 3); 4 plus 3 plus 3 equals 10 (score is 0); and 4 plus 3 plus 2 equals 9 (score is 9). The closest hand to 9 wins.

Each player has a chance to deal the cards. The shoe passes to the player on the right each time the bank loses. If the player wishes, he may pass the shoe at any time.

Note: When you bet on the bank and the bank wins, you're charged a 5% commission. This must be paid at the start of a new game or when you leave the table.

Blackjack

In this, the most popular casino card game, the dealer starts by dealing each player two cards. In some casinos, they're dealt to the player face up, in others face down, but the dealer always gets one card up and one card down. Everybody plays against the dealer. The object is to get a total that is higher than that of the dealer without exceeding 21. All face cards count as 10; all other number cards, except aces, are counted at their face value. An ace may be counted as 1 or 11, whichever you choose it to be.

Starting at her left, the dealer gives additional cards to the players who wish to draw (be "hit") or none to a player who wishes to "stand" or "hold." If your count is nearer to 21 than the dealer's, you win. If it's under the dealer's, you lose. Ties are a "push" (standoff) and nobody wins. After all the players are satisfied with their counts, the dealer exposes her face-down card. If her two cards total 16 or less, the dealer must hit until reaching 17 or over. If the dealer's total exceeds 21, she must pay all the players whose hands have not gone "bust." It is important to note here that the blackjack dealer has no choice as to whether she should stay or draw. A dealer's decisions are predetermined and known to all the players at the table.

If you're a novice or just rusty, do yourself a favor and buy one of the small laminated cards available in shops all over town that illustrate proper play for every possible hand in blackjack. Even longtime players have been known to pull them out, and they can save you from making costly errors.

Craps

The most exciting casino action is usually found at the craps tables. Betting is frenetic, play is fast-paced, and groups quickly bond while yelling and screaming in response to the action.

While it can be intimidating, it's very easy to play a basic game of craps, but figuring out the various bets and the odds associated with the advanced bets is sort of like learning rocket science, only with dice. Entire books are written about the game, so it would be impossible to explain it all in a couple of paragraphs. Here is enough to at least get you started.

The table is divided into marked areas (Pass, Come, Field, Big Six, Big Eight, and so on), where you place your chips to bet. Novices should stick with the "Pass Line" or "Come" bets until they get used to the rhythm of the game.

PASS LINE   A "Pass Line" bet pays even money. If the first roll of the dice adds up to 7 or 11, you win your bet; if the first roll adds up to 2, 3, or 12, you lose your bet. If any other number comes up, it becomes your "point." If you roll your point again, you win, but if a 7 comes up again before your point is rolled, you lose.

DON'T PASS LINE   Betting on the "Don't Pass Line" is the opposite of betting on the Pass Line. This time, you lose if a 7 or an 11 is thrown on the first roll, and you win if a 2 or a 3 is thrown on the first roll.

If the first roll is 12, however, it's a "push" (standoff), and nobody wins. If none of these numbers is thrown and you have a point instead, in order to win, a 7 will have to be thrown before the point comes up again. A Don't Pass bet also pays even money.

COME   Betting on "Come" is the same as betting on the Pass Line, but you must bet after the first roll or on any following roll. Again, you'll win on 7 or 11 and lose on 2, 3, or 12. Any other number is your point, and you win if your point comes up again before a 7.

DON'T COME   This is the opposite of a Come bet. Again, you wait until after the first roll to bet. A 7 or an 11 means you lose; a 2 or a 3 means you win; 12 is a push, and nobody wins. You win if 7 comes up before the point. (The point, you'll recall, was the first number rolled if it was none of the above.)

Poker

For most of the new millennium, poker was just about the biggest thing going, thanks to the popularity of celebrity poker TV shows, poker tours, books, and magazines. Just about every casino had a poker room and those that didn't wanted one.

That popularity has waned a bit in the last few years, with several of the poker rooms getting smaller, offering fewer games, or closing altogether. What's behind the trend? Nothing more than the cooling of a hot fad, really.

The game is still played by lots of people and you can easily find a table, but these days you probably won't have to wait as long to get a seat.

There are lots of variations on the basic game, but one of the most popular is **Texas Hold 'Em.** Two cards are dealt, face down, to the players. After a betting round, five community cards (everyone can use them) are dealt face up on the table. Players make the best five-card hand, using their own cards and the "board" (the community cards), and the best hand wins. The house dealer takes care of the shuffling and the dealing and moves a marker around the table to alternate the start of the deal. The house usually rakes around 10% (it depends on the casino) from each pot. Most casinos also provide tables for playing Seven-Card Stud, Omaha High, and Omaha Hi-Lo. A few even have Seven-Card Stud Hi-Lo split. To learn how these variations are played, either read a book or take lessons.

PAI GOW

Pai Gow is a variation on poker that has become popular. The game is played with a traditional deck plus one joker. The joker is a wild card that can be used as an ace or to complete a straight, a flush, a straight flush, or a royal flush. Each player is dealt seven cards to arrange into two hands: a two-card hand and a five-card hand. As in standard poker, the highest two-card hand is two aces, and the highest five-card hand is a royal flush. The five-card hand *must* be higher than the two-card hand (if the two-card hand is a pair of 6s, for example, the five-card hand must be a pair of 7s or better). Any player's hand that is set incorrectly is an automatic loser. The object of the game is for both of the players' hands to rank higher than both of the banker's hands. Should one hand rank exactly the same as the banker's hand, this is a tie (called a "copy"), *and the banker wins all tie hands.* If the player wins one hand but loses the other, this is a "push," and no money changes hands. The house dealer or any player may be the banker. The bank is offered to each player, and each player may accept or pass. Winning hands are paid even money, less a 5% commission.

LET IT RIDE

Let It Ride is another popular game that involves poker hands. You place three bets at the outset and are dealt three cards. The dealer is dealt two cards that act as community cards (you're not playing against the dealer). Once you've seen your cards, you can choose to pull the first of your three bets back or "let it ride." The object of this game is to get a pair of 10s or better by combining your cards with the community cards. If you're holding a pair of 10s or better in your first three cards (called a "no-brainer"), you want to let your bets ride the entire way through. Once you've decided whether to let your first bet ride, the dealer exposes one of his two cards. Once again, you must decide to take back your middle bet or keep on going. Then the dealer exposes the last of his cards; your third bet must stay. The dealer then turns over the hands of the players and determines whether you've won. Winning bets are paid on a scale, ranging from even money for a single pair up to 1,000 to 1 for a royal flush.

These payouts are for each bet you have in play. Similar to Caribbean Stud, Let It Ride has a bonus that you can win for high hands if you cough up an additional $1 per hand, but be advised that the house advantage on that $1 is obscene. But hey, that's why it's called gambling.

THREE-CARD POKER

Three-Card Poker has become one of the most popular table games in Las Vegas, with gamblers appreciating the relatively low mental input requirements and relatively high payout possibilities. It's actually more difficult to explain than to play. For this reason, we recommend watching a table for a while. You should grasp it pretty quickly.

Basically, players are dealt three cards with no draw and must make the best poker hand out of those three cards. Possible combinations include a straight flush (three sequential cards of the same suit), three of a kind (three queens, for example), a straight (three sequential cards of any suit), a flush (three cards of the same suit), and a pair (two queens, for example). Even if you don't have one of the favored combinations, you can still win if you have cards higher than the dealer's.

On the table are three betting areas—Ante, Play, and Pair Plus. There are actually two games in one on a Three-Card Poker table—"Pair Plus" and "Ante and Play." You can play only Pair Plus or only Ante, or both. You place your chips in the areas in which you want to bet.

In Pair Plus, you are betting only on your hand, not competing against anyone else at the table or the dealer. If you get a pair or better, depending on your hand, the payoff can be pretty fab—straight flush: 40 to 1; three of a kind: 30 to 1; straight: 6 to 1; flush: 3 to 1; and pair: 1 to 1.

In Ante and Play, you are betting that your hand will be better than the dealer's, but you're not competing against anyone else at the table. You place an Ante bet, view your cards, and then, if you decide you like your hand, you place a bet in the Play area equal to your Ante bet. If you get lousy cards and don't want to go forward, you can fold, losing only your Ante bet and your Pair Plus bet, if you made one. Once all bets are made, the dealer's hand is revealed—he must have at least a single queen for the bet to count; if not, your Ante and Play bets are returned. If you beat the dealer's hand, you get a 1 to 1 payoff, but there is a bonus for a particularly good winning hand: straight flush, 5 to 1; three of a kind, 4 to 1; straight, 1 to 1.

Your three cards are dealt. If you play only Pair Plus, it doesn't matter what the dealer has—you get paid if you have a pair or better. If you don't, you lose your bet. If you play the Ante bet, you must then either fold and lose the Ante bet or match the Ante bet by placing the same amount on the Play area. The dealer's hand is revealed, and payouts happen accordingly. Each hand consists of one fresh 52-card deck.

There are several variants to this game, including a bonus bet that can win a progressive jackpot (usually $1) and a six-card version where your cards are combined with the dealer's cards to come up with the best five- or six-card hand. Caesars Entertainment casinos are even offering a million-dollar top prize in their six-card games if, between you and the dealer, you come up with the 9-10-J-Q-K-A of diamonds. Don't scoff—several people have actually won it already!

OTHER POKER VARIANTS

Meanwhile, as if all this weren't enough, new variations on poker games keep popping up. There's Crazy 4 Poker, similar to Three-Card Poker, only with five cards dealt, no draw, and make your best four-card poker hand out of it; a version of Texas Hold 'Em, where you are not competing against other players; several riffs on Three-Card poker that include secondary bonus bets, progressive jackpots, and multiple betting strategies; and more. All of them follow the basic tenets of poker (highest hand wins), but each has its own set of rules, betting strategies, and payouts; if you see one of these games, look for an instructional pamphlet at the table or ask the dealer for a quick lesson.

Roulette

Roulette is an easy game to play, and it's really quite colorful and exciting to watch. The wheel spins and the little ball bounces around, finally dropping into one of the slots, numbered 1 to 36, plus 0 and 00. You can place bets "Inside" the table and "Outside" the table. Inside bets are bets placed on a particular number or a set of numbers. Outside bets are those placed in the boxes surrounding the number table. If you bet on a specific number and it comes up, you are paid 35 to 1 on your bet. Bear in mind, however, that the odds of a particular number coming up are actually 38 to 1 (don't forget the 0 and 00!), so the house has an advantage the moment you place an inside bet. The methods of placing single-number bets, column bets, and others are fairly obvious. The dealer will be happy to show you how to make many interesting betting combinations, such as betting on six numbers at once. Each player is given different-colored chips so that it's easy to follow the numbers you've bet on.

Slots

You put the coin in the slot and pull the handle. What, you thought there was a trick to this?

Actually, there is a bit more to it. But first, some background. Old-timers will tell you slots were invented to give wives something to do while their husbands gambled. Slots used to be stuck at the edges of the casino and could be counted on one hand, maybe two. But now they *are* the casino. The casinos make more from slots than from craps, blackjack, and roulette combined. There are more than 150,000 slot machines (not including video poker) in the county. Some of these are at the airport, steps away from you as you deplane. It's just a matter of time before the planes flying into Vegas feature slots that pop up as soon as you cross the state line.

To keep up with the increasing competition, the plain old machine, where reels just spin, has become nearly obsolete. Now they are all computerized and have buttons to push so you can avoid getting carpal tunnel syndrome from yanking the handle all night (though the handles are still there on some of them). Many don't even have reels anymore but are entirely video screens, which offer several little extras that have nothing to do with actual play. The idea is still simple: Get 3 (or 4, or 10) cherries (clowns, sevens, dinosaurs, whatever) in a row, and you win something. Each machine has its own combination. Some will pay you something with just one symbol showing; on most, the more combinations there are, the more opportunities for loot. Some will even pay if you get three blanks. Study each machine to learn what it does. *Note:* The **payback** goes up considerably if you bet the limit—from 2 to hundreds of coins on penny slots, for instance.

Progressive slots are groups of linked machines (sometimes spread over several casinos) where the jackpot gets bigger every few moments, just as lottery jackpots build up. Some machines have their own progressive jackpot, which can be slightly less stressful because you're not competing with other players to win the top prize.

Themes and interactivity are the watchwords these days. Pick a pop culture reference and there's probably a slot machine dedicated to it. *Wizard of Oz, The Walking Dead, Airplane!* ("Don't call me Shirley!"), *Sex and the City,* **Michael Jackson,** and *The Hangover* are just a few of the familiar titles you'll see on casino floors. Each of them features bonus rounds and side games that have animations, video clips, music, competitions between other players, and, in some cases, even motion-activated seats.

Penny and nickel slots, which for a long time had been overlooked, relegated to a lonely spot somewhere by a back wall because they were not as profitable for the casinos as quarter and dollar slots, have made a comeback. You can bet just a penny or nickel, but maximum bets for the bigger jackpots are usually in the $2 to $3 range, sometimes even more. As a result, more cash is pocketed by the casino (which keeps a higher percentage of cash off lower-denomination slots than it does off higher ones), which is happy to accommodate this trend by offering up more and more cheaper slots. See how this all works? Are you paying attention?

Cashless machines are the standard these days. Now when gambling, players insert their money, they play, and when they cash out, they get—instead of the clanging sound of coins cascading out into the tray—a little paper ticket with their total winnings on it. Hand in your ticket at a cashier's window or use the omnipresent ATM-style redemption machines, and you get your winnings. Or continue to feed the beast and slip your ticket right back into another slot machine in the same casino. Purists howl, bemoaning the loss of the auditory and tactile thrill of dealing with coins, but most of them are the type of people who would put $5 in a machine, lose it, and then be done with gambling for the rest of the trip. Those who are more than just casual players love the convenience and simplicity of the tickets and wouldn't go back to the days of having to lug big buckets of change around if you promised them better payoff odds.

Are there surefire ways to win on a slot machine? No. But you can lose more slowly. The slot machines use minicomputers known as random number

CASINO royale

When it comes right down to it, all casinos are basically the same—they all have slot machines, table games, too many people (often), lots of cigarette smoke (usually), and a general sense of hullaballoo that is completely unlike anyplace else on Earth.

But not all casinos are created equally. Some are big and feel like it, some are big and don't feel like it, some are loud, some are bright, some are light, some are cheap, some are overwhelming, and on and on it goes. Where you decide to gamble away little Billy's college fund really is a matter of taste, budget, and timing, but here are a few of our favorites, and not just because we have won money in them. Well, not *entirely* because we have won money in them.

If you are looking for a classic Las Vegas casino, go no further than **Caesars Palace,** 3570 Las Vegas Blvd. S. (www. caesarspalace.com; © **702/731-7110**). The domed ceiling over the main pit just off the lobby dates all the way back to 1966, but it has been kept up-to-date and sparkling. Plus, you might still see a toga-clad wench or an armor-plated gladiator wandering around posing for pictures.

If you prefer modern, try either **Aria Las Vegas,** 3730 Las Vegas Blvd. S. (www.arialasvegas.com; © **702/590-7111**), or the **Cosmopolitan of Las Vegas,** 3708 Las Vegas Blvd. S. (www. cosmopolitanlasvegas.com; © **702/698-7000**). Both offer dramatic, art-inspired rooms bursting with eye candy, with Aria's dramatic sculptures and natural lighting and the Cosmo's three-story chandelier and evocative decor.

The themed madness has been toned down at most casinos, but you can still

generators (RNGs) to determine the winning combinations on a machine, and though each spin may indeed be random, individual machines are programmed to pay back different percentages over the long haul. As a result, a machine programmed to return a higher percentage might be "looser" than others. A bank of empty slots probably (but not certainly) means the machines are tight. Go find a line where lots of people are sitting around with lots of credits on their meters. A good rule of thumb is that if your slot doesn't hit something in four or five pulls, leave it and go find another. Also, each casino has a bank of slots that they advertise as looser or with a bigger payback. Try these. It's what the casinos want you to do, but what the heck.

Sports Books

Most of the larger hotels in Las Vegas have sports-book operations, which look a lot like commodities-futures trading boards. In some, almost as large as theaters, you can sit comfortably, occasionally in recliners, and sometimes with your own video screen, and watch ball games, fights, and, at some casinos, horse races on huge TV screens. To add to your enjoyment, there's usually a deli/bar nearby that serves sandwiches, hot dogs, soft drinks, and beer. As a matter of fact, some of the best sandwiches in Las Vegas are served next to the sports books. Sports books take bets on virtually every sport (and not just who'll win but what the final score will be, who'll be first to hit a home run, who'll be MVP, who'll wear red shoes; you name it). They are best get a geo-location giggle with the Big Apple silliness at **New York–New York,** 3790 Las Vegas Blvd. S. (www.newyork newyork.com; ℭ **702/740-6969**), complete with the facades of famous Gotham landmarks looming around you; the iconic pyramid of **Luxor Las Vegas,** 3900 Las Vegas Blvd. S. (www.luxor.com; ℭ **702/262-4444**), which still lights up the night even if the interior has been transformed, or the Gallic-inspired romance of **Paris Las Vegas,** 3655 Las Vegas Blvd. S. (www.parislasvegas.com; ℭ **702/946-7000**), including legs of the Eiffel Tower replica sticking down into the casino.

If luxury and high limits are your thing, go to the fraternal twin casinos at **Wynn Las Vegas/Encore Las Vegas,** 3131 Las Vegas Blvd. S. (www.wynnlasvegas.com; ℭ **800/320-7125**). The former is a large, garden-inspired space with luxurious

seating and fabrics, while the latter is a more intimate, European-gambling-parlor–style room infused with natural light.

If you prefer your gambling more down-to-earth and affordable, check out one of the Downtown or locals' casinos. Our personal favorites are the lovely earth-toned space at the **Golden Nugget,** 129 Fremont St. (www.golden nugget.com; ℭ **702/385-7111**); the retro-modern industrial chic at the **Downtown Grand,** 206 N. 3rd St. (www. downtowngrand.com; ℭ **702/719-5100**); the richly textured stunner at **Red Rock Resort,** 10973 W. Charleston Ave. (www.redrocklasvegas.com; ℭ **702/767-7773**); and the warm, Mediterranean-inspired space at **Green Valley Ranch,** 2300 Paseo Verde Dr., Henderson (www. greenvalleyranchresort.com; ℭ **702/617-7777**).

during important playoff games or big horse races, when everyone in the place is watching the same event—shrieking, shouting, and moaning, sometimes in unison. Joining in with a cheap bet, so you feel like you, too, have a personal stake in the matter, makes for bargain entertainment.

Video Poker

Video poker works the same way as regular poker, except you play against the machine. You are dealt a hand, you pick which cards to keep and which to discard, and then you get your new hand. And, it is hoped, you collect your winnings. This is somewhat more of a challenge than slots because you have some control (or at least the illusion of control) over your fate, and it's easier than playing actual poker with a table full of serious poker players.

There are several varieties of video poker machines, including **Jacks or Better, Deuces Wild,** and so forth. Be sure to study your machine before you play. (The best returns are offered on the **Bonus Poker** machines; the payback for a pair of jacks or better is two times your bet and three times for three of a kind.) The Holy Grail of video-poker machines is the 9/6 (it pays nine coins for a full house, six coins for a flush), but you'll need to pray a lot before you find one in town. Some machines offer **double down:** After you have won, you get a chance to draw cards against the machine, with the higher card the winner. If you win, your money is doubled, and you are offered a chance to go again. Your money can increase nicely during this time, and you can also lose it all very quickly, which is most annoying.

Other options include multi-hand video poker, where you play anywhere from 3 to 100 hands at the same time; bonus spin poker, allowing you to spin a wheel for extra credits when you get certain hands; and progressive jackpots for things like royal flushes or four aces.

OUTDOOR ACTIVITIES

Biking

You really don't want to ride a bicycle anywhere near the Strip, or as a means of transportation, but bicycle rentals can be arranged through the concierge at most of the major hotels in town. Downtown Las Vegas is a bit more bike-friendly, with 21 grab-and-go bicycle stations at convenient locations; rent a bike for up to 24 hours for only $8 (bikeshare.rtcsnv.com; ✆ **844/641-7823**). For outdoor excursions, check out **Las Vegas Cyclery** (www.lasvegascyclery.com; ✆ **702/596-2953**), a rental and tour operator offering everything from street to mountain to tandem bikes and the necessary safety equipment and accessories. Guided tours of Red Rock Canyon, Mount Charleston, and more are also offered. Prices for mountain bike rentals start at around $40 for a half-day and guided tours at around $140.

Boating & Fishing

The bulk of the water-based activities in the area take place at the **Lake Mead National Recreation Area,** located about 20 miles east of Las Vegas. Several harbors offer rentals of power and fishing boats, as well as houseboats and personal watercraft. They can also help you with fishing licenses and equipment. For more information, see chapter 9.

Golf

See "Fore! Great Desert Golf" (p. 186).

Gyms

All the major hotels (and many of the minor ones) have fully stocked gyms on the premises. The size and quality vary, of course, but the bigger resorts have facilities that would make most commercial fitness centers green with envy. Entrance to most is covered by the nightly resort fee, but if the hotel you are staying in doesn't have a gym, expect a charge of anywhere from $15 to $35 per day. Several national chains, including **24 Hour Fitness,** have outlets in Las Vegas, and your membership may allow you to use the local branch.

Hiking

We consider the length you have to walk between hotels on the Strip, or from your room to the front door, enough of a hike, but if you are looking for something more traditional, the **Red Rock Canyon** and **Mount Charleston** areas have numerous hiking trails. For more information, see chapter 9.

striking OUT

Las Vegas is one of the favorite cities in the world for bowlers of all levels, with several huge alleys offering everything from regular bowling to rock-'n'-roll-style action.

- The Strip got its first serious bowling alley in 2014 at **Brooklyn Bowl,** 3545 Las Vegas Blvd. S. (at the LINQ; ℂ **702/862-2695**). The 32-lane facility has two floors of state-of-the-art scoring from Brunswick, swank couches at the lanes instead of hard plastic seats, and high-definition projection screens over the alleys. Be warned that the nice surroundings come with a high price ($25 and up per lane per hour). It's open Sunday through Thursday from 11am until 2am and Friday and Saturday until 4am.

- **Gold Coast Bowling Center,** 4000 W. Flamingo Rd. (at Valley View; ℂ **702/367-7111**), has a 70-lane bowling center; open daily 24 hours.

- The **Orleans Bowling Center,** 4500 W. Tropicana Ave. (ℂ **702/365-7400**), has 70 lanes, a pro shop, lockers, meeting rooms, and more; open daily 24 hours.

- **Red Rock Lanes,** 11011 W. Charleston Ave. (ℂ **702/797-7467**), is a luxury bowling center with 72 lanes, plasma TVs, and VIP suites where you can pick your own music and get bottle service. It's open daily from 8am until 2am.

- **Santa Fe Station Bowling Center,** 4949 N. Rancho Rd. (ℂ **702/658-4995**), has a 60-lane alley with modern scoring equipment, nice furnishings, a fun and funky bar, a small cafe, and much more.

Open Sunday through Thursday 8am until midnight, and Friday and Saturday 8am until 1am.

- **Sam's Town Bowling Center,** 5111 Boulder Hwy. (ℂ **702/456-7777**), offers 56 lanes plus a snack shop, cocktail lounge, video arcade, day-care center, pro shop, and more. It's open daily 24 hours.

- **South Point Bowling Center,** 9777 Las Vegas Blvd. (ℂ **702/797-8080**), has a 64-lane facility with a similar divided layout to its sister at Suncoast (see below). It has all the latest gee-whiz scoring and automation, plus the usual facilities, and is open 24 hours. A separate 60-lane facility hosts pro-bowling tournaments.

- **Strike Zone** at Sunset Station, 1301 W. Sunset Rd., in Henderson (ℂ **702/547-7467**), has a high-tech, 72-lane facility with all the latest automated scoring gizmos, giant video screens, a full bar, a snack shop, a pro shop, a video arcade, and more. It's open daily 24 hours.

- **Suncoast Bowling Center,** 9090 Alta Dr., in Summerlin (ℂ **702/636-7111**), offers 64 lanes divided by a center aisle. The high-tech center with touch-screen scoring has become a regular stop on the Pro Bowlers tours. It's open daily 8am-2am.

- **Texas Star Lanes,** 2101 Texas Star Lane (ℂ **702/288-7728**), offers a 60-lane alley, video arcade, billiards, a snack bar and lounge, and more. It's open Sunday to Thursday 7:30am to midnight, Friday to Saturday 7:30am to 2am.

Horseback Riding

Looking to indulge your inner cowboy/girl? There are several stables and horseback-tour companies in town, most of which are near **Red Rock Canyon** and **Mount Charleston**. For more information, see chapter 9.

Ice Skating

The **SoBe Ice Arena** at the Fiesta Rancho, 2400 N. Rancho Rd. (https://fiesta rancho.sclv.com; © **702/631-7000**), features an NHL regulation–size rink and offers daily open skating hours, lessons, and equipment rental. Public skating times vary from week to week based on the schedules of the various hockey leagues that use the facility. Usually the rink is open for at least a couple of hours every afternoon and after 8pm on Friday and Saturday nights, which is when a DJ and nightclub-worthy lighting may help mask the sound and sight of you falling down a lot.

During the holiday season, the **Cosmopolitan** transforms its pool into an outdoor skating rink, complete with faux snow, hot cocoa vendors (with an option to add a little booze for extra warmth), and occasional Olympic skaters.

Skiing & Snowboarding

See information about **Lee Canyon** in the Mount Charleston section of chapter 9.

Swimming

Vegas resort complexes have some fabulous pools. To find the best one for you, see "So Your Trip Goes Swimmingly…" (p. 66).

Tennis

Tennis used to be a popular pastime in Vegas, but these days, buffs only have a couple of choices at hotels in town that have courts. **Bally's** (© **702/967-4598**) has eight night-lit hard courts. Fees start at $20 per hour per court for guests of Bally's or Paris Las Vegas and $25 per hour for nonguests, with rackets available for rental. Facilities include a pro shop. Hours vary seasonally. Reservations are advised. The **Westgate Las Vegas** (© **702/732-5009**) has six outdoor hard courts (four night-lit) and a pro shop. It's open to the public but hours vary seasonally. Rates are $20 per hour for guests and $25 per hour for nonguests. Lessons are available. Reservations are required.

FORE! GREAT DESERT GOLF

In addition to the listings below, there are dozens of local courses, including some very challenging ones that have hosted PGA tournaments. *Note:* Greens fees vary radically depending on time of day and year. Also, call for opening and closing times, because these change frequently. Because of the heat, you will want to take advantage of the cart that in most cases is included in the greens fee.

Angel Park Golf Club ★★ This 36-hole, par-70/71 public course is a local favorite. Arnold Palmer originally designed the Mountain and Palm courses. (The Palm Course was redesigned several years later by Bob Cupp.) Players call this a great escape from the casinos, claiming that no matter how many times they play it, they never get tired of it. The Palm Course has gently rolling fairways that offer golfers of all abilities a challenging yet forgiving layout. The Mountain Course has rolling natural terrain and gorgeous panoramic views. Facilities include a pro shop, night-lit driving range, 18-hole putting course, restaurant, cocktail bar, snack bar, and more.

100 S. Rampart Blvd. (btw. Summerlin Pkwy. and Alta St., 20 min. NW of the Strip). www. angelpark.com. ✆ **888/446-5358** or 702/254-4653. Greens fees $35–$135. Internet specials available.

Arroyo Golf Club ★ Like Angel Park, Arroyo was also designed by Arnold Palmer, and this 18-hole, par-72 course is one of the more scenic in town owing to its location along Red Rock Canyon. Stunning mountains on one side and Las Vegas in the distance on the other side; what more could you want? Well, you get a challenging (but not insanity-inducing) course that will keep all but the most competitive of golfers entertained. Facilities include a pro shop, night-lit driving range, 18-hole putting course, restaurant, cocktail bar, snack bar, and more.

2250 C Red Springs Dr. (just west of the 215, 25 min. NW of the Strip). www.thearroyo golfclub.com. ✆ **866/934-4653** or 702/258-2300. Greens fees $65–$175.

Bali Hai Golf Club ★★★ One of the most exclusive golf addresses belongs to this multimillion-dollar course on the Strip, just south of Mandalay Bay. Done in a wild South Seas theme, the par-72 course has over 7 acres of water features, including an island green, palm trees, and tropical foliage everywhere you look. Not impressed yet? How about the fact that all their golf carts are equipped with GPS? Okay, if that doesn't convince you of the upscale nature of the joint, check out the greens fees. Even at those prices, premium tee times are often booked months in advance. Among the many facilities are a pro shop, putting green, gourmet restaurant, grill, and lounge.

5150 Las Vegas Blvd. S. www.balihaigolfclub.com. ✆ **888/427-6678.** Greens fees $200–$300.

Bear's Best Las Vegas ★★★ Golf legend Jack Nicklaus has designed hundreds of courses around the world, but here he has taken 18 of his favorite holes and put them all together in one delightfully challenging package. From courses in Mexico to Montana and back again, the bunkers, water features, and traps have all been faithfully re-created, giving you an opportunity to try the best of "the Bear." Facilities include a pro shop, putting green, restaurant (with Nicklaus memorabilia), and clubhouse.

11111 W. Flamingo Rd. www.clubcorp.com. ✆ **702/804-8500.** Greens fees $75–$235.

Las Vegas National Golf Club ★ This 18-hole, par-71 public course is one of the most historic in town. Built in 1961, it was at various times associated with, or run by, the Stardust, Sahara, and the Las Vegas Hilton. Yes, the Rat Pack played here, and you can, too. The course itself is classically designed (not the desert layout that most in Vegas have), and although it's not the most challenging in town, it will keep you entertained. Facilities include a pro shop, driving range, restaurant, cocktail lounge, and golf school.

1911 Desert Inn Rd. (btw. Maryland Pkwy. and Eastern Ave.). www.lasvegasnational. com. ℭ **866/695-1961.** Greens fees $79–$119.

Rio Secco Golf Club ★★   You don't have to be staying at the Rio Suites (or another Caesars Entertainment property) to play this gorgeous 18-hole course, but you get preferred tee times and discounts if you do. Set in the foothills of the mountains overlooking Las Vegas, the Rees Jones–designed course has incredible views and is one of the most in demand in town. Facilities include a pro shop, driving range, restaurant, and bar.

2851 Grand Hills Dr., Henderson. www.riosecco.net. ℭ **702/777-2400.** Greens fees $69–$199.

TPC Las Vegas ★★   Justin Timberlake has held his charity golf tournament at this course, so if it's good enough for him, it should be good enough for you, right? Luckily the "SexyBack" guy has good taste, as this scenic course, which follows the arroyos and plateaus of the terrain, is also a favorite of the PGA. That should tell you there are no windmills or clown's mouths here. It's a very challenging course, so bring your A game. Facilities include a pro shop, driving range, restaurant, clubhouse, and golf school.

9851 Canyon Run Dr. www.tpc.com. ℭ **702/256-2500.** Greens fees $119–$219.

SPAS

Most of the major resorts in Las Vegas have spa facilities that range from pretty basic (sauna, Jacuzzi, some treatment rooms for massages) to extravagant (is that a rock-climbing wall?), but many are only available to guests of the hotels in which they are located.

The spas that follow all have hours during which they are open to the general public. Those hours change seasonally and sometimes even weekly based on hotel guest demand, so call ahead or visit the websites.

Canyon Ranch SpaClub ★   The largest spa in Las Vegas has more than 130,000-square-feet worth of treatment rooms, workout facilities, and even a rock-climbing wall. Although the spa does a good job of keeping things relatively peaceful, the sheer size of the place and the number of people who visit may inhibit your relaxation efforts. Note that prices are more expensive on the weekends, so go on a weekday if you can.

At the Venetian, 3355 Las Vegas Blvd. S. www.canyonranch.com. ℭ **877/220-2688.** Massage and treatments $105–$385.

Hibiscus Spa ★★★   Westin's spa may not be as opulent as some of the other spas on the Strip, but it is just as indulgent. Plus, services such as deep tissue massages and facials are even more relaxing when you know your wallet won't take a beating. Before or after your treatment, feel free to spend some quality time schvitzing in the sauna, detoxing in the steam room, or simply chilling out in the quiet room. The spa may be aesthetically perfunctory, but the caliber of treatment and high level of service will still leave you feeling like a million bucks.

At Westin Las Vegas, 160 E. Flamingo Rd. www.westinvegas.com. © **702/836-5945.** Massage and treatments $70–$225.

Qua Baths & Spa ★★
Check out the Environment rooms at this lavishly designed spa, which include the Arctic Ice room complete with snow showers and a Roman Baths section that would make Caesar proud. Treatments and massages are not cheap, but the spa faithful say this is one of the best in town.

At Caesars Palace, 3570 Las Vegas Blvd. S. www.caesarspalace.com. © **866/782-0655.** Massage and treatments $185–$650.

Red Rock Resort Adventure Spa ★★★
The facility has the requisite spa accoutrements—a Zen-like space, massages, facials, sauna, and so on—but it's the "Adventure" part of the program that makes it truly unique. Capitalizing on the hotel's location on the edge of the Red Rock Canyon National Conservancy Area, the spa offers horseback riding, river rafting, kayaking, hiking, rock climbing, biking, and more. Go get a great outdoors workout and then come back for a massage to soothe your aches and pains.

At Red Rock Resort, 11011 W. Charleston Ave. (at I-215). www.rr-spa.com. © **702/797-7878.** Massage and treatments $165–$285.

Spa Aquae ★★
The centerpiece here is the "Ritual," a series of dunks and soaks in cold, warm, hydrotherapy, and floating pools, some of which are outside in a gorgeously landscaped grotto. It's totally unique and worth the 20-minute drive from the Strip.

At the JW Marriott, 221 N. Rampart Blvd. (at Summerlin Pkwy.). www.jwlasvegasresort.com. © **877/869-8777.** Massage and treatments $70–$215.

Spa at Bellagio ★★
The surroundings are luxe, and the staff is so soothingly attentive that you just know it's going to cost you a fortune to get worked on here—but it's totally worth it. Few other spas in town will make you feel so richly pampered.

At Bellagio, 3600 Las Vegas Blvd. S. www.bellagio.com. © **702/693-7472.** Massage and treatments $95–$350.

Spa at Encore ★★★
At what is by far the most beautifully designed spa in Las Vegas, the Moroccan garden decor is both breathtaking and calming. Your bill can get shocking really fast, but one walk down the lantern-lit treatment room hallway will make all your cares melt away.

At Encore Las Vegas, 3121 Las Vegas Blvd. S. www.encorelasvegas.com. © **702/770-4772.** Massage and treatments $170–$800.

The Spa at Park MGM ★★ With its clean lines and stark white tiles, this spa may seem a bit minimalist if you're used to the ornate baths at other resorts, but it's an oasis nonetheless. The Welcome Home package makes you feel just that, with an 80-minute full-body massage that works in another aesthetician for a 20-minute facial at the end, providing a four-handed experience.

At Park MGM, 3770 Las Vegas Blvd. S. www.parkmgm.com. (℅ **702/730-7010.** Massage and treatments $75–$280.

GETTING MARRIED

Getting hitched is one of the most popular things to do in Las Vegas. See that total stranger/childhood friend standing next to you? Grab him or her and head down to the **Clark County Marriage License Bureau,** 201 Clark Ave. (℅ **702/761-0600;** daily, including holidays, 8am–midnight), to get your license. Find a wedding chapel (not hard, as there are about 50 of them; they line the north end of the Strip, and most hotels have them) and tie the knot. Just like that. No blood test, no waiting period—heck, not even an awkward dating period.

Even if you have actually known your intended for some time, Las Vegas is a great place to get married. The ease is the primary attraction, but there are several other appealing reasons. You can have any kind of wedding you want, from a big, traditional production to a small, intimate affair (see the box "Vows with a Wow," on p. 192). The wedding chapels take care of everything; many will even provide a limo to take you to the license bureau and back. Most offer all the accessories, from rings to flowers to a videotaped record of the event.

More than 100,000 couples who yearly take advantage of all this can't be wrong. If you want to follow in the footsteps of Elvis and Priscilla (at the first incarnation of the Aladdin Hotel); Michael Jordan; Jon Bon Jovi; Richard Gere and Cindy Crawford; Pamela Anderson and husband no. 3; Angelina Jolie and Billy Bob; and Britney and What's-His-Name, peruse this list of the most notable wedding chapels on or near the Strip.

You can also call **Vegas Weddings** (www.702wedding.com; (℅ **702/933-3464** [which spells WEDDING]), which offers one-stop shopping for wedding services.

Weddings can be very inexpensive in Vegas: A license is $77 and a basic service not much more. Even a full-blown shebang package—photos, music, flowers, video, cake, and other doodads—will run only about $500 total. We haven't quoted any prices here because the ultimate cost depends entirely on you. Go cheap, and the whole thing will set you back maybe $150, including the license; go elaborate, and the price is still reasonable by today's standards. Remember that there are often hidden charges, such as expected gratuities for the minister (about $25 should do; no real need to tip anyone else), and so forth. If you're penny-pinching, keep those in mind.

AN ELVIS IMPERSONATOR'S TOP 10 REASONS TO get married IN LAS VEGAS

Jesse Garon has appeared in numerous Las Vegas productions as "Young Elvis." He arrives at any special event in a 1955 pink, neon-lit Cadillac, and does weddings, receptions, birthdays, conventions, grand openings, and so on. For all your Elvis impersonator needs, call ℭ **702/588-8188,** or visit his website at www.vegaselvis.com.

1. It's the only place in the world where Elvis will marry you, at a drive-up window, in a pink Cadillac—24 hours a day.
2. Chances are, you'll never forget your anniversary.
3. Where else can you treat all your guests to a wedding buffet for only 99¢ a head?
4. Four words: One helluva bachelor party.
5. On your wedding night, show your spouse that new "watch me disappear" act you learned from Siegfried & Roy.
6. Show your parents who's boss—have your wedding your way.
7. Wedding bells ring for you everywhere you go. They just sound like slot machines.
8. You can throw dice instead of rice.
9. It's easy to lie about your age on the marriage certificate—just like Joan Collins did!
10. With all the money you save, it's dice clocks for everyone!

Valentine's Day is a very popular day to get married in Vegas. Some of the chapels perform as many as 80 services on February 14. Halloween is the second most popular. On other dates, though, you can just show up, get your paperwork, close your eyes, and pick a chapel. And above all, have fun. Good luck and best wishes to you both.

Chapel of the Bells ★   Sporting the largest and gaudiest wedding chapel sign on the Strip, this is one of the longest-running chapels, operating since 1957. This combination of classic Vegas "style" and "tradition" is most of what this place has going for it. The chapel is pretty, garnished with swaths of white material and light green accents, seating 25 to 35, but nothing dazzling. It's not particularly distinctive; still, Kelly Ripa got married here, so there is that. The chapel prefers advance booking but can do same-day ceremonies.

2233 Las Vegas Blvd. S. (at Sahara Ave.). www.chapelofthebellslasvegas.com. ℭ **800/233-2391** or 702/735-6803. Sun–Thurs 10am–9pm; Fri–Sat 9am–midnight.

Chapel of the Flowers ★★   This chapel's claim to fame is that Dennis Rodman and Carmen Electra exchanged their short-lived vows here—but don't hold it against the place. They offer full services from photos to flowers, and more, with three chapels to choose from. The La Capella Chapel fits 50 and has a rustic Tuscan feel, with wood pews and frosted-glass sconces. The Victorian chapel, which holds only 30, has white walls and dark-wood pews and doesn't look very Victorian at all—but as the plainest, it's also the nicest. The smallest is the Magnolia Chapel, done in simple white marble with a

VOWS **WITH A WOW**

Simply getting married is not a big enough deal for some people. No, they can't trust that the exchange of vows with the person they love will create memories that will last forever. They must make sure it is truly memorable by throwing in a volcano, a giant fountain, or maybe even a roller coaster. If you are such a person, Las Vegas has plenty of places to put a little wow into your vows.

If you want to have the iconic dancing waters as a backdrop, you can get married on a balcony overlooking the Fountains at **Bellagio**, 3600 Las Vegas Blvd. S. (www.bellagio.com/weddings; ✆ **702/693-7700**). As you might expect, it ain't cheap, but you can time your "I do" to the fountains' big climax.

An almost aerial view of the fountains is available across the street from the Eiffel Tower at **Paris Las Vegas**, 3655 Las Vegas Blvd. S. (www.parislv.com; ✆ **877/650-5021**). You can get married on the observation deck at the top of the tower replica. Similar wow-worthy vistas are available at the world's tallest observation wheel, **High Roller,** 3545 Las Vegas Blvd. S. (✆ **800/CAESARS**).

An even higher view is available at the top of the **Strat,** 2000 Las Vegas Blvd. S. (www.chapelintheclouds.com; ✆ **800/789-9436**). Their chapels overlook the city from more than 100 stories up, or you can get married on the indoor or outdoor observation decks. They even have packages that will include the thrill rides, so you can take the plunge both metaphorically and literally.

Adrenaline junkies can also join in holy matrimony while zooming along at nearly 70 mph on the roller coaster at **New York–New York,** 3790 Las Vegas Blvd. S. (www.newyorknewyork.com; ✆ **702/740-6616**).

If you want to add a little fire to the festivities, try getting married in front of the volcano at the **Mirage,** 3400 Las Vegas Blvd. S. (www.mirage.com; ✆ **702/791-7155**). You can have the ceremony during the day, or at night when the thing is all lava-riffic.

Finally, several of the city's most popular museums offer themed wedding packages with very interesting backdrops, including the **Mob Museum** (p. 163) and the **Neon Museum** (p. 165).

freestanding arch. If you want an outdoor ceremony, you might choose the gazebo by a running stream and waterfall that nearly drowns out the Strip noise. There's also a medium-size reception room and live organ music upon request, plus Internet streaming of services is available for those of you who have second thoughts about not inviting the family. It's a pretty, friendly place, owned by the same family for more than 50 years. It does not allow rice or confetti throwing.

1717 Las Vegas Blvd. S. (at E. Oakey Blvd.). www.littlechapel.com. ✆ **800/843-2410** or 702/735-4331. Mon–Thurs 7am–8pm; Fri–Sat 7am–9pm.

Graceland Wedding Chapel ★   Housed in a landmark building that's one of the oldest wedding chapels in Vegas, the Graceland bills itself as "the proverbial mom and pop outfit." No, Elvis never slept here, but one of the owners was friends with Elvis and asked his permission to use the name. This is a tiny New England church building with a small bridge and white picket fence out front. Inside is a 30-seat chapel; the walls are off-white, with a large, modern, stained-glass window of doves and roses behind the pulpit. It's not the nicest of the chapels, but Jon Bon Jovi and Billy Ray Cyrus got married here (though not to each other). Naturally, an Elvis package is available.

619 Las Vegas Blvd. S. (at E. Bonneville Ave.). www.gracelandchapel.com. ✆ **800/824-5732** or 702/382-0091. Daily 9am–11pm.

Little Church of the West ★★ Built in 1942 on the grounds of the Frontier, this gorgeous traditional chapel has been moved three times in its history and has hosted weddings for everyone from Judy Garland to Angelina Jolie. Elvis even got married here, at least on film—the building played the backdrop for his nuptials to Ann-Margret in *Viva Las Vegas*. There are rich wood walls, ceiling, and pews; stained-glass windows; and a traditional steeple among the well-landscaped grounds, making it a really lovely option for those looking to walk down the aisle.

4617 Las Vegas Blvd. S. (at Russell Rd.). www.littlechurchlv.com. ✆ **800/821-2452** or 702/739-7971. Daily 8am–11pm.

Little White Wedding Chapel ★ This is arguably the most famous of the chapels on the Strip, maybe because there is a big sign saying Michael Jordan and Joan Collins were married here (again, not to each other), maybe because they were the first to do the drive-up window, or maybe because this is where Britney and what's-his-name began their 51 hours of wedded bliss. There are four separate chapels plus a drive-thru (allegedly the first of its kind), and an outdoor gazebo. It's all fine, but it has a factory-line atmosphere, processing wedding after wedding all day. Move 'em in and move 'em out. If you want something special, there are probably better choices.

1301 Las Vegas Blvd. S. (btw. E. Oakey and Charleston blvds.). www.alittlewhitechapel. com. ✆ **800/545-8111** or 702/382-5943. Daily 8am–midnight.

A Special Memory Wedding Chapel ★ This is absolutely the place to go if you want a traditional, big-production wedding; you won't feel it's the least bit tacky. It's a New England church–style building, complete with steeple. The interior looks like a proper church (well, a plain one—don't think ornate Gothic cathedral), with a peaked roof, pews with padded red seats, modern stained-glass windows of doves and flowers, and lots of dark wood. It's all very clean and seats about 87 comfortably. The area outside the chapel is like a mini-mall of bridal paraphernalia stores. Should all this be just too darned nice and proper for you, they also offer a drive-up window. They have a photo studio on-site and will do receptions featuring a small cake, cold cuts, and champagne. There's a gazebo for outside weddings, and they sell T-shirts!

800 S. 4th St. (at Gass Ave.). www.aspecialmemory.com. ✆ **800/962-7798** or 702/384-2211. Sun–Thurs 8am–10pm; Fri–Sat 8am–midnight.

Viva Las Vegas Weddings ★★★ Yes, you could come to Las Vegas and have a traditional wedding in a tasteful chapel where you walk down the aisle to a kindly minister. But wouldn't you rather literally ride into the chapel in the back of a pink Cadillac and get married by Elvis? Or wade in through dry ice fog while Dracula performs your ceremony? Or float in from the ceiling a la *Cirque du Soleil?* This is the mecca of the wacky-themed Vegas wedding, complete with indoor and outdoor spaces, tux and costume rentals, florists, theme rooms for receptions, and a staff of former stage performers who love to put on a show. *This* is what a Vegas wedding should be like.

1205 Las Vegas Blvd. S. (btw. Charleston and Oakey blvds.). www.vivalasvegas weddings.com. © **800/574-4450** or 702/384-0771. Sun–Thurs 9am–9pm; Fri–Sat 8am–10pm.

Wee Kirk O' the Heather ★★   The oldest wedding chapel in Las Vegas (it's been here since 1940; ah, Vegas, and its mixed-up view of age), it's the one at the very end of the Strip, right before Downtown and thus close to the license bureau. It was originally built as a house in 1925 for a local minister, but marriage bureau officials kept sending couples there to get married, and they eventually just gave up and turned it into a chapel. The decor is entirely fresh, and while that means gold-satin-patterned wallpaper in the chapel, we like it a great deal. It has just the right balance between kitsch and classic, and that's what you want in a Vegas wedding chapel. Plus, if there were a competition for the friendliest chapel in town, this one would win hands down.

231 Las Vegas Blvd. S. (btw. Bridger and Carson aves.). www.weekirk.com. © **800/843-5266** or 702/382-9830. Daily 10am–8pm.

SHOPPING

Las Vegas is one of the top shopping destinations in the world, and many visitors list the malls, stores, outlets, and boutiques as one of their primary reasons for coming to the city. Several top-grossing retail outlets are in Las Vegas, including the Forum Shops at Caesars Palace, which makes more money per square foot than any other mall in the United States. But in between the big malls and high-end luxury stores are lots of fun and offbeat boutiques that help to make Vegas a shopper's paradise, no matter your taste or budget.

Because they are as much tourist attractions as shopping destinations, the malls, stores, and boutiques on the Strip are open longer than you may expect, generally from 10am until 11pm on weekdays, and until midnight on weekends. Once you get off the Strip, things become more normal, with typical operating hours between 9am and 6 or 7pm. Some of the smaller independent stores are closed on Sundays.

Generally speaking, the farther away you get from the Strip, the cheaper the prices. This applies to just about all categories of merchandise, even at name-brand chain stores where they will bump up prices by a few bucks just because they can. So, if you're planning on getting a pair of shoes or jeans at a familiar chain store, check to see if it has an outlet elsewhere in the city; you can often save yourself some dough.

This also holds true for sundry items like toothpaste, shampoo, and deodorant. If you buy these at the hotel gift shops, expect to pay significantly more than you would if you go off the Strip to a regular retailer like Target or Walmart.

SOUTH STRIP

Hershey's Chocolate World ★★   Heaven forbid that when the apocalypse happens, this and M&M's World across the street lose power at the same time, resulting in Wonka-proportion rivers of chocolate spilling onto Las Vegas Boulevard. A fantasy, for sure, but one that's welcome at the flagship at New York–New York. At this scaled-down, no-ride version of the original theme park in Hershey, Pennsylvania, the lures include an 800-pound chocolate Statue of Liberty, the ability to customize your own candy bar wrapper, and a bakery serving cookies, cupcakes, and plenty of other choco-late-infused goodies. Unlike its neighbor M&M's World, this store is dedi-cated to more than just the iconic Hershey's chocolate, including interactive displays about Reese's Peanut Butter Cups and Jolly Ranchers. It's open Sunday through Thursday 9am to 11pm, and Friday and Saturday 9am to midnight. In New York–New York, 3790 Las Vegas Blvd. S. www.hersheyschocolate worldlasvegas.com. ℂ **702/437-7439.**

M&M's World ★★   The four stories dedicated solely to the chocolate that melts in your mouth, but not in your hand, is a great place to get the kids all hopped up on sugar before passing out from the inevitable crash. Part of a bright, frenetic facade for the Showcase Mall (that includes a giant Coca-Cola bottle and an equally frenetic GameWorks sign), this shop draws kids like flies to honey. Where else would you go to pay for overpriced M&Ms in a rainbow of colors you've never seen before? There's a 3-D movie that tracks the famed Red and Yellow M&Ms as they search for the monogram they apparently lost in Vegas. It's cute, and the good teen employees who introduce the film are seemingly more excited about their jobs than one would expect. If you've ever wanted your M&Ms to read something other than their original imprint, you can print a personal message—it'll be short and sweet because of the surface area, but that's kind of the point of M&Ms. M&M's World is open daily from 9am until midnight. In the Showcase Mall, 3785 Las Vegas Blvd. S. (just north of the MGM Grand Hotel). www.mmsworld.com. ℂ **702/740-2504.**

The Shops at Crystals ★   The jagged, sparkly facade that is front and center on Las Vegas Boulevard is a dramatic come hither for the high-end shops within: Fendi, Gucci, and Tiffany & Co. The Shops at Crystals has often been called the jewel of Las Vegas retail for the 1%. There's not only the larg-est Louis Vuitton in North America and the biggest Prada in the United States, but also the 10,000-square-foot Tiffany & Co. All that ultramodern design of the exterior is offset by high ceilings and plenty of white space inside. If there weren't stores lining the walls, you might think this was an art gallery, with plenty of art installations inside the shops themselves as well. Louis Vuitton has a permanent installation by light and space artist James Turrell, which you can see by appointment only, while an 8,000-Swarovski-crystal horse chande-lier dazzles inside Stella McCartney. Have a nosh at Wolfgang Puck's pizzeria or take a quick stroll over to Aria next door for lunch at **Bardot Brasserie** (p. 96). The two-story wooden structure that stands in the middle is called the Treehouse and houses tony seafood restaurant **Mastro's Ocean Club** on the second floor, as well as concierge shopping services on the first. And yes, it does look like a bong. The mall is open Sunday through Thursday 10am until 11pm, and Friday and Saturday 10am to midnight, but individual store and restaurant hours may vary. 3720 Las Vegas Blvd. S. (at CityCenter). www.simon.com/mall/the-shops-at-crystals. ℂ **702/590-9299.**

Las Vegas Shopping

Bonanza Gift and
  Souvenir Shop **9**
The Boulevard **11**
The Cosmopolitan **17**
Downtown Container Park **2**
Fashion Show **10**
Forum Shops at
  Caesars Palace **13**
Gamblers General Store/
  Gambler's Book Club **4**
Gold & Silver Pawn Shop **5**
Grand Bazaar Shops **16**

•••■••• Las Vegas Monorail
•••●••• Free monorail

The Grand Canal Shoppes/
  Shoppes at Palazzo **12**
Hershey's Chocolate
  World **21**
Las Vegas Premium Outlets
  North **3**
Las Vegas Premium Outlets
  South **23**
The LINQ Promenade **14**
M&M's World **20**
Miracle Mile Shops at
  Planet Hollywood **18**
Retro Vegas **7**
Rick's Restorations **6**
The Shops at Crystals **19**
Town Square **22**
The Toy Shack **1**
Via Bellagio **15**
Zia Record Exchange **8**

MID-STRIP

The Cosmopolitan ★★★ There are few real boutique shopping options on the Strip, but most of them can be found on the second floor of the Cosmopolitan. Local kicks shop CRSVR is a destination for sneaker-heads, and you can complete your hipster look with threads from AllSaints. The art-driven resort also features repurposed cigarette machines that dispense tiny works by local artists for about $5 a pop. Finally, those of you who may have forgotten your extra bling or cutting-edge fashion don't need to worry. Jason of Beverly Hills is home to one-of-a-kind diamond pieces, while sartorial-minded gents can dress up their suits from Stitched. Most of the shops are open daily from 10am to 11pm. 3708 Las Vegas Blvd. S. www.cosmopolitanlasvegas. com. ✆ **702/698-7000.**

The Forum Shops at Caesars Palace ★★★ A shopping spree at the Forum Shops is one of those events you'd see in the movies, after the hero has beaten the house and wants to spend his casino winnings. He steps off the carpeted casino floor through the 48-foot Roman archway and onto the bright, cold, marble floor, surrounded by enormous columns and stone carvings, with a painted blue sky on the domed ceiling. A statue of the goddess Fortuna smiles down at our hero, welcoming him and his money. Cue the montage of luxury brand storefronts: John Varvatos, Gucci, Louboutin, Fendi, Henri Bendel, Ferragamo.

For those of us who haven't hit the Megamillions progressive, it's still easy to appreciate the glory of the Forum Shops, the 675,000 square feet of retail space that set the tone for the Vegas shopping experience when it opened in 1992. It's not just high-end stores but also an elaborate maze with fantastic details. Many just walk through to see the sights.

And those sights are pretty swell. The three-story annex with an entrance directly on Las Vegas Boulevard features arched cathedral ceilings with frescos painted on them, acres of marble columns, and one of the few spiral escalators in the world. Look for the silly but fun "Fall of Atlantis," a fountain display in the Roman Great Hall with animatronic statues of gods that spring to life for 11 minutes every hour, on the hour. The multisensory experience is completed with 14 LED screens playing video elements relevant to the story, pyrotechnics, and 40 speakers in a surround sound system so powerful it reverberates in your chest as you feel the gods' wrath.

Even if you don't have Ferragamo money, there are still plenty of middle-of-the road retail options to enact your own shopping spree, like the largest H&M in the United States, Banana Republic, AllSaints, and Diesel. If all the window-shopping makes you peckish, you have the choice of classic red-sauce Italian from **Carmine's** (p. 118), old-school steakhouse **the Palm,** or modern sushi from **Sushi Roku.**

The majority of the shops are open Sunday through Thursday from 10am to 11pm, and Friday and Saturday from 10am to midnight. In Caesars Palace, 3500 Las Vegas Blvd. S. www.forumshops.com. ✆ **702/893-4800.**

Grand Bazaar Shops ★★ Flamingo and Las Vegas Boulevard is one of the busiest intersections on the Las Vegas Strip, with millions of pedestrians strolling past it daily. The Grand Bazaar Shops seeks to corral these people, hoping they'll spend their casino winnings (cough!) at this Moroccan-inspired shopping mecca. The Grand Bazaar Shops are, most definitely, a colorful place to shop, anchored by a Swarovski outlet that has a 14-foot sphere composed of 911 custom-cut crystals and more than 1,800 points of light. Nightly, from 9pm to midnight, the Swarovski Starburst coordinates its lights with music and those multicolored mosaic panels on the roofs of the shops for a dazzling show. Under the canopies, you'll find mainstream but eclectic stores such as Superdry and Swatch, plus essentials like Lush, Havaianas, and Hammitt. Snack-wise, the Grand Bazaar Shops houses one of the largest Starbucks stores in the country, complete with grandstand seating. Wahlburgers, the burger joint from the reality show of the same name, has arrived, along with Chicago deep dish pizza emporium Giordano's. The shops are open Sunday through Thursday from 10am to 10pm and Friday and Saturday from 10am to 11pm. 3635 Las Vegas Blvd. S. (in front of Bally's). www.grandbazaarshops.com. *©* **702/736-4988.**

The Grand Canal Shoppes ★★ The 160 shops and restaurants of this meandering mall are divided between the Venetian and Palazzo, though one side is definitely more ornate than the other. Wander through the Venetian part and you'll see that the meticulous attention to detail in the hotel's recreation of an Italian village is carried through here, including a ceiling that's cunningly painted like a cloud-dappled sky. Canals flow through the mall, complete with gondoliers who will take you (for a fee, of course) on a slow float on the water. An extra tip will ensure that your captain serenades you as well, from classic opera arias to vintage Rat Pack tunes. Pick up the gondolas near St. Mark's Square, entertainment central with wandering minstrels, living statues, and more opera singers. The Venetian stores include such affordable choices as Kenneth Cole, Ann Taylor, and Victoria's Secret. For food, we recommend a stop at Mercato della Pescheria, an antipasti and wine bar. There's "outdoor" seating on the faux patio, so order some antipasti and a glass of wine and watch the world go by, as you'd do in Italy.

The Shoppes at Palazzo aren't as exciting, partially because their setting is elegant but bland, and partially because the Palazzo houses crazy-expensive retailers like Barney's New York, Jimmy Choo, and Cartier, along with Bauman Rare Books—the only bookstore on the Strip. Navigating from one mall to the other isn't exactly intuitive, so you may have to ask for directions if you have a specific destination in mind. The shops are open Sunday through Thursday from 10am to 11pm and Friday and Saturday from 10am to midnight. In the Venetian/Palazzo, 3327-3377 Las Vegas Blvd. S. www.grandcanalshoppes. com. *©* **702/414-4525.**

The LINQ Promenade ★★ The ongoing trend in Las Vegas has been to capture the visitors while they're walking elsewhere. You turn into this unexpected gap between the Flamingo and the LINQ and boom, you're no longer *on* the Strip. Suddenly, you're on a long, narrow urban thoroughfare, complete with palm trees lining either side of the street, along with stores and restaurants. The High Roller, at 550 feet the world's tallest observation wheel, is the anchor of this block. You'll pass **Brooklyn Bowl** (p. 117), which offers great fried chicken and happens to be a concert venue featuring indie acts, and a Goorin Brothers hat shop. Need a cupcake to go? You can purchase one, 24 hours, at the cupcake ATM on the side of **Sprinkles,** a Los Angeles–based bakery that is now on this block. This little stretch has a Miami vibe to it, which all dissipates once you board one of the pods of the High Roller to see what surrounds you. That's okay; you didn't come to Vegas for that SoFlo feel anyway. Hours vary by store. 3454 Las Vegas Blvd. S. (btw. the LINQ and the Flamingo). www.thelinq.com. ℰ **800/CAESARS.**

Miracle Mile Shops at Planet Hollywood ★   The retail outlets here are just prettier, Vegas-ier versions of the stores at the nice mall in your hometown, like White House Black Market, Lucky Brand, Guess, H&M, and a giant Urban Outfitters that looms over the Strip. There are some one-off boutiques, such as an Original Penguin, and interesting art galleries to peruse like that of olive-loving artist Michael Godard and marine-life conservationist Wyland. The Zappos Theatre has become the home for major pop residencies, where the Backstreet Boys have returned *Larger Than Life,* Gwen Stefani shows she's not *Just a Girl,* and Def Leppard *Hits Vegas.* One thing to note about this mall: It's not the easiest to navigate. It's essentially one big circle, so if the shop you want is on one side and you don't realize you've gone the wrong way from the entrance, you might end up taking an entire lap of the mall to get to your destination. The shops are open Sunday through Thursday from 10am to 11pm and Friday and Saturday from 10am to midnight. In Planet Hollywood Resort & Casino, 3663 Las Vegas Blvd. S. www.miraclemileshopslv.com. ℰ **702/866-0704.**

Via Bellagio ★★   There are only about a dozen boutiques in this well-lit corridor of the Bellagio, and like most everything else at this hotel, they'll cost you a pretty penny. On the clothing side, that means Prada, Chanel, Gucci, Louis Vuitton, Dior, and Armani; sparkly, pretty things are on sale from Tiffany & Co., and a timeless timepiece from watchmaker Breguet (open since 1775) is also available here. Everybody gets a peek into Carrie's closet now that Sarah Jessica Parker has branched out here with another SJP boutique. It's worth a stroll, even if you're there just to window-shop. That's still free. Hours vary by store. In Bellagio, 3600 Las Vegas Blvd. S. www.bellagio.com. ℰ **702/693-7111.**

NORTH STRIP

Bonanza Gift and Souvenir Shop ★★   Even though it says it's the "World's Largest Gift Shop" outside, it isn't, and we don't care! It's 36,000 square feet of pure Vegas-oriented kitsch, from T-shirts to tchotchkes, Native American crafts and jewelry, casino accoutrements like retired dice and decks of playing cards, Elvis stuff, Rat Pack stuff, atomic age stuff—the Vegas things that run from tacky to tasteful—all for really good prices. Besides, no one really wants that plastic yard you drank warm daiquiris from all day when you stumbled down the Strip. It's open daily from 9am until 2am. 2440 Las Vegas Blvd. S. (at Sahara Ave.). www.worldslargestgiftshop.com. ✆ **702/385-7359.**

Fashion Show ★★   That saucer-looking thing hovering over the exterior may make you wonder when it will return to the mothership, but it's actually the front for probably the best mall on the Strip. The 250 stores here are comprehensive, covering the basics of a mall you're already familiar with (Gap, Banana Republic, Zara) and some higher-end, cooler options (Scotch & Soda, Top Shop, Diesel), all anchored by department stores like Dillard's, Neiman Marcus, and the Silver State's only Nordstrom. On select weekends, the place lives up to its name and has actual fashion shows within the mall itself. A hydraulic runway lifts out of the floor, sometimes with fog, and models march down. It's all very dramatic, as you'd expect from a mall front and center on the Strip. Fashion Show is open Monday through Saturday from 10am to 9pm, and Sunday from 11am to 7pm. 3200 Las Vegas Blvd. S. (at the corner of Spring Mountain Rd.). www.thefashionshow.com. ✆ **702/369-8382.**

DOWNTOWN

Downtown Container Park ★★★   In an attempt to revitalize Downtown Las Vegas into an urban counterpart to the Strip, it wasn't enough to add loft apartments, trendy restaurants, and mixology bars. The area needed a playground—a communal space for locals and visitors to gather—and Downtown Container Park has filled that role. You're greeted by the 40-foot Praying Mantis, straight from Burning Man, which breathes fire at night. No matter how many times I've passed it, I'm always startled when it happens. The retail side of the venture is housed in an assortment of stacked shipping containers and prefabricated cubes that contain independent fashion and art boutiques, jewelers, confectioners, bars, and restaurants. The 20,000-square-foot structure features a courtyard in the middle with a treehouse, complete with a 33-foot slide. Kids are welcome during the day, but after 9pm the whole complex is 21 and over. Live entertainment and outdoor movie nights (when it's not blazing hot) make this a nice neighborhood oasis for getting away from the real Vegas. The center is open Sunday through Thursday from 11am to 11pm, and Friday and Saturday from 11am to 1am, although store hours vary. 707 Fremont St. (at 7th St.). www.downtowncontainerpark.com. ✆ **702/637-4244.**

Gamblers General Store/Gambler's Book Club ★   If you can't bear to leave the gambling in Las Vegas, this is your ultimate resource. Everything you need to furnish your own casino at home is here, and not just dice and decks of cards. We're talking full-size blackjack and craps tables, slot machines, and roulette wheels too. Need an extra edge on your game? More than 3,000 titles are available with tips and tricks of the trade. As the house is almost always guaranteed to win, we question the veracity of the tips in some of these books, but they're not bad guides to learning every game inside and out. Want to have casino chips or cards customized? They'll do that, too. The only thing that would make this place better is if there was a Gamblers Anonymous meeting being held in the basement. Just kidding; Las Vegas doesn't have basements. The store is open Monday through Saturday from 9am to 5:30pm and Sunday from 9am to 4:30pm. 800 S. Main St. (Downtown). www.gamblersgeneralstore.com. © **800/522-1777** or 702/382-9903.

Las Vegas Premium Outlets North ★ The good news: This shopping emporium is situated between the Strip and Downtown Las Vegas, so it's more convenient to get to than its counterpart, **Outlets South** (see below). The bad news: It's outdoors. So, on summer days, despite the water misters and misguided attempts at shade, shopping here is unbearable. But if the weather is okay, you'll get to navigate some decent outlet shopping that includes brands like Diesel, AllSaints, Diane von Furstenberg, Dolce & Gabbana, True Religion, and Calvin Klein. The mall is open Monday through Saturday from 9am to 9pm, and Sunday from 9am to 8pm. 875 S. Grand Central Pkwy. (at I-15). www.premiumoutlets.com. © **702/474-7500.**

Retro Vegas ★★ Though it's got Vegas in its name, this little boutique has so much more than vintage Vegas design in its selection. There's a good chunk of beautiful Danish and midcentury modern furniture that many collectors would love to get their hands on. And for those who want to take home a bit of Sin City history, there are all kinds of items that evoke the best of Vegas vices, including old-school, sturdy, colored glass ashtrays from casinos of Vegas past and delicate, ornate cocktail glasses from the *Mad Men* era. It's open Monday through Saturday from 11am to 6pm, and Sunday from noon to 5pm. 1131 S. Main St. (at Charleston Ave.). www.retro-vegas.com. © **702/384-2700.**

The Toy Shack ★★★ One of the only reasons to visit Neonopolis (besides parking and the Cannabition Cannabis Museum), the Toy Shack is where Jimmy Jiminez, a toy expert who makes frequent appearances on the History Channel's *Pawn Stars,* actually works. The store carries everything from pristine collectibles to new-fangled toys, dolls, and action figures. Comic book nerds (and the people who love them) use the goods here for superhero cosplay parties; the country's biggest collection of Hot Wheels is a big draw for those sorts of aficionados. Who says you can't play with toys when you're an adult? The Toy Shack is open Mondays through Saturdays from 11am until 10pm. In Neonopolis, 450 E. Fremont St. © **702/538-8600.**

JUST OFF THE STRIP

The Boulevard ★ Las Vegans off the Strip; they're just like you! They need large appliances and new backpacks for the kids for school and sensible shoes, and they get them at malls like this one. The selection of stores here is of the everyday kind: Foot Locker, Lane Bryant, Macy's. They come in handy when you need to buy a pair of shoes that aren't wrecking your feet, or if you forgot to pack khakis for your conference, at prices that are probably a little more reasonable than at boutiques on the Strip. It's close enough that it won't

SHOPPING gets real

Reality TV shows have turned an island's worth of Average Joes, from ice road truck drivers to tanned Jersey boys, into pop-culture stars. Although you can't go trawling on a fishing boat with your favorite demi-celebrities, in Las Vegas you can visit the shopkeepers-turned-stars from popular current or past History Channel shows.

Pawn Stars is set at the **Gold & Silver Pawn Shop,** 713 Las Vegas Blvd. S. (www.gspawn.com; *C* **702/385-7912**). Operated by the colorful Harrison family, the store is heavy on hocked jewelry—but there are lots of other odds and ends worth a quick browse. The bad news is that the Harrisons themselves are rarely on-site anymore, which can be a disappointment to the hordes of people waiting in line (seriously!) to get inside. If you can't leave Vegas without an autograph, you could always pony up and schedule yourself for the 4-hour VIP meet and greet tour, which also takes you to various other Las Vegas reality show locations. But if $70 is a bit much just to meet the gang, there is a life-sized cut-out of Chumlee, Rick, Corey, and Richard to pose in front of. The store is open daily from 9am until 9pm.

You'll have a much better chance of seeing people you've seen on TV at **Rick's Restorations,** 1112 S. Commerce St. (www.ricksrestorations.com; *C* **702/366-7030**), where *American Restoration* was filmed. It also happens to be a stop on the Pawn Stars VIP tour. Owner Rick Dale, his wife Kelly, and a crew of lovable oddballs restore classic Americana (soda machines, gas pumps, bicycles, slot machines, and more) in a rambling facility that offers tours, a showroom, a gift shop, and more. Big windows in the public areas give visitors a glimpse into the working facility, and people from the show, including Rick, will often pop out to say hi and sign autographs. The restorations themselves are stunning accomplishments, but you're going to need a high credit limit to afford any of it. Recently offered gas pumps, for instance, started at around $7,000 and went up from there. The store is open Monday through Friday from 9am until 5pm.

cost you too much in cab fare, and it's a nice little taste of what real life is like in Sin City. The mall is open Monday through Saturday from 10am to 9pm, and Sunday from 11am to 7pm. 3528 S. Maryland Pkwy. (btw. Twain Ave. and Desert Inn Rd.). www.boulevardmall.com. *C* **702/735-8268.**

Zia Record Exchange ★★ Record stores? They still have these? Yes, and this is actually a very good one. Okay, so there are more CDs than vinyl on the shelves (but still way more vinyl than we've seen in quite some time), and the selection is vast. Hunting through the crates, you might find anything from Mumford and Sons and Tech N9ne to Rolling Stones' classic *Sticky Fingers* and Willie Nelson and Merle Haggard's *Django and Jimmie*—it's an eclectic collection. Vegas bands, obviously, get a lot of love, with a bin dedicated exclusively to local up-and-comers, who sometimes even do in-store performances and signings. Both locations are open daily from 10am to midnight. 1216 S. Rainbow Blvd. www.ziarecords.com. *C* **702/233-4942.** 4225 S. Eastern Ave., Ste. 17. *C* **702/735-4942.**

SOUTH & EAST OF THE STRIP

Las Vegas Premium Outlets South ★   The sister location at the north end of the Strip might have fancier brands, but this one has the real bargains. There are a few shared names between the two outposts, like the BCBG-MaxAzria, DKNY, and Calvin Klein. For the most part, the rest on the south side are old familiar faces like Dress Barn, Levi's, and Tommy Hilfiger, and it seems like these stores often have better deals than the ones up north. It's also a straight shot down Las Vegas Boulevard to get here, in the event you're driving. But the real reason this one wins out? The added bonus of being indoors and air-conditioned. The mall is open Monday through Saturday from 9am to 9pm and Sunday from 9am to 8pm. 7400 Las Vegas Blvd. S. (at Warm Springs Rd.). www.premiumoutlets.com. ℭ **702/896-5599.**

Town Square ★   This is the closest shopping center to the Strip where you'll see actual Las Vegans spending time, thanks to its townlike design. The 150 or so stores and restaurants are along tree-lined streets set up in a grid like city blocks. You can even park in front of the stores if there's a spot open; if not, there are also a couple of parking lots and covered garages. Stroll past quaint storefronts of an Apple store, Armani Exchange, Paper Source, and Tommy Bahama. Catch a blockbuster at the 18-screen movie theater, chill out with a pint or three at Yardhouse, or grab a bite at one of the dozen (mostly chain) restaurants, like **Brio Tuscan Grille** or **Texas de Brazil.** For kids, there's even a park in the center to play in, and a giant GameWorks, complete with a bowling alley, arcade, and laser tag. Baobab Stage is a live theater venue where performers from Strip productions spend their night off doing cabaret shows. It's pretty much all the stuff you'd do at this type of mall in your hometown—this one just happens to have a Las Vegas Boulevard address. Hours vary by store. 6605 Las Vegas Blvd. S. (at I-215). www.mytown squarelasvegas.com. ℭ **702/269-5000.**

ENTERTAINMENT & NIGHTLIFE

According to an advertising slogan, Hollywood is the "Entertainment Capital of the World." But consider for a moment the sheer number of shows, headliners, bars, nightclubs, lounges, and other forms of entertainment and nightlife in Las Vegas. Your options are almost limitless: Cirque du Soleil has more than a half-dozen permanent shows here; virtually every hotel has at least one showroom, if not four; Lady Gaga, Madonna, and Bruno Mars are now among the big names who perform regularly, and sometimes exclusively, in Vegas; most bars are open 24 hours a day; 7 of the 10 top-grossing nightclubs in the U.S. are in Vegas, and visitors seem to want to spend their money on an experience rather than gambling the night away. Hollywood may have the slogan, but Las Vegas is the real capital.

You certainly won't be lacking in things to do; in fact, the opposite may be true in that there are simply not enough hours in your vacation to do all the things you may want to do. The key is to cover the basics—a Cirque show if you've never seen one; a headliner, if one is in town; a fun bar; a high-energy nightclub—and then start layering in the off-the-beaten-track, the one-of-a-kind, and the less-high-profile shows, clubs, and entertainment offerings that will make your trip more memorable.

What follows are the things you should not miss—and some that are not worth your time no matter what you may have heard—in the category of performing arts, which includes shows big, small, and in between; the bar scene, including lounges, piano bars, and pubs; the club and music scene, covering the big dance clubs, ultralounges, comedy clubs, and more; and, of course, the strip clubs, which are big business in Vegas. There are also recommendations for gay and lesbian visitors showcasing some of the best and brightest bars and clubs around town.

THE PERFORMING ARTS

This category covers all the major Las Vegas production shows and a few of the minor ones as well. Note that shows can close without warning, even ones that have been running just shy of forever, so please call first. You might also want to double-check the days and times of performances; schedules can change without notice. *Note:* Most ticket prices do not include taxes, fees, or drinks, so you might also check for those potential hidden costs.

Absinthe ★★★ Like the supposedly hallucinatory drink it is named after, this Cirque du Soleil–style revue may leave you reeling. But, boy, will that hangover be worth it. The show is performed in the round in a small tent-like structure in front of Caesars Palace, with a tiny circular stage and only a few rows of seating. That means all the "death-defying stunts"—by acrobats, trapeze artists, high-wire walkers, and even high-speed roller skaters—will be just feet, and in some cases inches, from your face. Adding to the thrills are the raunchy host, the Gazillionaire, and his faithfully dimwitted sidekick assistant, who introduce the acts with a dirty glee and X-rated humor that will leave you laughing so hard you'll forget to be offended or shocked. Sidekick Joy Jenkins' hilarious, jaw-dropping potty-mouthed rant is worth the price of admission alone. The cast rotates, so the show differs from performance to performance. Definitely not for kids or prudes! Shows are nightly at 8 and 10pm. In Caesars Palace, 3570 Las Vegas Blvd. S. www.absinthevegas.com. ℂ **800/745-3000.** Tickets $99–$139.

Blue Man Group ★ Are they blue? Indeed, they are—three bald, non-speaking men dipped in azure paint, doing decidedly odd stunts with marshmallows, art supplies, smoke-ring-blowing cannons, and giant inflatable balls, commenting on the use of technology and social media without saying a word. The group's amazing array of percussion instruments is fashioned fancifully from PVC piping. Blue Man, back at its original Las Vegas home, Luxor, since 2015, has an updated and reimagined show to fit into the new, smaller space. Moments of silly genius are a staple—those oddly compelling,

Las Vegas Shows

Absinthe **7**
Blue Man Group **16**
Bruno Mars **11**
Cher **11**
Chippendales **6**
Cirque du Soleil's *KÀ* **14**
Cirque du Soleil's *LOVE* **4**
Cirque du Soleil's *Michael Jackson ONE* **17**
Cirque du Soleil's *Mystère* **2**
Cirque du Soleil's *O* **9**
Cirque du Soleil's *Zumanity* **13**
David Copperfield **14**
Gwen Stefani **10**

Human Nature: *Jukebox* **3**
Jabbawockeez: *JREAMZ* **14**
Jennifer Lopez **10**
Lady Gaga **11**
Legends in Concert **8**
Le Rêve **1**
Mac King **5**
Magic Mike Live **12**
Mariah Carey **7**
Penn & Teller **6**
Piff the Magic Dragon **8**
Reba, Brooks & Dunn **7**
Rod Stewart **7**
Terry Fator **4**
Thunder From Down Under **15**
Tournament of Kings **15**
V: The Ultimate Variety Show **10**
Vegas! The Show **10**

8

ENTERTAINMENT & NIGHTLIFE | The Performing Arts

HOW THE magic HAPPENS

Cirque du Soleil is about so much more than the performers onstage. Take a peek behind the scenes at these free daytime tours:

○ **Cirque du Soleil's KÀ**, at the MGM Grand, offers a complimentary Theater Experience on Tues and Sat at noon and 12:30pm (see below).

○ **Cirque du Soleil's LOVE**, at the Mirage, takes you on a Magical Technical Tour on Fri 1–1:30pm (p. 209).

○ **Cirque du Soleil's Mystère**, at Treasure Island, gives you a 30-minute sneak peek at their dress rehearsal on Sat at 3pm (p. 210).

giant smoke rings, for example, and a routine with a Twinkie and a hapless audience member are classics—but the cozier theater allows the troupe to create a more intimate, immersive experience and a few surprises. In the end, the show that used to be unique in Vegas is now uniquely Vegas, as much a part of the entertainment landscape as Cirque du Soleil, and for that alone it is worth a visit. Shows are nightly at 7 and 9:30pm. At Luxor, 3900 Las Vegas Blvd. S. www.blueman.com. ✆ **702/262-4400**. Tickets $64–$125; VIP and backstage tour packages available.

Brad Garrett's Comedy Club ★ Set off a walkway between the MGM Grand parking garage and the casino, this comedy club isn't the easiest to find. But for *Everybody Loves Raymond*'s Brad Garrett's self-deprecating style of stand-up, this underground lair, with its cabaret-style stage and intimate seating, has just the right pretension-free ambience. The star appears here regularly, along with an ever-revolving roster of talented comedians. The humor tends to run on the raunchy side; if you're easily offended, remember you're in Vegas. Lighten up. Photos of comedy legends hang on the walls; reserve a booth to feel like a VIP. There's no food, but there are three different types of flavored popcorn to snack on; specialty cocktails are a must, but be aware that there will be a pre-added gratuity on your bill. Shows are nightly at 8pm. In MGM Grand, 3799 Las Vegas Blvd. S. ✆ **866/740-7711**. Tickets $47–$65.

Cirque du Soleil's KÀ ★★★ *KÀ* overturns expectations by largely ignoring the usual Cirque format—acrobatic-style acts and ethereal performance art trappings with a tenuous-at-best connective tissue—in favor of an actual plot, as a sister and brother from some mythical Asian kingdom are separated by enemy raiders and have to endure various trials and tribulations before being reunited. Gleefully borrowing imagery from magical realist martial-arts movies such as *Crouching Tiger, Hidden Dragon,* the production makes use of a technically extraordinary set that shifts the stage not just horizontally but vertically, as the action moves from under the sea to the side of a steep cliff and beyond. The circus elements—clowns and acrobats—are incorporated into the show in a way that makes loose narrative sense.

The story is by turns funny, whimsical, and pulse-pounding, with moments of exquisitely perfect bits of theater. It might be too long and intense for younger children, but older ones will be enthralled—and so will you.

The tragic death of one of the show's performers during a show in 2013 has had only a minor impact on the fundamentals of this production but should have profound impact on the audience's interpretation of what Cirque does, reminding us that these are real human beings performing dangerous stunts for our amusement. Stand up at the end of the show and applaud that.

Performances are held Saturday through Wednesday at 7 and 9:30pm. In the MGM Grand, 3799 Las Vegas Blvd. S. www.cirquedusoleil.com/ka. ℂ **866/740-7711.** Tickets $69–$250.

Cirque du Soleil's LOVE ★ A collaboration between the Beatles (by way of Sir George Martin's son, who reconfigured and remixed the music with a free hand that may distress purists) and Cirque du Soleil, this is the usual Cirque triumph of imaginative design, but it also feels surprisingly hollow. Yes, there's inspiration in the idea of pairing Beatles' music with Cirque's joyous spectacle. But while Cirque shows have never been big on plot, the intense aimlessness of this production means that the show too quickly dissolves into the introduction of one novel staging element after another. In other words, its visual fabulousness ends up repetitious rather than thrilling. Still, the familiar music provides an aura of accessibility to the sometimes-dense world of Cirque du Soleil that other Vegas productions don't, so it could be good for Cirque newbies. Shows are held Thursday through Monday at 7 and 9:30pm. At the Mirage, 3400 Las Vegas Blvd. S. www.cirquedusoleil.com/love. ℂ **800/963-9634** or 702/792-7777. Tickets $55–$209.

Cirque du Soleil's *Michael Jackson ONE* ★★★ Unlike *LOVE,* Cirque's Beatle-themed show, *Michael Jackson ONE* works like gangbusters. Its blend of the brilliantly conceived pop music (and pop-culture touchstones) created by Michael Jackson and the pop-art interpretive lens of Cirque du Soleil is a perfect union. Massive walls of video seem to envelop the audience while speakers, built into the seats, pump the timeless soundtrack of Jackson classics, remixed and remastered, directly into your brain. Each is presented with a set piece that ranges from evocative to stunning to giddy glee-inducing. "Bad" features a gang zooming in on zip lines and bouncing around on what amounts to a giant rubber band stretched across the stage; "Wanna Be Starting Something" showcases an acrobatic troupe using Jackson's iconic fedoras as twirling and twisting props; a mash-up of "Human Nature" and "Never Can Say Goodbye" has a solo dancer doing expert human animation; "Billie Jean" evokes the lighted sidewalk in the music video with lighted suits on dancers performing in an otherwise darkened theater. By the time they get to the part where it "snows" on the audience, or the "Thriller" homage with zombies on trampolines, you'll want to stand up and cheer. And when the company dances with a so-realistic-it-hurts hologram of Jackson during "Man in the Mirror," you may have a lump in your throat. You need to be at least an appreciator of

BIG NAMES, bigger shows

During its fallow days in the 1970s and 1980s, Las Vegas was the place where an entertainer's act went to die. The headliner showrooms were the refuge for singers whose best career days were years, and sometimes decades, behind them.

That all changed when Céline Dion came to town in 2003. Her 5-year engagement at Caesars Palace shattered box office records and made it safe for big-name headliners to call Vegas their home. In the last decade and a half, we have seen marquee-topping extended runs from Elton John, Cher, Bette Midler, Garth Brooks, Tim McGraw & Faith Hill, Shania Twain, Rod Stewart, and more. Now that Céline has gone, a new crop of A-list talent has moved in.

Tickets are expensive, with the best seats going for upward of $300, and the concerts are not performed every week, so if you want to see one, you must plan your vacation around their schedule rather than yours. But many of the shows are exclusive engagements, meaning if you want to see the stars, you have to come to Vegas.

Sting announced his first headlining run at Caesars Palace, 3570 Las Vegas Blvd. S. (www.sting.com; ℭ **877/423-5463;** show times vary; tickets $55–$250). Starting in May 2020, *Sting: My Songs* reprises his greatest hits, which is to be expected of any Vegas headliner, but these are retooled versions that have been released on his album of the same name. Sting may not have the 31-piece orchestra that backed Céline during her last tenure in this theater, but sometimes you don't need more than Sting and his guitar in a spotlight.

Sharing the same stage (but not at the same time, sadly), **Rod Stewart,** at Caesars Palace, 3570 Las Vegas Blvd. S.

---

the music and willing to overlook the subtle hagiography of the (fallible) guy who created it to properly enjoy the show. But anyone who ever danced to a track of "Thriller"—which is pretty much everybody—will be, in a word, thrilled. Shows are held Friday through Tuesday at 7 and 9:30pm. At Mandalay Bay, 3950 Las Vegas Blvd. S. www.cirquedusoleil.com/one. ℭ **877/632-7400** or 800/745-3000. Tickets $75–$250.

Cirque du Soleil's Mystère ★★★ It's been running since 1993, and *Mystère* will always be fondly known as the first (and many say the best) of Cirque du Soleil's multiple Las Vegas productions. Although there have been some tweaks here and there and a few new acts added and subtracted here and there, the show is pretty much the same as it always has been, which, in a word, is *stunning.* It's the closest to the original ethos of the Montréal-based company's unique circus experience, which focuses on feats of human strength and agility all wrapped up in performance art elements both absurd and surreal. The show features one unbelievable act after another (breathtakingly beautiful aerial maneuvers, seemingly boneless contortionists and acrobats), interspersed with Dadaist/*commedia dell'arte* clowns. All this and a giant snail! The thesaurus runs dry trying to describe it: dreamlike, suspenseful, erotic, funny, mesmerizing, and just lovely. At times, you might even find yourself moved to tears. I'm not ashamed to admit I was. Catch it Saturday (www.rodstewart.com; ℂ **888/435-8665;** show times vary; tickets $49–$250), continues to tour with his show, simply and aptly titled *The Hits*. Stewart's canon of work is irreproachable: "Forever Young," "You Wear It Well," "Maggie May," and of course his iconic "Do You Think I'm Sexy." After 5 decades' worth of hits, yes, Rod, we do.

Country stars unite in **Reba, Brooks & Dunn: Together in Vegas** at Caesars Palace, 3570 Las Vegas Blvd. S. (www.thecolosseum.com; ℂ **800/745-3000;** show times vary; tickets $60–$205), a show exclusively created for Las Vegas. Reba McEntire collaborated with country duo Kix Brooks and Ronnie Dunn for this fun, 90-minute honky-tonk, packed with plenty of number-one songs from both their extensive catalogs.

Finally, icon **Lady Gaga** has taken up residency at the newest venue on the block, the Park Theater at Park MGM, 3770 Las Vegas Blvd. S. (https://vegas.ladygaga.com; ℂ **866/919-7472;** show times vary; tickets $78 and up, and much higher for resale tickets), rotating performance schedules with other heavy hitters such as Bruno Mars and Cher. There are two iterations of the show: The first is the dynamic *Enigma*, where Gaga performs her huge pop hits with all the spectacle and costume changes for which she is known. The other is the more sedate *Jazz & Piano*, where she plays acoustic versions of her songs and other American standards. During her opening weekend, this was the show where her *A Star Is Born* co-star Bradley Cooper joined her on stage to sing their Oscar-winning duet, "Shallow," proving that even without big production values, Gaga is still full of surprises.

through Wednesday at 7 and 9:30pm, or pop in for free dress rehearsals on Saturdays from 3 to 3:30pm. In Treasure Island, 3300 Las Vegas Blvd. S. www.cirquedusoleil.com/mystere. ℂ **800/392-1999** or 702/894-7722. Tickets $75–$137, discounts for children under 12 based on availability.

Cirque du Soleil's O ★★★ Franco Dragone, the director, gave Cirque's smash hit its one-letter-name because it's a symbol for infinity; moreover, "O" is the phonetic pronunciation of "eau," the French word for water. Go to see *O*, and turn your attention from the stage for a moment. You'll find another reason for this odd title: the saucer eyes and open mouths of the audience. This is simply the most astounding, profound, exhilarating, eye-poppingly beautiful show in Vegas. That's a long chain of superlatives, but if I had more space, I'd probably add a couple more. The show is centered around a 1.5-million-gallon pool, an engineering marvel: In seconds flat, it transforms from pool to a shallow African watering hole, to a dry platform filled with dancers and acrobats, to a plateau with dancing fountains, or to a shimmering lake studded with islands and clown-steered houseboats. Synchronized swimmers plunge into its depths, staying submerged for what seems like 10 minutes. Meanwhile, above-the-water divers twist and knife in, as brilliantly costumed parades traverse the edges of the water. Running since 1998, this is a spectacle like no other and does the impossible: It tops all the other brilliant Cirque shows. Performances are held Wednesday through Sunday at 7 and 9:30pm. In Bellagio, 3600 Las Vegas Blvd. S. www.cirquedusoleil.com/o. ✆ **888/488-7111** or 702/796-9999. Tickets $99–$295.

Cirque du Soleil's *Zumanity* ★ Most controversial among Cirque's offerings, *Zumanity* is an erotic circus that celebrates sexuality in all its myriad incarnations: men with women, women with women, men with men, senior citizens with other seniors or with young folks, little people with Amazon-sized women, group sex, masturbation—you name it. Which means that when two strong men are lifting one another in the classic "watch our veins pop out as we imitate Atlas" act, it's clear that there's a lot more than just lifting going on between these two. And when the aerialist hanging from the long silk ribbon is flinging herself around the stage, it's all about S&M and autoerotic asphyxiation. Those who are open-minded will find the Cirque magic here, as much of it is visually arresting. One of the last times I was there, however, several people did walk out, so think honestly about what makes you squeamish before you book. Shows are held Friday through Tuesday at 7 and 9:30pm (show times vary seasonally). In New York–New York, 3790 Las Vegas Blvd. S. www.cirquedusoleil.com/zumanity. ✆ **866/606-7111** or 702/740-6815. Tickets $69–$125. Only ages 18 and over admitted.

David Copperfield ★ Illusionists don't come any more illustrious than David Copperfield, who has been in the business for decades and has done everything from making the Statue of Liberty disappear to walking through the Great Wall of China. He has played semi-regular sets at the MGM Grand for years, but now is making the hotel his home with his name on the showroom. He mixes small, up-close magic like popping balloons "with his mind" and making a small piece of tissue dance up someone's arm, with larger stunts like making a car appear out of nowhere and causing an entire group from the audience to disappear (from the stage, not their seats). His laconic, "I'm so good at this I don't need to make a big deal about it" stage presence is a welcome relief from the hyper-dramatic theatrics that other magicians of his caliber often embrace, and Copperfield's ever-evolving act means that even if you have seen one of his TV specials, you'll witness new tricks here. Shows are held nightly at 7 and 9:30pm, with an additional 4pm show on Saturday. In the MGM Grand, 3555 Las Vegas Blvd. S. www.davidcopperfield.com. ✆ **877/880-0880.** Tickets $83–$240.

Human Nature: *Jukebox* ★★ It might have been crooning Motown hits that put Australian quartet Human Nature on the map, but after a long run on the Strip, the other guys from Down Under have expanded their repertoire with *Jukebox* (which also happens to be the name of their platinum-selling album). Their tight harmonies are delightful throwbacks to the era when the Miracles, the Supremes, the Four Tops, and the Jackson 5 ruled the charts, but they whip audiences into the 21st century with just as exciting pop covers of Taylor Swift, Bruno Mars, and the Beatles. Human Nature started as a boy band (though at this age, they really are a man band), so you'll also be

The Performing Arts

ENTERTAINMENT & NIGHTLIFE

family-friendly SHOWS

Appropriate shows for kids, all described in this chapter, include:

- **Cirque du Soleil's KÀ,** at the MGM Grand (p. 208)
- **Cirque du Soleil's LOVE,** at the Mirage (p. 209)
- **Cirque du Soleil's *Mystère*,** at Treasure Island (p. 210)
- **David Copperfield,** at MGM Grand (p. 212)
- **Mac King,** at Harrah's (p. 216)
- ***Tournament of Kings,*** at Excalibur (p. 219)

delighted by renditions of other all-male groups like the Beach Boys, Boyz II Men, and Backstreet Boys. Save your quarters. This is a jukebox where you won't want to skip any songs. Shows are Tuesday through Saturday at 7pm. At the Venetian/Palazzo, 3355 Las Vegas Blvd. S. www.humannaturelive.com. ℂ **866/641-7469** or 702/414-9000. Tickets $67–$121.

Jabbawockeez ★★ The shtick here is that each of the crew of hip-hop dancers is totally covered with clothes and serene blank masks, so issues of race, gender, and physical perfection are left at the door. It's interesting and sporadically amusing as they use their bodies to communicate everything from lust to disgust, but the real benefit is that it allows the group to function as a single unit. They're almost like a multicell organism, only one that pops and locks. The show's latest incarnation, at MGM Grand, is set on a smaller stage, which may seem confining for their acrobatic dance style, but the addition of video mapping and intricate lighting effects makes the stage as big a part of the show as the dancers. Shows are Thursday through Monday, 7 and 9:30pm. In the MGM Grand, 3799 Las Vegas Blvd. S. www.jbwkz.com. ℂ **702/531-3826.** Tickets $55–$120.

Jimmy Kimmel's Comedy Club ★ Somewhere while hosting his successful late-night talk show, Las Vegas native Jimmy Kimmel found the time to create his own comedy club in 2019. He designed a two-story, 300-person, 8,000-square-foot showroom, accented with memorabilia from his career, across from the Brooklyn Bowl on the LINQ Promenade. Kimmel even selected a small-bites menu of handheld dishes—think sliders and Neapolitan-style pizza—so that the clinking of utensils doesn't distract the audience. The bar opens at 4pm, offering creative cocktails named for some of the comedian's favorite people (like the tequila-based Guillermo, his sidekick on his show) and his favorite Vegas places (as in the vodka-and-ginger-beer-infused Neon Boneyard), presumably to lube you up for the funny people he and his team have curated to headline. But sorry, *Jimmy Kimmel Live!* fans, the man himself likely won't be performing here, though surprise guests could stop in from time to time. Shows are held Thursday through Sunday at 8pm, with additional shows Friday and Saturday at 10pm. In the LINQ, 3535 Las Vegas Blvd. S. www.kimmelscomedyclub.com. ℂ **855/234-7469.** Tickets $29–$69. Only ages 18 and over admitted.

Pretty much every singer worth their Twitter followings makes a stop in Vegas on their national tour. While the big acts usually play the big arenas, some go for the more intimate rooms, so you may get a chance to see your favorites up close and in person. Major headliner showrooms in Vegas include the following:

- The Cosmopolitan of Las Vegas, 3708 Las Vegas Blvd. S. (www. cosmopolitanlasvegas.com; ℂ 877/551-7778), has two venues, the laid-back, open-air **Boulevard Pool** overlooking the Las Vegas Strip, and the **Chelsea,** a surprisingly intimate venue considering that it can accommodate more than 3,000 people. This converted ballroom feels less like that and more like an industrial-chic play space complete with reclaimed-wood accents, subway tile, and a cheeky attitude perfect for the hotel in which it is located. Both draw big names including Lorde, Adele, and Bruno Mars.

- The 4,000-seat **Colosseum,** in Caesars Palace, 3570 Las Vegas Blvd. S. (www.caesarspalace.com; ℂ 866/227-5938), has been home to extended runs for big-name artists like Sting, Mariah Carey, Rod Stewart, and more,

with shorter stands by big-name singing and comedy acts like Madonna and Jerry Seinfeld.

- Hard Rock Hotel's **Joint,** 4455 Paradise Rd. (www.hardrockhotel. com; ℂ 800/693-7625 or 702/693-5000), was rebuilt in 2009 and now holds 4,000 people for rock concerts and special events. The smaller **Vinyl** club is like a rock-'n'-roll haven on the Sunset Strip.

- The **House of Blues** can hold several hundred people for smaller rock and blues concerts and the weekly gospel brunch (in Mandalay Bay, 3950 Las Vegas Blvd. S.; www.hob.com; ℂ 877/632-7400 or 702/632-7600).

- **Brooklyn Bowl** has cornered the indy-rock market for Vegas. The concert venue is intimate and relaxed, a perfect place to catch the general-admission shows from artists both edgy (Jane's Addiction, Fishbone, and so on) and safe—hey, where have you been, Steve Winwood? (at the LINQ, 3545 Las Vegas Blvd. S., Ste. 22; www.brooklynbowl.com; ℂ 702/862-2695).

- **Mandalay Bay Events Center** seats 12,000 people for arena-style concert tours and indoor

The Laugh Factory ★   Another comedy institution, this one was born in Hollywood with names like George Carlin and Ellen DeGeneres on its roster. But at the Strip outpost, you'll find more unknowns and rising stars, with new comedians putting their comedic skills to the test each week. Shows are nightly at 8:30 and 10:30pm, plus additional shows at midnight Friday and Saturday. In the Tropicana Las Vegas, 3801 Las Vegas Blvd. S. www.troplv.com. ℂ 800/829-9034. Tickets $38–$55.

Le Rêve ★★   Set in a dramatic theater in the round, the "stage" at the center of the bowl-shaped room can be solid, a shallow pool, or deep enough

- sporting events (in Mandalay Bay, 3950 Las Vegas Blvd. S.; www.mandalaybay.com; ✆ **877/632-7400** or 702/632-7580).
- **MGM Grand Garden Events Arena** can hold over 17,000 people and is home to big-name concert tours and events (in the MGM Grand, 3799 Las Vegas Blvd. S.; www.mgmgrand.com; ✆ **800/929-1111** or 702/891-7777).
- **Park Theater** anchors the Park MGM as an intimate, 5,200-seat space where the furthest you can be from the stage is a mere 145 feet. Current residents include Cher, Ricky Martin, and Bruno Mars (in Park MGM, 3770 Las Vegas Blvd. S.; www.mgmresorts.com; ✆ **844/600-7275**).
- The **Orleans Showroom** seats 9,500 people and often has concerts, ice hockey, traveling circuses, and other events (in the Orleans, 4500 W. Tropicana Ave.; www.orleanscasino.com; ✆ **800/675-3267**).
- The **Pearl Theater** is a three-level venue that seats up to 2,500 people for pop, rock, R&B, and comedy concerts (in the Palms, 4321 W. Flamingo Rd.; www.palms.com; ✆ **866/942-7770**).

- **Sam Boyd Stadium** is a 36,800-seat stadium that features big concerts and sporting events (7000 E. Russell Rd.; www.ticketmaster.com; ✆ **800/745-3000**).
- The **Smith Center for the Performing Arts** has a 2,000-seat concert hall for big stage shows (including a Broadway series), a 300-seat Cabaret Jazz theater, and a 200-seat theater for smaller productions. See p. 218 for more details (361 Symphony Park Ave.; www.thesmithcenter.com; ✆ **702/614-0109**).
- **T-Mobile Arena** seats up to 20,00 people for large-scale concerts (count Billy Joel among the inaugural acts) and is home to Las Vegas's hockey team, the Vegas Golden Knights (3780 Las Vegas Blvd. S.; www.t-mobilearena.com; ✆ **702/692-1600**).
- The **Thomas and Mack Center** is a 19,522-seat arena that hosts concerts and sporting events (UNLV Campus; www.ticketmaster.com; ✆ **800/745-3000**).
- The **Fremont Country Club** is Downtown Las Vegas's only real concert venue, hosting rock shows and other special events (601 E. Fremont St.; www.fcc.backstagebarlv.com/; ✆ **702/382-6601**).

to dive into from what seem like insane heights—proven in a gasp-inducing moment. The decision to base this Cirque-like show around a stage of water prompted inevitable comparisons with *O* down the street. Certainly the acrobatics, diving, aerial work, and ballroom dance are as good as what you'll see in any Cirque show, but the moody atmosphere and visually arresting staging really set the show apart. The wordless storyline concerns a woman considering love but needing to face her own demons and past as she wanders through a dreamscape of betrayal, passion, fear, and ultimately salvation. Provocative moments include a sultry tango performed in ankle-deep water and a set piece involving performers descending from the rafters, limp and motionless until they hit the water and spring to life. The latter ends with some of them being jerked back up into the smoky ceiling, screaming as they go. It, like much of the rest of the show, is dark and a bit disconcerting at times, but in a good way, staying with you long after you leave the showroom. Glimpse behind-the-scenes action without ever leaving the theater with a VIP package that gives you your own theater box, bottle of champagne, and video screens of the underwater action as the show happens. Shows are held Friday through Tuesday at 7 and 9:30pm. In Wynn Las Vegas, 3131 Las Vegas Blvd. S. www.wynnlasvegas.com. ℂ **888/320-7110.** Tickets $115–$175. Only ages 13 and over admitted.

Legends in Concert ★   In this parade of faux celebrities, performers vary depending on when you see the show; you may catch "Janet Jackson" and "Diana Ross," or you could get "Lady Gaga" and "Prince," but you will almost always get "Elvis." Unlike other impersonator shows, the singing is live (no lip-syncing), which can enhance the illusion or destroy it. Some performers succeed more in appearance and others do better with vocal mimicry, and while most are at least passable, there are a few that will leave you wondering if he or she is the real thing playing a joke on the audience. Don't scoff; Ellen DeGeneres did that very thing during a 2008 show and captured the audience reactions ("didn't look anything like her") for her daytime talkfest. Shows are daily at 4pm, 7:30pm, and 9:30pm. In the Flamingo, 3555 Las Vegas Blvd. S. www.flamingolasvegas.com. ℂ **855/234-7469.** Tickets $53–$82.

Mac King ★★★   The best daytime show, in fact one of the most exceptional shows in Vegas, period, the *Mac King* show is that rare breed of entertainment that's not only appropriate for all ages, but also a show that junior, grandma, and the hot date you met in Vegas will enjoy. A comedian with a big talent for magic—King is the only magician who was asked to appear on all five of NBC's "World's Greatest Magic Show" specials—King looks like a refugee from *The Music Man,* wearing an old-fashioned plaid suit and a goofy aw-shucks expression. His tricks are oddball illusions (featuring fellows in bear suits, a "cloak of invisibility," and disappearing heads) that he performs with a generous dose of whimsy and intelligence. If there's any justice in the world, this longtime performer will soon be headlining his own evening show. He's that good. Shows are held Tuesday through Saturday at 1 and 3pm. In Harrah's, 3475 Las Vegas Blvd. S. www.mackingshow.com. ℂ **800/427-7247** or 702/369-5222. Tickets $36–$47.

Penn & Teller ★★★   The most intelligent show in Vegas, as these two—magicians? illusionists? truth-tellers? BS artists? geniuses?—put on 90 minutes of, yes, magic and juggling, but also acerbic comedy, mean stunts, and quiet beauty. Looking like two characters out of Dr. Seuss, big, loud Penn and smaller, silent Teller (to reduce them to their basic characteristics) perform magic, reveal the secrets behind a few major magic tricks, discuss why magic is nothing but a bunch of lies, and then turn around and show why magic is as lovely an art form as any other. We won't tell you much about the various

PENN & TELLER'S TOP 10 THINGS ONE SHOULD NEVER DO IN A VEGAS magic show

Penn & Teller have been exercising their acerbic wit and magical talents in numerous forums together since the late 1970s, and their show at the Rio is one of Vegas's best and most intelligent. We must confess that we couldn't get the quieter half of the duo, Teller, to cough up a few words, but the more verbose Penn Jillette was happy to share.

1. Costume yourself in a gray business suit totally lacking in rhinestones, animal patterns, Mylar, capes, bell bottoms, shoulder pads, and top hats.

2. Wear your hair in any style that could *not* be described as "feathered" or "spiked."

3. Use really good live jazz music instead of canned, sound-alike, cheesy, rip-off, fake pop "music."

4. Cruelly (but truthfully) make fun of your siblings in the magic brotherhood.

5. Do the dangerous tricks on each other instead of anonymous show women with aftermarket breasts and/or endangered species.

6. Toss a cute little magic bunny into a cute little chipper-shredder.

7. Open your show by explaining *and* demonstrating how other magicians on the Strip do their most amazing tricks, and then do that venerable classic of magic, "the Cups and Balls," with transparent plastic cups.

8. Treat the audience as if they have a brain in their collective head.

9. Allow audience members to sign real bullets, load them into real guns, and fire those bullets into your face.

10. Bleed.

(You will find many of these "don'ts" in the Penn & Teller show at the Rio All-Suite Hotel & Casino.)

tricks and acts for fear of ruining the illusions, but watching Teller fish money out of an empty glass aquarium or play with shadows is to belie Penn's earlier caveats about learning how tricks are done—it doesn't ruin the wonder of it, not at all, nor the serenity that settles in your Vegas-sensory-overloaded brain. Hang around the lobby after the show for a free meet-and-greet, something other Vegas headliners charge a hefty fee for. Shows are held Saturday through Wednesday at 9pm. In the Rio All-Suite Hotel & Casino, 3700 W. Flamingo Rd. www.riolasvegas.com. © **888/746-7784.** Tickets $87–$97. Only ages 5 and over admitted.

Piff the Magic Dragon ★★★ If a grown man in a dinosaur costume doesn't make you laugh, just wait until he starts doing magic. A finalist on *America's Got Talent,* Piff (and his sidekick, Mr. Piffles, The World's Only Magic Performing Chihuahua) lets a dry sense of humor and blasé attitude take audiences through 90 minutes of some actually quite astonishing magic tricks. He's not making monuments disappear like Copperfield, or even an African spotted pygmy elephant à la Penn and Teller. Piff's magic works on a smaller scale, using everyday items like a toaster or a can of dog food as vehicles for his illusions. A word: Although he's dressed like he can work your kid's birthday party, this isn't a show for kids (and no, they don't do

BROADWAY & beyond

Although Las Vegas has been synonymous with entertainment for decades, filled with showrooms and theaters galore, the one thing the city never had was a true performing arts venue—the kind of place where symphonies and true Broadway shows (not the cut-down versions that happen on the Strip) could spread their wings. Opened in 2012, the **Smith Center for the Performing Arts** changed all that and firmly established Sin City as a cultural center to be reckoned with.

The buildings are stunning, designed with a timeless Art Deco style inspired by the Hoover Dam—notice the chandeliers, which look like an inverted version of the water intake towers. The whole thing is bright, modern, and dramatic, yet comfortable and built to last. While many Vegas buildings attempt scope and grandeur, they feel impermanent somehow. The Smith Center feels like the kind of place that will be here for centuries.

The main space, **Reynolds Hall,** is a finely tuned, Carnegie Hall–worthy, 2,050-seat concert venue that hosts philharmonics, headliners, and touring versions of Broadway shows like *Hamilton* and *The Book of Mormon*. The 240-seat **Cabaret Theater** is a classic, nightclub-style space with big windows, giving it a sense of airiness missing in most theaters. It features a jazz series and more intimate concerts from acts that run from swing to doo wop to funk. A third, 200-seat "black box"-style theater holds smaller theater and dance productions. Outside is a beautiful park that can also be used for performances, or just a place to sit and enjoy the view. 361 Symphony Park Ave. (at Grand Central Pkwy.). www.thesmithcenter.com. ✆ **702/749-2000.** Prices and times vary by show.

children's parties, either). Also, occasionally Mr. Piffles might be shot from a cannon. Show nights vary, with shows at 5:30 and 8pm. In the Flamingo, 3555 Las Vegas Blvd. www.flamingolasvegas.com. ✆ **888/746-7784.** Tickets $63–$103.

Terry Fator ★ *America's Got Talent* winner Fator is no Susan Boyle, that's for sure, but his shtick—ventriloquism meets impersonation—is entertaining. The format of the 80-minute show is fairly standard: A series of puppets joins Fator on stage, and they proceed to do a song or three impersonating a famous voice. Winston the Turtle does a serviceable Justin Bieber and a very good Kermit the Frog, while Walter the Cowboy kills on a Brooks & Dunn song—or rather Fator does, of course. Even the less-than-perfect impressions are still impressive considering the fact that he's doing it all with his mouth closed. Fator's overall demeanor is a little too laconic, especially when he doesn't have a piece of felt on his hand, but the show mostly hits its middle-of-the-road target on the bull's-eye, offering up some decent chuckles and a nice night of music. Try to get a seat in the center section; otherwise you'll spend most of your time watching the giant TV screens instead of the guy (and his friends) on stage. Shows are Monday through Thursday at 7:30pm. At the Mirage, 3400 Las Vegas Blvd. S. www.mirage.com. ✆ **800/963-9634** or 702/792-7777. Tickets $65–$163.

Tournament of Kings ★ "Lords and Ladies, Wizards and Wenches, hasten thee to thy throne, for the battle is about to commence." Yes, that's how they talk at this dinner show—like a Renaissance fair, only with better production values. There's nothing different here than you'll find at one of those Medieval Times chain restaurants, with a decent dinner and lots of knights-in-shining-armor–style theatrics. It's not *Game of Thrones* (now THAT would be an interesting Vegas show), so it's one of the few family-friendly options in town; younger kids will like it, teenagers will be too jaded, and adults will probably be bored. Shows are Monday and Friday at 6pm and Wednesday, Thursday, Saturday, and Sunday at 6 and 8:30pm. In Excalibur, 3850 Las Vegas Blvd. S. www.excalibur.com. ℂ **800/933-1334** or 702/597-7600. Tickets $45–$56.

V: The Ultimate Variety Show ★ Although not as big budget as the Cirque productions, *V* can still offer some big thrills if you happen to see it on the right night. It's a collection of variety acts that could include acrobats, magicians, musicians, dancers, and more, but since the acts vary, so does the quality. Check to see if the thrilling roller-skating couple Vittorio and Jenny Aratas are on the roster. They only do 5 minutes of a 70-minute show, but their hold-your-breath stunts performed mere inches from the audience will make whatever you have to watch in the other 65 minutes totally worth it. Shows are nightly at 7 and 8:30pm. In the Miracle Mile Shops at Planet Hollywood Resort, 3667 Las Vegas Blvd. S. www.vtheshow.com. ℂ **866/932-1818** or 702/260-7200. Tickets $80–$100.

Vegas! The Show ★★★ What would happen if you took the best bits of classic Las Vegas entertainment from the last 70 years or so and put it in one package? That's the basic question behind this loving look back at the ghosts of the Sin City stages, and the answer is this: It would be a heck of a lot of fun. A gateway to the days of Vegas past, with beautiful showgirls in skimpy costumes and big headdresses; headliners like the Rat Pack and Elvis; variety acts (tap dancing! magic!); dancing; singing; even Elton John and implosions. The show plays like a TV history special done by Busby Berkeley. The singing and dancing are among the best you'll find in Vegas, which may very well make you long for the days before those French-Canadian acrobats took over the showrooms. Shows are nightly at 7 and 9pm. In the Miracle Mile Shops at Planet Hollywood Resort, 3667 Las Vegas Blvd. S. www.vegas theshow.com. ℂ **866/932-1818** or 702/260-7200. Tickets $99–$120.

THE BAR SCENE

In addition to the venues listed below, you might check out the incredible nighttime view at the bars and lounges atop the **Strat** (p. 72) or midway up on the **Eiffel Tower Experience** (p. 156)—nothing beats them, except for maybe the more up-close view of the bar adjacent to the 23rd-floor lobby at the **Waldorf Astoria.** The floor-to-ceiling windows make you feel like you're floating in the middle of the Strip, especially at night.

JUST FOR laughs

Depressed over all the money you lost in the casino? A surefire way to get cheered up is to check out one of the shows from stand-up comics currently playing in Las Vegas.

Aces of Comedy, at the Mirage, 3355 Las Vegas Blvd. S. (www.mirage.com; ℓ **702/792-7777;** select Fri–Sun at 10pm; tickets $75–$104), features a rotating list of headliners who are already making you laugh on cable television, including Trevor Noah, Bill Maher, Daniel Tosh, and Kathy Griffin.

If you're feeling absurdist, you can try the outrageous, stream-of-consciousness prop comedy of **Carrot Top,** at Luxor Las Vegas, 3900 Las Vegas Blvd. S. (www.luxor.com; ℓ **800/557-7428;** Mon and Wed–Sun 8:30pm; tickets $50–$65).

Also be sure to see who is playing at the comedy clubs in Vegas, all described in this chapter, which include:

o **Brad Garrett's Comedy Club,** at MGM Grand (p. 208)
o **The Laugh Factory,** at Tropicana (p. 214)

Bars & Cocktail Lounges

SOUTH STRIP

Franklin ★★ Just like the hotel, this bar in the Delano is named for the 32nd president of the United States, and it's a welcome watering hole in this casino-free venue. (Having it here means you don't have to walk all the way over and through the casino of adjoining Mandalay Bay to get a drink.) Franklin has a sleek, contemporary look, all browns and blues, though the twinkling lights above the bar make us think of fireflies—or maybe we had one too many on the last visit. Classic cocktails are the focus, prepared with high-end spirits, like the Delano Daiquiri with Bacardi 1909 Heritage Rum or the barrel-aged drinks, made with the resort's own exclusive reserve of bourbon. Open nightly until midnight. In Delano, 3940 Las Vegas Blvd. S. www.delanolasvegas.com. ℓ **877/632-5400.** No cover.

MID-STRIP

Alibi ★★ Set right in the center of Aria's casino floor, this opulent, back-lit gem of a bar has a lovely, vintage vibe. I especially like the crystal decanters on display and the ornate wooden and faux mother-of-pearl accents. Don't mistake the large, round *objet d'art* above the bar for a clock, though; this is on a casino floor, after all. More often than not, you'll find tourists stopping in to re-up their Bud Light, but you're missing out if you don't put the bartenders through their paces. They're expert at giving classic cocktails modern twists and have a really fun "craft ice" program (you'll see what I mean). At night, the curtains around the round space are drawn, creating a nice barrier between the bar and the buzz of the casino. It's open 24 hours. In Aria, 3730 Las Vegas Blvd. S. www.alibiloungelv.com. ℓ **702/590-9777.** No cover.

Beer Park ★ Based on the name, you'd think that this beer garden on the Strip would be at the Park, but surprise! This one is on the rooftop of the Paris

Las Vegas Nightlife

1 Oak **18**
Aces of Comedy **18**
Alibi **27**
Artifice **5**
Atomic Liquors **4**
Backstage Bar
  & Billiards **3**
The Bar at Times
  Square **32**
Beauty Bar **3**
Beerhaus **31**
Beer Park **25**
Bound **24**
Brad Garrett's
  Comedy Club **33**
Carnaval Court **20**
Carrot Top **35**
The Chandelier **26**

Chateau **25**
Cheetah's **8**
Commonwealth **3**
Dino's Lounge **7**
Don't Tell Mama **3**
The Dorsey **17**
Double Down
  Saloon **30**
Downtown Cocktail
  Room **3**
Drai's **24**
Franklin **36**
Funhog Ranch **19**
Gilley's **16**
The Griffin **3**
Hakkasan **33**

Herbs & Rye **9**
Hogs & Heifers
  Saloon **2**
Intrigue **13**
Jimmy Kimmel's
  Comedy Club **23**
Larry Flynt's
  Hustler Club **37**
The Laugh Factory **34**
Light **36**
Marquee **26**
Mizuya Lounge **36**
O'Sheas **23**
Omnia **22**
On the Record **28**
The Palomino **1**
Park on Fremont **3**
Peppermill Fireside
  Lounge **11**
Piranha Las Vegas **29**
Rosina **17**
Sand Dollar
  Lounge **14**
Sapphire Gentleman's
  Club **15**
Spearmint Rhino **12**
Surrender **13**
Tao Nightclub **17**
Treasures **10**
Vanguard Lounge **3**
Velveteen Rabbit **6**
Vesper **26**
VooDoo Rooftop
  Nightclub **21**
XS **13**

8

ENTERTAINMENT & NIGHTLIFE | The Bar Scene

hotel, and produced by the king of beers itself, Budweiser. There's way more than just the classic red label beer being served from the more than 36 taps and additional 60 or so bottle and can selections. Not surprisingly, most are Budweiser products, even those that give the appearance of being craft beer labels (or once were craft beers, only to be bought up by the likes of Anheuser-Busch), like Goose Island, Shock Top and Firestone Walker. Nevada local Joseph James brewery does make an appearance, though. As far as outdoor beer-drinking vibes go, compared to the Beerhaus across the street, the Beer Park is less yuppie and more sports-oriented, while giant Jenga games and burgers from the grill make it feel more like an evening in your own backyard. It's open daily from 11am until late. In Paris Las Vegas, 3655 Las Vegas Blvd. S. www.beerpark.com. ✆ **702/444-4500.** No cover.

Beerhaus ★★ The stretch of real estate between the T-Mobile Arena and Las Vegas Boulevard is intended to coax pedestrians to pause from traipsing up and down the Strip. And there's no better way to keep tourists in one spot than giving them somewhere to drink, preferably outdoors and with games. Billing itself as a "modern American beer hall," Beerhaus is where you might fondly relive your college days, complete with live cover bands, foosball, Ping-Pong, cornhole, and shuffleboard. Two beers average around $22, so these are definitely not college bar prices, but beer aficionados will welcome a selection that includes Delirium Tremens, crafty IPAs, and local brews. The patio seating allows guests to soak up the sun while people-watching. Large garage doors open between the main dining room and the elements, in the event you'd rather soak up the air-conditioning while still eyeing the crowds. Servers only serve drinks, so if you want some of their fun and casual but well-executed bar bites like pretzels with cheese, cheese-filled brats, and such—it's served fast-casual style. Order from the bar and they'll give you a buzzer to pick up your snacks when the food is ready. It's open Sunday through Thursday from 11am until 1am and Friday and Saturday until 2am. In the Park, 3784 Las Vegas Blvd. S. www.theparkvegas.com. ✆ **702/692-2337.** No cover.

Bound ★★ This lobby bar at the Cromwell features a drink list created by famed mixologist Salvatore Calabrese. Located near registration, it's a sophisticated oasis before you enter the madness of the casino floor. The bar is done up in lots of gold, with plush seating and a cabinet full of rare spirits. Calabrese, who once set the Guinness World Record for creating the World's Most Expensive Cocktail, left that one off this list, but he does serve up his Breakfast Martini here. Legend has it that he created it after his wife implored him to eat breakfast (as opposed to drinking it, we're assuming), so he made this with the orange marmalade he puts on his toast. To go along with this theme, Bound also has a selection of nice, strong coffee cocktails that give you a nice jolt as well as a buzz. Bound is open Monday through Thursday from 4pm to midnight and Friday through Sunday from noon to midnight. In the Cromwell of Las Vegas, 3595 Las Vegas Blvd. S. www.thecromwell.com. ✆ **702/777-3777.** No cover.

bachelorette party SHOWS

Las Vegas gained its Sin City reputation for gambling, free-flowing alcohol, and entertainment that often involved big, feathered headdresses and bare breasts. But women also get their titillation in Sin City. Of the several beefcake revues in town, **Chippendales** ★ at the Rio, 3700 W. Flamingo Rd. (www.chippendales.com; ✆ 855/234-7469; nightly 8:30pm with an additional 10:30pm show Thurs–Sat; tickets $50–$73), gets the most attention simply because of its well-known brand name. The show ticks all the boxes: insanely handsome and fit men; fantasy fulfillment sketches featuring the guys as cowboys and firefighters and the like; and an audience of (mostly) women who go quite, quite crazy. Bring earplugs because the screaming is non-stop. Check the website for frequent guest appearances by "famous" hunks like Tyson Beckford, Ian Ziering, or Antonio Sabato Jr. (it's okay if you don't know who they are).

If we were the ones screaming for more skin, we'd probably do so for the hunks of **Thunder From Down Under** ★★ at Excalibur, 3850 Las Vegas Blvd. S. (www.thunderfromdownunder.com; ✆ 702/597-7600; Mon–Wed at 9pm; Thurs and Sun at 9 and 11pm; and Fri and Sat at 7, 9, and 11pm; tickets $51–$71). It's not that the guys are any hotter or the dancing any better, but this production has an edgier, anything-could-happen vibe that amps up the energy and the fun. Plus, the guys here are all Australian. Oh, those accents.

And finally, since 2017 there's some fresh meat on the block in **Magic Mike Live** ★★★ at Hard Rock Hotel, 4455 Paradise Rd. (www.magicmikelivelasvegas.com; ✆ 800/745-3000; Wed–Sun 7:30 and 10pm; tickets $49–$128). Even if you've never seen the original (artsy, and surprisingly good) Steven Soderbergh film *Magic Mike* or its (dumber, but way hotter) sequel, *Magic Mike XXL*, you'll get the gist pretty quickly. When I say fresh, I don't just mean the men—while there's plenty of buff, well-sculpted eye candy baring (almost) all, they're not relegated to just sweating on a single stage. The show replicates a locale from the second film called Club Domina, an immersive, 360-degree cabaret where men cater to the needs and whims of women. Magic Mike himself, Channing Tatum, had a hand in this production of life imitating art, and it's a fun, raucous ride that has women screaming "Shut up and take my money!"

The Chandelier ★★★   The Cosmopolitan of Las Vegas really does love its chandeliers. So much so that it's got a three-story one in the middle of its casino, made of millions of crystals strung together in one towering, shimmering masterpiece. The crystal curtains envelop the top two floors of this elaborate space, while one stunning centerpiece chandelier hangs above the ground-level bar. The main floor on the casino floor features plush seating and a raised platform where live trios sometimes play; the mezzanine is more secluded, featuring a mixology-driven menu; the top level is a stark white lounge, where you can often find folks hanging out with a drink while they wait to get into the adjacent Marquee nightclub. No matter what level you choose, this is one of the most unique places to sip a cocktail on the Strip. The Chandelier is open 24 hours. In the Cosmopolitan of Las Vegas, 3708 Las Vegas Blvd. S. www.cosmopolitanlasvegas.com. ✆ **702/698-7979.** No cover.

The Dorsey ★★　One of two newer bars at Venetian and Palazzo, the Dorsey (opened 2016) is the louder, bigger, and livelier sister, with cocktails and decor of a more contemporary caliber. Often mixologists can create a drink on the fly to your specifications, or you can sip your way through interesting drinks with fun names such as Spicy Flamingo, Depeche Mode, and Easy Street. Grown-up punch bowls are ideal to share if you've got a good group (or one other really thirsty friend; we don't judge), and the space's open plan is ideal for people-watching on the bustling casino floor. Open nightly 3pm until 4am. In the Venetian, 3355 Las Vegas Blvd. S. www.venetian.com. ℂ **702/414-1945.** No cover.

O'Sheas ★　With its beer pong and omnipresent host Mr. Lucky, O'Sheas is like a fraternity bar that celebrates St. Patrick's Day year-round. When its home, the stretch between the former Imperial Palace and Flamingo, was imploded in 2012 to make way for the LINQ promenade, many wondered if that was the end of the rowdy casino/bar. Fortunately, Mr. Lucky (a little person dressed as a leprechaun) and O'Sheas have been reinstated to their rightful spot on the Strip. The current O'Sheas is smaller and slightly less seedy than the original, but the now 5,000 square feet is still the place for cheap beer (they've got more than 50 brews), some gaming, and those always-popular daily beer pong tournaments. Plus, its access to the LINQ and High Roller makes it a great place to pre-game before taking a ride on the observation wheel. The bar is open 24 hours a day. In the LINQ, 3535 Las Vegas Blvd. S. www.thelinq.com. ℂ **800/634-6441.** No cover.

Rosina ★★　The other lounge at Venetian and Palazzo, Rosina is the vintage answer to the more modern Dorsey (see above). High-backed, round booths with curtains that can be drawn makes this spot the more clandestine and intimate of the two, while tones of gold and mauve add to the subdued and relaxed atmosphere. In-the-know guests ask for the secret Manhattan, old-fashioned, or julep menus, each of which features fresh takes on old favorites. Classic cocktails befitting its Art Deco interior are meant to be sipped slowly, as well as appreciated for their appropriate glassware: heavy crystal tumblers for the old-fashioned, a funky skull mug for a mai tai. But one truly modern amenity? The Champagne Call Button—which you should absolutely press—that dispatches a lovely server to top off your bubbly. Open nightly 4pm until 3am. In the Palazzo, 3325 Las Vegas Blvd. S. www.palazzo.com. ℂ **702/607-1945.** No cover.

Vesper ★★　The most low-key of the three main bars of Cosmopolitan, Vesper is relatively small, and that's how we like it. While tourists might be cramming themselves into the Chandelier bar, this is where you'll find savvy locals and hotel executives unwinding after their days (we wonder if it's because of its proximity to the parking-garage elevators). Named for an obscure cocktail created by James Bond in *Casino Royale,* Vesper focuses on other cocktails of the same ilk: classic and with a twist. The music can get a little loud on weekend nights, but the steady stream of stumbling club-goers through the lobby makes the people-watching pretty hilarious. Vesper is open daily 24 hours. In the Cosmopolitan of Las Vegas, 3708 Las Vegas Blvd. S. www. cosmopolitanlasvegas.com. ② **702/698-7969.** No cover.

NORTH STRIP

Dino's Lounge ★★   This dive bar on Las Vegas Boulevard marks the divide between the glitzy part of the Strip and grittier Downtown, and chances are you've breezed right past it. Which, if you ask the locals perched on stools at the bar, is just fine with them. The family-run watering hole has been an unofficial landmark since 1962, as the city has grown around it. If you've ever wondered what a bona fide locals bar looks like in Las Vegas, this is it, complete with smoky atmosphere, video poker nestled into counters, cheap, no-frills drinks, cold beer, and not a lick of sunlight, even in the daylight hours. Come in often enough and you've got a shot at being nominated by bartenders as Drunk of the Month. On weekends you'll find some of the best karaoke in town, hosted by a guy named Danny whose pipes are so good, you'll wonder why he doesn't just sing the whole show himself. The kiosk in the parking lot has served as an incubator for several dining concepts that have gone on to become brick-and-mortar restaurants. Whoever's cooking in the kiosk when you're there is bound to be putting out great food, which you can eat inside the bar. Dino's is open daily 24 hours. 1516 Las Vegas Blvd. S. (at Wyoming Ave.). www.dinoslv.com. ② **702/382-3894.** No cover.

Peppermill Fireside Lounge ★★   Austin Powers would be in his element at the Peppermill Fireside Lounge. With its bubbling fire pool, mirrored walls, circular booths, neon tubes of blue and pink, and cocktail servers dressed in elegant black gowns, it harkens back to a groovier era, baby. With that kind of vibe, this is not the bar to bring someone who wants to be "just friends." It is, however, the bar to bring someone who appreciates old-fashioned cocktails (Harvey Wallbanger, anyone?) and who can hold his or her liquor—the signature Scorpion is an alky's dream come true, with six different kinds of liquor and ice cream. It's served in what looks like a fishbowl, and it tastes great going down, but by the time you get to the bottom of the 64-ouncer, the flavor will be the least of your concerns. The Peppermill is open daily 24 hours. 2985 Las Vegas Blvd. S. www.peppermilllasvegas.com. ② **702/735-4177.** No cover.

DOWNTOWN

Atomic Liquors ★   Las Vegas history is on glorious display in this reinvention of a classic watering hole. The building dates to 1945 and is the oldest freestanding bar in the city. It got its name in 1952 when people used to go up on the roof to watch the aboveground nuclear blasts from the Atomic Test Site north of Las Vegas. The bar became a go-to spot for everyone from the Rat Pack to Barbra Streisand, who has her own memorial stool at the bar. Atomic has a classic neon sign out front and a big bar and plenty of comfy seating inside, plus nearly two dozen microbrews, a craft cocktail menu (featuring some classic "Atomic" concoctions), and a variety of events to keep things interesting. In 2017 it added the Kitchen at Atomic, with great bar bites to go along with your beverages. Atomic Liquors is open Monday through Wednesday from 4pm until 2am; Thursday from 2pm until 3am, Friday from 2pm until 4am; Saturday from noon until 4am; and Sunday from noon until 2am. 917 Fremont St. (at 9th St.). www.atomic.vegas. ℭ **702/982-3000.** No cover except for special events.

Backstage Bar & Billiards ★   Though it was intended to be the actual backstage area for Fremont Country Club, local producers and musicians transformed it into an intimate, cool hangout, complete with rock paraphernalia, band equipment crates from Anvil Cases as furnishings, and 8 decades of DJ and turntable history as decor. It's basically where you want to be for an after-party with the band. Live performances by mostly punk rock bands are a big draw for the tatted-and-pierced set, as are cheap beers and lack of pretentious attitude. Maybe it's a little rough around the edges compared to the other wannabe posh bars in the area, but it wouldn't be punk rock any other way. It's open nightly from 7pm until late. 601 E. Fremont St. (at 6th St.). www.back stagebarandbilliards.com. ℭ **702/382-2227.** No cover except for special events.

Beauty Bar ★   Take a vintage beauty parlor and add cocktails: That's the formula that's been so popular it's turned into a hipster chain with outlets in New York City, Chicago, and San Francisco. At Las Vegas's Downtown version, you get a lot of diversity thanks to its location near Fremont Street Experience. During the day, it's a more chill experience where you can get a decent manicure and pedicure while sipping on fruity cocktails; the evening features live bands and DJs on both its indoor and outdoor stages. It's open nightly from 9pm until 4am. 517 E. Fremont St. www.thebeautybar.com. ℭ **702/598-3757.** No cover except for special events.

The Commonwealth ★★   Part speakeasy, part neighborhood bar, Commonwealth has earned itself a reputation as one of the true hot spots to come out of the revitalization of this stretch of Fremont Street. The 6,000-square-foot, swanky, multilevel space has a pre-Prohibition-era vibe, with a mix of vintage and modern artwork (peacocks are a big deal here) and stiff cocktails. The main floor is a bustling mix of folks from the neighborhood and tourists who found their way here from the Fremont Street Experience, while the rooftop patio is one of the few outdoor spaces comfortable for hanging out above the hubbub of the main drag. Cocktail aficionados should secure themselves an invite into the Laundry Room, the true speakeasy behind the main floor (ask and they'll walk you there). This intimate room allows for a one-on-one session with one of Commonwealth's expert mixologists, who are at the ready to dazzle you with custom concoctions based on your tastes. Open Tuesday through Saturday 7pm until late. 525 E. Fremont St. (at 6th St.). www.commonwealthlv.com. ℭ **702/445-6400.** No cover except for special events.

Double Down Saloon ★★   Leave the multiple-ingredient cocktails to the Strip. Here you're going to be listening to live punk, rock, or blues bands while pounding PBR and shots of Ass Juice, a fruity, if not unappealing-looking mystery concoction that the bar has been selling since the early 1990s. If the idea of Ass Juice isn't your idea of a good time at a place whose motto is "You puke, you clean," then try their other house specialty, the bacon martini, which Double Down claims to have invented. It's like every other punk bar you've been to in other cities, with psychedelic murals, secondhand furniture, weird videos playing on the TVs, and a very punk rock jukebox, but this one just happens to be the antithesis of the city surrounding it. The Double Down is open daily 24 hours. 4640 Paradise Rd. (at Naples Dr.). www.doubledownsaloon.com. ✆ **702/791-5775.** No cover except for special events.

The Griffin ★★   This is one of the few bars you can walk into in Las Vegas that doesn't feel like Las Vegas at all. The strong brickwork and arched ceiling inside offer that post-industrial feel you'd get in old-school-turned-hipster bars in Chicago or New York, while two firepits give it almost an Aspen vibe (the lack of video poker machines set into the bar also helps). There are better mixology programs in the surrounding bars, but this is where you'd come to relax, maybe have a real conversation with real people, and get out of that Vegas mindset, if only for a little while. Live bands and DJs play on weekends. It's open Monday through Friday from 5pm until 3am; Saturday from 7pm until 3am; and Sunday from 8pm until 3am. 511 E. Fremont St. ✆ **702/382-0577.** No cover except for special events.

Herbs & Rye ★★   This local watering hole is where you'll find the city's best drink slingers, as well as other industry folk, when they want someone else to make a drink for them. Owner and head bartender Nectaly Mendoza has won numerous awards for his innovative and cool cocktail program that reads as if it came straight from a speakeasy. Drink your way through history with classics such as the Pimm's Cup or the Boulevardier all the way through the tiki craze, artfully made with select spirits and fresh ingredients. While you're there, nosh on a steak or Italian-inspired small plates for a full experience. It's open Monday through Saturday from 5pm until 3am and is closed Sunday and major holidays. 3713 W. Sahara Ave. http://herbsandrye.com. ✆ **702/982-8036.** No cover except for special events.

Hogs & Heifers Saloon ★   Hot, midriff-revealing chicks dancing on the bars, screaming at you with bullhorns; cold cans of PBR; all this and a collection of bras hanging above your head: That's the scene at Hogs & Heifers and it's not my idea of a good time, but I may be in the minority. This outlet is part of a chain started in New York City, where the original outpost of Hogs (as in motorcycles) & Heifers was born and inspired a movie and a competing outfit called Coyote Ugly. It's open daily, usually 1pm to 6am (call, as hours vary by month). 201 N. 3rd St. (btw. Ogden and Stewart aves., 1 block from the Fremont Street Experience). www.hogsandheifers.com. ✆ **702/676-1457.** No cover.

Park on Fremont ★   While Commonwealth (p. 226), Vanguard (below), and Downtown Cocktail Room (p. 236) are more sophisticated drinking establishments, Griffin (see above) and this spot are casual watering holes, which is perfect considering its proximity to the Fremont Street Experience.

There are fine cocktails on the menu at Park, along with a decent bar food menu (Sunday brunch, complete with stacked Bloody Marys, is a busy time), but Park is a much more relaxed, come-as-you-are spot to throw back some brewskies. The front patio offers great people-watching on Fremont Street, while behind the bar is another, walled-in backyard that you'd kill to find at your own neighborhood bar, complete with a fireplace, murals, and artwork from local artisans. Tucked behind that is another secret alcove with a seesaw. It is called a "park," after all. Open Monday through Friday from 11am to 11pm, and Saturday and Sunday from 10am until 11pm. 506 Fremont St. (at Las Vegas Blvd.). www.parkonfremont.com. ✆ **702/834-3160.** No cover.

Vanguard Lounge ★★ The long, narrow bar is the most minimally appointed one that you'll find on this stretch of Fremont Street, but that is by design. Cocktails take center stage here, made by a team of talented mixologists who use seasonal, artisanal, and house-made ingredients for well-executed tipples that focus on balance and flavor. Be prepared for the use of lots of bitters and stuff like Falernum and amaro in some pretty mind-blowing drinks. These folks can do more than just sling a gin and tonic or pour you a beer (though they do have an excellent craft selection, too). On weekends, house and techno DJs liven things up. Vanguard is open Monday through Friday from 4pm until 2am, and Saturday from 6pm until 2am. 516 E. Fremont St. www.vanguardlv.com. ✆ **702/868-7800.** No cover.

Velveteen Rabbit ★★ Located in the ever up-and-coming Arts District near Downtown, this is probably the most hipster of the hipster bars in Las Vegas, complete with boho-chic vintage furniture decor, and tatted-up, mustachioed mixologists furiously shaking their metal Boston shakers. While each drink might take about 10 minutes to make, they're worth the wait, running on the herbal, floral, and savory side of the palate and arriving in beautiful vintage crystal tumblers and coupes. If you can't wait that long, they have interesting craft beers. And at $10 to $13 a pop, you can't beat these prices, considering you'd be paying twice as much for the same caliber of cocktail on the Strip. It's open Monday through Wednesday 5pm until 1am, Thursday through Saturday 5pm until 2am, and Sunday 5pm to midnight. 1218 Main St. (near Colorado Ave.). www.velveteenrabbitlv.com. ✆ **702/685-9645.** No cover.

JUST OFF THE STRIP

The Sand Dollar Lounge ★★ In its glory days, the Sand Dollar was an iconic blues bar that was a mandatory stop for legends such as Muddy Waters and B. B. King. It took a hit during the recession and closed in 2007, then was renovated on a bar makeover show and somehow stayed afloat, trying on a few different identities until it finally took off again in 2015. Part of the Sand Dollar's resurrection is thanks to the introduction of a fantastic craft cocktail menu. Also helping are the surprisingly gourmet pizzas coming out of its kitchen, which have made this an unofficial chef clubhouse after the pros leave their Strip kitchens for the night. Live blues and rock bands still grace the stage nightly. Open daily 3pm until 4am. 3355 Spring Mountain Rd. S. www.thesanddollarlv.com. ℂ **702/485-5401.** No cover.

Piano Bars

The Bar at Times Square ★   Much like the actual Times Square, this bar is usually jam-packed with tourists looking for a night of revelry. Dueling pianos are the draw and create the perfect soundtrack for a booze-driven night of camaraderie with your fellow Vegas visitors. Heaven help you when they start playing Billy Joel's *Piano Man.* If you're inclined to do a crawl through the bars at New York–New York, you can purchase an all-access pass here starting at $15 that gets you into the hotel's two other festive watering holes, Nine Fine Irishmen and Coyote Ugly. The bar is open Monday through Thursday from 1pm until 2:30am, and Friday and Sunday from 11am through the wee hours. Shows are from 8pm to 2am, but if you want to be able to have a conversation without shouting over the music, stop in for happy hour, weekdays from 3pm to 7pm. In New York–New York, 3790 Las Vegas Blvd. S. www.newyork newyork.com. ℂ **702/740-6466.** No cover before live show, after $5–$25.

Don't Tell Mama ★   This piano bar, named for a New York City classic, is less group sing-along (like the Bar at Times Square, above) and more live karaoke. Audience members get up to sing standards with the crack pianists (they can play anything). While in other towns this would lead to hours of painful howling, there's so much talent in Vegas that the impromptu show is often darn good. In fact, many of the performers who appear in visiting Broadway musicals and other Strip shows often head here to belt out a tune or two after they've finished their paid performance, just for fun. Not that that should intimidate you from getting up there and singing a heartfelt version of *Me and Mr. Jones* with a live pianist backing you. Don't Tell Mama is ready for you Tuesday through Sunday 8pm until late. 517 E. Fremont St. www.dont tellmama.com. ℂ **702/207-0788.** No cover; one-drink minimum.

THE CLUB & MUSIC SCENE

Most of the clubs in town have DJs, often famous ones, and on those rare occasions when they do have live entertainment, it's usually a pop or cover band. If you prefer alternative or real rock music, your choices used to be limited, but that's all changed. Most touring rock bands make at least one stop in the city. But otherwise, the alternative club scene in town is no great shakes. If you want to know what's playing during your stay, consult the free local alternative paper, the *Las Vegas Weekly* (with great club and bar descriptions in its listings; see www.lasvegasweekly.com). If you're looking for good alt-culture tips, try asking the cool staff at **Zia Records** (ℂ **702/735-4942**); not only does it have bins dedicated to local artists, but local acts also play live in stores on the weekend.

Dance Clubs

In many ways, especially monetarily, the nightclub scene in Vegas has eclipsed famous party spots like Ibiza, New York, and Los Angeles. Almost every hotel has at least one club, and almost all of them are packed whenever their doors are open.

Many of the following have insanely high cover charges ($30 and up), outrageously priced drinks ($10 for a domestic beer), and seating that is reserved for patrons willing to pay hundreds or even thousands of dollars to get bottle service. For the uninitiated it sounds crazy, and is, but the hordes of people willing to pay those kinds of costs seem to be having a good time, so maybe they know something we don't.

One bright note: Women are usually charged less for admission than men (sometimes even allowed in free), and any guest can get a comped ticket to even the hottest clubs, if you play it right. If you are gambling for any length of time, ask the pit boss for comps.

1 OAK ★   In a town where celebrities are often paid to make appearances (read: They get paid stupid money to hang out in a private booth and drink free booze), this is one of the few clubs where the celebrities actually go of their own free will. The New York transplant opened with a bang in 2012: Performances by Fergie and a legendary 3-hour DJ set by none other than Kanye West set the tone for the star-studded years to come. The 16,000-square-foot space is actually visually interesting, with cool modern artwork, dark woods, track lighting, and elevated poles ready to be danced around. Low ceilings, and clusters of booths ready for bottle service, make this a tight space to walk through if you're not seated at a table, but mostly you're just there to see and, hopefully, be seen by any number of A-listers that stop in, like Katy Perry, Joseph Gordon-Leavitt, and Adam Levine, who all just want to have a good time like everyone else. Though 1 OAK stands for One Of A Kind, there are also 1 OAKs in New York, Los Angeles, and Dubai. It's open Wednesday, Friday, and Saturday from 10:30pm until 4am. In the Mirage, 3400 Las Vegas Blvd. S. www.1oaklasvegas.com. ✆ **702/588-5656.** Cover $30 and up.

Artifice ★   While not a nightclub per se, this multipurpose space is one of the few places in town where you'll hear decent local DJs who aren't bumping only mainstream electronic pop music. Fitting in with its Arts District locale, Artifice also features a gallery space with work from up-and-coming artists. Its eclectic assortment of events takes in singles mixers to neo-burlesque shows to open mic nights. Open Monday through Saturday from 5pm until close, and Sunday from 8pm until close. 1025 First St., #3 (at Charleston Blvd.). www.artificebarlv.com. ✆ **702/489-6339.** No cover except for special events.

Chateau ★   This is definitely not a Paris, France, nightclub: Chateau may sport some lovely French touches in the decor, but the club is all high-energy, high-rent Las Vegas. Three distinct spaces offer three different nightlife experiences. Head up the spiral staircase from the casino floor to enter the nightclub, a long, narrow room flanked by bottle service tables. The sultry red

crowd CONTROL

Huge lines outside are a point of pride for Vegas clubs. So, if you're into dancing, you may spend a good chunk of the night single-file, double-file, or in an enormous, unwieldy cluster out in front of a club—particularly on Friday or Saturday. We're not kidding: Lines can be hours long (see below), and once you get to the front, you'll find that there's no actual order. You're at the mercy of a power-wielding, eye-contact-avoiding "executive doorman"—aka bouncer—who gives attractive women priority. To minimize your time in line, try the following strategies:

Arrive before 11pm. You'll have a harder time getting in if you show up between 12:30 and 1am, the busiest period at clubs.

Group yourself smartly. The larger the group, the longer the wait—especially a large group of mostly (or all) guys. Split up if you must, but always keep some women with each part of your group. It's much harder for unaccompanied men to get into the clubs.

If you're trying to tip your way in, don't make it obvious. It's a negotiation. Don't wave cash above your head (the IRS has been clamping down on unreported tip income, so that tactic will make you *very* unpopular). Discreetly and respectfully hand the doorman $20 and ask if he can take care of you.

Don't buy a VIP Pass. Can you say "scam"? Many passes require you get there before midnight (a time when there'd normally be no line), and with others you're paying big bucks just to have someone make the call ahead that you could have made yourself. Again: *Don't* fall for this scam.

Do check the websites. Many clubs will offer front-of-line passes, cover discounts, and drink specials via text alerts and/or if you check in via a social networking site like Facebook or Twitter. Details change often, so check the club's website for the latest offer.

Dress to impress. For women: Antediluvian but true—showing more cleavage is a line-skipping tactic. If that's not an option, stick with a little black dress or nice jeans and a sexy or club-wear–style top. For men: Look good. Avoid baggy jeans, shorts, tennis shoes, or work boots. Nice jeans or pants and a collared shirt work well.

Look confident. While cockiness never helps, assertiveness never hurts.

lights complement the modern, French-inspired furnishings, complete with crystal chandeliers hanging from the high ceilings. There are also classy touches like the DJ booth planted atop a 10-foot-tall marble fireplace mantel. When it gets too crammed inside, head out to one of two outdoor sections. The first is a VIP deck two stories above the Strip, with unobstructed views of the Fountains of Bellagio; it's the perfect spot to have a more intimate conversation with that stranger you just met on the dance floor. There's also the 22,000-square-foot rooftop garden, set at the base of the Eiffel Tower, that is essentially a whole other club with its own dance floor and bars. You won't convince yourself that you're in Paris proper, but as far as romantic locations go, this is just as effective. Chateau is open Wednesday through Saturday from 10:30pm until 4am. In Paris Las Vegas, 3655 Las Vegas Blvd. S. www.chateaunights. com. ☎ **702/776-7770.** Cover varies, usually $20 and up.

Drai's ★ Nightlife impresario Victor Drai ruled the underground—literally—in Las Vegas. His after-hours club (which still exists in the underbelly of the Cromwell) was around for nearly 2 decades as one of the only house music–fueled after-parties, with attendees who often spilled back on to the Strip when the sun was already well up in the sky. Now the sunlight shines on Drai's all day long at his 65,000-square-foot rooftop club atop the Cromwell, which hosts the beach club around the hotel pool until the sun goes down, when it transitions into a dance club. A roster of well-known resident DJs provides the EDM-heavy soundtrack, but hip-hop acts such as Big Sean, Fabolous, and Ty Dolla $ign have been making their way into the residential rotation as well. The dress code still applies here—even if you've been hanging out at the pool party all day, you still must put on more clothes to attend the club at night. The nightclub is open Thursday through Sunday from 10:30pm until 4am. In the Cromwell, 3595 Las Vegas Blvd. S. www.draislv.com. ℂ **702/777-3800.** Hotel guests are free; nonguests are $20 and up.

Hakkasan Las Vegas ★★ At one of the biggest nightclubs in the world, you'll have to navigate through five levels in the course of an evening. These include an elegant modern Chinese restaurant, an ultralounge, tables with exorbitantly priced bottle service, and a booth where a roster of world-famous EDM DJs spin their magic. Kudos to whatever lighting designer strung the LED lighting along the ceiling of the club and behind the DJ booth—the effect is mesmerizing. Lines to get in are long and filled with young and excited partiers who don't mind being crammed onto a dance floor, so long as they can get a glimpse of the world's highest-paid DJ Calvin Harris or watch Steve Aoki take a ride on the crowd in an inflatable boat. Open Thursday through Sunday from 10:30pm until close. In the MGM Grand, 3799 Las Vegas Blvd. S. www.hakkasanlv.com. ℂ **702/891-3838.** Cover varies, usually $40 and up.

Intrigue ★★ Occupying the space formerly known as Tryst, Intrigue opened in 2016 to much fanfare, but mixed reviews. Tryst was a groundbreaking club for its time (that time being the mid-'00s), one of the first to fully capitalize on the growing EDM scene and create what we know as bottle service today. Intrigue promised to move away from overpaid DJs and focus more on the guest experience for ALL the guests, not just the ones who paid for table service. Yet opening night featured a big-name DJ. Even more telling: One of the most noted features of Intrigue is a club-within-a-club that only the true elite will ever see. The social media–free zone is hidden behind a secret door, and admittance can only be gained through approval by some cabal of executives. So, what *is* new? Well, they've added a "selfie wall," choreographed pole dancers, and cocktail waitresses who wear different uniforms every night. The rest of the club was lightened up, and the 94-foot man-made waterfall that was the centerpiece to Tryst's outdoor section remains. Intrigue is open Thursday through Saturday from 10pm until late. In Wynn Las Vegas, 3131 Las Vegas Blvd. S. www.intriguevegas.com. ℂ **702/770-7070.** Cover varies, usually $30 and up.

Light ★★★ While once upon a time Cirque du Soleil "powered" this nightclub at Mandalay Bay, that is no longer the case; Cirque pulled out of the venture in 2015. So, while periodic performances by acrobats, dancers, and other artists have gone away, the light show is still spectacular. It's a lot of fun, as are the massive video wall that projects ambient visuals while illuminating the room, and the killer, well-balanced sound system (your entire sternum will quiver from the reverberation of the bass used by acts like Disclosure and Baauer). Light is the only major club on the Strip to host any semblance of non-mainstream electronic acts, though bottle service—and the crowds that love bottle service—still reigns supreme. Its sun-up component, Daylight, is one of the cooler pool parties on the weekend, if only because the music is slightly better than the other options. Open Wednesday, Friday, and Saturday from 10:30pm until 4am. In Mandalay Bay, 3950 Las Vegas Blvd. S. www.thelight vegas.com. ✆ **702/632-4700.** Cover varies, usually $30 and up.

Marquee ★★★ At more than 60,000 square feet and containing three different party atmospheres within, the mega club at Cosmopolitan is here to say: Size matters. It's exactly what you'd expect from a Vegas club: massive main floor; huge LED wall behind the DJ booth that projects an amazing laser show while internationally renowned house DJs play; and lots of low booths to be sold to the highest bidder for bottle service. The main room can be over-whelming, especially when people are wall-to-wall and it's six deep even to get a drink. Hole up in the Library, the more exclusive lounge, where the music is more chill, there are pool tables, and you can actually pull a seat up to the bar. Need a break from all the EDM? The hip-hop and pop-driven soundtrack in the intimate Boombox will clear your head from all those synths. There's also an outdoor patio with cabana seating (tables will run cheaper than inside the main club) and gaming. The line to enter will snake across the second floor of the Cosmopolitan, so unless you've got a table, be prepared to wait for a long time. Marquee is open Monday, Friday, and Saturday from 10:30pm until 5am. The pool club is open seasonally on weekend afternoons. In the Cosmopolitan of Las Vegas, 3708 Las Vegas Blvd. S. www.marqueelasvegas.com. ✆ **702/333-9000.** Cover varies, usually $30 and up.

Omnia ★ Occupying the space of former mega club Pure, the mega club Omnia was created by the same people who did Hakkasan at MGM Grand. The 75,000-square-foot space underwent a $100-million renovation in 2015, gaining a dark, ultra-modern vibe, accented by the multimillion-dollar, space-ship-looking chandelier above the middle of the dance floor. It's really a high-tech installation of eight concentric rings that slowly drop from the ceiling while projecting lights and lasers and move and shift along with the music played by star DJs (like Afrojack and Calvin Harris). It's breathtaking to watch: Get a better view of it from the second level, where you won't be nearly as jam-packed as on the main floor. Omnia also inherited Pure's prime terrace, which overlooks the Strip and offers an exclusive VIP lounge, the Heart of Omnia. People clamor to get in here, so dress to impress and employ

cool BY THE POOL

A critical part of the nightclub scene is that it takes place at night. Maybe that's why they call them "night" clubs. But you don't have to wait until the sun goes down to start partying, especially in Vegas, where a host of daytime pool clubs give vacationers an opportunity to boogie down while working on your tan.

Most of the major hotels have some form of a poolside day club that usually operates on weekends and only in season (Mar–Oct, mostly). They all feature DJs or live music, bars, private cabanas, and lots of opportunity to splash around in pools that are separated from the main recreational facilities, for people over 21 years of age only. All charge a cover (although they vary as much as nightclub covers do), and some offer table games (like blackjack) and topless sunbathing. All are open to the general public; you don't have to be staying at the host hotel.

It should go without saying that these usually draw a younger, fit crowd who aren't embarrassed about how they look in a bikini or board shorts. If that isn't you, you may want to consider alternate afternoon entertainment.

Here are the most noteworthy of the current pool clubs:

- **Bare** At the Mirage, 3400 Las Vegas Blvd. S. (⟨ **702/696-8300;** www.barepool.com). Small pool, cabanas, DJ, and bar. Topless sunbathing allowed. Open daily 11am–6pm. Cover $20 and up.

- **Daylight** At Mandalay Bay, 3950 Las Vegas Blvd. S. (⟨ **702/ 693-8300**). 50,000-square-foot beach area with pool, three wet decks, private cabanas, DJ, bars, and food service. No topless sunbathing. Open Wednesday 11am to 3am and Friday to

some pre-game as needed. It's open Tuesday and Thursday through Saturday from 10pm until close. In Caesars Palace, 3570 Las Vegas Blvd. S. www.omnianight club.com. ⟨ **702/785-6200.** Cover varies, usually $30 and up.

On The Record ★★★ The newly minted Park MGM adds to its off-the-beaten-path experience with this spot from Los Angeles nightlife kings Mark and Jonnie Houston. Moving the trend away from the massive, one-room club where everyone's focused on the DJ, On the Record instead has a more nostalgic vibe. Similar to the Houstons' other venues, this outpost has multiple, relatively intimate spaces offering different experiences, including a private speakeasy off the main room for VIPs. But don't worry: There's still plenty of room to dance. As you walk in, you're greeted by, well, records, as the entry to the venue is a fully functioning record store for you to peruse and even purchase some vinyl for yourself. The outdoor patio features a 1963 Bristol Lodekka double-decker bus doubling as a DJ booth. Open Wednesday through Saturday from 10:30pm until 4am. In Park MGM, 3770 Las Vegas Blvd. S. www.parkmgm.com. ⟨ **702/730-6773.** Cover varies, usually $30 and up.

Tao Nightclub ★ Once the palace where the Hiltons, Kardashians, and other reality TV celebrities partied the night away, the Asian-themed club at the Venetian has lost a bit of the limelight to bigger, newer Strip clubs. Ah

Sunday 11am to 6pm. Cover $25 and up.

o **Encore Beach Club** At Encore Las Vegas, 3121 Las Vegas Blvd. S. (www.encorebeachclub.com; ✆ **702/770-7300**). 60,000-square-foot facility, three pools, cabanas, DJ, gaming, bar, grill. No topless sunbathing. Open Friday noon to 6pm and Saturday to Sunday 11am to 6pm. Cover $25 and up.

o **Liquid** At Aria Las Vegas, 3730 Las Vegas Blvd. S. (www.arialas vegas.com; ✆ **702/693-8300**). Three pools, cabanas, DJ, bar, restaurant. No topless sunbathing. Open daily 11am to 6pm. Cover $20 and up.

o **Marquee Dayclub** At the Cosmopolitan of Las Vegas, 3801 Las Vegas Blvd. S.

(www.marqueelasvegas.com; ✆ **702/333-9000**). Two pools, cabanas with private pools, DJ, gaming, bar, food service. No topless sunbathing. Open daily 10am to sunset. Cover $25 and up.

o **Tao Beach** At the Venetian, 3355 Las Vegas Blvd. S. (www. taobeach.com; ✆ **702/388-8588**). One pool, cabanas, DJ, bar, food service. Topless sunbathing allowed. Open daily 10am to sunset. Cover $20 and up.

o **Wet Republic** At MGM Grand, 3799 Las Vegas Blvd. S. (www. wetrepublic.com; ✆ **800/851-1703**). Two pools, cabanas, DJ, bar, food service. No topless sunbathing. Open Thursday to Monday 11am to 6pm. Cover $20 and up.

well, it's still fun. Enter the Buddhist temple—if Buddhist temples were opulent palaces that offered high-end bottle service—under the arched hallway, flanked by bathtubs that appear again on raised platforms on the dance floor. Where you'd usually find go-go dancers inciting the crowd, bathing beauties are trying not to splash water everywhere to the beat of the pounding bass. The footprint of the main floor of the club is small compared to current standards, which ensures that everyone dancing gets to know each other really well. Bottle service tables line up against a long banquette, so unless you pony up for a truly private table, your party will have to mingle with the one next to you. But that's okay. You came to make new friends, didn't you? It's open Thursday through Saturday from 10pm until 5am. In the Venetian, 3355 Las Vegas Blvd. S. www.taolasvegas.com. ✆ **702/388-8588**. Cover varies.

XS ★★★ As the abbreviated name suggests, this gold-plated crown jewel of Wynn nightlife is excessive. A $10-million redesign in 2015 upgraded the entire space—both the inside area and its outdoor pool deck—to include a pyrotechnic system that shoots flames above the pool. It also added a DJ booth with 14,000 LED lights, movable video screens, and more lasers. An update like this costs a pretty penny, but as the highest-grossing nightclub in the country (thanks to the contributions of appreciative visitors like yourself), XS can afford lots of lasers. XS is open Friday through Monday from 10pm to 4am. In Encore Las Vegas, 3121 Las Vegas Blvd. S. www.xslasvegas.com. 🕐 **702/770-0097.** Cover varies, usually $30 and up.

Ultralounges

What, you may be asking, is an ultralounge? That's an excellent question, since it is loosely defined at best. Generally speaking, ultralounges are smaller than traditional nightclubs, offering a more intimate vibe. Some have dance floors, and some don't, although even the ones that don't usually have DJs, and people will dance wherever they can find the room to do so. You'll also usually find a lot more seating at an ultralounge, but most of it will probably be reserved for people willing to pay for bottle service. Drink and cover prices may be a bit less than at the big nightclubs. The crowd they draw depends on the location and theme, with the most popular bringing in the same young, pretty crowd that goes to the hot dance clubs. (They'll often come to an ultralounge first, and then head to the dance floor elsewhere.)

Downtown Cocktail Room ★★   This intimate mixology bar is a go-to joint for those who want a chill evening without all the craziness that comes with other bars, both on and off the Strip. Its entrance on Las Vegas Boulevard, across from the Fremont Street Experience, hides in plain sight; a big metal sheet that looks like it shouldn't move opens when you pull it. Sheer drapes and low banquettes offer private seating when you maneuver them to your liking. Low ceilings, large Picasso-esque paintings, and deep red tones make things cozy and calm, while talented mixologists behind the bar whip up avant-garde cocktails. The punch bowls, delicious and dangerous, are meant to be shared. It's open Monday through Friday from 4pm until 2am and Saturday from 7pm until 2am. 111 Las Vegas Blvd. www.downtowncocktailroom.com. 🕐 **702/880-3696.** No cover.

Surrender ★★   Another feather in the cap of the Wynn and Encore resorts, the intimate Surrender is a stunning space. A giant, golden snake poses on the wall above the bar, while curved white, plush leather couches dot the room, enticing partiers to take a seat and pay through the nose for it (with outrageously costly bottle service). The real party happens outside, however, when the wall of windows opens to **Encore Beach Club** (p. 235), and big-name DJs like David Guetta, Diplo, and Martin Solveig set the soundtrack for the biggest day party in town. Surrender is open Wednesday, Friday, and Saturday from 10:30pm until dawn. In Encore Las Vegas, 3121 Las Vegas Blvd. S. www.surrendernightclub.com. 🕐 **702/770-7300.** Cover varies, usually $30 and up.

VooDoo Rooftop Nightclub ★   The two-floor behemoth, on the 50th and 51st floors of the Rio, was one of the original mega clubs before night-clubs became a huge deal. The steakhouse component occupies the first level. After a dinner there, head up to the club, which has two sections: the lounge with voodoo-themed decor and furniture (yeah, it feels a bit dated) and the more contemporary dance floor area. The two-story rooftop terrace is the winning feature here, affording some of the best views of the city; you can head even higher up if you take the spiral staircase. The lounge portion is open nightly 5pm to 3am, and the nightclub operates Sunday through Thursday from 8pm until 2am, and Friday and Saturday until 3am. In the Rio All-Suite Hotel & Casino, 3700 Las Vegas Blvd. S. www.riolasvegas.com. ✆ **702/777-6875.** Cover varies, usually $20 and up.

Hotel Lounges

Most of the nightclubs in town are ruled by the young and pretty—you know who we mean: the 23-year-olds in impossibly short dresses, with tiny waists, and an attitude that can be seen from space. Not that there's anything wrong with that. If I were thin and pretty, I'd want to hang out at these nightclubs, too.

But what about the rest of us? What about older people who may no longer be a size 0 but still want to go out, dance, and have a good time?

For them we offer what some consider to be a dinosaur of a bygone age: the hotel lounge. Don't roll your eyes! Many hotel lounges offer entertainment, dance floors, low or no cover charge, cheaper drink prices, and an almost total absence of the kind of "hey, look at me" posing that's *de rigueur* at the trendy nightclubs. These are great places to simply have a night out of fun that doesn't involve a slot machine or blackjack table. All the major hotels have at least one, so you can just wander by to see if it strikes your fancy. Here are a couple that might be worth the extra effort to visit.

Carnaval Court ★ If partying front and center right on the Las Vegas Strip is on your bucket list, you can cross it off here. This open-air party blares music day and night, luring in passersby, and the party just gets bigger and bigger as the night goes on. Lounge bands channeling the '70s and '80s get a ton of play here, so you're guaranteed to know just about every song . . . if you're of a certain age. If the faux "hair band" acts aren't entertaining enough, the bartenders' flair will get your attention: Watch them flipping bottles and shakers around before mixing a cocktail. All in all, when what you want to do is dance like no one's watching, to music that you actually recognize, it's a nice alternative to the casino nightclubs. Carnaval Court is open daily from noon until 3am. At Harrah's Las Vegas, 3475 Las Vegas Blvd. S. www.harrahslv.com. ✆ **702/731-7778.** Cover varies.

Gilley's ★★ One of the few country-and-western spots on the Strip, Treasure Island inherited Gilley's from the Frontier after that hotel closed, opening it in 2010. The mechanical bull gets a workout all night, while live honky-tonk bands and country rock bands perform several nights a week. Think you sound like Reba or Garth? There's Cowboy Karaoke on Tuesdays and Wednesdays. Line dancing is, of course, a must, with lessons offered Monday through Friday at 7pm. The BBQ is worth a taste, as well. The saloon opens at 11am daily, while the nightclub portion of the facility gets going around 7 or 8pm and stays open until 2am weeknights and later on weekends. In Treasure Island, 3300 Las Vegas Blvd. S. www.gilleyslasvegas.com. ☏ **702/894-7111.** Cover varies.

Mizuya Lounge ★★ This Japanese-themed lounge serves sushi but also happens to be an incredibly chill place to take a break from the casino floor. Nightly entertainment is usually provided by local cover bands, who play classic rock and some pop. While there's no cover, there is a two-drink minimum when the band is playing, but they're usually decent enough that you don't mind paying to stick around. It's open Monday through Thursday from 11am until 3am, Friday from 11am until 4am, Saturday from 9am until 4am, and Sunday from 9am until 3am, but the party part doesn't usually start until evening. In Mandalay Bay, 3950 Las Vegas Blvd. S. www.mandalaybay.com. ☏ **702/632-6112.** No cover; two-drink minimum when band plays.

THE GAY & LESBIAN SCENE

Hip and happening Vegas locals know that some of the best scenes and dance action can be found in the city's gay bars. And no, they don't ask for sexuality ID at the door. All are welcome at any of the following establishments—as long as you don't have a problem with the people inside, they aren't going to have a problem with you. For women, this can be a fun way to dance and not get hassled by overeager Lotharios.

If you want to know what's going on in gay Las Vegas during your visit, pick up a copy of *Q Life,* also available at the places described below. You can also check out the online edition at www.qvegas.com.

Funhog Ranch ★ Forget lines, high cover charges, and overpriced drinks: This is not the place for those things. Funhog Ranch is the dive bar of Vegas's gay bars, which isn't a bad thing; it's tiresome to be surrounded by so much manufactured opulence all the time. This is a relaxed, casual environment where partiers have no expectations beyond having a good time. The atmosphere is rustic, with wooden booths, a jukebox, video poker, and cheap drinks. Fetish and leather gear is encouraged, though you're not required to be a bear to have fun. Funhog is open daily 24 hours. 495 E. Twain Ave. (just east of Paradise Rd.). www.funhogranchlv.com. ☏ **702/791-7001.** No cover.

Piranha Las Vegas ★★ The jewel of the Fruit Loop—the small "boystown" of Las Vegas—is this see-and-be-seen club for the city's gay elite. The brick facade makes the building look unassuming, but once you enter, it's a whole new world. The small, but banging, blue-lit nightclub is constantly teeming with bodies. For a better view, and some air, head to the lounge on the second floor. Even more air (and a break from the loud music) is available on the outdoor patio, a popular spot where partiers warm up by the fireplace. It's not open 24 hours, but a 5am closing is still plenty of time to pack in plenty of fun. Open 10pm-dawn. 4633 Paradise Rd. (at Naples Dr.). www.piranha vegas.com. ☏ **702/791-0100.** No cover.

STRIP CLUBS

No, we don't mean entertainment establishments on Las Vegas Boulevard South. We mean the other kind of "strip." Yes, people come to town for the gambling and the wedding chapels, but the lure of Vegas doesn't stop there. Though prostitution is not legal within the city, the sex industry is an active and obvious force in town. Every other cab carries a placard for a strip club, and a walk down the Strip at night will have dozens of men thrusting fliers at you for clubs, escort services, phone-sex lines, and more. And some of you are going to want to check it out.

And why not? An essential part of the Vegas allure is decadence, and naked flesh would certainly qualify, as does the thrill of trying something new and daring. Of course, by and large, the nicer bars aren't particularly daring, and if you go to more than one in an evening, the thrill wears off, and the breasts don't look quite so bare.

In the finest of Vegas traditions, the "something for everyone" mentality extends to strip clubs. Here is a guide to the most prominent and heavily advertised; there are plenty more, of increasing seediness, out there. You don't have to look too hard. The most crowded and zoo-like times are after midnight, especially on Friday and Saturday nights. Should you want a "meaningful" experience, you might wish to avoid the rush and choose an off-hour for a visit.

Cheetah's ★   The club that was featured in the 1995 movie *Showgirls* employs 500 women in a 24-hour period on the weekends, quite possibly outnumbering the number of men who are there at the same time. This is a good thing, as variety is the spice of life in a lively club like this. Mirrored walls around the booths give you a good look at all the flesh around you, and yes, there are lots of fake cheetahs prowling around the main and five smaller stages. Lap dances are $20. Cheetah's is open daily 24 hours. 2112 Western Ave. www.cheetahlv.com. ⓒ **702/384-0074.** Topless. Cover $30.

Larry Flynt's Hustler Club ★   Comparable in size to the "World's Largest Strip Club" Sapphire, the interior of porn king Larry Flynt's joint is just as gaudy as its "you can't miss it from the highway" exterior. The three floors of entertainment feature spaces with names like the "Beaver Stage" and "Honey Suites." It's a maze to navigate, and easy to get separated from your group. In the event one of you gets a private dance, make sure you can locate

---

Question Your Cabbie

If there's a particular strip club you want to visit, don't let your cabdriver talk you out of it. Clubs give cabdrivers kickbacks for delivering customers. So be leery of drivers who suggest one club over another. They may be making $20 for delivering you there. And don't accept a higher cover charge than we've listed here; the clubs are trying to get you to cover the kickback they just gave the cabbie.

For Men Only?

Many of the strip clubs will not allow women in unless they're escorted by a man—presumably to protect ogling husbands from suspicious wives. If you're looking for a ladies' night out and want to check out the topless action, be sure and call ahead to find out what each individual club allows.

---

him, lest you lose him and he loses too much money. There's also a 25,000-square-foot adult superstore. Lap dances are $30. The Hustler Club is open daily 24 hours. 6007 Dean Martin Dr. www.vegashustlerclub.com. ✆ **844/795-3131.** Topless. Cover $30 (includes first lap dance).

The Palomino ★ What the Palomino lacks in convenient location or gorgeous decor, it makes up for in nudity. Yes, this is the only strip club in Vegas where all the bits are revealed, thanks to the club's license being grandfathered in before selling alcohol and being totally nekkid were banned from happening in the same place. But with great power comes great responsibility: You don't have to sit on your hands during private dances (as is required in other similar establishments), but you must keep your phones in your pockets. Photos are strictly *verboten.* Call ahead to arrange free transportation to and from the club. Topless lap dances are $20; totally nude dances are $40. The Palomino is open Sunday through Thursday from 4pm to 5am and Friday and Saturday from 4pm to 7am. 1848 Las Vegas Blvd. N. www.palominolv.com. ✆ **702/642-2984.** Totally nude. Cover $30.

Sapphire Gentleman's Club ★★★ Charlie Sheen publicly endorsed Sapphire, so yes, things do get crazy here. It's the largest strip club in the world at 70,000 square feet and features three stages joined together as a bridge across the room, and one big room where multiple dancers vie for your attention from their respective poles. But what might be the most unusual part of the experience is that the women look just like women you'd find on the street: more natural-looking than at other strip clubs and of all shapes and sizes. Sheen isn't the only celebrity to make it rain here; others who choose to remain anonymous take to the private and expensive rooms upstairs for VIP action. During the day, you can spend the day getting hotter under the sun with the girls at the Sapphire Pool. Lap dances start at $20. Sapphire is open daily 24 hours. 3025 S. Sammy Davis Jr. Dr. www.sapphirelasvegas.com. ✆ **702/796-6000.** Topless. Cover $30 6pm–6am.

Spearmint Rhino ★★ Ask any man who has never been to Vegas before if he knows of a strip club here, and he'll mention the Spearmint Rhino. If anything, the Rhino, as it's affectionately called, is one of the best-looking clubs in town. It's 18,000 square feet of opulence, divided into three main viewing areas done in black and gold notes, along with plenty of tables and VIP rooms for those private encounters with the girl of your dreams. The dancers are as comely as the club; in fact, many would say that the Rhino gets the hottest performers in town. Lap dances are $20 and up. Spearmint Rhino is open daily 24 hours. 3340 S. Highland Dr. www.spearmintrhinolv.com. ✆ **702/796-3600.** Topless. Cover $30.

Treasures ★★★ The most Vegas-y of the Vegas strip clubs, Treasures is a favorite of both locals and visitors alike. The outside looks like it was lifted right from Caesars Palace, while the interior is as ornate, modeled after a Victorian brothel. The main stage is a spectacle with two staircases descending to a platform, where a neon-lit pole is used by dancers who actually take pride in their work. There's no disaffected shimmying here; these dancers put on a show, complete with special effects, props, and feats of athleticism. And while we'd normally shy away from eating at a strip club, the steakhouse is actually quite good. Lap dances are $20 and up. Treasures is open daily from 4pm to 6am. 2801 Westwood Dr. www.treasureslasvegas.com. ✆ **702/257-3030.** Topless. Cover $40.

DAY TRIPS FROM LAS VEGAS

9

Though Vegas is designed to make you forget that there is an outside world, it might do you and your wallet some good to reacquaint yourself with the non-Vegas realm. The good news: As Vegas is the most geographically isolated major city in America, there's nothing but nature in every direction outside its neon-lit borders.

It's a startling contrast between the artificial wonders of Sin City and the natural wonders that lie, in some cases, just a few miles away. Few places are as developed and modern as Vegas; few places are as untouched as some of the canyons, desert, and mountains that surround it. The electrical and design marvel that is the Strip couldn't exist without the extraordinary structural feat that is Hoover Dam. Need some fresh air? There are plenty of opportunities for outdoor recreation, all in landscapes that are completely un-Vegas, in the best ways.

HOOVER DAM & LAKE MEAD

30 miles SE of Las Vegas

This is one of the most popular excursions from Las Vegas, visited by upward of 7 million people annually. Why should you join them? Because Hoover Dam is an engineering and architectural marvel, and it changed the Southwest forever. Without it, you wouldn't even be going to Vegas. Kids may be bored, unless they like machinery or big things, but expose them to it anyway, for their own good. Buy them ice cream and a Hoover Dam snow globe as a bribe. If you are visiting Lake Mead, the dam is a must.

Getting There

Drive east on Flamingo Road or Tropicana Avenue to U.S. 515 S, which automatically turns into I-93 S and takes you right to the dam. This involves a dramatic drive as you go through Boulder City and come over a rise, and Lake Mead suddenly appears spread out before you. It's a beautiful sight. After the 2010 opening of a bypass bridge (dramatic on its own for its soaring height over the canyon), vehicles no longer pass directly over the bridge to get from Nevada to Arizona, but despite hopes that the bypass would make the commute better, it hasn't helped much. On a normal day, getting to the dam will take about an hour.

Go past the turnoff to Lake Mead to Nevada State Route 172, the well-marked Hoover Dam Access Road. As you near the dam, you'll see a five-story parking structure tucked into the canyon wall on your left. Park here ($10 charge) and take the elevators or stairs to the walkway leading to the visitor center.

If you would rather go on an **organized tour,** check out **Gray Line** (www.grayline.com; © **800/472-9546**), which offers a half-day tour of the dam from $57 or a daylong tour that includes a visit to the Welcome to Fabulous Las Vegas sign and a tour of the Ethel M Chocolates factory from $66.

Hoover Dam ★★★

There would be no Las Vegas as we know it without Hoover Dam. Certainly, the neon and glitz that we know and love would not exist. In fact, the growth of the entire Southwest can be tied directly to the electricity created by this dam in the Black Canyon of the Colorado River.

Construction on the dam began in 1931. An army of more than 5,200 laborers was assembled, and work proceeded 24 hours a day. Though 96 workers were killed during construction, contrary to popular myth, none were accidentally buried as the concrete was poured (it was poured only at a level of 8 in. at a time). Look for a monument outside dedicated to the workers who were killed—"they died to make the desert bloom"—along with a tombstone for their doggy mascot who was also killed, albeit after the dam was completed. Compare their wages of 50¢ an hour to those of their Depression-era peers, who made 5¢ to 30¢.

Completed in 1936, 2 years ahead of schedule and $15 million under budget (it is, no doubt, a Wonder of the Modern Fiscal World), the dam stopped the annual floods and conserved water for irrigation, industry, and domestic uses. Equally important, it became one of the world's major electricity-generating plants, providing low-cost, pollution-free hydroelectric power to a score of surrounding communities. Hoover Dam's $165-million cost has been repaid with interest by the sale of inexpensive power to a number of California cities and the states of Arizona and Nevada. The dam is a government project that paid for itself—a feat almost as awe-inspiring as its engineering.

The dam itself is a massive curved wall, 660 feet thick at the bottom, tapering to 45 feet where a road crosses it at the top. It towers 726 feet above bedrock (about the height of a 60-story skyscraper) and acts as a plug between the canyon walls to hold back up to trillions of gallons of water in Lake Mead, the reservoir created by its construction. Four concrete intake towers on the lake side drop the water down about 600 feet to drive turbines and create power, after which the water spills out into the river and continues south.

All the architecture is on a grand scale, and the design has beautiful Art Deco elements, unusual in an engineering project. Note, for instance, the monumental 30-foot bronze sculpture, *Winged Figures of the Republic,* flanking a 142-foot flagpole at the Nevada entrance. According to its creator, Oskar Hansen, the sculpture symbolizes "the immutable calm of intellectual resolution, and the enormous power of trained physical strength, equally enthroned in placid triumph of scientific achievement."

TOURING THE DAM

The **Hoover Dam Visitor Center** is a vast three-level circular concrete structure with a rooftop overlook. This facility is where you can buy tour tickets; peruse informational exhibits, photographs, and memorabilia; and view videos about the dam and its construction. The Overlook Level additionally provides an unobstructed view of Lake Mead, the dam, the power plant, the Colorado River, and Black Canyon. Have your camera ready.

It costs $10 to visit just this portion, but for an extra $5 you can get the Powerplant Tour as well (see below). Open every day except for Thanksgiving and Christmas, the center closes at 5pm (4:15pm is the last admission time), though hours vary seasonally.

There are two tours available, the Powerplant Tour and the Hoover Dam Tour. The cost of the former is $15 for adults; $12 for seniors, children 4 to 16, and military personnel and their dependents; and free for children 3 and under and military in uniform. It is self-guided and takes about 2 hours if you really stop to look at and read everything (less if you're a skimmer). The more extensive Hoover Dam Tour includes the self-guided portion but adds an hour-long guided tour into the deeper recesses of the facility. It is $30 per person; no children age 7 and under are allowed. Tickets for the Hoover Dam Tour must be purchased at the visitor center, while admission to the visitor center and tickets for the Powerplant Tour are available online. Parking is $10 no matter which tour you take, and the lot takes cash only. There is no need to call ahead to reserve a place, but for more information, call ☎ **866/730-9097** or 702/494-2517.

On the Powerplant Tour, visitors go to the center, see a movie, and walk on top of the dam. While both tours include a 530-foot descent via elevator into the dam to view the massive generators, the Powerplant Tour is a self-guided tour aided by the occasional information kiosk or guide/docent stationed at intervals along the way; the pricier Hoover Dam Tour offers the same attractions and viewing opportunities, but it is guided, lasts an hour, and is limited to 20 people. If you plan on taking that tour, be aware that it covers over a mile and a half of walking on concrete and gravel, with no handicapped access. The Hoover Dam Tour is offered every half-hour, with the last tour at 3:30pm, while the final Powerplant Tour admission is at 4:15pm.

For more information on the dam, visit www.usbr.gov/lc/hooverdam.

Lake Mead National Recreation Area ★★

Under the auspices of the National Park Service, 1.5-million-acre Lake Mead National Recreation Area was created in 1936 around Lake Mead (the

Day Trips from Las Vegas

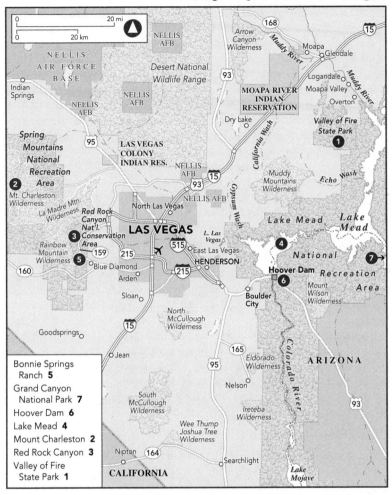

Map legend:

- Bonnie Springs Ranch **5**
- Grand Canyon National Park **7**
- Hoover Dam **6**
- Lake Mead **4**
- Mount Charleston **2**
- Red Rock Canyon **3**
- Valley of Fire State Park **1**

reservoir lake that is the result of the construction of Hoover Dam) and later Lake Mohave to the south (formed by the construction of Davis Dam). Before the lakes emerged, this desert region was brutally hot, dry, and rugged—unfit for human habitation. Today it's one of the nation's most popular playgrounds, attracting millions of visitors annually. The two lakes comprise 247 square miles. At an elevation of just over 1,000 feet, Lake Mead itself extends some 110 miles upstream toward the Grand Canyon. Its 700-mile shoreline, backed by spectacular cliff and canyon scenery, forms a perfect setting for a wide variety of watersports and desert hiking.

Having said all that, Lake Mead is in the beginning stages of a crisis so large that if unchecked, it would spell the end for Vegas entirely. The nation's largest reservoir has experienced a severe drop-off in levels since 2000, due to a combination of drought, global warming, and increased use. Whole portions of the lake's edges are now dry, in the process exposing the remains of some of the small towns that were flooded to build the thing in the first place. These have become tourist spots themselves. In 2018, the lake was at 40% of its capacity and hit a record low height of 1,077 feet above sea level. Despite some recent years with increased water flow into the lake, it is still a fraction of its former self, and the long-term risk is still present. Because the lake supplies water to Las Vegas (not to mention hydroelectric power), this has grave implications for that city. Let's encourage those fancy new hotels to put in drought-tolerant plants instead of more grass. And don't ask for your towels to be changed every day.

The **Lake Mead Visitor Center** is 4 miles northeast of Boulder City on U.S. 93, at NV 166 (© **702/293-8990**). Here, you can get information on all area activities and services, pick up trail maps and brochures, view informative films, and find out about scenic drives, accommodations, ranger-guided hikes, naturalist programs and lectures, bird-watching, canoeing, camping, lakeside RV parks, and picnic facilities. The center has some informative exhibits about the area and is staffed by friendly folks full of local pride. It's open daily from 9:00am to 4:30pm except Thanksgiving, Christmas, and New Year's Day.

For information on camping, boat rentals, fishing, tours, and more, visit the National Park Service website at www.nps.gov/lake.

The **entry fee** for the area is $25 per vehicle, which covers all passengers, $20 if you're motorcycling, or $15 per person if you're walking or biking in. Entry fees cover 1 to 7 days, and yearly passes are available for $45 per vehicle or individual.

Outdoor Activities

This is a lovely area for scenic drives amid the dramatic desert landscape. One popular route follows the Lakeshore and Northshore scenic drives along the edge of Lake Mead. From these roads, there are panoramic views of the blue lake, set against a backdrop of the browns, blacks, reds, and grays of the desert mountains. Northshore Scenic Drive also leads through areas of brilliant red boulders and rock formations, and you'll find a picnic area along the way.

BOATING & FISHING   Nonresidents can get a fishing license online ($81 for a year or $19 for 1 day plus $7 for each additional day; discounts for children 15 and under are available; additional fees apply for special fishing classifications, including trout, which require a $10 stamp for taking or possessing that fish). Largemouth bass, striped bass, channel catfish, crappie, and bluegill are found in Lake Mead; rainbow trout, largemouth bass, and striped bass are in Lake Mohave. The **Las Vegas Boat Harbor** (www.boatinglakemead.com; © **702/451-2901**) rents powerboats, pontoon boats, personal watercraft, and watersports equipment. It also carries groceries, clothing, marine supplies, sporting goods, water-skiing gear, fishing equipment, and bait and tackle. Similar services are offered at the **Callville Bay Resort & Marina** (www. callvillebay.com; ✆ **800/255-5561** or 702/565-8958), which not only features a few RV and campground sites but also rents small watercraft as well as fully equipped houseboats.

CAMPING Lake Mead's shoreline is dotted with campsites, all of them equipped with running water, picnic tables, and grills. Available on a first-come, first-served basis, they are administered by the **National Park Service** (www.nps.gov/lake; ✆ **702/293-8990**). There's a charge of $20 per night at each tent campsite, and up to $45 for RVs.

CANOEING The **Lake Mead Visitor Center** (see above) can provide a list of outfitters that rent canoes for trips on the Colorado River. A canoeing permit ($22 per person) is required in advance and is available from livery services licensed by the Bureau of Reclamation. Questions about launch permits should be directed to Willow Beach/Black Canyon River Adventures (www.willowbeachharbor.com; ✆ **800/455-3490** or 702/294-4267). You can apply for and receive the permit on the same day that you plan to canoe.

HIKING The best season for hiking is November through March; it's too hot the rest of the year. Three trails, ranging in length from .75 mile to 6 miles, originate at the **Lake Mead Visitor Center** (see above), which stocks detailed trail maps. The 6-mile trail goes past remains of the railroad built for the dam project. Be sure to take all necessary desert-hiking precautions. (See "Desert Hiking Advice," below.)

LAKE CRUISES A delightful way to enjoy Lake Mead is on a cruise aboard the **Lake Mead Cruises** boat *Desert Princess* ★ (www.lakemead cruises.com; ✆ **866/292-9191**), a Mississippi-style paddle wheeler. It's a relaxing, scenic trip (enjoyed from an open promenade deck or one of two fully enclosed, climate-controlled decks) through Black Canyon and past colorful rock formations known as the Arizona Paint Pots en route to Hoover Dam, which is lit at night. Options include narrated midday cruises ($26 adults, $13 children), Sunday Champagne brunch cruises ($45 adults, $19.50 children), and dinner cruises ($61.50 adults, $25 children). Dinner is served in a pleasant, windowed, air-conditioned dining room. There's a full onboard bar. Brunch and dinner cruises run April through October, and the midday cruises run February through November. Call for departure times.

VALLEY OF FIRE STATE PARK ★★

60 miles NE of Las Vegas

The 36,000-acre Valley of Fire State Park typifies the mountainous, red Mojave Desert that surrounds Las Vegas. It derives its name from the brilliant sandstone formations that were created 150 million years ago by a great shifting of sand, and that continue to be shaped by the geologic processes of wind and water erosion. These are rock formations like you'll never see anywhere else. There is nothing green, just fiery red rocks swirling unrelieved as far as the eye can see. No wonder various sci-fi movies have used this place as a stand-in for another planet. The entire place is very mysterious, loaded with petroglyphs, and totally inhospitable. It's not hard to believe that for the Indians it was a sacred place where men came as a test of their manhood. The area is a natural wonder that must be seen to be appreciated.

Although it's hard to imagine in the sweltering Nevada heat, for billions of years these rocks were under hundreds of feet of ocean. This ocean floor began to rise some 200 million years ago, and the waters became more and more shallow. Eventually the sea made a complete retreat, leaving a muddy terrain traversed by ever-diminishing streams. A great sandy desert covered much of the southwestern part of the American continent until about 140 million years ago. Over eons, winds, massive fault action, and water erosion sculpted fantastic formations of sand and limestone. Oxidation of iron in the sands and mud—and the effect of groundwater leaching the oxidized iron—turned the rocks the many hues of red, pink, russet, lavender, and white that can be seen today. Logs of ancient forests washed down from faraway highlands and became petrified fossils, which can be seen along two interpretive trails.

Getting There

From Las Vegas, take I-15 N to exit 75 (Valley of Fire turnoff). However, the more scenic route is I-15 N to Lake Mead Boulevard east to Northshore Road (NV 167); then proceed north to the Valley of Fire exit. The first route takes about an hour, the second, 1½ hours.

There is a $10-per-vehicle admission charge to the park, regardless of how many people you cram inside.

Plan on spending a minimum of an hour in the park, though you can spend a great deal more time. It can get very hot in there; there is nothing to relieve the sun beating down and reflecting off all that red. There is also no water, so be certain to bring a liter, maybe two, per person in the summer. Without a guide you must stay on paved roads, but don't worry if they end; you can always turn around and go back to the main road. You can see a great deal from the car, and there are also hiking trails.

Numerous **sightseeing tours** go to the Valley of Fire; inquire at your hotel.

What to See & Do

There are no food concessions or gas stations in the park; however, you can obtain meals or gas on NV 167 or in nearby **Overton** (15 miles northwest on NV 169).

At the southern edge of town is the **Lost City Museum ★**, 721 S. Moapa Valley Blvd. (✆ **702/397-2193**), a sweet little museum, very nicely done, commemorating an ancient ancestral Puebloan village that was discovered in the region in 1924. Artifacts dating back 12,000 years are on display, as are clay jars, dried corn and beans, arrowheads, seashell necklaces, and willow baskets from the ancient Pueblo culture that inhabited this region between A.D. 300 and 1150. Other exhibits document the Mormon farmers who settled the valley in the 1860s. A large collection of local rocks—petrified wood, fern fossils, iron pyrite, green copper, and red iron oxide—along with manganese blown bottles turned purple by the ultraviolet rays of the sun, are also displayed here. The museum is surrounded by reconstructed wattle-and-daub pueblos. Admission is $5 for adults, free for children 17 and under. It's open daily from 8:30am to 4:30pm, but closed Thanksgiving, December 25, and January 1.

Information headquarters for Valley of Fire is the **Visitor Center** on NV 169, 6 miles west of Northshore Road (© **702/397-2088**). It's open daily 8:30am to 4:30pm and is worth a quick stop for information and a glance at some of the informational exhibits before entering the park. Postcards, books, slides, and films are for sale here, and you can pick up hiking maps and brochures. Rangers can answer your park-related questions. For online information about the park, which is open sunrise to sunset, go to www.parks.nv.gov/parks/valley-of-fire-state-park.

There are **hiking trails, shaded picnic sites,** and **two campgrounds** in the park. Most sites are equipped with tables, grills, water, and restrooms. A $20-per-vehicle, per-night camping fee is charged for use of the campground (plus $10 for utility hookups); if you're not camping, it costs $10 per vehicle to enter the park.

Some of the notable formations in the park have been named for the shapes they vaguely resemble—a duck, an elephant, seven sisters, domes, beehives, and so on. Mouse's Tank is a natural basin that collects rainwater, so named for a fugitive Paiute called Mouse, who hid there in the late 1890s. **Native American petroglyphs** etched into the rock walls and boulders—some dating from 3,000 years ago—can be observed on self-guided trails. Petroglyphs at Atlatl Rock and Petroglyph Canyon are both easily accessible. In summer, when temperatures are usually over 100°F (38°C), you may have to settle for driving through the park in an air-conditioned car.

RED ROCK CANYON ★★★

19 miles W of Las Vegas

If you need a break from the casinos of Vegas, Red Rock Canyon is a balm for your overstimulated soul. Less than 20 miles away—but a world apart—this is a magnificent, unspoiled vista that should cleanse and refresh you (and if you must, a morning visit should leave you enough time for an afternoon's gambling). You can drive the panoramic 13-mile **Scenic Drive** (daily 6am–dusk, $7 per vehicle) or explore more in depth on foot, making it perfect for athletes and armchair types alike. There are many interesting sights and trail heads along the drive itself. The **National Conservation Area** (www.nv.blm.gov/redrockcanyon) offers hiking trails and internationally acclaimed

Red Rock Canyon

DESERT hiking ADVICE

Except in summer, when temperatures can reach 120°F (49°C) in the shade, the Las Vegas area is great for hiking. The best hiking season is November through March. Great locales include the incredibly scenic Red Rock Canyon (p. 249) and Valley of Fire State Park (p. 247).

Hiking in the desert is exceptionally rewarding, but it can be dangerous. Here are some safety tips:

1. Don't hike alone.
2. Carry plenty of water and drink it often. Don't assume that spring water is safe to drink. A gallon of water per person per day is recommended for hikers.
3. Be alert for signs of heat exhaustion (headache, nausea, dizziness, fatigue, and cool, damp, pale, or red skin).
4. Gauge your fitness accurately. Desert hiking may involve rough or steep terrain. Don't take on more than you can handle.
5. Check weather forecasts before starting out. Thunderstorms can turn into raging flash floods, which are extremely hazardous to hikers.
6. Dress properly. Wear sturdy walking shoes for rock scrambling, long pants (to protect yourself from rocks and cacti), a hat, and sunglasses.
7. Wear sunscreen and carry a small first-aid kit.
8. Be careful when climbing on sandstone, which can be surprisingly soft and crumbly.
9. Don't feed or play with animals, such as the wild burros in Red Rock Canyon. (It's actually illegal to approach them.)
10. Be alert for snakes and insects, though they're rarely encountered. You'll want to look into a crevice before putting your hand into it.
11. Visit park or other information offices before you start out, and acquaint yourself with rules and regulations and any possible hazards. It's also a good idea to tell the staff where you're going, when you'll return, how many are in your party, and so on. Some park offices offer hiker-registration programs.
12. Follow the hiker's creed: Take only photographs and leave only footprints.

rock-climbing opportunities. Especially notable is 7,068-foot Mount Wilson, the highest sandstone peak among the bluffs; for information on climbing, contact the **Red Rock Canyon Visitor Center** at ✆ **702/515-5350.**

There are picnic areas along the drive and in nearby **Spring Mountain Ranch State Park** (www.parks.nv.gov; ✆ **702/594-7529**), 5 miles south, which also offers plays in an outdoor theater during the summer. The entrance fee is $10 per vehicle.

Getting There

Just drive west on Charleston Boulevard, which becomes NV 159. As soon as you leave the city, the red rocks will begin to loom around you. The visitor center will be on your right.

You can also go on an **organized tour. Gray Line** (www.grayline.com; ✆ **800/634-6579**), among other companies, runs bus tours to Red Rock Canyon. Inquire at your hotel tour desk.

Finally, you can go **by bike.** Not very far out of town (at Rainbow Blvd.), Charleston Boulevard is flanked by a bike path that continues for about 11 miles to the visitor center/scenic drive. The path is hilly but not difficult, if you're in reasonable shape. However, exploring Red Rock Canyon by bike should be attempted only by exceptionally fit and experienced bikers.

Just off NV 159, you'll see the turnoff for the **Red Rock Canyon Visitor Center** (www.redrockcanyonlv.org; © **702/515-5350**), which marks the entrance to the park. It features outdoor exhibits on the flora and fauna found in the canyon, and you can pick up info on trails and the driving route. The center is open daily from 8am to 4:30pm.

About Red Rock Canyon

The geologic history of these ancient stones goes back some 600 million years. Over eons, the forces of nature have formed Red Rock's sandstone monoliths into arches, natural bridges, and massive sculptures painted in a stunning palette of gray-white limestone and dolomite, black mineral deposits, and oxidized minerals in earth-toned sienna hues ranging from pink to crimson and burgundy. Orange and green lichens add further contrast, as do spring-fed areas of lush foliage. Some formations, such as **Calico Hill,** are brilliantly white where groundwater has leached out oxidized iron. Cliffs cut by deep canyons tower 2,000 feet above the valley floor.

During most of its history, Red Rock Canyon was below a warm, shallow sea. Massive fault action and volcanic eruptions caused this seabed to begin rising some 225 million years ago. As the waters receded, sea creatures died, and the calcium in their bodies combined with sea minerals to form limestone cliffs studded with ancient fossils. Some 45 million years later, the region was buried beneath thousands of feet of windblown sand. As time progressed, iron oxide and calcium carbonate infiltrated the sand, consolidating it into cross-bedded rock.

About 100 million years ago, massive fault action began dramatically shifting the rock landscape here, forming spectacular limestone and sandstone cliffs and rugged canyons punctuated by waterfalls, shallow streams, and serene oasis pools.

Red Rock's valley is home to more than 45 species of mammals, about 100 species of birds, 30 reptiles and amphibians, and an abundance of plant life. Ascending the slopes from the valley, you'll see cactus and creosote bushes, aromatic purple sage, yellow-flowering blackbrush, yucca and Joshua trees, and, at higher elevations, clusters of forest-green pinyon, juniper, and ponderosa pines. In spring, the desert blooms with extraordinary wildflowers.

In the latter part of the 19th century, Red Rock was a mining site, and later a sandstone quarry that provided materials for many buildings in Los Angeles, San Francisco, and early Las Vegas. In 1990, Red Rock Canyon became a National Conservation Area that comprises approximately 197,000 acres.

What to See & Do

Begin with a stop at the **Red Rock Canyon Visitor Center;** while there is a $15-per-vehicle fee for entering the park, you also can pick up guides, trail maps, and lists of flora and fauna. You can also view exhibits that tell the history of the canyon and depict its plant and animal life, including the thousands of wild horses and burros, protected by an act of Congress since 1971. Call ahead to find out about ranger-guided tours as well as informative guided hikes offered by such groups as the Sierra Club and the Audubon Society.

The easiest thing to do is to **drive the 13-mile scenic loop ★★★** (or give it a go on your bike for a moderately difficult ride). It really is a loop, and it only goes one way, so once you start, you are committed to driving the entire thing. You can stop the car to admire a number of fabulous views and sights along the way, have a picnic, or hike. As you drive, observe how dramatically the milky-white limestone alternates with iron-rich red rocks. Farther along, the mountains become solid limestone with canyons running between them, which lead to an evergreen forest—a surprising sight in the desert.

If you're up to it, however, we can't stress enough that the way to really see the canyon is by **hiking.** Every trail is incredible—glance over your options and decide what you might be looking for. You can begin from the visitor center or drive into the loop, park your car, and start from points therein. Hiking trails range from a .7-mile-loop stroll to a waterfall (its flow varying seasonally) at Lost Creek to much longer and more strenuous treks. Actually, all the hikes involve a certain amount of effort, as you must scramble over rocks on even the shortest hikes. Unfit or less dexterous people should beware. Be sure to wear good shoes, as the rocks can be slippery. You must have a map; cell coverage is spotty to nonexistent. You won't get lost forever (there usually are other hikers around to help you out, eventually), but you can still lose your way. Once you're deep into the rocks, everything looks the same, even with the map, so give yourself extra time for each hike (at least an additional hour), regardless of its billed length.

A popular 2-mile round-trip hike leads to **Pine Creek Canyon** and the creek-side ruins of a historic home site surrounded by ponderosa pine trees. Our hiking trail of choice is the **Calico Basin,** which is accessed along the loop. After an hour walk up the rocks (which is not that well marked), you end up at an oasis surrounded by sheer walls of limestone that, alas, make the oasis itself inaccessible. In the summer, flowers and deciduous trees grow out of the walls.

As you hike, keep your eyes peeled for lizards, the occasional desert tortoise, herds of bighorn sheep, birds, and other critters. But the rocks themselves are the most fun, with small caves to explore and rock formations to climb on. On trails along Calico Hills and the escarpment, look for "Indian marbles," a local name for small, rounded sandstone rocks that have eroded off larger sandstone formations. Petroglyphs are also tucked away in various locales.

Biking is a tremendous way to travel the loop. There are also terrific off-road mountain-biking trails, with levels from amateur to expert. No need to haul your bike with you; you can rent one from one of the recommended shops linked on Friends of Red Rock (www.friendsofredrockcanyon.org).

The gleaming, luxurious **Red Rock Resort** (p. 92) gives day-trippers a highly desirable refueling point on a trip to the canyon. Stop by the food court Capriotti's, the economical submarine sandwich shop. The subs are ideal for takeout for picnics in the park (buy a cheap ice chest at a convenience store) or for in-room dining as you rest up in your hotel post-hike.

Nearby **Bonnie Springs Ranch** (www.bonniesprings.com; ✆ **702/875-4191**) has a cute Wild West old town, horseback riding, a petting zoo, and more. Horseback riding is $60 for 1 hour; pony rides are $7.50 per child. Zoo admission is $7 Monday and Tuesday, and Wednesday through Sunday $10 adults, $7 children.

MOUNT CHARLESTON ★★

About 35 miles NW of Las Vegas

Although officially known as the Springs Mountains National Recreation Area, this region is more popularly referred to by the name of its most prominent landmark, the 11,918-foot-high Mount Charleston. Visible from Las Vegas proper, the mountain and its surrounding recreation areas have been a popular getaway for locals and vacationers alike for decades.

Comprising more than 316,000 acres of the Humboldt-Toiyabe National Forest (the largest in the lower 48), the area is practically an earth science class covering geography of such variety that it almost causes whiplash. As you start up the road toward the peak, you are surrounded by the kind of desert sagebrush and Joshua trees that are most predominant at the lower levels. Suddenly the road takes a curve and a dip, and the desert gives way to a pinyon- and juniper-based ecosystem, full of craggy canyons and trees. Finally, you dive into the full-on forests of ponderosa and bristlecone pines, which create a lush oasis powered by more than 100 natural springs formed by water and snow runoff that soaks through the porous limestone rock and eventually bubbles to the surface.

Outdoor activities are the predominant lure and include hiking, camping, rock climbing, and, during the winter months, skiing and snowboarding.

Getting There

Head north on I-15 away from the Strip and then transition to U.S. 95 N. About 18 miles of freeway-style driving will bring you to the first of two roads in the Mount Charleston area. Kyle Canyon Road/NV 157 will take you about 17 miles up toward the summit and is where you'll find the **Spring Mountain Visitor Center,** open 9am to 4pm daily (www.gomtcharleston.com; ✆ **702/872-5486**), many of the campgrounds and hiking trails, the Mount Charleston Resort, and the Mount Charleston Lodge. A few miles farther is NV 156, which runs about 18 miles up to the Lee Canyon (see "Snow Sports,"

THE grand canyon

The geographically challenged among us believe that the Grand Canyon is just a hop, skip, and a jump from Las Vegas and therefore a great idea for a side trip while visiting Sin City. While this may be true from a strictly comparative basis—the canyon is closer than say, London—it's not exactly what you'd call "close."

While the West Rim is closer to Las Vegas at 180 miles and about 2 hours away, the more popular side for visitors is the South Rim at 270 miles and another 2 hours farther, as there's more to see and do.

The quickest and easiest way to get to the West Rim is via helicopter. **Papillon** (www.papillon.com; © **888/635-7272**), a popular charter service, offers several packages to the west side, including a bird's-eye view of Hoover Dam, Lake Mead, and possibly the Grapevine Mesa. The shorter, 4-hour tour ($129–$219) is just a quick fly-by over the canyon, but the narrated guide, available in multiple languages, is thorough, informative, and excellent. A more expensive package (that extends the tour by an hour for about $100 more) allows for a landing at the bottom of the canyon, 4,000 feet below the rim, where you're treated to a champagne picnic in

one of the most gorgeous settings you'll ever dine in. If you want a full-day excursion, there's an option to combine the flight to the canyon, a boat trip on the Colorado River, and VIP passes on the SkyWalk bridge ($449–$539).

The North Rim is the unsung hero of the Grand Canyon, where visitors can be closer to nature without all the crowds. But that solitude comes at a price, as the North Rim is the most difficult to get to. Despite its being the same distance from Vegas as the South Rim, this side is more wild and secluded, so a day trip by car isn't advised. Fortunately, between April and November, Papillon heads there for an overnight tour ($319–$369). The day starts with a prop plane ride with views of Hoover Dam, Lake Mead, and the Colorado River before dropping you off at an isolated landing strip at Bar 10 Ranch. Your guide will take you via ATV on a 2-hour round-trip tour down to the North Rim, 3,000 feet above the Colorado River, where you can appreciate the majesty of the canyon and not fight tourists to breathe in the landscape. You'll eat like a cowboy for lunch and dinner, ride a horse, and sleep in one of the bunk rooms or in a converted covered wagon. After a country breakfast, you

below). It's only about 35 miles or so from Downtown Las Vegas, but traffic on the freeways in town is often difficult (to say the least), so plan an hour of travel time to be safe. *Note:* Chains are often required during or after snowfalls, which can be epic in the area. A December 2010 storm dumped a record 90 inches here over the course of several days.

Also note that there are no gas stations, convenience stores, or other services (and that often includes cellphone service) in the area, so be sure to fill up the tank and bring whatever supplies you may need with you.

Outdoor Activities

You might well be satisfied with driving up to the region and, if it's wintertime, gazing at the snow from the warmth of your vehicle. We know that many of you come to Las Vegas in the winter to get away from the snow, but for spend a few leisurely hours on a hike or shooting skeet, and then fly back to the Strip.

Whenever you bring up the West Rim, folks always mention the SkyWalk, and it's usually not in a favorable manner. More than 1 million pounds of steel went into the construction of this U-shaped footbridge that extends 70 feet from the rim over the canyon. The transparent glass base is supposed to allow visitors to look down and absorb the awesomeness of the Grand Canyon. However, exorbitant fees (about $82, part of which goes to the Hualapai tribe whose reservation the bridge is on) and relatively unreasonable demands—no cameras, no backpacks—keep a lot of visitors away. Before you decide to pay the price of admission, consider that just a few yards from the bridge, Eagle's Point offers similar, if not better, views absolutely free.

To visit the South Rim, there are more helicopter tours available, but we suggest that if you've got a whole day, get up early and catch the Papillon Bus Tour ($89–$150). The coach is air-conditioned and comfortable and makes frequent rest stops. You'll get off the bus for photo opps at Hoover Dam, drive through the 900-year-old Joshua tree forest, and receive a voucher for lunch at the National Geographic food court. Like a trip in school, this will be a learning experience, thanks to a knowledgeable driver well-versed in the history and geology of the American Southwest.

Or be the captain of your ship! Renting a car and driving is an excellent and affordable option, especially if you've got a group. Four to 5 hours over the two-lane highway (three to the West Rim) is doable, but not unheard of. Plus, you'll have the luxury of staying as long as you like and exploring on your own terms. We find that many visitors decide to stay overnight just for the pleasure of seeing the canyon at dusk and dawn.

If you're taking your own car, head east on Flamingo Road or Tropicana Boulevard to I-515 S. This becomes NV 93, which crosses over Hoover Dam into Arizona and leads to I-40 at Kingman. Take the interstate east to NV 64 at Williams, Arizona, and follow the signs north. Drivers should be advised that much of the route to the Grand Canyon from Las Vegas is along narrow, twisty roads that can be a challenge and are often jammed with traffic.

those who don't get to see it very often, snow-covered peaks could very well be an entertaining sight. If you want to actually get out of the car, a number of recreational activities are available.

CAMPING There are seven campgrounds in the Mount Charleston area, although only the McWilliams, Fletcher View, and Kyle Canyon sites are open year-round. Some have hookups if you are bringing your camper with you, while others are good for just tents and your sleeping bag; most have toilets, fire pits, and other outdoorsy conveniences. Fees range from around $10 to $50, depending on the number of people, type of vehicle, and facilities or hookups. A full listing of the campgrounds is available at the USDA Forest Service website at www.recreation.gov (then search for the Spring Mountains National Recreation Area). To make reservations for any of the sites, use the National Recreation Reservation Service at ☏ **877/444-6777** or book online.

HIKING   Whether you are an expert hiker or a casual walker, there is probably a trail here for you—more than two dozen total. The Echo/Little Falls trail is a relatively easy mile or so through forests that lead to a small waterfall. On the other end of the scale is the South Loop, an 8-mile trek that leads you almost all the way to the summit of Mount Charleston more than 11,000 feet up. You can pick up a trail guide at the Spring Mountain Visitor Center. There is no fee to use the trails. Follow all the admonitions about bringing plenty of water and not drinking from the natural springs, which may contain parasites that can make you sick.

ROCK CLIMBING   There are several rock-climbing opportunities available in the Mount Charleston area, but all of them are do-it-yourself—no cushy controlled environments here. The most popular sites are the Hood along the unfortunately named Trail Canyon Trail, or Robber's Roost, accessed from the trail head along Highway 158. For more information, pick up a guide at the Spring Mountain Visitor Center.

SNOW SPORTS   Lee Canyon (formerly Las Vegas Ski and Snowboard Resort), Hwy. 156, Mount Charleston (www.leecanyonlv.com; ℂ **702/385-2754**), offers three chairlifts and more than 30 trails ranging from beginner to advanced, plus terrain parks for snowboarders and a tubing area. Lift tickets are $40 to $60 for adults, and $30 to $45 for children 12 and under and seniors 60 and over. The facility offers a full array of equipment and clothing rentals; there's also a small snack bar and sundry shop if you forgot to bring a camera with which to record yourself in full downhill glory (or falling repeatedly, if you are like us). It is usually open late November through early April from 9am until 4pm, but that may vary based on conditions.

Where to Stay & Dine

In addition to the aforementioned snack shop at the Lee Canyon, there is only one other dining option outside of the Mount Charleston Resort (see below). The **Mount Charleston Lodge,** 5375 Kyle Canyon Rd. (www.mtcharleston lodge.com; ℂ **702/872-5408**), has a rustic dining room with 20-foot ceilings in an A-frame, ski-lodge type of building; a big bar; an open fireplace in the center of the room; big windows; and an outdoor patio from which you can enjoy the scenic views from its 7,717-foot elevation. Best known for boozy but warming Mount Charleston Coffee (spiked with a bit of Drambuie and brandy), the dining room also serves a wide range of American comfort food. It's open from 8am to 8pm Sunday through Thursday and from 8am to 9pm on Friday and Saturday. The lounge is open daily until midnight.

The Resort on Mount Charleston ★   This woodsy retreat has undergone some serious improvements over the last few years that have kept the charm of the place but modernized it and moved it upscale a notch or two. The ski chalet–style buildings (log and stone exteriors) are tucked into a canyon, providing a gorgeous backdrop for a peaceful respite. The lobby has a big fireplace perfect for warming up after a winter hike, along with a small menagerie of stuffed animals that seem *de rigueur* in a place like this.

The rooms range from standard motel size to presidential suites, all with comfortably modern furnishings, flatscreen TVs, faux fireplaces, iPod radios, DVD players, and more.

On-site there are a small spa and fitness center; a full-service restaurant (classic American fare); a sundry store/bistro with quick bites; and a bar complete with billiards and even a few video poker machines if you're going into gambling withdrawal.

2275 Kyle Canyon Rd. www.mtcharlestonresort.com. © **888/559-1888** or 702/872-5500. 61 units. $99 and up double. Resort fee $16.95 tax included. Free self-parking. Extra person $15. Children 17 and under stay free in parent's room. Pets under 25 pounds permitted, $50 per animal up to 2. Amenities: 2 restaurants; bar/lounge; spa; free property-wide Wi-Fi.

PLANNING YOUR TRIP TO LAS VEGAS

Whether you are visiting Las Vegas for the first time or the 50th, planning a trip here can be an overwhelming experience—as overwhelming as the city itself. With more than 150,000 hotel rooms, nearly as many slot machines, thousands of restaurants, and dozens of shows and attractions, there are seemingly endless ways to lose or waste your money. This chapter is designed to help you navigate the practical details of designing a Vegas experience that is tailored to your needs, from getting to and around the city to advice on the best times to visit and more.

10

Lots of people, both from the U.S. and abroad, believe that Las Vegas is the way it is portrayed in movies and television. For the most part, it isn't. Well, okay, you are more likely to run into a random showgirl or Elvis impersonator here than you are in say, Wichita, but they aren't in the background of every photo opportunity. International visitors, especially, should pay close attention to the material that follows in order to prepare for the most common non-showgirl issues you may encounter in Las Vegas or on your way here.

GETTING THERE
By Plane

Las Vegas is served by **McCarran International Airport,** 5757 Wayne Newton Blvd. (www.mccarran.com; ✆ **702/261-5211,** TDD 702/261-3111), just a few minutes' drive from the southern end of the Strip, where the bulk of casinos and hotels are concentrated. The airport is known by the code **LAS.**

Most major domestic and many international airlines fly into Las Vegas, and the city acts as a major routing point for low-cost Southwest Airlines.

The airport has two terminals. Terminal 1 serves mostly domestic carriers with four sets of gates. A and B gates are accessible to the main ticketing area and baggage claim by (very long) hallways, while most of the C and all the D gates are reached by tram. The ultramodern Terminal 3 primarily services international and some domestic carriers like United with its 14 gates.

In case you're wondering what happened to Terminal 2, it closed when Terminal 3 opened. Why they didn't renumber things is a mystery.

Each terminal has its own baggage-claim facility and services such as dining, shopping, and traveler assistance, along with ground transportation areas for taxis, buses, and shuttles to the rental-car facility.

And yes, all the terminals and baggage claims have slot machines just in case you want to lose a few bucks while you're waiting for your luggage.

By Car

The main highway connecting Las Vegas with the rest of the country is **I-15;** it links Montana, Idaho, and Utah with Southern California. The drive from Los Angeles is quite popular and can get very crowded on weekends as revelers make their way to and from Las Vegas.

From the east, take **I-70** or **I-80** west to Kingman, Arizona, and then **U.S. 93** north to Downtown Las Vegas (Fremont St.). From the south, take **I-10** west to Phoenix, and then U.S. 93 north to Las Vegas. From San Francisco, take I-80 east to Reno, and then **U.S. 95** south to Las Vegas.

Vegas is 286 miles from Phoenix, 759 miles from Denver, 421 miles from Salt Lake City, 269 miles from Los Angeles, and 586 miles from San Francisco.

International visitors should note that insurance and taxes are almost never included in quoted rental-car rates in the U.S. Be sure to ask your rental agency about these. They can add a significant cost to your car rental.

For information on car rentals and gasoline (petrol) in Las Vegas, see "Getting Around: By Car," below.

By Bus

Bus travel is often the most economical form of public transit for short hops between U.S. cities, but it's certainly not an option for everyone. Though getting to Vegas this way is cheaper, especially if you book in advance, it's also time-consuming (a 1-hour flight from L.A. becomes a 5- to 8-hour trek by bus) and usually not as comfortable. So, you need to figure out how much time and comfort mean to you. **Greyhound** (www.greyhound.com; ✆ **800/231-2222** in the U.S.; ✆ **001/214/849-8100** outside the U.S. without toll-free access) is the sole nationwide bus line.

The main Greyhound terminal in Las Vegas is located Downtown next to the Plaza hotel, 200 S. Main St. (✆ **702/384-9561**), and is open 24 hours. Although the neighborhood around it has improved dramatically, it is still a busy bus station, so normal safety precautions should be taken in and around it.

Megabus (www.megabus.com; ✆ **877/462-6342**) operates coaches from Los Angeles to the Regional Transportation Commission's South Strip Transfer Terminal at 6675 Gillespie St. near McCarran International Airport. From there you can easily transfer (hence the name) to many of the city's bus routes, including those that travel to the Strip (see "Getting Around: By Bus," below).

By Train

Amtrak (www.amtrak.com; ☏ **800/872-7245**) does not currently offer direct rail service, although plans have been in the works for years to implement a high-speed railway between Los Angeles and Las Vegas. We've been hearing these reports for so long now, they just make us roll our eyes.

In the meantime, you can take the train to Los Angeles or Barstow, and Amtrak will get you to Las Vegas by bus, which takes 5 to 6 hours depending on traffic.

GETTING AROUND

It isn't too hard to navigate your way around Vegas. But do remember: Thanks to huge hotel acreage, often very slow traffic, and lots and lots of people—like you—trying to explore, getting around takes a lot longer than you might think. Heck, it can take 15 to 20 minutes to get from your room to another part of your hotel! Always allow for plenty of time to get from point A to point B.

Getting into Town from the Airport

Getting to your hotel from the airport is a cinch. You can grab one of the roughly nine gajillion cabs that are lined up waiting for you (see "By Taxi," p. 264), summon your favorite ride-share service such as Lyft or Uber (designated pickup areas are in the parking garages of each terminal), or you can grab a shuttle bus. **Bell Transportation** (www.airportshuttlelasvegas.com; ☏ **800/274-7433**) runs 24-passenger minibuses daily (3:30am–1am) between the airport and all major Las Vegas hotels and motels. The cost is $7.50 per person each way to hotels on the Strip or around the Convention Center, and $8.50 to Downtown and other off-Strip properties (north of Sahara Ave. and west of I-15). Several other companies run similar ventures—just look for the signs for the shuttle bus queues, located just outside of the baggage-claim area. Buses from the airport leave every few minutes. When you want to check out of your hotel and head back to the airport, call the shuttle at least 2 hours in advance to be safe (though often you can just flag down one of the buses outside any major hotel).

Even less expensive are **Citizens Area Transit (CAT)** buses (www.rtcsnv.com/transit; ☏ **702/228-7433**). The no. 109 bus goes from the airport to the South Strip Transfer Terminal at Gillespie St. and Sunset Rd., where you can transfer to the Strip and Downtown Express (SDX) or Deuce line that runs along the Strip into Downtown. Alternately, the no. 108 bus departs from the airport and takes you Downtown. The fares for buses on Strip routes are $6 for adults for 2 hours or $8 for 24 hours. Other routes are $2 for a single ride. *Note:* You might have a long walk from the bus stop to the hotel entrance, even if the bus stop is right in front of your hotel. Shuttles and taxis can get right up to the entrance, so choose one of those if you're lugging lots of baggage.

If you have a large group with you, you might also try one of the limos that wait curbside at the airport and charge $45 to $65 for a trip to the Strip. The price may go up with additional passengers, so ask about the fee very carefully. The aforementioned Bell Transportation is one reputable company that operates limousines in addition to their fleet of shuttle buses (call in advance).

By Car

We used to recommend renting a car to explore further, but now that the hotels charge for parking, we've changed our tune. In 2016, MGM Resorts properties announced they would institute fees for both valet and self-parking, and most other Strip resorts followed suit. The fees go up incrementally depending on how long and at which property you're visiting stay (the max you'll pay overnight is $18). But hey, you still get your first hour free. The days of free valet are also gone, with most casinos now charging $13 to $24, and that's not including the $2 to $5 tip. But you're paying for convenience at this point. Valet usually fills up on busy nights and is restricted at some hotels to elite players' club members. To avoid a parking headache, leave your car where it is; or stay at one of the Strip properties where parking is still free (see p. 59).

Our REAL advice? If you plan to confine yourself to one part of the Strip (or one cruise down) or to Downtown, your feet will suffice. Ride-sharing is the way to go these days. The Strip is too spread out for walking (and Las Vegas is often too hot or too cold to make strolls pleasant); and public transportation is often ineffective in getting you where you want to go. But renting a car is still the way to go for exploration in more remote parts of the city, and especially if you want to do any side trips at your own pace.

You should note that places with addresses some 60 blocks east or west of the Strip are actually less than a 10-minute drive—provided there is no traffic.

But when is there no traffic? It's a rare occurrence. A general rule of thumb is to avoid driving on the Strip whenever you can and give yourself plenty of extra time during rush hour to get where you want to go (see p. 266 for some helpful tips on how to get around the worst of the traffic).

If you're visiting from abroad, note that insurance and taxes are almost never included in quoted rental-car rates in the U.S. Be sure to ask your rental agency about these. They can add a significant cost to your car rental.

At press time, in Nevada, the cost of gasoline is around $3.34 per gallon and tends to vary unpredictably. Taxes are already included in the printed price. One U.S. gallon equals 3.8 liters or .85 imperial gallons. Fill-up locations are known as gas or service stations. Las Vegas prices typically fall near the nationwide average. You can also check **www.gasbuddy.com** for recent costs.

RENTING A CAR

All the major car rental companies have outlets in Las Vegas, as do **E-Z Rent-A-Car** (www.e-zrentacar.com) and **Payless** (www.paylesscar.com).

Rental policies vary from company to company, but generally speaking, you must be at least 25 years of age with a major credit or debit card to rent a vehicle in Las Vegas. Some companies will rent to those between 21 and 24 but will usually charge extra ($20–$30 per day) and will require proof of insurance and a major credit card; also, they may restrict the type of vehicle you are allowed to rent (forget those zippy convertibles).

All the major car-rental companies are located at a consolidated facility at 7135 Gillespie St., just a block off Las Vegas Blvd. near Warm Springs Rd. and about 2½ miles from the airport. When you arrive, look for the signs for BUSES AND SHUTTLES in the baggage-claim area and follow them outside, where you'll find blue-and-white buses marked MCCARRAN RENT-A-CAR CENTER. It takes about 10 minutes to make the trip, although it's worth noting that the lines for buses and at the car-rental counters can be long—budget some extra time if you have somewhere to be right after you get to town.

The rental-car facility is modern and easily navigable, and just in case you resisted while at the airport, there are slot machines next to the rental counters as well. Welcome to Vegas!

When exiting the facility, take three right turns and you are on the Strip, about 2 miles south of Mandalay Bay.

Car-rental rates vary even more than airline fares. The price you pay depends on the size of the car, where and when you pick it up and drop it off, the length of the rental period, where and how far you drive it, whether you purchase insurance, and a host of other factors. Finding the answers, online or at the counter, to a few key questions could save you hundreds of dollars:

o **Are weekend rates lower than weekday rates?** In Vegas this is usually true, although holiday or special events weekends can be more costly. Ask if the rate is the same for pickup Friday morning, for instance, as it is for Thursday night.

o **Is a weekly rate cheaper than the daily rate?** Even if you need the car for only 4 days, it may be cheaper to keep it for 5.

o **Does the agency assess a drop-off charge if you don't return the car to the same location where you picked it up?** Is it cheaper to pick up the car at the airport than at a Downtown location?

o **Are special promotional rates available?** Terms change constantly, and reservations agents are notorious for not mentioning available discounts unless you ask.

o **Are discounts available for members of AARP, AAA, frequent-flier programs, or trade unions?** If you belong to any of these organizations, you may be eligible for discounts of up to 30%.

o **Are there additional fees?** In Las Vegas, expect to add about 35% to 40% on top of the rental fee, including a $1.60-per-day vehicle license fee, a $3.75-per-day facility fee, a 10% concession fee, and about 20% in taxes and state government surcharges. Ouch.

o **What is the cost of adding an additional driver's name to the contract?**

o **How many free miles are included in the price?** Free mileage is often negotiable, depending on the length of the rental.

Some companies offer "refueling packages," in which you pay for an entire tank of gas up front. The price is usually fairly competitive with local gas prices, but you don't get credit for any gas remaining in the tank; and because it is virtually impossible to use up every last bit of fuel before you return it, you will usually wind up paying more overall than you would if you just filled it up yourself. There are several gas stations within a few blocks of the car-rental center, including three at the intersection of Las Vegas Blvd. and Warm Springs Rd. You may pay a few extra pennies at them than you would at stations elsewhere in town, but in the long run it's still a better deal.

SURFING FOR SAVINGS ON RENTAL CARS

We find the best resource for renting cars is a site called **Autoslash.com**. Not only does it apply every coupon on the market to your rental, it also monitors your booking between the time you make it and when you pick up the car. If the price drops, it rebooks you at the lower rate. It is smart one-stop shopping for car rentals, and *always* beats the competition.

DEMYSTIFYING RENTAL-CAR INSURANCE

Before you drive off in a rental car, be sure you're insured. Hasty assumptions about your personal auto insurance or a rental agency's additional coverage could end up costing you tens of thousands of dollars—even if you are involved in an accident that was clearly the fault of another driver.

If you already hold a **private auto insurance** policy in the United States, you are most likely covered for loss of, or damage to, a rental car, and liability in case of injury to any other party involved in an accident. Be sure to find out whether you are covered in Vegas, whether your policy extends to all persons who will be driving the rental car, how much liability is covered in case an outside party is injured in an accident, and whether the type of vehicle you are renting is included under your contract. (Rental trucks, sport utility vehicles, and luxury vehicles may not be covered.)

Most **major credit cards** provide some degree of coverage as well—provided they were used to pay for the rental. Terms vary widely, however, so be sure to call your credit card company directly before you rent. If you don't have a private auto insurance policy, the credit card you use to rent a car may provide primary coverage if you decline the rental agency's insurance. This means that the credit card company will cover damage or theft of a rental car for the full cost of the vehicle. If you do have a private auto insurance policy, your credit card may provide secondary coverage—which basically covers your deductible. *Credit cards do not cover liability* or the cost of injury to an outside party and/or damage to an outside party's vehicle. If you do not hold an insurance policy, you may want to seriously consider purchasing additional liability insurance from your rental company. Be sure to check the terms, however: Some rental agencies cover liability only if the renter is not at fault; even then, the rental company's obligation varies from state to state. Also bear in mind that each credit card company has its own peculiarities; call your own credit card company for details before relying on a card for coverage.

DRIVE IN style

If the idea of tooling around Las Vegas in a pedestrian rent-a-box just doesn't sound appealing, you can always indulge your fantasies by going with something more exotic.

Las Vegas Exotic Car Rentals (www.vegasexoticrentals.com; © **866/871-1893** or 702/736-2592) has a fleet from makers such as Lamborghini, Bentley, Ferrari, and Lotus, plus classic American muscle cars like the Chevrolet Corvette. The company even features an Aston Martin, if you want to work out your inner James Bond while buzzing between casinos. Rates start at about $400 for 6 hours and go up from there—sometimes, way up. At press time, the Lamborghini Gallardo Spyder was $995 per day, or roughly what you'll pay for a week in a room at a nice Vegas hotel.

Speaking of cards, members of AAA should be sure to carry their membership ID card with them, which provides some of the benefits touted by the rental-car agencies at no additional cost.

The basic insurance coverage offered by most rental-car companies, known as the **Loss/Damage Waiver (LDW)** or **Collision Damage Waiver (CDW)**, can cost $20 per day or more. The former should cover everything, including the loss of income to the rental agency, should you get in an accident (normally not covered by your own insurance policy). It usually covers the full value of the vehicle, with no deductible, if an outside party causes an accident or other damage to the rental car. You will probably be covered in case of theft as well. Liability coverage varies, but the minimum is usually at least $15,000. If you are at fault in an accident, you will be covered for the full replacement value of the car—but not for liability. In Nevada, you can buy additional liability coverage for such cases. Most rental companies require a police report in order to process any claims you file, but your private insurer will not be notified of the accident. Check your own policies and credit cards before you shell out money on this extra insurance because you may already be covered.

It's worth noting that rental-car companies seem to be pushing the extra coverage especially hard these days. Doing your research on what types of coverage you do and do not need will allow you to smile politely and decline if it is appropriate. Don't let them pressure or scare you into spending extra money for items you don't need.

By Taxi

Because cabs line up in front of all major hotels, an easy way to get around town is by taxi. Cabs charge $3.50 at the meter drop and $2.76 per mile after that, plus an additional $2.00 fee for being picked up at the airport and time-based penalties if you get stuck in traffic. A taxi from the airport to the Strip will run you $15 to $20, from the airport to Downtown $18 to $25, and between the Strip and Downtown about $12 to $18. You can often save money by sharing a cab with someone going to the same destination (up to five people can ride for the same fare).

All this implies that you have gotten a driver who is honest. Long-hauling—the practice of taking people on a longer route to the destination to increase fares—is rampant in Las Vegas these days. A 2016 audit by the state found an estimated $47 million in overcharges, making Clark County one of the most expensive places in America to catch a cab.

The simplest way to avoid the long-way 'round is to always know where you are going and roughly how much it should cost to get there. Use the maps on your phone or online to gauge the distance and calculate the approximate fare or let a website like **taxifarefinder.com** do the math for you. When you get into the cab and state your destination, don't be afraid to add something like "that will cost about $20, right?" It puts the cabbie on notice that you are not a hapless tourist ready to be taken for a metaphorical ride.

If you suspect that you have been long-hauled, call the taxi company to complain and be sure to file a report with the Nevada Taxicab Authority at **taxi.nv.gov**.

Also be aware that in addition to various fuel surcharge fees, there's an additional $3 fee to pay with your credit card, which definitely adds up after a weekend of cab rides.

If you just can't find a taxi to hail and want to call one, try the following companies: **Desert Cab Company** (✆ **702/386-9102**), **Whittlesea Blue Cab** (✆ **702/384-6111**), or **Yellow/Checker Cab/Star Company** (✆ **702/873-2000**).

By Uber or Lyft

On-demand car service companies Uber and Lyft operate in Las Vegas. As in other cities, you can order either service via mobile app to come collect you and take you wherever you need. Rides are slightly cheaper than taxis, though price surging still happens on busy nights and will wipe out any savings. And because of traffic on the Strip, it will often take longer to snag a car from one of these services then it will to get a taxi (as they'll be parked outside every major hotel). An Uber or Lyft from the airport to the Strip will run you $11 to $19, from the airport to Downtown $21 to $38, and between the Strip and Downtown about $12 to $21. Hotels now have designated ride-share pickup areas, often near valet.

By Monorail

The 4-mile monorail route runs from the MGM Grand, at the southern end of the Strip, to the Sahara at the northern end, with stops at Paris/Bally's, the Flamingo, Harrah's, the Las Vegas Convention Center, and Westgate along the way. Note that some of the actual physical stops are not particularly close to their namesakes, so there can be an unexpected—and sometimes time-consuming—additional walk from the monorail stop to wherever you intended to go. Factor in this time accordingly.

TRAFFIC tips

Traffic in Las Vegas can be frustrating at times, especially near the Strip on evenings and weekends. Here are a few tips to help you get around the worst of it:

○ **Spaghetti Bowl:** The "Spaghetti Bowl" is what locals call the mess where I-15 intersects U.S. 95, but a construction overhaul completed in mid-2019 has improved it.

○ **Do D.I. Direct:** Most visitors seem to get a lot of mileage out of the Strip and I-15. But if you're checking out the local scene, you can bypass both of those, using Desert Inn Road, which is now one of the longest streets running from one side of the valley to the other. Plus, the 2-mile "Superarterial" section between Valley View and Paradise zips you nonstop over the interstate and under the Strip.

○ **Grin and Bear It:** Yes, there are ways to avoid traffic jams on the Strip. But at least these traffic jams are entertaining! If you have the time and patience, go ahead and take a ride along the Strip from Mandalay Bay to the Strat. The 4-mile drive might take an hour, but while you're grinding along, you'll see a sphinx, an active volcano, a water ballet, and some uniquely Vegas architecture.

○ **Rat Pack Back Doors:** Frank Sinatra Drive is a bypass road that runs parallel to the Strip from Russell Road north to Industrial. It's a great way to avoid the traffic jams and sneak in the back of hotels such as Mandalay Bay, Luxor, and Park MGM, and T-Mobile Arena. On the other side of I-15, a bunch of high-end condo developers talked the city into rechristening a big portion of Industrial Road as Dean Martin Drive. From near Downtown to Twain, Industrial is now called Sammy Davis Jr., Drive, and it lets you in the back entrances to Circus Circus, Treasure Island, and others. It's a terrific bypass to the Strip and I-15 congestion.

○ **Beltway Bypass:** The 53-mile 215 Beltway wraps three-quarters of the way around the valley, allowing easy access to the outskirts while bypassing the Resort Corridor.

These trains can accommodate more than 200 passengers (standing and sitting) and make the end-to-end run in about 15 minutes. They operate Monday from 7am until midnight, Tuesday through Thursday from 7am until 2am, and Friday through Sunday from 7am until 3am. Fares are $5 for a one-way ride, whether you ride from one end to the other or just to the next station; discounts are available for round-trips and multiride/multiday passes.

For more information, visit the Las Vegas Monorail website at **www.lvmonorail.com**.

By Bus

The Deuce and SDX (Strip to Downtown Express) buses operated by the **Regional Transportation Commission** (**RTC;** www.rtcsnv.com/transit; ℭ **702/228-7433**) are the primary public transportation on the Strip. The double-decker Deuce and double-carriage SDX run a route between the Downtown Transportation Center (at Casino Center Blvd. and Stewart Ave.) and a few miles beyond the southern end of the Strip. The fare is $6 for adults for 2 hours; an all-day pass is $8 and a 3-day pass is $20. There are no discounts for children or seniors. RTC buses run 24 hours a day and are wheelchair accessible. Exact change is required.

In late 2017, Las Vegas also launched its very own driverless shuttle—which crashed on the first day (it was the other driver's fault!). It's free, holds up to 12 passengers, cruises along at a maximum 27 mph, and only does a short loop through the Downtown area on Fremont Street between Las Vegas Boulevard and 8th Street. The tech company that created it assures that the shuttle is now safer than ever, so if you're feeling exceptionally curious as to how it works, and maybe even exceptionally lazy, it might be fun.

Although buses are certainly economical transportation choices, they are not the most efficient in terms of time or convenience. They run often but are usually very crowded and are not immune to the mind-numbing traffic that clogs the Strip at peak times. Patience is required.

There are also several **free transportation services,** courtesy of the casinos. A free monorail connects Mandalay Bay with Luxor and Excalibur; another connects Park MGM, Bellagio, and Crystals and Aria; and a free tram shuttles between the Mirage and Treasure Island. Given how far apart even neighboring hotels can be, thanks to their size, and how they seem even farther apart on really hot (and cold and windy) days, these are blessed additions.

[FastFACTS] LAS VEGAS

Area Codes The local area codes in Las Vegas are 702, 775 and 725. The full 10-digit phone number with area code must be dialed to complete the call.

Business Hours Casinos and most bars are open 24 hours a day; nightclubs are usually open only late at night into the early morning hours; and restaurant and attraction hours vary.

Cannabis Laws Count Nevada among the states where it's now legal to use recreational marijuana, except you might lack an actual place to smoke it. As of right now, the only place a person can legally smoke the pot they have legally purchased is in a private residence with the blinds drawn. You also cannot smoke pot anywhere you can consume alcohol, and most of the city's hotel rooms are non-smoking anyway, so that's out. Getting caught smoking in a vehicle might net you a DUI and a $600 fine. The solution: edibles. You'll find them for sale wherever buds are sold.

Customs Every visitor 21 years of age or older may bring in, free of duty, the following: (1) 1 liter of alcohol as a gift or for personal use; (2) 200 cigarettes, 100 cigars (but not from Cuba), or 3 pounds of smoking tobacco; and (3) $100 worth of gifts. These exemptions are offered to travelers who spend at least 72 hours in the United States and who have not claimed them within the preceding 6 months. It is forbidden to bring into the country almost any meat products (including canned, fresh, and dried-meat products, such as bouillon, soup mixes, and so forth). Generally, condiments, including vinegars, oils, pickled goods, spices, coffee, tea, and some cheeses and baked goods are permitted. Avoid rice products, as rice

267

can often harbor insects. Bringing fruits and vegetables is prohibited since they may harbor pests or disease. International visitors may carry in or out up to $10,000 in U.S. or foreign currency with no formalities; larger sums must be declared to U.S. Customs on entering or leaving, which includes filing form CM 4790. For details regarding U.S. Customs and Border Protection, consult your nearest U.S. embassy or consulate, or **U.S. Customs** (www.cbp.gov).

For information on what you're allowed to take home, contact your home country's Customs agency.

Disabled Travelers
On the one hand, Las Vegas is fairly well equipped for travelers with disabilities, with virtually every hotel having wheelchair-accessible rooms and ramps and other requirements. On the other hand, the distance between hotels (particularly on the Strip) makes a vehicle of some sort virtually mandatory for most people with disabilities, and it may be extremely strenuous and time-consuming to get from place to place (even within a single hotel) because of the crowds. Even if you don't intend to gamble, you still may have to go through the casino, and casinos can be quite difficult to maneuver in, particularly for a guest in a wheelchair. Casinos are usually crowded, and the machines and tables are often arranged close together, with chairs,

people, and such blocking easy access. You should also consider that it is often a long trek through larger hotels between the entrance and the room elevators (or, for that matter, anywhere in the hotel), and then add a crowded casino to the equation.

Doctors Hotels usually have lists of doctors, should you need one, or you can use the physician referral service at **Desert Springs Hospital** (www.desertsprings hospital.com; ✆ **702/733-8800**). Hours are Monday to Friday from 8am to 8pm and Saturday from 9am to 3pm except holidays. Also see "Hospitals," below.

Drinking Laws The legal age for purchase and consumption of alcoholic beverages is 21; proof of age is required and often requested at bars, nightclubs, and restaurants, so it's always a good idea to bring ID when you go out.

Beer, wine, and liquor are sold in all kinds of stores pretty much around the clock in Vegas; trust us, you won't have a hard time finding a drink in this town.

Do not carry open containers of alcohol in your car or any public area that isn't zoned for alcohol consumption, which includes the Strip and the Fremont Street Experience downtown. The police can fine you on the spot. And nothing will ruin your trip faster than getting a citation for DUI (driving under the influence), so don't even think

about driving while intoxicated.

While walking around on the Strip with an alcoholic beverage is generally safe (provided you're of age, of course), don't tempt fate by walking around with glass bottles. You'll see plenty of folks stumbling around with large, novelty-size yards and boots, but that doesn't give you an excuse to act like a total fool when out in public. If the drink you ordered in the hotel came in a glass, you can ask the bartender to transfer it to a plastic cup so you can take your roadie to go.

Electricity Like Canada, the United States uses 110–120 volts AC (60 cycles), compared to 220–240 volts AC (50 cycles) in most of Europe, Australia, and New Zealand. Downward converters that change 220–240 volts to 110–120 volts are difficult to find in the United States, so bring one.

Emergencies Dial ✆ **911** to contact the police or fire department, or to call for an ambulance.

Family Travel Family travel can be immensely rewarding, giving you new ways of seeing the world through smaller pairs of eyes. That said, Vegas is hardly an ideal place to bring the kids. For one thing, they're not allowed in casinos at all. Because most hotels are laid out so that you frequently must walk through their casinos to get to where you are going, you can see how this becomes a headache.

The Strip is often peppered with people distributing fliers and other information about adult entertainment options in the city. Sex is everywhere. Just walking down the Strip might give your kids an eyeful of items that you might prefer they avoid. (They don't call it "Sin City" for nothing!)

On top of everything else, there is a curfew law in Vegas: Kids younger than 18 are not permitted on the Strip without a parent after 9pm on weekends and holidays. In the rest of the county, minors can't be out without parents after 10pm on school nights and midnight on the weekends.

Although discounts are still an option at most smaller chain hotels and motels, the major casino-hotels on the Strip offer no discount for children staying in your room, so you may pay an additional fee ($10–$40 per person per night) to have them bunk with you. You'll definitely want to book a place with a pool. Some hotels also have enormous video arcades and other diversions.

Health By and large, Las Vegas is like most other major American cities in that the water is relatively clean, the air is relatively clear, and illness-bearing insects and animals are rare. However, in a city with this many people coming and going from all over the world, there are a couple of specific concerns worth noting:

o **Food Poisoning** Food preparation guidelines in Las Vegas are among the strictest in the world, but when you're dealing with the sheer volume that this city is, you're bound to run into trouble every now and then. All restaurants are required by law to display a health certificate and letter grade (A, B, or C) that indicate how well they did on their last Health Department inspection. An A grade doesn't mean you won't get food poisoning, but it does mean the staff does a better-than-average job in the kitchen.

o **Norovirus** Over the past few years, there have been a few outbreaks of norovirus at Las Vegas hotels. This virus, most commonly associated with cruise ships, is rarely serious but can turn your vacation into a very unpleasant experience of intestinal illness. Because it is spread by contact, you can protect yourself by washing your hands often, especially after touching all of those slot machines.

o **Sun Exposure** Las Vegas is in the middle of a desert, and the sun shines particularly bright here. Heat and sunstroke are dangers that all visitors should be concerned about, especially if you are considering spending any amount of time outdoors. Sunscreen (stick to a minimum SPF 30) is a must even if you are just traveling from one hotel to another, and you should always carry a bottle of water with you to stay hydrated even when temperatures are moderate. The low desert humidity means that your body must work harder to replenish moisture, so help it along with something other than a free cocktail in the casino.

Hospitals The closest full-service hospital to the Strip is **Sunrise Hospital,** 3186 Maryland Pkwy. (www.sunrisehospital.com; (C) **702/731-8000**), but for lesser emergencies, **Las Vegas Strip Urgent Care** (www.lasvegasstripurgent care.com; (C) **702/796-1116**) offers an on-call doc 24 hours a day who consults right in your hotel room. Additionally, most major hotels in Las Vegas can provide assistance in finding physicians and/or pharmacies that are well suited to your needs.

Insurance Traveler's insurance is not required for visiting Las Vegas, and whether it's right for you depends on your circumstances. For example, most Las Vegas travel arrangements that include hotels are refundable or cancelable up to the last moment, so insurance is probably not necessary. If, however, you have prepaid a nonrefundable package, then it could be worth considering insurance.

Internet & Wi-Fi   Most major hotels in Vegas offer wireless access as a part of their nightly resort fee, although some still require an additional fee that can run upward of $20 per day. Some hotels offer free, advertiser-supported Wi-Fi in public areas, meaning you won't have to pay to surf the Web when you're hanging out at the pool, but you'll have to put up with banner ads on your browser. In Las Vegas, you can find free Wi-Fi at most stand-alone McDonald's, Starbucks, and in the Fashion Show mall.

Most major airports have Internet kiosks that provide basic Web access for a per-minute fee that's usually higher than hotel prices. Check out copy shops, such as FedEx Office, which offer computer stations with fully loaded software (as well as Wi-Fi).

Legal Aid   While driving, if you are pulled over for a minor infraction (such as speeding), never attempt to pay the fine directly to a police officer; this could be construed as attempted bribery, a much more serious crime. Pay fines by mail or directly into the hands of the clerk of the court. If accused of a more serious offense, say and do nothing before consulting a lawyer. In the U.S., the burden is on the state to prove a person's guilt beyond a reasonable doubt, and everyone has the right to remain silent, whether he or she is suspected of a crime or actually arrested. Once arrested, a person can make one telephone call to a party of his or her choice. The international visitor should call his or her embassy or consulate.

LGBT Travelers   For such a licentious, permissive town, Las Vegas has its conservative side, and for a long time it was not the most gay-friendly city. But in the past decade the town has become one of the most inclusive and tolerant destinations, and in 2016 was even named one of the best cities for gay-friendly retirement. It *is* called Fabulous Las Vegas, after all. See listings for gay bars in chapter 8.

Mail   At press time, domestic postage rates were 35¢ for a postcard and 55¢ for a letter. For international mail, a first-class letter of up to 1 ounce or a postcard costs $1.15. For more information go to **www.usps.com**.

Always include a zip code when mailing items in the U.S. If you don't know a zip code, visit www.usps.com/zip4.

The most convenient post office to the Strip is immediately behind Circus Circus at 3100 S. Industrial Rd., between Sahara Ave. and Spring Mountain Rd. (© **800/275-8777**). It's open Monday through Friday from 8:30am to 5pm. You can also mail letters and packages at your hotel.

Mobile Phones   Hotel rooms and casinos are notoriously bad places to be if you want to chat with someone back home on your cellphone, but step outside and things usually improve dramatically. Note that if you can get a signal in a casino, don't try to use your phone while sitting at a gaming table—that's a big no-no.

Once you leave Las Vegas proper, you are in the wilds of the Nevada desert, so unless you are near a major byway (like I-15), expect to get very few, if any, bars on your phone.

Money & Costs
Because Las Vegas is a town built on the concept of separating you from your money, it should come as

THE VALUE OF THE U.S. DOLLAR VS. OTHER POPULAR CURRENCIES

US$	Aus$	Can$	Euro (€)	NZ$	UK£
1	A$1.42	C$1.35	€0.90	NZ$1.51	£0.78

WHAT THINGS COST IN LAS VEGAS	US$
Taxi from the airport to the Strip	15.00–25.00
Taxi from the airport to Downtown Las Vegas	18.00–27.00
One-way Las Vegas monorail ticket	5.00
All-day Deuce or SDX bus pass	8.00
Standard room at Bellagio, Fri–Sat	179.00–499.00
Standard room at MGM Grand, Fri–Sat	165.00–249.00
Standard room at Bally's, Fri–Sat	100.00–200.00
Dinner for two at Guy Savoy, prix fixe	770.00
Dinner for two at Nacho Daddy	45.00
Wynn Las Vegas buffet, weekend champagne brunch	35.00
Main Street Station Garden Court buffet champagne brunch	16.00
Ticket to Cirque du Soleil's O	99.00–295.00
Ticket to Mac King (comedy magic show)	36.00–47.00
Domestic beer at Light	10.00
Domestic beer at the Double Down Saloon	5.00

no surprise that gaining access to money is very easy—sometimes too easy. There are many ATMs; and check cashing, credit card–advance systems are omnipresent. Note that using any of these to access your money will cost you money; ATMs charge upward of $6 per transaction, and that's before whatever fees your bank will add.

Today few, if any, slots and other gaming machines now accept coins. All machines take bills in most denominations, and you get "change" in the form of a credit slip that appears when you cash out. You then take this slip to the nearest cashier's cage to exchange for actual money.

So, getting to your money isn't a problem. Keeping it may be.

Las Vegas has grown progressively more expensive, with the concept of a cheap Sin City vacation a distant memory. The average room rate on the Strip on weekends is over $200 a night, those formerly cheap buffets have been replaced by $40-a-person lavish spreads, and top-show tickets easily surpass $100 a head. Then there are the casinos, a money-losing proposition if there ever was one.

But there are Las Vegas vacations available for just about any budget. See chapter 4, "Where to Stay," and chapter 5, "Where to Eat," which break down your choices by cost.

Beware of hidden credit card fees while traveling. International visitors should check with their credit or debit card issuer to see what fees, if any, will be charged for transactions in the U.S.

Newspapers & Magazines The *Las Vegas Review-Journal*, the major daily periodical in the city, is now partnered with the *Las Vegas Sun*, its former newspaper rival. Both offer the latest news, weather, and information and can be valuable resources for coupons and up-to-the-minute show listings.

LVM is a local magazine usually available in-room, listing shows, restaurants, and more, and it often features discount offers to attractions.

Packing Most Las Vegas hotel rooms are fully stocked with basics—shampoo, conditioner, hand lotion, mouthwash, and in some cases things like sewing kits and cotton swabs. If you don't have allergy or skin sensitivity issues to contend with, you may want to consider leaving those types of sundry items at home. The same goes for your travel iron, as most rooms have a full-size iron and ironing board, or these items are available by request through housekeeping.

Comfortable walking shoes are a must for Las Vegas. Yes, your Jimmy Choo's will look fabulous for your night out at the party spots, but do you really want to navigate the crowds across a 100,000-square-foot casino in them?

Check the weather forecast before your trip for guidance, but packing a light sweater or jacket even during the summer months is not a bad idea. It gets windy in Las Vegas, and there can be a chill in the evenings. Many of the casinos and showrooms set the air-conditioning on "Siberia," so light layers are recommended.

If you are bringing your computer or other mobile devices, don't forget to bring your power cords and chargers.

Lastly, toss in a small flashlight. During an emergency, this could become invaluable in helping you navigate your way out of a 4,000-room hotel.

Police For non-emergencies, call ☎ **702/795-3111.** For emergencies, call ☎ **911.**

Safety The mass shooting in 2017, when a man opened fire from the 32nd floor of the Mandalay Bay into a music festival, killing 58 people and wounding nearly 500, brought new safety concerns to the Strip. Almost all the hotels revamped their security measures. Some are obvious, like added security at elevators and large-scale events, and some are a little more aggressive, like doing welfare checks on rooms that have had their "Do Not Disturb" sign hanging on the door for two consecutive days.

On your end, always take a minute to know where your exits are, and the rule "if you see something, say something" should trump "what happens here stays here."

One also must ward against petty crime. With all that cash floating around town, pickpockets and thieves are predictably active. At gaming tables and slot machines, men should keep wallets well concealed and out of the reach of pickpockets, and women should keep handbags in plain sight (on laps). If you win a big jackpot, ask the slot attendant to cut you a check rather than give you cash. Outside the casinos, popular spots for pickpockets and thieves are restaurants and outdoor shows, such as the volcano at the Mirage or the fountains at Bellagio. Stay alert. Unless your hotel room has an in-room safe, check your

valuables into a safe-deposit box at the front desk.

When in your room, be sure to always lock and bolt the door, and only open it to hotel employees whom you are expecting (such as room service).

A special safety concern for women (and even men occasionally) centers on behavior at nightclubs. Do not ever accept a drink from a stranger, no matter how handsome he is, and keep your cocktail in your hand at all times, even while on the dance floor. Instances of people getting something slipped into their drink are rare, but they have happened, so it's best to take precautions.

Senior Travel One of the benefits of age is that travel to most destinations often costs less—but that's rarely true in Las Vegas. Discounts at hotels, shows, restaurants, and recreation are rare. About the only discounts offered to seniors are at some of the local attractions, which will give a few bucks off to those over 62 or 65 (see chapter 6).

Members of **AARP** (www.aarp.org; ☎ **888/687-2277**) get discounts on hotels, airfares, and car rentals. But be sure to check them against the discount websites we recommend earlier in the book, because sometimes these "special discounts" aren't as good as the normal ones.

The U.S. National Park Service (NPS) offers an **America the Beautiful— National Park and Federal**

Recreational Lands Pass— Senior Pass. You'll find it useful for some of the day trips covered in chapter 9. The pass gives U.S. residents 62 years or older lifetime entrance to all properties administered by the National Park Service— national parks, monuments, historic sites, recreation areas, and national wildlife refuges—for a one-time processing fee of $80. An annual Senior Pass is $20. The pass must be purchased in person at any NPS facility that charges an entrance fee. Besides free entry, the America the Beautiful Senior Pass also offers a 50% discount on some federal-use fees charged for such facilities as camping. For more info, go to **www.nps.gov/find apark/passes.htm**.

Smoking Increasingly strict smoking laws prohibit puffing virtually everywhere indoors except in designated hotel rooms, nightclubs, bars, and on the casino floor. Hotels still have dedicated floors for smokers and nonsmokers. There is a significant charge, approximately $300, for smoking anything in a nonsmoking room.

Taxes The United States has no value-added tax (VAT) or other indirect tax at the national level. Every state, county, and city may levy its own local tax on all purchases, including hotel and restaurant checks and airline tickets. These taxes will not appear on price tags but are added when you make a purchase.

The sales tax in Las Vegas is 8.25% and is added to food and drink bills. Hotel rooms both on the Strip and Downtown come with a 13.35% tax. Taxes are also added to show tickets.

Telephones Generally, Vegas hotel surcharges on long-distance and local calls are astronomical. You are often charged even for making a toll-free or phone-card call. You're better off using your **cellphone.** Most hotels resort fees cover local calls. The fee can range from $3 to $25 per day.

Most long-distance and international calls can be dialed directly from any phone. **To make calls within the United States and to Canada,** dial 1 followed by the area code and the seven-digit number. **For other international calls,** dial 011 followed by the country code, city code, and the number.

Calls to area codes **800, 888, 877, 866,** and **855** are toll-free.

For **reversed-charge or collect calls,** and for person-to-person calls, dial the number 0, then the area code and number; an operator will come on the line, and you should specify whether you are calling collect, person-to-person, or both. If your operator-assisted call is international, ask for the overseas operator.

For **directory assistance** ("Information"), dial 411 for local numbers and national numbers in the U.S. and Canada. For dedicated long-distance information, dial 1, then the appropriate area code plus 555-1212.

Time The continental United States is divided into **four time zones:** Eastern Standard Time (EST), Central Standard Time (CST), Mountain Standard Time (MST), and Pacific Standard Time (PST). Alaska and Hawaii have their own zones. Las Vegas is in the Pacific Time zone, 8 hours behind Greenwich Mean Time (GMT), 3 hours behind the East Coast, and 2 behind the Midwest. For example, when it's 9am in Las Vegas (PST), it's 7am in Honolulu (Hawaii Standard Time), 10am in Denver (MST), 11am in Chicago (CST), noon in New York City (EST), 5pm in London (GMT), and 2am the next day in Sydney.

Daylight saving time (summer time) is in effect from 1am on the second Sunday in March to 1am on the first Sunday in November, except in Arizona, Hawaii, the U.S. Virgin Islands, and Puerto Rico. Daylight saving time moves the clock 1 hour ahead of standard time.

Tipping Las Vegas is a hospitality-driven economy, meaning many people you encounter depend on tips for their livelihood. This doesn't necessarily mean you *need* to tip more than you would anywhere else, but average tips in other cities can be viewed as somewhat stingy.

In the casinos, it's common to tip **cocktail waitresses** $1 to $2 per drink and to tip **dealers** 5% of any big wins.

In hotels, tip **bellhops** at least $1 per bag ($2–$3 if you have a lot of luggage) and tip the **chamber staff** $3 to $5 per day (more if you've left a big mess to clean up). Tip the **doorman** or **concierge** only if he or she has provided you with some specific service (for example, calling a cab or obtaining theater tickets). Tip the **valet-parking attendant** $2 to $5 every time you get your car.

In restaurants, bars, and nightclubs, tip **service staff** and **bartenders** 15% to 20% of the check, and tip **checkroom attendants** $1 per garment.

As for other service personnel, tip **cabdrivers** 15% of the fare; tip **skycaps** at airports at least $1 per bag ($2–$3 if you have a lot of luggage); and tip **hairdressers** and **barbers** 15% to 20%.

Toilets In Las Vegas, you are almost always near a bathroom if you are in one of the tourist areas, with the casinos being the most obvious example. All have multiple facilities, and they are usually among the cleanest you'll find in any public location. Many hotel restaurants do not have their own restrooms, meaning you may need to go into the casino to find the nearest one.

Large hotels and fast-food restaurants are often the best bet for clean facilities. Restaurants and bars in resorts or heavily visited areas may reserve their restrooms for patrons.

Visitor Information

The Las Vegas Convention and Visitors Authority (www.visitlasvegas.com; (C) **877/ 847-4858** or 702/892-7575) provides information, hotel reservation assistance, show guides, convention calendars, and more.

Other popular Las Vegas travel websites include www.vegas.com, www.vegas4visitors.com, and www.cheapovegas.com.

Many hotels have their own mobile apps with special information and offers.

Water Ongoing drought conditions mean water is a concern in terms of its long-term availability, but for now it is plentiful from faucets, drinking fountains, and endless bottles of the stuff. As in most of the United States, the drinking water is considered safe, and there have been no reported instances of sickness from it. Bottles of water are often free in the casinos.

Women Travelers

Thanks to the crowds, Las Vegas is as safe as any other big city for a woman traveling alone. A woman on her own should, of course, take the usual precautions and should be wary of hustlers and drunken businessmen. Many of the big hotels have security guards stationed at the elevators at night to prevent anyone other than guests from going up to the room floors. If you're anxious, ask a security guard to escort you to your room. *Always* double-lock your door *and* deadbolt it.

Index

See also Accommodations and Restaurant Indexes.

General Index

1 OAK, 230
18b Arts District, 20, 25, 165
1900s, early, 29
1940s, 26–30
1950s, 30
1960s, 31
1970s, 31–33
1980s, 33
1990s, 34
2000s, 34–36
2020 convention dates, 38

A

Absinthe, 9, 19, 206
Accommodations, *See also*
  Accommodations Index
  best hotels, 5–6
  chains, 83
  deals, 42–43
  discounts, 44
  Downtown, 73–79
  extras, hidden, 43
  family-friendly, 54
  Lake Las Vegas, 91
  locals' hotels, 86–87
  luxury, 43–44
  Mid-Strip, 56–68
  North & West of Strip, 91–93
  North Strip, 68–73
  off the Strip, 80–88
  online bookings, 42, 44
  pet-friendly, 53
  prices, 41–42
  resort fees, 42–43, 50
  social media, 42
  South & East of Strip, 88–91
  South Strip, 45–56
  suites, 43
Aces of Comedy, 220
Adapting, 28–29
Adventuredome, 153, 159
Afternoon activities
  foodies' Las Vegas, 23
  girls' getaway, 19
  guys' getaway, 17–18
  iconic Las Vegas, 11
  over-the-top Las Vegas, 15–16
  unlikely/unusual Las Vegas, 21
Air tours, 15
Air travel, 258–259
Alibi, 220
American cuisine, 94
Amtrak, 260
Angel Park Golf Club, 187
Antiques, 7
Area codes, 267
Aria Fine Art Collection, 153
Aria Las Vegas, 8, 182

Arroyo Golf Club, 187
Artifice, 230
The Arts Factory, 153, 162
Asian cuisine, 94
Atomic Liquors, 225–226
Autoslash.com, 263
AVN Adult Entertainment Expo, 38

B

Baccarat, 175–176
Bachelorette party entertainment, 223
Backstage Bar & Billiards, 226
Bali Hai Golf Club, 187
Barbecue, 94
Bare, 234
The Bar at Times Square, 229
Bars, 219–229
  Downtown, 225–228
  Mid-Strip, 220–225
  North Strip, 225
  off the Strip, 228–229
  piano bars, 229
  South Strip, 220
Bear's Best Las Vegas, 187
Beauty Bar, 226
Beer Park, 220–222
Beerhaus, 222
Bell Transportation, 260
Bellagio Conservatory, 6, 152, 160
Bellagio Fountains, 6, 14, 16, 152, 160
Bellagio Gallery of Fine Art, 153, 156
Big Apple Coaster & Arcade, 153–154
Biking, 184, 253
Bistro, 94
Blackjack, 176
Blue Man Group, 206–208
Boating, 184
Bodies. . . The Exhibition, 153–154
Bonanza Gift and Souvenir Shop, 15, 200–201
Bonnie Springs Ranch, 253
Bonus Poker, 183
Book of Mormon, 7
The Boulevard, 202–203
Boulevard Pool, 214
Bound, 222
Bowling, 185
Brad Garrett's Comedy Club, 208, 220
Broadway shows, 7
Brooklyn Bowl, 152, 185, 214
Buffets, 14, 94–95, 115, 144–151
Burgers, 95
Bus travel, 259–260, 266–267
Business hours, 267

C

Cab drivers, 239
Cabaret Theater, 218

Caesers Palace, 8, 182
Calendar of Events, 38–40
Calico Basin, 252
Camping, 255
Cannabition Cannabis Museum, 2, 21, 153, 162
Canyon Ranch SpaClub, 188
Car rentals, 261–264
Car travel, 259, 261–264
Carlo's Bakery, 22
Carnival Court, 237
Carrot Top, 220
Cascata, 15
Casinos
  Aria Las Vegas, 182
  best, 8
  Caesars Palace, 182
  Cosmopolitan of Las Vegas, 182
  Downtown Grand, 183
  Golden Nugget, 183
  Green Valley Ranch, 183
  hopping, 1–2
  Luxor Las Vegas, 183
  New York-New York, 183
  Paris Las Vegas, 183
  Red Rock Resort, 183
  sports books, 182–183
  Wynn Las Vegas/Encore Las Vegas, 183
Chains, hotels, 83
Chamber of Commerce, 24, 38
The Chandelier, 223
Chapel of the Bells, 191
Chapel of the Flowers, 191–192
Chateau, 230–231
Cheetah's, 239
Chelsea, 214
Chinese cuisine, 95
Chippendales, 19, 223
Circus Circus Midway, 8, 152, 160
Cirque du Soleil, 8, 14, 16, 208
Citizens Area Transit (CAT), 260
City layout, 24
Civillico, Jeff, 9, 21
Clark County Marriage License Bureau, 190
Clark County Museum, 153, 169
Clubs, 229–238
  crowds, 231
  dance, 230–236
  hotel lounges, 237–238
  poolside, 234–235
  strip, 239–241
  ultralounges, 236–237
Colosseum, 214
Comedy, 220
Commonwealth, 18, 22, 226
Consumer Electronics Show, 38
Continental cuisine, 95
Convention dates, 2020, 38
Cosmopolitan of Las Vegas, 8, 182, 198
Costs, 270–271
Craps, 177
Currencies, 270
Customs, 267

D

D Las Vegas, 8
Dance clubs, 230–236
David Copperfield, 212–213
Daylight Beach Club, 17, 234
Deals, accommodations, 42–43
Delis, 95
Deuces Wild, 183
Dig This!, 152, 166–167
Diners, 95
Dining, see also **Restaurants Index**
    American cuisine, 94
    Asian cuisine, 94
    barbecue, 94
    bistro, 94
    buffets, 14, 94–95, 115, 144–151
    burgers, 95
    Chinese cuisine, 95
    continental cuisine, 95
    delis, 95
    diners, 95
    discounts, 103, 108
    Downtown, 128–134, 150
    eclectic cuisine, 95
    food courts, 105, 115
    food halls, 95
    French cuisine, 95
    German cuisine, 95
    half-price, 103
    health inspections, 148
    Irish cuisine, 95
    Italian cuisine, 95
    Japanese cuisine, 95
    kid-friendly, 115
    Mexican/Latin cuisine, 95
    Mid-Strip, 108–125, 147–149
    New American cuisine, 95
    North & West of Strip, 142–144
    North Strip, 125–128, 150
    off the Strip, 135–142, 150–151
    pizza, 95
    pubs, 95
    reservations, 98
    sandwiches, 95
    seafood, 96
    soul food, 96
    South Strip, 96–108, 145–146
    Southwestern cuisine, 96
    Spanish cuisine, 96
    steaks, 96
    Thai cuisine, 96
    themes, 106, 115
    Venezuelan cuisine, 96
Dino's Lounge, 225
Disabled travelers, 268
Discounts
    accommodations, 44
    dining, 103, 108
**Discovery Children's Museum,
153, 162–163**
Doctors, 268
Don't Tell Mama, 229
The Dorsey, 224
Double Down Saloon, 226–227
Downtown, 2, 25–26
    accommodations, 73–79
    attractions, 162–166
    bars, 225–228
    buffet, 150

    dining, 128–134
    resurgence, 165
    shopping, 201–202
**Downtown Cocktail Room, 22,
236**
**Downtown Container Park, 153,
165, 201**
Downtown Grand, 8, 183
Drai's, 232
Drinking laws, 268
Drives, 9

E

Early 1900s, 29
Eastside Cannery, 8
Eclectic cuisine, 95
EDO Gastro Tapas & Wine, 7
**Eiffel Tower Experience, 153,
156–157, 219**
Eiffel Tower Light Show, 152, 160
Electric Daisy Carnival, 39
Electricity, 268
Ellis Island, 21
Elvis impersonator, 191
Emergencies, 268
Encore Beach Club, 17, 235
**Entertainment complexes,
152–153**
Entertainment, see **Performing
Arts**
Ethel M Chocolates, 22, 153, 169
Excalibur, 11
Exhibits, 153
E-Z-Rent-A-Car, 261

F

Family-friendly
    accommodations, 54
    entertainment, 213
    travel, 268–269
Fantasy, 18
Fashion Show, 15, 201
**Fast Lap Indoor Kart Racing, 152,
167**
**First Friday Las Vegas, 7, 23, 25,
165**
Fishing, 184
Food courts, 105, 115
Food halls, 95
Food poisoning, 269
Forum Shops, 11, 15, 19, 198
Fountains, Bellagio, 6, 14, 16
Four Queens, 8
Franklin, 220
Free things, 6–7, 160–161
Fremont Country Club, 215
**Fremont East Entertainment
District, 22, 25, 165**
**Fremont Street Experience, 6, 14,
25, 152–153, 163, 165**
French cuisine, 95
Funhog Ranch, 238

G

Galleries, 153
**Gamblers General Store/
Gambler's Book Club, 201–202**

Gambling, 174–184
    Baccarat, 175–176
    Blackjack, 176
    Bonus Poker, 183
    Craps, 177
    Deuces Wild, 183
    Jacks or Better, 183
    lessons, 175
    Let It Ride, 178–179
    Pai Gow, 178
    poker, 177–180
    progressive slots, 181
    Roulette, 180
    slots, 180–182
    Texas Hold 'Em, 178
    Three-Card Poker, 179–180
    video poker, 183–184
Garon, Jesse, 191
Gay and lesbian nightlife, 238
German cuisine, 95
Gilley's, 17, 237–238
Girls' getaway, 19–20, 223, 240
Glitter Gulch; see **Downtown**
Gold & Silver Pawn Shop, 203
Gold Coast Bowling Center, 185
Gold Spike, 18
Golden Nugget, 8, 183
Golf, 9, 186–188
**Graceland Wedding Chapel,
192–193**
Grand Bazaar Shops, 15, 199
**Grand Canal Shoppes, 2, 11, 15,
19, 199**
Grand Canyon, 254–255
Gray Line, 174, 243
**Green Valley Ranch Resort, 7–8,
183**
Greyhound, 259
The Griffin, 227
Guinness World Records, 2
Guys' getaway, 17–18
Gyms, 184

H

Hakkasan Las Vegas, 14, 35, 232
Half-price dining, 103
Halloween, 40
Hamilton, **7**
The Hangover, **17**
Health, 269
**Health inspections, restaurants,
148**
Help of Southern Nevada, 16
Herbs & Rye, 227
**Hershey's Chocolate World, 53,
195–196**
Hibiscus Spa, 188–189
High Roller, 2, 16, 192
**High Roller Observation Wheel,
153, 157**
Hiking, 184, 250, 252, 256
Historic Las Vegas, 29–36
    1900s, early, 29
    1940s, 26–30
    1950s, 30
    1960s, 31
    1970s, 31–33

1980s, 33
1990s, 34
2000s, 34–36
Hogs & Heifers Saloon, 227
Holidays, 38
Hoover Dam, 9, 242–247
Horseback riding, 186
Hospitals, 269
Hotels, *see also* Accommodations
Index
best, 5–6
chains, 83
deals, 42–43
discounts, 44
Downtown, 73–79
extras, hidden, 43
family-friendly, 54
Lake Las Vegas, 91
locals' hotels, 86–87
luxury, 43–44
Mid-Strip, 56–68
North & West of Strip, 91–93
North Strip, 68–73
off the Strip, 80–88
online bookings, 42, 44
pet-friendly, 53
prices, 41–42
resort fees, 42–43, 50
social media, 42
South & East of Strip, 88–91
South Strip, 45–56
suites, 43
Hotel lounges, 237–238
House of Blues, 214
Human Nature (*Jukebox*), 9,
212–213

I
Ice skating, 186
Iconic Las Vegas, 10–14, 152
Insanity, 18
Insurance, 269–270
International Builders Show, 38
Internet, 270
Int'l Esthetics Cosmetic and Spa
Conference, 38
Intrigue, 18, 35, 232
Irish cuisine, 95
Italian cuisine, 95

J
Jabbawockeez, 213
Jacks or Better, 183
Japanese cuisine, 95
Jewel, 18
Jimmy Kimmel's Comedy Club,
213
Joint, 214
Jukebox (Human Nature), 9,
212–213

K
KÀ, Cirque du Soleil, 8, 14, 16,
208–209, 213
Kid-friendly dining, 115
KISS by Monster Mini Golf, 152,
167

L
Lady Gaga, 16, 211
Lagasse's Stadium, 18
Lake Las Vegas, 91
Lake Mead National Recreation
Area, 242–247
boating, 246–247
camping, 247
canoeing, 247
cruises, 247
fishing, 246–247
hiking, 247
Larry Flynt's Hustler Club, 239
240
Las Vegas Convention and Visitors
Authority, 24, 38, 42
Las Vegas Exotic Car Rentals, 264
Las Vegas Market Furniture Show,
38
Las Vegas Metro Chamber of
Commerce, 24, 38
Las Vegas Mini Gran Prix, 152,
171
Las Vegas Motor Speedway, 9,
17, 39, 152, 172
Las Vegas National Golf Club,
187–188
Las Vegas Natural History
Museum, 153, 163
Las Vegas Premium Outlets
North, 19, 202
Las Vegas Premium Outlets South,
204
Las Vegas Strip Urgent Care, 269
Las Vegas Weekly, 229
Laugh Factory, 214, 220
Le Rêve, 214–216
Lee Canyon, 256
Legal aid, 270
Legends in Concert, 216
Lessons, gambling, 175
Let It Ride, 178–179
LGBTQ
nightlife, 238
travel, 270
Life Is Beautiful Festival, 40
Lifestyle, 28–29
Light, 14, 16, 20, 233
LINQ Promenade, 15, 199–200
Lion Habitat Ranch, 153, 170
Liquid, 235
Little Church of the West, 193
Little White Wedding Chapel, 193
Locals, 7, 86–87
Love, Cirque du Soleil, 208–209,
213
Luxor, 10, 183
Luxury accommodations, 43–44
Lyft, 265

M
Mac King, 9, 21, 213, 216
Madame Tussauds Las Vegas, 153,
157–158
Magazines, 271
Magic Mike Live, 223
Mail, 270

Main Street Arts District, 22
Mandalay Bay Events Center, 214
Mandalay Bay, 9
March Madness, 39
Marquee Dayclub, 235
Marquee, 16, 18, 35, 233
Marriage, 190–194
Maverick Helicopters, 15
McCarran International Airport,
258
Megabus, 259
Mexican/Latin cuisine, 95
MGM Grand Garden Events
Arena, 215
Michael Jackson ONE, Cirque du
Soleil, 8, 14, 209–210
Mid-Strip, 25
accommodations, 56–68
attractions, 156–159
bars, 220–225
buffets, 147–149
dining, 108–125
shopping, 198–200
Miracle Mile Shops, 15, 19, 200
Mirage Volcano, 6, 14, 152, 160
Mirage, 9
Mizuya Lounge, 238
M&M's World, 22, 196
Mob Museum, 11, 152–153,
163–164, 192
Mob, 32
Mobile phones, 270
Modern Las Vegas, 27–29
Money, 270–271
Monorail, 265–266
Morning activities
foodies' Las Vegas, 22
girls' getaway, 19
guys' getaway, 17
iconic Las Vegas, 10–11
over-the-top Las Vegas, 14–15
unlikely/unusual Las Vegas,
20–21
Mount Charleston, 9, 184, 186,
253–257
Museums, 2, 153
Music clubs, 229–238
crowds, 231
dance, 230–236
hotel lounges, 237–238
poolside, 234–235
ultralounges, 236–237
Mystère, Cirque du Soleil, 8, 14,
208, 210–211, 213

N
NASCAR, 39
National Association of
Broadcasters, 38
National Atomic Testing Museum,
2, 11, 21, 153, 167–168
National Finals Rodeo, 40
National Hardware Show, 38
National Museum of Organized
Crime and Law Enforcement,
11
Neighborhoods, 25–26

GENERAL INDEX

Neon Museum, 2, 152–153, 165–166, 192
Nevada Commission on Tourism, 24
Nevada State Museum, 153, 172
New American cuisine, 95
New Year's Eve, 40
New York–New York, 10, 183
Newspapers, 271
NFR Cowboy Christmas Gift Show, 40
Night activities; see also Casinos, Clubs, Comedy, Performing arts
    foodies' Las Vegas, 23–24
    girls' getaway, 19–20
    guys' getaway, 18
    iconic Las Vegas, 11–14
    over-the-top Las Vegas, 16–17
    unlikely/unusual Las Vegas, 21–22
Norovirus, 269
North Strip, 25
    accommodations, 68–73
    attractions, 159–162
    bars, 225
    buffets, 150
    dining, 125–128
    shopping, 200–201
North & West of Strip
    accommodations, 91–93
    attractions, 171–174
    dining, 142–144

O

O, Cirque du Soleil, 14, 16, 211–212
Off the Strip, 26
    accommodations, 80–88
    attractions, 166–168
    bars, 228–229
    buffets, 150–151
    dining, 135–142
    shopping, 202–203
Omnia, 20, 233–234
Online bookings, 42, 44
On The Record, 234
Orleans, 8
Orleans Bowling Center, 185
Orleans Showroom, 215
O'Sheas, 224
Outdoor activities, 9, 184–186
Over-the-Top itineraries, 14–16

P

Packing, 271–272
Pai Gow, 178
Palace Station, 8
The Palomino, 240
Papillon Tours, 15, 254
Paris Las Vegas, 183
The Park, 153, 158
Park on Fremont, 227–228
Park Theater, 215
Parking, 59
Passion Pit, 18
Patisserie, 23

Pawn Stars, 203
Payless, 261
Pearl Theater, 215
Penn & Teller, 9, 216–217
Penny slots, 7
Peppermill Fireside Lounge, 17, 24, 225
Performing arts, 205–219
    Absinthe, 206
    Blue Man Group, 206–208
    Boulevard Pool, 214
    Brad Garrett's Comedy Club, 208
    Brooklyn Bowl, 214
    Cabaret Theater, 218
    Chelsea, 214
    Cirque du Soleil, 208
    Colosseum, 214
    David Copperfield, 212–213
    family-friendly, 213
    Fremont Country Club, 215
    House of Blues, 214
    Human Nature: Jukebox, 212–213
    Jabbawockeez, 213
    Jimmy Kimmel's Comedy Club, 213
    Joint, 214
    KÀ, Cirque du Soleil, 208–209, 213
    Lady Gaga, 211
    Laugh Factory, 214
    Legends in Concert, 216
    Le Rêve, 214–216
    Love, Cirque du Soleil, 208–209, 213
    Mac King, 213, 216
    Mandalay Bay Events Center, 214
    MGM Grand Garden Events Arena, 215
    Michael Jackson ONE, Cirque du Soleil, 209–210
    Mystère, Cirque du Soleil, 208, 210–211, 213
    O, Cirque du Soleil, 211–212
    Orleans Showroom, 215
    Park Theater, 215
    Pearl Theater, 215
    Penn & Teller, 216–217
    Piff the Magic Dragon, 217–218
    Reba, Brooks & Dunn: Together in Vegas, 211
    Reynolds Hall, 218
    Sam Boyd Stadium, 215
    Smith Center for the Performing Arts, 215, 218
    Stewart, Rod, 210
    Sting, 210
    Terry Fator, 218
    Thomas and Mack Center, 215
    Tix4Tonight, 206
    T-Mobile Arena, 215
    Tournament of Kings, 213, 219
    Vegas! The Show, 219
    venues, 214–215

V: The Ultimate Variety Show, 219
Zumanity, Cirque du Soleil, 212
Pet-friendly accommodations, 53
Petroglyphs, 249
Piano bars, 229
Piff the Magic Dragon, 217–218
Pinball Hall of Fame, 7, 21, 153, 170
Pine Creek Canyon, 252
Piranha Las Vegas, 20, 238
Pizza, 95
Poker, 177–180
Pole Position Raceway, 153, 172–173
Police, 272
Pools, 9, 66
Poolside clubs, 234–235
Progressive slots, 181
Pubs, 95

Q

Q Life, 238
Qua Baths & Spa, 189

R

Rat Pack, 31
Reality TV, 203
Reba, Brooks & Dunn: Together in Vegas, 211
Red Rock Adventures, 17
Red Rock Canyon, 2, 184, 186, 249–253
Red Rock Lanes, 185
Red Rock Resort, 7–8, 183, 253
Red Rock Resort Adventure Spa, 189
Red Rock scenic drive, 9
Reservations, dining, 98
Resort fees, 42–43, 50
Resort on Mount Charleston, 256–257
Restaurants, see also Restaurants Index
    best, 4–5
    American cuisine, 94
    Asian cuisine, 94
    barbecue, 94
    bistro, 94
    buffets, 14, 94–95, 115, 144–151
    burgers, 95
    Chinese cuisine, 95
    continental cuisine, 95
    delis, 95
    diners, 95
    discounts, 103, 108
    Downtown, 128–134, 150
    eclectic cuisine, 95
    food courts, 105, 115
    food halls, 95
    French cuisine, 95
    German cuisine, 95
    half-price, 103
    health inspections, 148
    Irish cuisine, 95
    Italian cuisine, 95

Japanese cuisine, 95
kid-friendly, 115
Mexican/Latin cuisine, 95
Mid-Strip, 108–125, 147–149
New American cuisine, 95
North & West of Strip, 142–144
North Strip, 125–128, 150
off the Strip, 135–142, 150–151
pizza, 95
pubs, 95
reservations, 98
sandwiches, 95
seafood, 96
soul food, 96
South Strip, 96–108, 145–146
Southwestern cuisine, 96
Spanish cuisine, 96
steaks, 96
Thai cuisine, 96
themes, 106, 115
Venezuelan cuisine, 96
Retreats, 9
Retro Vegas, 7, 202
Reynolds Hall, 218
Richard Petty Driving Experience, 17
Rick's Restorations, 203
Rides, 153
Rio Secco Golf Club, 188
Rock climbing, 256
Rosina, 20, 224
Roulette, 180

S

Safety, 272
Sam Boyd Stadium, 39, 215
Sam's Town Bowling Center, 185
The Sand Dollar Lounge, 228–229
Sandwiches, 95
Santa Fe Station Bowling Center, 185
Sapphire Gentleman's Club, 17, 240
Seafood, 96
SEMA/Automotive Aftermarket Industry Week, 38
Senior travel, 272–273
Shark Reef at Mandalay Bay, 153–156
Shelby American Heritage Center, 153, 170–171
Shooting, Hunting & Outdoor Trade Show, 38
Shopping, 2, 19, 195–204
Downtown, 201–202
Mid-Strip, 198–200
North Strip, 200–201
off the Strip, 202–203
South & East of Strip, 204
South Strip, 195–197
Shops at Crystals, 15, 19, 196
Shows, 2, 7–9
best, 8–9
Broadway, 7
Siegfried & Roy's Secret Garden & Dolphin Habitat, 153, 158–159

Skiing, 186
SkyJump, 18
SkyZone, 153, 171
Sleeping in, 2
Slots, 7, 180–182
SlotZilla, 2, 18, 153, 166
Smith Center for the Performing Arts, 7, 21–22, 153, 215, 218
Smoking, 273
Snowboarding, 186
Snow sports, 256
SoBe Ice Arena, 186
Social media, 42
Soul food, 96
South & East of Strip
accommodations, 88–91
attractions, 169–171
shopping, 204
South Point Bowling Center, 185
South Rim, Grand Canyon, 254–255
South Strip, 25
accommodations, 45–56
attractions, 153–156
bars, 220
buffets, 145–146
dining, 96–108
discount packages, 154
shopping, 195–197
Southern Nevada Health District, 148
Southwestern cuisine, 96
Spas, 19, 188–190
Spa Aquae, 189
Spa at Bellagio, 189
Spa at Encore, 15, 189
Spa at Park MGM, 190
Spanish cuisine, 96
Spearmint Rhino, 240–241
Special Memory Wedding Chapel, 193
SpeedVegas, 153, 168
Sports books, 18, 182–183
Spring Mountain Ranch State Park, 250
Springs Preserve, 20, 153, 173
Sprinkles, 23
Steaks, 96
Stefani, Gwen, 16
Stewart, Rod, 210
Sting, 210
Stratosphere Tower & Thrill Rides, 2, 18, 152–153, 160–162, 192, 219
Street fair, 7
Strike Zone, 185
Strip, 1–2, 26
beginnings, 29–30
parking, 59
Strip clubs, 18, 239–241
Suites, 43
Sun exposure, 269
Suncoast Bowling Center, 185
Sunrise Hospital, 269
Super Bowl, 38–39
Surrender, 236
Swimming, 66, 186

T

Tao Beach, 235
Tao Nightclub, 234–235
Taxes, 273
Taxis, 264–265
Telephones, 273
Temperature, 36
Tennis, 186
Terry Fator, 218
Texas Hold 'Em, 178
Texas Star Lanes, 185
Thai cuisine, 96
Theme parks, 153
Theme restaurants, 106, 115
Thomas and Mack Center, 215
Three-Card Poker, 179–180
Thunder from Down Under, 19, 223
Time, 273
Tipping, 273–274
Titanic: The Exhibition, 153, 156
Tix4Tonight, 103, 206
T-Mobile Arena, 18, 215
Toilets, 274
Topgolf, 153, 168
Tournament of Kings, 213, 219
Tours, 174
Grand Canyon
Hoover Dam, 243–244
Red Rock Canyon, 250
Town Square, 204
The Toy Shack, 202
TPC Las Vegas, 9, 188
Traffic, 266
Train travel, 260
Transportation services, 267
Travelers Aid Society, 16
Treasure Island, 59
Treasures, 241

U

Uber, 265
Ultralounges, 236–237
Unlikely/unusual Las Vegas, 20–22
USA Sevens, 39

V

V: The Ultimate Variety Show, 219
Valentine's Day, 39
Valley of Fire State Park, 2, 247–249
Vanguard Lounge, 22, 228
Vegas! The Show, 9, 219
VegasTours.com, 15
Vegas Uncork'd, 39
Vegas Weddings, 190
Velveteen Rabbit, 22, 228
Venezuelan cuisine, 96
Venues, entertainment, 214–215
Vesper, 224–225
Via Bellagio, 200
Video poker, 183–184
Visitor information, 274
Viva Las Vegas Weddings, 193–194
Volcano, 6, 14, 152, 160
VooDoo Rooftop Nightclub, 236–237

W

Water 274
Weather, 36–37
Wee Kirk O' the Heather, 194
Welcome to Fabulous Las Vegas sign, 7, 10, 152, 161
West Rim, Grand Canyon, 254
Wet 'n Wild, 153, 173–174
Wet Republic, 235
Wi-Fi, 270
Women travelers, 274
World Series of Poker, 39
Wynn Conservatory, 153, 161
Wynn Las Vegas/Encore Las Vegas, 8, 183
Wynn Lake of Dreams, 152, 161

X

X Burlesque, 18
XS, 16, 20, 235–236

Z

Zia Record Exchange, 203, 229
Zoos, 153
Zumanity, Cirque du Soleil, 212

Accommodations

Aliante Casino and Hotel, 87
Aria Las Vegas, 6, 45–46
Arizona Charlie's East, 86
Bally's Las Vegas, 62
Bellagio, 11, 19, 56–57, 192
Best Western Mardi Gras, 83
Best Western McCarran, 83
Boulder Station, 86
Caesars Palace, 5, 11, 14–15, 17, 19, 57–58
California Hotel & Casino, 75
Candlewood Suites, 83
Canyon Ranch SpaClub, 6
Circa, 73
Circus Circus Hotel & Casino, 5, 54, 59, 71–72
Clarion Hotel, 83
The Cosmopolitan of Las Vegas, 5, 58–60
Courtyard by Marriott, 83
Cromwell, 5, 60
The D Las Vegas Casino Hotel, 73–74
The Downtown Grand, 74
Drew, 73
Eastside Cannery, 86
El Cortez Hotel & Casino, 75–76
Embassy Suites, 83
Excalibur, 51–52, 54
Fairfield Inn by Marriott, 83
Fairfield Inn Suites, 83
Fiesta Henderson, 87
Fiesta Rancho, 87
Flamingo Las Vegas, 62–63
Four Queens, 76
Four Seasons Hotel Las Vegas, 6, 46–48, 54

Fremont Hotel & Casino, 77
Gold Coast, 84–85
Golden Gate, 5, 77–78
Golden Nugget, 74–75
Green Valley Ranch Resort, Spa & Casino, 88–89
Hampton Inn Express, 83
Hampton Inn, 83
Hard Rock Hotel & Casino, 80
Harrah's Las Vegas, 63–64
Hilton Lake Las Vegas Resort & Spa, 91
Hyatt Place, 83
JW Marriott, 92
La Quinta Inn and Suites, 83
Las Vegas Marriott, 83
The LINQ, 64
Luxor Las Vegas, 52–53
M Resort, 89–90
Main Street Station, 78
Mandalay Bay/Delano Las Vegas, 48–49, 54
MGM Grand Hotel & Casino, 49–51
The Mirage, 64–65, 192
Mount Charleston Lodge, 256
New York–New York Hotel & Casino, 53–55, 192
Oasis at Gold Spike, 78–79
The Orleans, 54, 85
Palace Station, 85–87
Palazzo Las Vegas, 61
Palms Casino Resort, 81–82
Paris Las Vegas, 11, 65–67, 192
Park MGM/NoMad Las Vegas, 55
Planet Hollywood Resort & Casino, 67–68
Plaza Hotel & Casino, 6, 79
Red Rock Resort, 5, 92–93
Renaissance Las Vegas, 83
Residence Inn, 83
Resorts World Las Vegas, 73
Rio All-Suite Hotel and Casino, 39, 82
Sahara Hotel and Casino, 59, 70–71
Sam's Town, 86
Silver Sevens, 88
Silverton, 86
South Point, 90–91
Spa at Encore, 6
Staybridge Suites, 83
The Strat Hotel, Casino and SkyPod, 54, 59, 72
Sunset Station, 87
Super 8, 83
Texas Station, 87
Travelodge, 83
Treasure Island, 59, 68
Tropicana Las Vegas, 56
Tuscany Suites & Casino, 82–83
Venetian, 5–6, 16, 19, 59, 61
Waldorf Astoria, 219
Westgate Las Vegas, 5, 83–84
Westin Lake Las Vegas, 91
Wynn/Encore Las Vegas, 6, 14, 17, 69–70

Restaurants

Alder & Birch, 137–138
American Coney Island, 132
Andiamo Steakhouse, 128–129
Aureole, 96
Bacchanal Buffet, 4, 147
Bardot Brasserie, 96–97
Bavette's Steakhouse, 98
Bazaar Meat, 4, 125–126
bBd's Burgers, Beers, Desserts, 4, 23, 138
Bellagio Patisserie, 144
Best Friend, 4, 98–99
Big Ern's BBQ, 132
Black Tap, 5, 23, 116, 145
Block 16 Urban Food Hall, 116
Blue Ribbon Brasserie, 108–109
Bobby's Burger Palace, 107
Border Grill, 103–104
Bouchon, 19, 110
Brio Tuscan Grille, 204
Brooklyn Bowl, 117
Buddy V's Ristorante, 117
Buffet at Aria, 145–146
Buffet at Bellagio, 11, 147
Buffet at Excalibur, 146
Buffet at Luxor, 146
Burger Bar, 107–108
Cabo Wabo Cantina, 117–118
Capriotti's, 23, 140–141
Carmine's, 118
Carnival World Buffet, 150–151
Carson Kitchen, 132–133
China Poblano, 118
Corner Market Buffet, 148
Costa di Mare, 126
Crush, 23, 99
Cupcakery, 145
Delmonico Steakhouse, 110
Dick's Last Resort, 104
Doña María Tamales, 133
Eat, 133–134
Eataly, 11, 104
EDO Gastro Tapas & Wine, 23, 138–139
Egg Slut, 5, 22, 123–124
Emeril's New Orleans Fish House, 99
Estiatorio Milos, 4, 110–111
Flavors Buffet, 148–149
Fleur by Hubert Keller, 16, 99–100
Flock & Fowl, 4, 21, 134
Forum Food Court, 124
Freed's Bakery, 144
Fulton Street Food Hall, 124
Garden Court Buffet, 4, 22, 150
Giada, 19, 118–119
Gilley's, 119
Goodwich, 134
Gordon Ramsay Burger, 23, 124–125
Gordon Ramsay Fish & Chips, 125
Gordon Ramsay Pub & Grill, 119–120
Gordon Ramsay Steak, 111
Greene St. Kitchen, 139

Guy Fieri's Vegas Kitchen, 120
Hakkasan, 100
Hard Rock Cafe, 106
Harley-Davidson Café, 106
Hash House a Go Go, 4, 17, 120
Heart Attack Grill, 133
Hell's Kitchen, 4, 111–112
Herringbone, 104–105
Hofbräuhaus, 139–140
Holstein's Shakes & Buns, 120–121
House of Blues, 106
Hugo's Cellar, 130
Joël Robuchon, 4, 16, 100
Julian Serrano Tapas, 101
Kitchen at Atomic, 4, 21, 130–131
L'Atelier de Joël Robuchon, 4, 23, 101
La Comida, 4, 131
Lagasse's Stadium, 121
Le Village Buffet, 149
Lotus of Siam, 141
Luv-It Frozen Custard, 145
M&M Soul Food Café, 20, 142
Mabel's BBQ, 140
Mandalay Bay's Bayside Buffet, 146

Margaritaville, 106
MB Steak, 135
Mercato della Pescheria, 121–122
Mesa Grill, 112
Mirage Cravings Buffet, 149
Momofuku, 122
Mon Ami Gabi, 11, 122
Morimoto, 101–102
Nacho Daddy, 125
Naked City Pizza, 141–142
Old Homestead Steakhouse, 112
Oscar's Steakhouse, 130
Other Mama, 21, 142
Pamplemousse, 135–136
Pantry, 22, 24
PBR Rock Bar & Grill, 106
Picasso, 113
Piero's Italian Cuisine, 136
Ping Pang Pong, 140
Pizza Rock, 131
Planet Hollywood, 106
Ports O' Call Buffet, 151
Pub 1842, 105–106
Raku Grill, 143
Rao's, 113
Red 8, 128
Red Square, 19, 102

Restaurant Guy Savoy, 4, 113–114
Rí Rá Irish Pub, 107
Rivea, 5
Rose.Rabbit.Lie, 114
Sadelle's, 22, 122–123
Sage, 102–103
Scotch 80 Prime, 136
Shake Shack, 23, 53, 108
Sinatra, 126–127
Spago, 114
Sparrow + Wolf, 4, 21, 143
Spice Market Buffet, 11, 149
Steakhouse, 23, 127–128
Sterling Brunch at BLT at Bally's, 14
STK, 19
Strip House, 11, 23, 115
StripSteak, 11
Tender Steakhouse, 53
Texas de Brazil, 204
Top of the World, 5, 128
Viva Las Arepas, 134–135
Wicked Spoon Buffet, 147–148
Wynn Las Vegas Buffet, 150
Yardbird, 23, 123
Zuma, 115–116

Map List

Las Vegas & Environs   3
Suggested Las Vegas Itineraries   12
Las Vegas Hotels   47
South Strip Restaurants   97
Mid-Strip Restaurants   109
North Strip Restaurants   127
Downtown Restaurants   129

Restaurants Beyond the Strip   137
Las Vegas Attractions   155
Las Vegas Shopping   197
Las Vegas Shows   207
Las Vegas Nightlife   221
Day Trips from Las Vegas   245

MAP LIST

Photo Credits

Frommer's EasyGuide to Las Vegas 2020, 7th Edition

Published by
FROMMER MEDIA LLC

ISBN 978-1-62887-458-7 (paper), 978-1-62887-459-4 (e-book)

Editorial Director: Pauline Frommer
Editor: Linda Cabasin
Production Editor: Heather Wilcox
Cartographer: Elizabeth Puhl
Photo Editor: Seth Olenick
Cover Design: Dave Riedy

For information on our other products or services, see www.frommers.com.

Frommer Media LLC also publishes its books in a variety of electronic formats. Some content that
appears in print may not be available in electronic formats.

Manufactured in the United States of America

5 4 3 2 1